# THE NATURE AND ORIGINS
# OF JAPANESE IMPERIALISM

# THE NATURE AND ORIGINS OF JAPANESE IMPERIALISM

## A reinterpretation of the Great Crisis of 1873

*Donald Calman*

London and New York

First published 1992
by Routledge
11 New Fetter Lane, London EC4P 4EE

Simultaneously published in the USA and Canada
by Routledge
a division of Routledge, Chapman and Hall, Inc.
29 West 35th Street, New York, NY 10001

1992 Donald Calman

Typeset in 10 on 12 point Baskerville by
Falcon Typographic Art Ltd, Fife, Scotland
Printed and bound in Great Britain by
Biddles Ltd, Guildford and King's Lynn

*British Library Cataloguing in Publication Data*
Calman, Donald, *1926–*
The nature and origins of Japanese imperialism:
reinterpretation of the great crisis of 1873.
I. Title
325.320952

ISBN 0–415–06710–3

*Library of Congress Cataloging in Publication Data*
Calman, Donald, 1926–
The nature and origins of Japanese imperialism : a reinterpretation of
the great crisis of 1873 / Donald Calman.
Includes bibliographical references and index.
ISBN 0–415–06710–3
1. Japan – Politics and government – 1868–1912. 2. Japan – Foreign
relations – Korea. 3. Korea – Foreign relations – Japan. 4. Imperialism.
I. Title.
DS882.C35   1992
952.031 – dc20   91–39194   CIP

72438

Dedicated to my brother Bruce
whose backing made this research possible.

# CONTENTS

# ACKNOWLEDGEMENTS

Most of the research was carried out at the Bodleian Library, Oxford, and at the Shaken and main libraries, Tokyo University. The kind assistance of their staff is gratefully acknowledged. Three months were also spent at Harvard's Yenching Library, and shorter periods at Columbia, UCLA and the University of Hawaii. In Japan, a year was spent at the Hokkaidō University and some months at the University of Kyushu, Fukuoka.

Special thanks go to the staff at Kurume's very fine public library for assistance and hospitality well beyond the call of duty and also to Kurume's two senior historians, Koga Yukiō and Tsuruku Jirō, who were willing to share their knowledge and source material. The public libraries of Fukushima and Saga, as well as the Parliamentary Library, Tokyo, also gave every assistance.

Other libraries used at Oxford were the Pusey Lane, Union and Nissan Institute Libraries and in Sydney the Fisher and Mitchell Libraries.

Thus the librarians who assisted this research are too numerous to list individually, and I can merely acknowledge the fact that without their help this research would have been impossible.

Finally, I am indebted to Suzanne Anderson, Supertype, Oxford, who undertook the task of typing the manuscript. I must also thank Helen Roesler of Sunny Corner, New South Wales, Australia for her important supplementary efforts.

# GLOSSARY OF JAPANESE TERMS

| | |
|---|---|
| *ahōkan* | 'Fools' Building or 'Fools' Institute |
| *Ainu* | Japanese aboriginal race |
| *aite* | opposing number; opponent; enemy |
| *aniki* | big brother |
| *ashigaru* | a low-ranking *samurai*; a footman |
| | |
| *Bakufu* | Shogunate |
| *Bakumatsu* | late Shogunate period |
| *bantō* | assistant (shop); clerk; servant |
| *batsu* | clique; faction; power group |
| *bugyō* | magistrate; high commissioner |
| *bummei kaika* | civilization and enlightenment |
| *bun to bu* | civil and military |
| *bushi* | *samurai*; warrior |
| *bussan kyoku* | production department |
| | |
| *chambara* | a movie or TV drama revolving around sword fights |
| *chigyō* | system whereby *samurai* allocated control over a certain area of land |
| *chikuba no tomo* | childhood friend |
| *chintai* | Meiji term for regular soldiers conscripted from all classes |
| *Chōkan* | chief; director; head |
| *chommage* | topknot |
| *chōteki* | enemy of the Emperor |
| | |
| *dai shōya* | village headman |
| *daimyō* | a feudal lord |

| | |
|---|---|
| *dainagon* | an old term for a high-ranking minister serving the Emperor |
| *Dajōkan* | Council of State |
| *den* | biography |
| | |
| *endai no saku* | great and distant plans |
| *Eta* | untouchables |
| | |
| *fudai* | (ministers) serving the same lord for generations |
| *fukko ishin* | revival of the old and making new |
| *fukoku kyōhei* | a rich country and strong troops |
| *funkei no tomo* | a friend to the death |
| *furyō no hai* | floating population; undesirable element |
| | |
| *gaijin* | foreigner |
| *gakusha* | scholar |
| *genrō* | elder statesmen |
| *Genyōsha* | the forerunner of the Black Dragon Society |
| *(genro in) gikan* | (Council of Elders) assistant minister |
| *gimu* | duties |
| *go* | the game of *go* |
| *gomen ne* | excuse me |
| *gōnō* | wealthy farmers |
| *goyō* | official |
| *gun* | district; administrative unit |
| *gunkoku shugi* | militarism |
| | |
| *haken* | supremacy; control of 'the world' |
| *han* | fief or clan |
| *hanbatsu* | fief-based power block |
| *hankan* | a local governor |
| *haragei* | psychological acting; putting on an act to disguise one's real intention |
| *haraisage* | to sell or dispose of, usually by the government |
| *hatten saku* | plan to expand and develop |
| *heimin* | the common people (non-*samurai*) |
| *hinin* | non-people; untouchables |
| *hinmin* | the extremely poor |

| | |
|---|---|
| *ikke shinjū* | family suicide |
| *ikki* | an agrarian uprising |
| *ishin* | the act of making new; restoration |
| *jikan* | deputy chief or head |
| *jikiyama* | mines under the direct management of the government |
| *jinmin kenri (minken)* | popular rights |
| *jitsuwa* | true stories |
| *Jiyū-tō* | the Liberal Party |
| *jōi* | drive out the foreigners |
| *juku* | private school |
| *kaientai* | a sea support force; Tosa's unofficial navy |
| *kaikoku* | the opening of the country; end of seclusion |
| *kaishaku* | decapitation with a sword |
| *Kaitakushi* | Colonial Department or Pioneering Department |
| *kambun* | Chinese read the Japanese way |
| *Kampaku* | from Heian Age the top minister assisting the Emperor |
| *kannemōke shugi* | money orientated |
| *Kannushi* | fort chiefs |
| *karō* | principal retainer; minister of a daimyō |
| *kazoku kaikan* | assembly hall for the nobles |
| *(Chōshū) kei* | in the Chōshū camp |
| *keiei* | management |
| *ken* | prefecture |
| *kenri* | rights |
| *kikiyaku* | an official who listens; spy |
| *kinnō ka* | a loyalist; one 'on the side of the Emperor' |
| *kisatsu (kika Satsujin)* | one who is in effect a naturalized Satsuma man |
| *kōbu gattai* | a policy of reconciling the nobles and the military, i.e. Emperor and Shogun |
| *kōdō fukkō* | restoration of the Imperial Way |
| *kokken* | state rights |
| *koku* | 4.9629 bushels |
| *kokugaku (sha)* | national studies (a nativist) |
| *Kokuryūkai* | the Black Dragon Society |
| *kokutai* | the national polity; the national essence |

| | |
|---|---|
| *konoe hei* | forces directly attached to the Emperor |
| *Kunai shō* | the Department of the Imperial Household |
| *machi-bugyō* | town magistrate |
| *meibutsu* | famous product |
| *mikuni (bito)* | (people of) the Imperial Country |
| *Minbu-shō* | a Ministry which dealt with matters relating to people |
| *minei* | private management |
| *minken* | popular rights |
| *Mombushō* | Education Ministry |
| *momme* | a unit of weight; $\frac{1}{1000}$ kan |
| *muzai ron* | the doctrine of not guilty (for war) |
| *nai-gai* | internal and external |
| *namban* | southern barbarians |
| *nanibō* | a certain person |
| *nanki* | difficult period |
| *Ōentai* | support forces; auxiliary force |
| *ōgosho* | a retired Shogun; the major power behind the scenes in the business world |
| *rangaku (sha)* | Dutch studies; Western studies (a student of . . .) |
| *Rikuentai* | land support force; name for unofficial Tosa land force in Nagasaki |
| *roku* | stipend; allowance; income measured in rice |
| *rōnin (rōshi)* | masterless samurai |
| *Saibansho* | in early Meiji a term for the administration set up in the open ports; in modern Japanese a law-court |
| *Sa-in* | Chamber of the Left |
| *sakoku* | seclusion; closing the country off from the world |
| *sambō (chō)* | staff officer (Chief of Staff) |
| *sangi* | a councillor |
| *sankin kōtai* | attendance by turns at the Shogun's Court |
| *sanyō* | a councillor |
| *Satchō* | Satsuma and Chōshū |

| | |
|---|---|
| *Seido kyoku* | Law System Office |
| *seihen* | political crisis |
| *Sei-in* | highest government body attended by Emperor; set up in 1871 when clans abolished |
| *seikan (ronsha)* | (one who advocates) an attack on Korea |
| *seishin (ronsha)* | (one who advocates) an attack on China |
| *sensō* | war |
| *seppuku (harakiri)* | to commit suicide by cutting open the stomach with a sword |
| *shimpei* | royal guards |
| *shinhan* | clans whose lords were Tokugawa family members |
| *shinsei* | forces led by the Emperor himself |
| *Shin-shū* | the holy land (Japan) |
| *Shintō* | the Holy Way (local Japanese religion) |
| *shishi* | men of spirit; activists |
| *shizoku* | samurai; warriors |
| *shosei* | live-in student-secretary |
| *shosei ron* | the kind of argument put forward by students |
| *shotai* | squad of troops – perhaps about 100 men |
| *shōya* | village headman |
| *sōdan yaku* | consultant |
| *sōmō tai* | grass-roots force |
| *sonnō joi* | revere the Emperor and drive out the barbarians |
| *sonnōka* | one who reveres the Emperor; pro-Emperor |
| *taigai ron* | advocacy of foreign wars |
| *taigi meibun* | historical justification |
| *tenka* | under heaven; the world |
| *tennō heika* | the Emperor |
| *tonden hei* | soldier settlers; local militia |
| *tozama* | outside clans not closely connected to the Tokugama shoguns |
| *tsubo* | a land measure of six *shaku* square |
| *ukeoi (system)* | a contract system; use of contractors |
| *wajin* | Japanese |
| *wakō* | Japanese pirates |
| *yakuza* | gangsters |

# GLOSSARY

| | |
|---|---|
| *yatoi gaijin* | an employed foreigner |
| *yōshi* | an adopted son and heir |
| *zaibatsu* | plutocracy; a power group based on money |

# PREFACE

History may or may not repeat itself, but the way men approach the task of writing history certainly does repeat itself. Generally speaking, writing history is a job. Therefore histories tend to be orthodox in the classical Greek meaning of the word: *orthos* (right), *doxa* (opinion). Rarely does the historian play a significant part in the formulation of this right opinion. His are the humbler tasks of refining and disseminating current orthodoxy, and using the weight of his authority to stifle tiresome public debate.

A case in point is the way Western historians have re-written modern Japanese history. The current Anglo-American orthodoxy has been summed up for us by London's senior professor, W. G. Beasley, in his 1987 volume, *Japanese Imperialism 1894–1945*. Beasley claims that 'Japanese imperialism dates from the Sino-Japanese War of 1894–5', and argues that 'There is no evidence that in declaring war on China in 1894 its government had any expectation of territorial gain, but the ease and rapidity of Japanese victories soon prompted them' (p. 55). Beasley also stresses the military threat posed by Russia and credits the German teacher Major Meckel, who arrived in 1885, with driving home the strategic importance of Korea (pp. 45–6). He also refers to the 'Enlightenment' leader, Fukuzawa Yukichi, and concludes that 'one purpose of establishing Japanese power in East Asia was to defend Asia's soul, not merely its territory' (p. 32).

This analysis places Beasley right up alongside the eminent Victorian Japanologist, Basil Chamberlain. Writing in 1905 during the Russo-Japanese War, Chamberlain gave the following explanation of Japan's imperial successes over the previous thirty-five years: 'some good fairy has presided over all their acts' (p. 43).

Though modern readers are unlikely to be carried away by the

Chamberlain fairy thesis, there is a very real danger that they will accept the Beasley picture, which is in fact equally fanciful. Therefore it should be noted that Beasley is merely pontificating: he is outside his own period of expertise. One must give careful consideration to the question of just what is meant by 'historical evidence'. For the moment let us merely state quite bluntly that this book will clearly demonstrate that, despite the current 'orthos doxa' Japanese imperial expansion was debated and planned for many years, and then carried out with extreme ruthlessness and cynicism.

It is inconceivable that the Beasley line could have been taken by an English Establishment historian in the thirties or forties. It is interesting that it comes in an age when the British government seems desperate to promote a Japanese presence and a Japanese capital inflow, and where university Japanese departments, starved of money, compete furiously for Japanese funds, rather like Third World children diving for coins.

It is interesting, too, that the Chamberlain fairy thesis comes from the early years of the century when Britain and America were keen to contain Russia's advance in the East, and were only too happy to delegate this task to Japan.

Hence Chamberlain ignored the appalling atrocities already committed by the Japanese military machine and the grievous burden it imposed on the Japanese people, and applauded their successes. That war, however, brought home to America that Japan was not a pliable American protégé but rather a steely and devious rival. Thereafter the Japanese Emperor system, Japanese militarism and Japanese imperialism were seen for the monstrosities they were.

Not the least of the victims were the Japanese people. Thus at war's end the Americans bestowed, and most Japanese eagerly embraced, a constitution renouncing war. Then within a few years came the Cold War, and Japan was pressured to resume her 'historic role' as a bulwark against Russia. However, this sudden volte-face had to be sold not only to the people of America and its allies but also to the Japanese people. The obvious person to lead this crusade would have been Matsuoka Yonosuke (1880–1946), a statesman of proven charisma, flexibility and strength. Matsuoka was from Chōshū, one of the two great western clans which had engineered the Meiji Restoration and thereafter had maintained a strong grip on the State and its armed forces. Matsuoka was in turn diplomat, politician and President of the Manchurian Railway. It was he who led Japan out of the League of Nations, then, as Foreign Minister in

the Second Konoe Cabinet, signed the Axis Pact with Germany and
Italy. Next he went to Russia to negotiate a non-aggression pact, but
once Hitler invaded Russia, Matsuoka demonstrated his flexibility
by urging a Japanese attack on Russia. Later he demonstrated
his strength by resigning from Cabinet because he was implacably
opposed to continued negotiations with America.

Unfortunately, in 1946 Matsuoka died of tuberculosis in Sugamo
Prison. Thus his services were lost to the Free World in its hour of
need. However, the rest of the old brigade were soon allowed back,
and with just a brief *gomen ne* to the Japanese people, they once more
took over the reins. Prominent among them were Matsuoka's young
relatives, the brothers Kishi Nobosuke and Sato Eisaku, who both
went on to become significant prime ministers. Kishi's career had
been sponsored by Matsuoka in Manchuria, then in Tōjō's wartime
cabinet he had done a splendid job organizing the economic arm of
the war machine.

I first went to Japan in 1957 when Kishi was Prime Minister,
and I found he inspired in most young Japanese feelings of deep
revulsion. He brought to mind the pictures of a benignly smiling,
baby-bedecked Russian leader which proliferated in our newspapers
after 1940. But Kishi was even more difficult to sell than Stalin. I
witnessed the violence of 1960 when Kishi was toppled over the
renewal of the military pact with America and I stayed on throughout
the turbulent sixties when Japan was closer to civil war than history
will recall.

For the historian, such periods of change are times of great activity.
As governments shuffle the pack and recycle or discard old friends,
the historian must keep up with the changing *orthos doxa*. For the
American historian, it was heady stuff, especially after 1960 when
Kennedy, in an attempt to mend fences after the furore of that
year, appointed Harvard historian Reischauer as Ambassador to
Japan. The son of missionaries, Reischauer had grown up in
Japan and relished his role as bridge-builder. He taught that the
two countries are natural friends and that the thirties were just
a temporary aberration. His academic colleagues rallied behind
him to form a Western Japanology establishment likewise devoted
to bridge-building.

Beasley's volume is basically an English version of the American
*orthos doxa*. The Emperor system sprang up in the nineties in
response to the needs of the day, and when Japan went to war
against China in 1894 she had no prior thoughts of territorial

aggrandisement. Thereafter her advance was merely a natural reaction to changing external circumstances. Thus the Emperor system, and its concomitant militarism and imperialism, have been prettified, truncated and explained away. They have been rendered irrelevant to our understanding of contemporary Japan.

Of course, the way Japanese history is presented is of even more concern for the Japanese people than it is for the rest of the world. Since 1945 it has been a battlefield. Traditionally the historian was a *goyō gakusha* serving the government. He continued this role after the Meiji Restoration of 1868 and the 'history' taught in schools was a combination of myths, legends and nationalistic propaganda.

After the war, there was an explosion of academic freedom, but this largely took the form of Marxist indoctrination. This made it easier for the government to justify regaining control of the history-teaching process, especially once the Chōshū Matsuoka–Kishi line was re-established. Thus we are now back to the stage where the national history taught in schools is little better than the pre-war myths and legends. This has been made possible by the fact that the Mombusho (Education Ministry) must approve all school texts.

The gravity with which a great proportion of the Japanese people view the current indoctrination is demonstrated by the Ienaga case. In the early sixties, Professor Ienaga submitted for Education Ministry approval high school history books which referred, for example, to the Nanking massacre of 1937 and to Japanese aggression in China. The Japanese government, however, has refused to allow Ienaga to describe Japan's 'advance' in China as 'aggression' or the events in Nanking as mass murder. Ienaga sued the government in 1965 and the court cases have dragged on to this day. More than seventy lawyers have represented Ienaga free of charge, distinguished writers and academics have appeared in court on his behalf, and there has been huge publicity. In 1989 the High Court finally decided in favour of Ienaga on one count and ordered damages of about $1,000. The major charges, however, have not been addressed so the matter will now be taken to the Supreme Court.

Of course, Japan has not been alone in distorting history. It has been observed that 'in war the first casualty is truth' and this is no less true in the case of a Cold War. Nor has Japan been alone in quietly ignoring those facts which don't fit in with the desired national image. There is not, I believe, a single American high school textbook which tells why peace negotiations were so protracted after the War of Independence. To tell American children that the British doggedly supported, and the Americans relentlessly opposed, Indian land rights would, of course, only 'confuse' them.

Again, it must be pointed out that Meiji Japan does have a case. Before the Restoration, Russia tried to set up a naval base in the Tsushima Islands between Japan proper and Korea. Japan was too weak to drive her out, but the British would have none of it and forced the Russians out. Britain for her part angled to get control of the key city of Shimonoseki at the juncture of Honshu and Kyūshū, in order to turn it into a second Hong Kong, while the kindly Americans were most insistent that they should be responsible for all shipping and railways which the quaint little Orientals thought they might possibly be able to manage by themselves. The Japanese soon showed that they were masters of the art of playing off one power against another. They also understood the fundamental rule that economic dependence leads to political dependence, and steadfastly refused to allow foreigners to buy their land and mines.

There is even a case for Japanese aggression in that attack is often the best defence, and it was therefore argued that Japan's security required an outer ring of possessions. Yet it still remains true that the Japanese Emperor system, and its concomitant militarism and imperialism, were monstrosities, and the combined teachings of Japanese *goyō gakusha* and the Western Japanology establishment add up to a grotesque and dangerous distortion which might be compared to that of the lunatic fringe which maintains that there was no holocaust in Europe.

Japanese imperialism was not simply a response to external conditions; its well-springs are to be found within Japanese history. In essence Japanese imperialism was economic imperialism. Once this fact is grasped it is easy to see that 1945 did not represent a complete break with the past. Japan's post-war obsession with becoming the world's economic super-power is a natural extension of her earlier history. Indeed, there is an essential unity in the Japanese story from the fourteenth century to the present day.

One cannot understand contemporary Japan by regarding it as a country born in 1945, nor can one understand Japanese imperialism by beginning the narrative with the China War of 1894–5. The Meiji Restoration came complete with a slogan *seikan-ron* (Let's attack Korea). Korea was to be conquered, occupied, exploited and used as a base for an advance into China and beyond until Japan's position as centre of the universe was 'restored'. It was a bitter debate over how and when to attack Korea which ostensibly brought on the great political crisis of 1873.

Japanese historians usually confine their analysis to the post-Restoration years, but contemporary Japan can be understood only if we trace certain themes over many centuries. Once the great 1873 crisis has been understood, the nature of Japanese imperialism becomes manifest; and a clear understanding of the nature and origins of Japanese imperialism is essential if we are to understand Japan – past, present and future.

# 1

# INTRODUCTION

Let us begin with a brief look at the period 1868–1940 in order to introduce some of the themes, concepts, personalities and terminology which will figure prominently in this study.

Certain Japanese words such as *geisha* and *samurai* have passed into the English language because there is no word in English which captures their true essence and special aura. In like manner, when dealing with Japanese imperialism, there are key words and phrases which lose much in translation. The very act of translation tends to make bland and familiar concepts which are chillingly alien. Such expressions shall be explained then left in the original Japanese.

Much of this book revolves around the *seihen* of 1873. *Seihen* may be translated as 'political crisis'; but a crisis may come and go leaving everything unchanged, whereas *seihen* contains the idea of a crisis which leads to far-reaching changes. Moreover, it is not just a political or constitutional crisis occurring in the capital, but usually involves much of the country, with the threat of civil war looming in the background. There was to be another *seihen* in 1881. Paradoxically, it was largely orchestrated by Mitsubishi, but it brought Japan to the verge of 'a Japanese French Revolution'. We shall refer throughout to the 1873 *Seihen* (or the Meiji year 6 *Seihen*) and to the 1881 *Seihen* (or Meiji year 14 *Seihen*).

*Kokugakusha* is another word best left in the original. It is usually translated as 'national scholars', or the somewhat dismissive 'nativists'. Analysing Japanese imperialism without dealing with the *kokugakusha* is rather like giving an account of Arab expansion without mentioning Mohammed, and referring to the *kokugakusha* as 'nativists' immediately tends to tone down the religious fanaticism and extreme racism.

1

The events of 1868 are described in English as the Meiji Restoration, which is taken to mean the termination of the Shogunate (or Bakufu) and the restoration of power to the Emperor. Such a restoration was, of course, a polite fiction. Many of the Shoguns, especially the recent ones, had been weak, sickly youths who were personally insignificant. In 1867 the future Emperor Meiji was a terrified fifteen year old who had been brought up by his mother's family and who probably shared the widespread suspicion that his father, the Emperor Kōmei, had been poisoned by the victors. The great western fiefs which had brought about the Restoration clearly regarded the young Emperor as a pliable figurehead. For them, restoration meant the restoration of their own political and economic power.

Tokugawa power dated from the great battle fought in 1600 at Sekigahara near modern Nagoya – virtually a battle between west Japan and east Japan. Sekigahara had been decided in the traditional manner when, at the height of the battle, a Hiroshima leader changed sides. The wealth and power of the great western fiefs had been based on their overseas trade and it was largely to prevent their revival that the Tokugawas imposed a policy of Seclusion.

The western clans' opposition to the Shogunate was the product not so much of ideological differences as of a determination to resume overseas trading and hence build up their own wealth and power. Even before 1868 people such as Iwasaki Yatarō, founder of Mitsubishi, and Godai Tomoatsu, an unscrupulous Satsuma entrepreneur, had been trying to get into Korea, and, quite predictably, those efforts were to be intensified once Sekigahara was reversed in 1868. Business sharks such as Godai have been virtually written out of Japanese history, but, as with the *kokugakusha*, the story of Japanese imperialism becomes grossly distorted if one does not give due prominence to the likes of Godai.

The long struggle against the Shogunate had largely been carried out by extreme, ideological followers of the *kokugakusha* with their doctrine of *fukko Shintō* and their goal of *fukko ishin*. Shintō (the holy way) was to become the State Religion, and for a while the Department of Religion figured prominently in the Meiji government. But the new pragmatic rulers from the West soon distanced themselves from the ideologues and their goal of *fukko ishin*. Fukko meant 'to restore the old', but it had a very special meaning: they were to go back to an Emperor-based theocracy and to the ethos of antiquity before 'corrupting' influences came in from China and India. The

gods had descended from the heavens and had made their home
in Japan. At first the whole world had been in harmony under the
rule of the Japanese Emperor, the descendant of those gods. In the
course of time, other countries had broken away and the world had
degenerated into a state of disharmony. Now the time had come to
'restore' not only Japan's own pure Japanism but also her position
as the centre of the universe. The world had to be brought once
more into 'harmony'.

In Japanese, the Meiji Restoration is referred to as the Meiji Ishin.
The term *ishin* means 'to make new', so the Meiji Ishin is often
thought of as a movement to modernize Japan. But *ishin* should
not be separated from *fukko*; it had strong revolutionary overtones,
and was concerned not with administrative and technological modernization but with making the spirit and the heart new again. Thus
Meiji Revolution would probably be a better translation than Meiji
Restoration.

There is a strong feeling of betrayal running through Japanese
history right down to 1940 (and indeed beyond), and that feeling
centres around the betrayal of their *ishin* (or revolution) of 1868.
In the 1930s, for example, the young officers were openly seeking
a second *ishin*. It is important to note that in the 1930s, as in the
1870s, this hostility sprang in part from the greed and corruption
of the government and its business partners, but in part it was a
reaction to the government's failure to proceed with sufficient speed
to implement the policy of foreign aggression implicit in the doctrine
of *fukko ishin*. The slogans *seikan* (Let's attack Korea) and *seishin* (Let's
attack Shin China), which had wide currency long before 1868, must
be regarded as specific planks in the doctrine of *fukko ishin*, and the
nature of the China War of 1894–5 is hopelessly distorted if one
concentrates on the immediate causes.

The first period of Meiji history, from 1868 to 1873, began with
the promise of a widely based modern state founded on the Rule
of Law. But soon the two great western fiefs, Satsuma and Chōshū
(Satchō), moved to concentrate power in their own hands. They
maintained a tight control of the armed forces, the Japanese Navy
being known ironically as 'the Satsuma Navy' and the Army as
'the Chōshū Army'. Continuing well into the twentieth century,
all senior Army promotions were decided informally at the *Ippin*
Club, a group open only to Chōshū officers, the name coming
from the Chōshū clan symbol which may be read *Ippin* (one
thing). The extremism of the young officers in the twenties and

3

thirties represented in part an attempt to break down this Chōshū monopoly.

This control of the armed forces enabled Satchō in 1871 to carry out a *coup d'état*, concentrating power in their own hands, with Tosa and Saga, two other western trading fiefs, as junior partners. Corruption was of a kind now usually associated with newly emerging Third World countries. This fuelled the extremists' sense of betrayal and led to a series of uprisings and scandals which culminated in the 1873 *Seihen*. The Boshin Civil War of 1868 had seen the Satchō forces defeat the supporters of the Shogun, notably in the east and north. Since that time the task of distributing the spoils of victory had been proceeding steadily, and after the 1873 *Seihen* the victors were able to proceed apace with the redistribution of Japan's mineral wealth. With the spoils of wars past thus settled attention could be focused on the spoils of wars – or 'incidents' – soon to come. The Satchō government, the *fukko* extremists and the great merchants were all determined that Korea should be opened. It was just a question of finding the right pretext.

Of course, this Satchō government under Satsuma's Ōkubo Toshimichi was widely detested. The ideologues returned to their home provinces and staged a series of uprisings. The most serious, the *Seinan* (West–South) Wars began in Satsuma itself in 1877. Ōkubo's old comrade-in-arms, the legendary Saigō Takamori, had stormed out of the government after the 1873 *Seihen* and had returned to Satsuma. There he became a rallying point and the war when it came had all the nastiness and bitterness usually associated with civil wars. At war's end Saigō committed *seppuku* and a year later Ōkubo was assassinated. Two of the younger generation, Chōshū's Itō Hirobumi and Ōkuma Shigenobu of Saga, now competed for the number one spot and their rivalry helped bring on the 1881 *Seihen*, though it was not, as some Japanese historians would have us believe, the major cause.

The 1873 *Seihen* had established the fact that Satchō were above the law. Having failed to set up an independent judiciary to restrain Satchō, many of those defeated in 1873 resigned from the government and embarked upon a campaign to achieve an elected parliament as a way of breaking the Satchō monopoly of power. Thereafter the government was constantly assailed both by the extremists still seeking *fukko ishin* and by the *minken* advocates demanding a Western-style parliament. There was also widespread agrarian unrest caused by the increased taxes, conscription ('the blood tax') and reforms such as giving the *Eta* (untouchables) full legal rights.

By the end of the seventies the government found itself being threatened by yet another force – Mitsubishi. Unlike Mitsui, Mitsubishi was a new company whose development had been sponsored by the government to prevent first American, then British, shipping from gaining control of Japanese waters. Yet even after this foreign threat had been beaten off, and Mitsubishi had gained a virtual monopoly of Japanese shipping, it continued to be heavily subsidized. However, the British and Dutch East India Companies were well known in Japan, and it was widely believed that Japan too would produce one such dominant trading company. To prevent Mitsubishi fulfilling such a role, a stop-Mitsubishi movement emerged. As a way of toppling Itō Hirobumi and the Satchō *hanbatsu* Ōkuma Shigenobu threw in his lot with Mitsubishi, as did Fukuzawa Yukichi, media-magnate and founder-president of Keio University. Things came to a head in 1881 when a new Satsuma company was virtually presented with the large northern island of Hokkaidō which was in danger of being engulfed by Mitsubishi shipping and trading interests. This created a nationwide storm, with Mitsubishi, the *minken* advocates and old ideologue forces all braying for blood. Ōkuma and his supporters were all driven out of the government and civil service, but Satchō was forced to compromise: the 'sale' of Hokkaidō was cancelled and a proclamation was issued in the name of the Emperor promising a parliament in ten years' time.

Satchō, however, remained vulnerable and isolated. The war with Mitsubishi was to continue for many years, while that with the democrats was just beginning. Thus it was that after 1881 the Satchō *hanbatsu* turned back once more to their old allies, the *fukko ishin* extremists. The Emperor was still their trump card, and with the help of the ideologues, the Emperor system was now elaborated and forced upon the country. Though its implementation dates from the 1890s, the general concept goes far back into Japanese history. In all essentials, it was what the extremists had been seeking in the Bakumatsu (late Bakufu or late Shogunate) period, except, of course, that they had not pictured it as a tool to prop up the Satchō *hanbatsu*.

This reactivating of the old alliance must be understood if we are to grasp the nature of Japanese imperialism. Ōkubo Toshimichi, Ōkuma Shigenobu, Itō Hirobumi and his *alter ego* Inoue Kaoru, were all modern, pragmatic men. In the seventies they had pushed on together with a policy of economic imperialism. It is hardly an exaggeration to speak of the Satchō–Tosa colonization of Japan. Tohoku, in particular, became a colony whose minerals were seized, whose labour trudged off to Hokkaidō, and whose shipping and banking became dependent on the southern colonizers.

Korea was forced open in 1875–6 by a Satchō government promoting the fortunes of Satchō business interests which moved swiftly to tie up Korean grain, banking, etc. This economic imperialism did not cease to exist after 1881, but once Mitsubishi defected and waged war on Satchō and its affiliated companies, the ongoing economic imperialism, already covered by an elaborate garb of phony 'national honour', was removed even further from the spotlight as the *fukko ishin* extremists and the militarists took centre stage.

Japan did get a parliament of sorts in 1890, and predictably this led to savage attacks on the Satchō prerogatives. The Emperor system proved to be an effective weapon for controlling both the parliament and the populace, but it could not control the extremists who were now let loose. The most notorious, the Fukuoka-based Black Dragon Society, provided the government with thugs to 'police' the 1892 election, and its agents pushed ahead on the mainland, laying the basis for the war that was sure to come. The government finally moved in 1894 when it was being sorely pressed in parliament – a move which, predictably, succeeded in uniting the parliament and the people behind it. As in 1904 against Russia, Japan seized the initiative by attacking before war was declared – acts of initiative generally applauded in the West. Tōgō sank Chinese troop ships making for Korea, then, with scrupulous care, rescued every one of their British officers. The Chinese troops and seamen, to the last man, were left to drown. Whatever the concern for Asia's 'soul', Asian bodies clearly did not rate highly.

That war produced acts of Japanese savagery which have gone unreported in Japan to this day. The sickened Western correspondents left Taiwan *en masse*. But back in Japan, the quick victories, territorial gains and large reparations produced a state of euphoria which was only partially dampened when Russia, Germany and France stepped in and demanded that most of the territorial gains be cancelled. The reparations were mostly spent on further military expansion, and a 1902 Treaty with Britain freed Japan for a showdown with Russia, now promoted to the status of traditional enemy.

Itō Hirobumi played almost a lone hand in seeking an accommodation with Russia, but he had little chance against the extremists who were increasingly calling the shots from behind the curtain. Thus in fairly quick succession there followed the Russian War of 1904–5, the annexation of Korea, the Great War plundering of China, the post-war occupation of Siberia, the China 'Incident' and subsequent 'advance', and then the Second World War.

The Satchō-*fukko ishin* extremist alliance reactivated after 1881 may be said to have ended with the extremists gradually taking over the reins. As the assassination of both political and business leaders was used as a major weapon, this struggle took place out in the open. However, the 1881 *Seihen* also marked the real beginning of an equally vital struggle – one which was conducted away from the public gaze. In Tokugawa days, and also in the early Meiji period, certain merchants were officially licensed to serve the government. These were termed *goyō* merchants. But when Mitsubishi, Ōkuma and Fukuzawa threw down the gauntlet in 1881, what they were really saying was that the great merchants were now stronger and more important than the politicians. It is clear that by the end of the century the great merchants with their *zaibatsu* had come out on top. Thereafter Japanese politics must generally be regarded as a case of *goyō* politicians serving the great merchants – a situation which continues to this day.

By the time of the 1894 China War, fear of a Japanese version of the British East India Company had receded and the feeling was now that the world, and especially China, was big enough for everyone to have a substantial slice. The tendency was now to form business associations or to hold informal *zaibatsu* summits at which spheres of influence were mapped out to prevent the great Japanese companies from competing against each other outside Japan – again a feature of Japanese economic imperialism which survives and flourishes to this day. This new *zaibatsu* chumminess is best illustrated by the cosy Saionji Cabinet of 1906, for all the major *zaibatsu* were directly represented by a relative or protégé.

It is, of course, highly dangerous to take a long period like 1895–1945 and to write of one power block, the *zaibatsu*, dominating the scene. One must identify five elements all struggling for dominance: the democrats, the Satchō oligarchy, the *zaibatsu*, the military and the old *fukko ishin* extremists. However, it was not a simple, clear-cut division. Ōkuma, for example, was a democrat, but he was also one of the Mitsubishi Prime Ministers. It must be said for Mitsubishi that they gave the Japanese people a political choice: they could have a Satchō Prime Minister or they could have a Mitsubishi

Prime Minister. Then, too, increasingly most of the Satchō Prime Ministers were Admirals or Generals, while a significant number of *fukko ishin* extremists from the disadvantaged prefectures were young officers. One must also note, for example, the great mining *zaibatsu*, Furukawa, which was 'asked' to take over mines in Korea. The main family behind Furukawa was that of Mutsu Munemitsu, the Foreign Minister who played an important role in engineering the 1894 China War. Thus one person or group could belong to more than one of the above five divisions, and there was a tangled mass of criss-crossing alliances, some short-lived, others ongoing, between different elements from the five divisions. Thus intensive research is required to say which element was dominant at any particular time. What can be said with reasonable certainty is that the democrats never really got off the bottom of the ladder and in the thirties suffered virtually complete eclipse; that politicians as a class became less important than both the *zaibatsu* and the military; and that Satchō power waned somewhat once the original Meiji leaders passed away.

Let us return to the Beasley–Conroy line that the Meiji government in 1894 had no thought of territorial aggrandisement. Be it Britain moving into Malaya, Fiji, New Zealand etc., or America taking Texas, Cuba and Hawaii, or Japan penetrating Korea and China, imperial expansion tends to be a messy process. Rarely is it a case of a rational government sitting down quietly and concluding that a certain acquisition would be in the national interest. More often than not, the central government, or important sections thereof, didn't want to be involved in the inevitable expense, the administrative problems and the possible international complications. But gradually its hand was forced by its own nationals who went on ahead of the flag, building up their own commercial interests and wreaking havoc on the local society. Christian missionaries, or *fukko ishin* ideologues, would also go in and urge the necessity of the government taking over to fulfil its historic role and protect the indigenous population; and the media would come in, be it the measured tones of *The Times* or Hearst's Yellow Press whipping America into war against Spain. At some point, the act of imperial expansion assumes an air of inevitability, and the government decides to go along, especially if its own popularity is waning.

Thus it is far too simplistic merely to talk about the Japanese government in 1894. It can be argued that Prime Minister Itō did not want war, that he finally agreed to a limited engagement, and that he was tricked into a full-scale war by Foreign Minister Mutsu and Army Chief of Staff Kawakami Soroku. Yet even this oft-repeated story must not be accepted as gospel. It rather recalls the popular saying that Itō was clean in financial matters, dirty in matters of sex, while Ōkuma was clean in matters of sex, dirty when it came to money. True, Ōkuma was not as *sukebe* (sex mad) as Itō, but he was not above boasting about his sexual exploits; and Itō was not as filthy in money matters as Ōkuma, but he spent lavishly on *geisha*. All the Meiji leaders were close to one or more of the great *zaibatsu* figures, and Itō was very close to Ōkura, a somewhat unsavoury figure who prospered as a gun-runner during the Boshin War of 1868. Ōkura was one of the most aggressive of the economic imperialists; he was among the first into Korea, and half a century later we find him still spending vast amounts to promote civil disturbances in China.

Yet even if we accept that there was a doubt about Itō's desire for an aggressive foreign war, surely only those quite convinced of the fairy thesis would deny important elements in the Cabinet, most notably Foreign Minister Mutsu and the armed forces' representatives, were determined on war. The *fukko ishin* extremists, the *zaibatsu* and the military were all demanding action, and the besieged government in 1894 embarked upon the politically expedient course of waging war on China. Considerations of Itō's 'true heart' are basically irrelevant. Japan in 1894 began an aggressive war which the nation applauded. Nor was there any surprise about the outcome. The intelligence reports had long been predicting the ease and rapidity of Japanese victories.

Thus historians who have focused on the cryptical and elliptical government statements and 'policies' have failed to grasp the glaringly obvious fact that, thanks to the extremists, the military, the *zaibatsu* and certain Satchō elements, as well as media magnates such as Fukuzawa, Japan had long been preparing for just such an aggressive imperialistic war. The bland assertions that 'there is no evidence that . . .' ignore the fact that for nations, as for individuals, 'evidence' consists mainly of what people do, not what they say, and there is voluminous evidence that Japan's war plans had a long period of gestation, and were worked out in minute detail. Here one may note, for example, the setting up in China and Korea of an elaborate network of spies and intelligence officers, mostly disguised as traders and students. Then there was the building of a modern naval base at Kure in the Inland Sea, the transferral of the officer training college to nearby Etajima and the sending of strongman Senda as Governor of Hiroshima to bully the fiercely protesting local population into bearing most of the expense of building a modern harbour complex at Ujina – a decision inextricably linked with the plans to wage an aggressive war. During the 1894–5 China War, the war cabinet, presided over by the Emperor, moved to Hiroshima, and it was from Ujina that most troops and supplies were shipped to the mainland. In one sense, Hiroshima's 1945 fate was decided by the decision six decades earlier to build Ujina.

The Japanese Emperor system devised after the 1881 crisis was based on the *fukko ishin* doctrine that Japan is the centre of the universe and the Japanese a super race. Thus in Korea an Iwasaki (Mitsubishi) son-in-law was made the first Minister of Agriculture and Commerce, and Mitsubishi duly became Korea's largest landowner; the *zaibatsu* such as Furukawa were 'asked' to be kind enough to take over Korea's mineral wealth; Korean labourers were sent as forced labour to work in Japan's mines, especially in Hokkaidō, and Korea was built up as a base from which to launch further expansion. On the cultural side, Korea was again denuded of her treasures; Japanese became the official language and the only language taught in schools; all Koreans were forced to use Japanese names; and the planting of the national trees became a prison offence (with liberation, the Japanese cherry trees were among the first to suffer).

After the war, the Emperor system was swept away, and the military were swept under the carpet, but the old commercial imperialism not only survived but grew stronger. It was now the businessman, flying off overseas, who prided himself on being 'the new *samurai*'. Japan's obsession with becoming number one – the world's economic super-power – is not really a break with the past but a natural extension of *fukko ishin*.

The above brief analysis differs from accepted dogma in several respects. Assertion, of course, must now be backed by detailed analysis. Unfortunately, the amount of material available in English is pitifully inadequate, and it is impossible in one volume to give a detailed analysis, for example, of the 1881 *Seihen*, Japanese economic penetration of Korea, the Mitsubishi–Satchō wars, the role of the intelligence networks and so on. What is required is to build up an outline knowledge of modern Japanese history, then to hone in on one period or aspect. This deeper knowledge must then be used to illuminate the wider story. This volume will pay particular attention to the 1873 *Seihen* as an event vital to the understanding of Japan's self-image and self-delusion. We shall examine the three interlocking threads: the teachings of the *kokugakusha* and the *fukko ishin* ideologues, the role of the great western fiefs, and the commercial expansion of Japan. But this is far more than just a study of that *Seihen* or that period in Japanese history: it provides many of the keys necessary for the understanding of later ages.

Let us take just one example. The young officers of the thirties, who wrought such havoc with the selective assassinations, liked to quote not contemporary writers but those of the Bakumatsu period. Especially revered was Yoshida Shōin, the extreme young teacher whose Hagi *juku* was attended, at least briefly, by most of the Meiji Chōshū leaders. He was executed by the Shogunate, and a very youthful Itō Hirobumi was one of those who washed and dressed the body and replaced the head. (Perhaps it was because of this incident that Itō, throughout his life, was extremely aware of the horror of such a death, and his own assassination, when it eventually came in Korea in 1909, was mercifully swift as he fell to a barrage of seven bullets fired from the six-shooter of 'a lone Korean assassin'.) The writings and deeds of the Bakumatsu period have generally been ignored by Japanese historians writing about the 1873 *Seihen* but they are vital to our understanding not only of the *seihen* but also of the opening of Korea, the 1894 War, the life and death of Itō Hirobumi, the young officers of the thirties and the student terrorists of the sixties.

It is in this longer story that one must seek the answers. For Western historians it is a two-way street: a long study of Japanese equips them to understand present-day Japan, but, at the same time, unless they are prepared to be absorbed into Japanese life for a considerable period of time, to feel the same pressures and frustrations and to come to think and react like Japanese, it is highly unlikely that they will be able to relive the Japanese historical experience. Almost inevitably, they will take the 'documents' at their face value and be unable to penetrate beyond a carefully erected façade. They will be prisoners of 'documents' usually collected by the Japanese Establishment.

11

# 2

# WESTERN WRITERS AND MEIJI HISTORY

Western writers who have contributed significantly to our understanding of Meiji Japan are few and far between. For this there are five main reasons: linguistic problems; a shortage of reliable source material; the Japanese propensity to disguise the truth; the tendency of Japanese historians to serve the State; and the fact that Western historians are prone to follow their current national orthodoxy.

The Bakufu policy of isolation involved keeping foreigners in the dark about Japan. Thus in 1830, when Takahashi Sazaemon gave Dr Siebold a map of Japan in response to Siebold's gift of a world map, he was arrested and soon 'suicided' in prison. Being a *rangakusha* was quite a dangerous business.

## EARLY WESTERN WRITERS

From the time of their first contacts, Westerners were frustrated by a mixture of secrecy, myth-making and bold deceit. Dr Hawks, Perry's official historian, was told by various Japanese that they were forbidden by law to tell foreigners anything about their country (Mossman 1873: 25). With perhaps a degree of foreign exaggeration, British envoy Alcock drew attention to

> the incorrigible tendency of the Japanese to withhold from Foreigners or disguise the truth on all matters great and small and consequently the absence of reliable information on almost every subject necessary to the full elucidation of their character, institutions and system of government.
> (Alcock 1863: Preface X)

Ten years later, Mossman (1873: 443–4) accused them of 'bad faith'

12

in communicating with the West. He instanced the Iwakura Mission which was shown everything they wished to see and which was able to fill volumes with their notes; but that same mission was prepared to reveal nothing about their own country.

Equally inhibiting was the fact that Britain had backed Satsuma against the Bakufu and claimed a special relationship with the new Meiji government. Early editions of the *Encyclopaedia Britannica* set out the official legends quite clearly in the articles on Ōkubo and Saigō. *The Times* generally restricted its criticism to issues affecting British trade, and when Japan opened Korea 'peacefully' in 1875 it applauded this 'triumph for diplomacy' (*The Times* 17.4.1876). That same year, W. E. Griffis, in his *The Mikado's Empire*, declared the Restoration to have been 'the flowering of the nation'. The government had to contend the 'stolidly conservative peasantry, backed by ignorance, superstition, priestcraft, and political hostility'. The peasants were simply 'too ignorant to see that local abuses of privileges were being adjusted to a national basis of just equality' (Griffis 1876: 9).

Even earlier, Mossman had acted as a spokesman for the government, praising 'the new reign of law and order' (1873: 410), and repeating everything he was told 'confidentially' about 'the inferior character and talents of Kōmei', the 'avaricious and irresolute' deceased Emperor.

In 1880, E. Reed published *Japan: Its History, Traditions and Religions*. He parroted the Japanese claim that Korean kings had traditionally paid tribute to Japan, and quoted an 1879 history by Mounsey, *The Satsuma Rebellion*, which concluded that Saigō had aimed to make himself a military despot under the Mikado, along the lines of Ieyasu and Yoritomo (Reed 1880: 332).

If we move on to Chamberlain's *Things Japanese* we find that, despite its charm and scholarship, it was a work of Japanese jingoism. In foreign affairs, 'some good fairy has presided over all their acts', and 'the civilized warriors of Japan are again inscribing glorious deeds on the page of history' (Chamberlain 1905: 43). Within Japan he had no time for the 'rowdies' who opposed the government. He admitted (ibid.: 353–4) that most newspapers had 'a prison editor', a figurehead whose sole purpose was to go to prison when the time came, and thus leave the real editor free to carry on; yet he refused to criticize press censorship, claiming that 'the thoughtful person' would judge *by the direction* and that things were improving.

13

Though his contemporary account is innocuous, Chamberlain performed a valuable service in pointing out the extent to which Japanese history had been 'cooked'. Modern Japanese history writing dates from 1657 when the second Mito clan lord, Mitsukuni, a grandson of Tokugawa Ieyasu, began the compilation of *Dai Nihon Shi* (the *Great Japan History*) modelled on the famous histories of Ancient China. A devout disciple of the Chu Hsi school of Confucianism, Mitsukuni believed that the purpose of history writing was moral uplift or edification. The compilation of this monumental work continued after Mitsukuni's death in 1700 and, indeed, with interruptions, down to modern times. It was partly with this work in mind that Chamberlain wrote:

> There seems little doubt that the ruling powers at any given time manipulated both the more ancient records and the records of their own age, in order to suit their own private ends. But the process of cooking still persists as may be seen by any critical pair of eyes that will take the trouble to examine contemporary official documents.
>
> A little reflection will show that such manipulations of history are likely to be the rule rather than the exception in Oriental countries. . . . The concern of ancient peoples, and of Oriental peoples, has always been not so much for truth as for edification. Outside Europe and her colonies, it is easy to manipulate records, because the people are told nothing about the matter, and, because even if they were told, they have neither the means nor the inclination to be critical.
>
> (Chamberlain 1905: 241ff.)

Chamberlain later criticized German scholars such as Kaempfer and Siebold:

> Surely it is not enough to get at the Japanese sources. The Japanese sources must themselves be subjected to rigorous scrutiny. It was reserved for the English school, represented by Satow and Aston, to do this – to explore the language with scientific exactness, and to prove, step by step, that the so-called history, which Kaempfer and his followers had taken on trust, was a mass of old wives' fables.
>
> (ibid.: 431)

Standard Japanese histories of the Meiji period cannot be dismissed as old wives' fables, but, broadly speaking, Chamberlain's strictures apply: they are victors' history.

It should be stressed that documents and source material on the Restoration were not assembled until well into the twentieth century. If one checks the historical encyclopaedias such as Kawade (1972) under *Dai Nihon Shiryō* (*Greater Japan Historical Source Materials*) one gets a somewhat different impression. A bureau for collecting historical material was set up in 1869; it underwent various changes of name, but apparently some sort of office remained in existence and in 1888 it was placed under the forerunner of the Tokyo University. The first volume, *Dai Nihon Shingō*, did appear in 1901, but it dealt with the fourteenth century, and this series was to be concerned only with Japanese history to the end of the Edo period. Thus in the nineteenth century the objective study of the Restoration had not really begun.

There were, of course, diaries and letters, but these, too, can be doctored. Selected letters, such as those in Vol. 17 of *Fukuzawa Yukichi Zenshū* (1958–64) generally avoid the issues we most wish to examine, while surviving Godai letters frequently contain the injunction 'Top Secret, please destroy'. Such letters do little more than alert us to the fact that we are being fed scraps.

In addition there were numerous newspapers, but for the historian they are something of a minefield. Foreign papers such as *The Times* and the *China Post* are worth consulting, but we must not lapse into believing that we are necessarily dealing with accurate and impartial journalists. There were, too, various local English language papers. The *Japan Herald*, with J. P. Black as editor (Black 1962: Intro.), was launched in 1861 and it at once became the official organ for the publications of the treaty powers' legations. In 1867 Black set up his own rival paper, the *Japan Gazette*, while in 1868 sixteen vernacular newspapers sprang up. Most, however, were so scandalous that in 1869 the government imposed censorship and required the licensing of papers.

To provide the vernacular press with a model, Black began the *Nisshin Shinjishi* (*Reliable Daily News*) in 1872. Its usually constructive criticisms of the government won it the right to publish the proceedings of the Council of the Left, but in 1873 it overstepped the boundaries of discretion by revealing confidential information about the crisis of that year. It also opposed the Formosan expedition of 1874; and so in 1875 regulations provided that only Japanese could publish vernacular papers. Black defiantly started the *Bankoku*

*Shimbun* in January 1876, but, with Parkes co-operation, the government soon had him closed down.

The ex-banker Rickerby (Black 1962: 377–8) had started the *Japan Times* in 1865, but it was bought out and became the *Japan Weekly Mail* in 1870. English papers also appeared in Nagasaki and Kansai, but it could be a dangerous business: in 1864 the proprietor of the *Rising Sun and Nagasaki Express* was attacked and lost an arm (ibid.: 297).

The English language papers, especially the *Mail*, remain a valuable source, but because of government oppression and secrecy, they frequently appear curiously unaware of what was happening and cannot be regarded as a major primary source.

The vernacular press cannot be quoted lightly. Papers rose and fell with great speed; they were subjected to government censorship and suppression; and they went in for editorials and polemics rather than for reporting. Though it would, of course, be a mistake to regard any newspaper as completely impartial, the historian researching British or Commonwealth history in the mid-nineteenth century can begin his or her researches by working through *The Times*, the *Sydney Morning Herald*, etc., and thereby get a basic understanding of the major events and issues. There is no Japanese vernacular paper of the early Meiji period which the historian can use thus as a starting point. Each paper quoted must be researched so that one understands the position of its writers, owners and affiliates. This is no simple task and really means that each paper requires its own specialist. For the non-specialist, such papers are best used towards the end of research to verify and flesh out conclusions. In this sense, the vernacular papers are secondary rather than primary sources.

In the search for information, the historian is often left merely to speculate. This speculation goes beyond questions of motive and interpretation, and extends to basic 'facts'. For example, in 1850, it seems one Kurume clan leader suddenly made a frenzied attack on another, but was overcome and killed. In the seventies, Kawashima Chōnosuke, an extremist turned chronicler, tried to get to the bottom of that incident (Kawashima 1911), only to find that the authorities had gone to such pains to conceal the truth that all he and subsequent historians could do was to speculate as to what might have happened (Yamaguchi 1973: 57–60).

Such unsolved mysteries are not confined to the provinces. In 1853 Perry brought a letter to the Shogun from the US President asking that diplomatic relations be established with Japan. Despite bitter opposition, Shogun Ieyoshi decided to accept the letter. Shortly afterwards he died suddenly, and in 1858 his successor, Iesada, likewise died suddenly just before the arrival of Elgin. The British envoy Alcock reported that on both occasions it was widely believed that the Shogun had been assassinated and gave detailed accounts of the rumours (Alcock 1863: 216ff.). Yet he had to add that it was quite impossible to get at the truth. Likewise, the death of Emperor Kōmei in 1866 is shrouded in mystery. Was he, too, assassinated? There were widespread rumours of poisoning (Tsuda 1915: 365–8). These are not matters of mere titillation but are central to our understanding of the realities of government and the nature of power in both Bakumatsu and Meiji Japan.

The historian is liable to misinterpret the lack of evidence. In *The Japanese Seizure of Korea 1868–1910*, Conroy concluded that the Japanese had had no long-range plans to absorb Korea and that they merely reacted to changing external situations. Conroy's conclusion seems to flow from his approach to evidence; 'this author has found no evidence that . . .' (Conroy 1960: 310) and 'the documents do not reveal it' (ibid.: 493) are statements which not so much lament the lack of evidence as imply that lack can in itself be used to support positive conclusions. Yet the Japanese government carefully managed its 'history' of relations with Korea. It was largely cloak and dagger stuff, with agents being sent not so much by the government as by factions or individuals within the government. Moreover, Fukuzawa and Rightist Tōyama (*Fukuzawa Zenshū* 1960, Vol. 17: 559–61; 615–16; 740), for example, also sent their own agents, while the great merchants such as Mitsui and Godai were quite ready to ignore the law. To take a modern analogy, finding out what the Japanese were up to in Korea is similar to, but more difficult than, following CIA activities in South America. If one simply studies official publications, and takes the view that lack of evidence is a kind of proof, one ends up as a propagandist rather than as a historian.

There are many examples of elaborate disinformation in Meiji and subsequent periods. After consulting official documents, diaries, newspapers, etc., the historian might have concluded that in the first decades of this century, Japan's policy aimed at preserving the unity and independence of China. Yet documents (*Kobun Shosen* 1985, Vol. 1: 133–5) released after the war clearly show that Japan had been playing a carefully conceived and executed double game. Unfortunately such revealing documents do not always come to light. Writing in 1904, Stead concluded that

> One great defect of the Japanese system of diplomacy is its unreasonable secrecy. . . . Here all questions are kept secret while they are pending and secret they remain until the end of time unless revealed in some fortuitous way.
>
> (Stead 1904: 218)

Probably a case in point is provided by Katsura's diplomacy. Not long after the Anglo-Japanese Treaty was renewed, Katsura went to Russia, presumably to negotiate with Britain's ally. However, according to a book by Sun Yat Sen's interpreter (Tai 1927), Katsura had told Sun that Japan's main enemy was Britain, and that he was going to Russia to have secret talks with the Kaiser.

The historian must take great care to choose an expression which accurately conveys the degree of probability. In discussing the role of the Genrō (Elder Statesmen) in a certain incident, Hackett struck just the right note when he declared that 'the logic of the situation and the available information compel one to conclude . . .' (Ward 1968: 94). Unfortunately, the available information is not always that compelling. In the Katsura case, a study of his character and policies does suggest that Tai Kito was telling the truth; yet even so his unsubstantiated statements provide the historian with stimulation rather than proof. Frequently, one is driven back to such models of Japanese circumspection as *de arō ka to mo sōzō sareru ga* (one can imagine that it might have been thus, but it is not clear). This is not scientific language, but no amount of research is going to obviate the need for some such expression. The main problem confronting the researcher is not digging out the available information but acquiring a knowledge of Japan and Japanese history deep enough to enable him or her to appreciate the logic of the situation and to develop skills in assessing the degree of probability.

### Japan by the Japanese

By any normal standard, *Japan by the Japanese*, the book Stead edited in 1904, must be regarded as a collection of valuable documents. It has a section on the Constitution by Itō Hirobumi, and others on finance and commerce by Inoue and Shibusawa. Itō gives the following explanation of the Constitution:

> The Emperor is Heaven-descended, divine and sacred; he is pre-eminent above all his subjects. . . . His Imperial Majesty has himself determined a Constitution, and has made it a fundamental law to be observed both by the Sovereign and by the people. He has further, made it clear that every provision in the said Constitution shall be conformed to without failure or negligence.
>
> (Stead 1904: 34)

It was, of course, Itō and not the Emperor who drew up the Constitution. The Emperor left no direct testimony in the form of letters or diaries, but it is fairly clear that he did not relish being turned into a symbol and strove instead to play the role of a modern constitutional monarch. For example, on 17 May 1890, Prime Minister Yamagata proposed bringing stormy-petrel Mutsu into the Cabinet, but the Emperor strongly objected because of his treachery during the Seinan War (Toriumi 1979: 92–3). Yamagata, with the support of Itō and Inoue, persisted, arguing that it was safer to have Mutsu inside the government. Nominally, the Emperor had the right to reject Mutsu and even to dismiss Yamagata, but like a good constitutional monarch, he allowed his objections to be over-ruled. Mutsu, as Foreign Minister, was to be a key figure in bringing about the China War. He was also a key figure in the great Furukawa mining *zaibatsu* which was basically a front organization for politicians and bureaucrats – a charming device for rewarding themselves, first in Japan, then in Korea and beyond, with other people's mines and land.

As for the respect Itō paid this divine personage, it is well illustrated by two incidents. From May 1888 to January 1889, the Privy Council held long sessions to consider the draft Constitution, and the Emperor hardly missed a meeting (ibid. 96). It would seem that it was at his own request that the Emperor participated in these deliberations. But in May he was furious because the Edict he had to read in setting up the Privy Council was not sent to him by Itō till the previous day. He was so incensed that, in effect, he threatened strike action.

Another illustration was provided during the China War. Out of their 'deep respect' for the Emperor, Itō and Inoue did not patronize the Hiroshima *geisha* houses, but went up to picturesque Onomichi.

Frequently, however, they did not get back in time for the meetings of the War Cabinet, inspiring the Emperor's famous lament: 'The only ones taking this war seriously are me and my horse' (Kimura 1979: 103).

Though the origins of the Meiji Constitution are now well known, successive generations of Japanese were forced to accept the Itō version as literal truth. Like *Japan by the Japanese*, many Meiji 'documents' were source material not for the historian but for the myth-maker whose task it was to glorify not only the Emperor but also the Satchō government. The standard claims that the Satchō leaders were 'persuaded' to take over mines and vast land-holdings, and that they accepted 'for the good of the nation', are as misleading as Itō's claims that the Emperor personally drew up the Constitution.

In *Japan by the Japanese* we see a common rhetorical device: instead of avoiding an incident which exposed their feet of clay, many Japanese leaders would draw attention to it and brazenly claim that it proved their morality and integrity. Before the Russian War, Katsura and other leaders were badgered and bullied by a stream of Army visitors. Yet Suematsu paid Katsura the following tribute:

> He told me that during that long-protracted negotiation with Russia, not one of our military or naval officers or men had come to him to disturb him with their opinions of diplomacy or politics. This will probably give you some idea of what are the characteristics of our army.
>
> (Stead 1904: 578)

Ōkuma used a similar rhetorical technique when writing for the New York *Independent* in 1899:

> That Japan entertained no idea of the permanent possession of the land which she conquered can be inferred from the readiness with which she evacuated Liaō-tung Peninsula under the friendly advice of some European powers.
>
> (Uchimura 1932–3, Vol. 16: 514)

In truth, of course, the Three Power intervention had produced a state of national hysteria which clearly indicated the depth of Japan's commitment to territorial expansion. According to Chamberlain (1905: 220), forty committed *seppuku* when the territory was handed back. In these two examples the events are too well known, and the deception too blatant, to be really effective, but when dealing

20

with relatively obscure questions where the evidence is far from compelling, the historian is apt to be intimidated by a bold assertion that black is white.

This tactic has undone several naive young Western historians. For example, Oxford wrote thus of the 1881 *Seihen*:

> As the prestige and fame of the Kōjunsha grew, so did the rumour that it was a subversive political party. The rumour was fed by another rumour – equally widespread and equally groundless – that Fukuzawa was conspiring with Ōkuma Shigenobu, then Minister of Finance, to overthrow the government.
>
> (Oxford 1973: 53)

The rumours were certainly widespread, but even a cursory investigation of the 1881 *Seihen* is enough to show that they were far from groundless, and such starry-eyed and unquestioning acceptance of Fukuzawa's protestations of innocence – the charges were 'fitting material for a cheap comedy' (*Fukuzawa Zenshū* 1960: 316) – reduces Oxford to the level of a publicist for Fukuzawa.

Akita's account of the same question is even more culpable (Akita 1967). Whereas Oxford simply accepted Fukuzawa's protestations, Akita tried to give weight to the argument by adding the testimony of Ōkuma and Treasury official Go Junzo. As Ōkuma is, in effect, on trial along with Fukuzawa, his only real witness is Go. But Akita simply plucked his quotation out of a collection of letters without checking on Go's own background.

Go was the son of a Gifu farmer (Hakushaku Go Seinosuke Den 1943: 14ff.). Becoming a low-ranking Bakufu official, he rose rapidly in the last days of the Bakufu when many officials backed away from their posts. His career took him to Ezochi (ibid.: 34), and for three years he was *machi bugyō* in Osaka where he developed extensive contacts in the business world (ibid.: 42–3). He stayed on to serve the Meiji government, soon became entrenched in the Treasury, and helped bring Shibusawa back into the government (Shiraishi 1933: 147). He lived like a feudal lord, and a *Jiji* article of 22 September 1901 listed him as one of the 150 Tokyo men with assets of over half a million yen (*Iwasaki Yatarō Den* 1967, Vol. 2: 606ff.).

Go's eldest son Seinosuke did his first day's work at the age of thirty-one, when he was made president of one of the Kawasaki companies. He went on to become *the* leader of the Japanese business world with the honorary title of Ōgosho, which his son prudently bestowed upon Ieyasu when he retired – a formal recognition that Ieyasu still wielded power from 'behind the curtain'. In modern Japan only three men have been known as ōgosho: Shibusawa, Go and Nagano Shigeru.

Go would not condescend to become Treasurer (Hakushaku Go Seinosuke Den 1943: 514), but stayed close to Tanaka Giichi, played a leading role in the development of China, and died in 1942 with full honours.

The key to understanding *Japan Incorporated* lies in the system of marriage and adoption alliances. In 1876 Go had given his fourth son, then aged two, to Iwasaki, and this 1876 Go–Iwasaki adoption alliance had been a significant step in the emergence of Mitsubishi and the later creation of 'Go ōgosho'. As Okuma is best seen as the most important of the prime ministers raised up by Mitsubishi, Akita's use of the testimonials of Go, Fukuzawa and Ōkuma as proof of Mitsubishi's and Fukuzawa's non-involvement in the 1881 *Seihen* is rather like concluding there was really no Watergate scandal because Nixon, Mitchell and Dean said so.

## MODERN HISTORIANS

A true appreciation of the 1873 *Seihen* is vital to an understanding of Meiji politics and Japanese imperialism. Whether they be thought of as bridge-builders, *goyō gakusha*, or as simply being naive, the few Western historians who have touched on the *seihen* of 1873 and 1881 have done little more than parrot Japanese propaganda. The handful of biographies are uncritically hagiographical. Iwata's *Ōkubo Toshimichi, the Bismarck of Japan* (1964) does not even mention Ōkubo's corrupt *alter ego*, Godai, while Lebra's biography of Ōkuma Shigenobu, the Prime Minister who presented China with the notorious Twenty-One Demands, praises him for his interest in China (Lebra 1980). Not surprisingly, Lebra, like Akita, has the distinction of being translated into Japanese.

Among senior historians we have Akita's 1967 account of the making of the Japanese Constitution and Conroy's 1960 version of Japanese–Korean relations. Both might well have been commissioned by the Satchō oligarchy, and could be presented in Japanese high schools without a single Mombusho amendment. Then there is Beasley's recent work, *Japanese Imperialism 1894–1945* (1987) which still sums up the 1873 crisis as a struggle between 'a war party' which sought to send 'a punitive expedition' against Korea, and a cautious group of leaders who regarded a Korean war as one which would be dangerously wasteful of resources and which would give Britain and Russia a chance to fish in troubled waters. 'Caution won' (Beasley 1987: 43). This Beasley version has advanced not one whit from the PR material put out at the time by the victors.

The difficulties involved in doing research into Meiji history are thus quite formidable. Where, then, should the researcher begin? Perhaps the least imperfect method is to start with the wealth of biographical and autobiographical material. Once one becomes familiar with the characters and careers of the leading politicians and merchants, and of various relatively unknown officials, the logic of the situation begins to emerge.

Various biographies have been written by Western historians, but generally they are 'banzai biographies', being naive and hagio-graphical. One such is Iwata's *Ōkubo* which claims that 'Emerson's statement that "all history resolves itself very easily into the biogra-phy of a few stout and earnest persons" . . . is particularly applicable to Japan during the Restoration period' (Iwata 1964: Intro.). I must strongly disagree. It is not a 'hero' approach that leads us to stress biographies. Indeed, they lead us in the opposite direction, showing – usually despite the biographers – that the 'leaders' were being swept along by the tide of events.

Again, it should be stressed that the emphasis placed on such sources is not due to a naive belief in the veracity of those involved. Each such work must be subject to intense critical scrutiny. When people such as Ōkuma and Ōkura reminisce about their own activities, it is simply ludicrous to take their statements at face value. However, their testimony does become more significant when they talk about others. As this comes to the very heart of Meiji history writing, let us take some specific examples.

Masuda Takashi's autobiography (Nagai 1939) is the gleeful narration of a garrulous old man. It does not add too much to our knowledge of the Osarisawa mine scandal, the Mint, the setting up of Mitsui Bussan or his subsequent war with Fukuzawa's nephew, Nakamigawa, for control of Mitsui. Yet it is full of throwaway gems, and helps piece together that tapestry of interlocking relationships which must be clearly perceived before one can begin to comprehend the stance of the principal actors. For example, in 1859 Masuda's father obtained a position in the foreign service due to the help of Go Junzo (ibid.: 24). Go later became a key Treasury official. In 1863 Masuda senior went to Europe with the Ikeda Mission (ibid.:

36ff.). There were strict laws against officials taking along members of their own family, but Takashi went along by simply changing his name – a nice example of how nepotism worked. When they called into port in China, a young Satsuma *samurai* asked to be taken along. He was refused and returned to Nagasaki where business-shark Godai became his protector, providing him with clothes and money and setting things right with the clan. This young *samurai*, Ueno Kagenori, must be regarded as a Godai protégé. He later joined the Foreign Office and became one of the officials most involved with the opening of Korea. The Godai connection is, of course, not mentioned in official documents but it should set us wondering how many of the officials involved in the opening of Korea were protégés of Godai.

Masuda throws much light on Inoue, Mutsu, etc., and tells too of an official who helped his young brother, a Bakufu soldier captured in the north. He was sent back to Edo and was to be sent into exile in Sanuki in Shikoku, making the dangerous crossing in August in a small local boat. However, Takashi heard of an official who could be relied upon to fix such things (ibid.: 158). His brother was freed, changed his name and enrolled at Keio, where his father was Fukuzawa's secretary. Takashi claimed (ibid.: 10) that his father wrote the first set of school rules and was the first to use the name Keio. Be that as it may, one should note this early Fukuzawa link with Masuda, and hence Mitsui. This little incident also tells us more than piles of documents about the official who, quite obviously for a price, could be relied upon to circumvent the law. His name was Ōkuma Shigenobu, and this incident should be borne in mind when assessing Ōkuma's 1873 dilemma. Of course, we have only Masuda's word, but he and Ōkuma were to remain close, and quite clearly he felt there was nothing reprehensible in either his own conduct or that of Ōkuma.

Many Japanese historians have cast a critical eye on such reminiscences. Sawada Akira (1966), for example, has shown that the official 1916 biography of Yuri Kimimasa is full of inconsistencies and mistakes. He analyses six of Yuri's *jitsuwa* which have been quoted as gospel by a succession of learned historians, and shows that they are full of errors. He also effectively ridicules Ōkuma's account of raising money in Osaka on his way up to Edo – 'a first-class Ōkuma story'.

Kido is another whose veracity has been seriously questioned. Tominari's 1972 biography reaches the conclusion that Kido's 'diaries' were subsequently amended to show his own actions in a more favourable light. Diaries, no less than tapes, can be erased and re-written, and can rarely receive unqualified acceptance.

Indeed, one is brought back to the logic of the situation. In 1873 the government was torn apart by the Korean question; two years later a 'conference' was held in Osaka to get Kido and Itagaki back into the government. There are no first-hand reports of what was said, so the historian must judge by second-hand reports and by the apparent results of the meetings. Itagaki and Kido returned to the government, and it has been assumed that the talks were confined to domestic matters. But here again one must suspect that Japanese historians have been blinkered by considerations of *taigi meibun*. As Itagaki and Kido had left the government in 1873 and 1874 over policy towards Korea and Formosa, surely it is logical to assume that these questions were raised in the 1875 meetings. The fact that there are no reports of such discussions is of little significance. The 1874 Formosan expedition became something of a fiasco because it received too much publicity and this mistake was not repeated in 1875 when a force was sent to cause an incident in Korea and thus provide a pretext for forcibly opening that country. One must ponder why it is that contemporary commentators and later historians made no attempt to link the Osaka Conference and the opening of Korea.

Thus the Western historian must be prepared to go beyond the perimeters laid down by his Japanese counterparts. Rather than accepting documents and 'authorities' at face value, he must be prepared to speculate and to search for the truth. He must never forget that all autobiographies and diaries are merely testimonials presented for the scrutiny of the historians' court. The much-quoted writings of both Sasaki Takayuki and Fukuzawa Yukichi drive home the message that in dealing with Meiji history, there are no short-cuts, no neat little collections of primary sources which can be pieced together to give us our story. What we have – even when it poses as primary sources – is a mass of evidence which must be sifted through, subjected to the closest scrutiny and, all too frequently, downgraded or even discarded. The witnesses, too, must be regarded as being on trial, and it is not enough simply to give name and occupation.

If one is mesmerized by documents and primary sources, one will finish up like Akita with his droll description of the wonderful and idealistic Meiji leadership – a leadership which was pocketing everything in sight 'for the good of the country'. For the Western historian collections of documents represent a special trap. They are useful if used to supplement and direct his own reading, but they tend to assume a special aura and to take the place of true, original research. Again this is nicely illustrated by Akita is his posthumous attack on the unorthodox Canadian historian, E. H. Norman (Akita 1977). Taking Dower's definition of 'primary source' as 'documents found in collections' Akita claimed that in 'Japan's Emergence' Norman had used primary sources only fourteen times as against 240 Japanese, and 449 Western, secondary refernces.

This definition, however, does not make sense. It leads to absurdities such as Akita's own attempt to exonerate Mitsubishi by quoting Okuma, Fukuzawa and Go.

The multi-volumed biographies usually have enough primary material to fill a volume. With a biography, we know the direction in which we are being led, and so can evaluate the letters. Separate collections of letters are usually better taken as a supplement to the biography. It serves little purpose – and, indeed, gives a false aura of authority – to flaunt certain sources as primary, for so often the 'secondary' sources are primary, and the 'primary' sources are secondary supplements.

Not the least valuable section of the official biographies is the list of mourners and the supplementary tributes. For instance, the Maruyama Kanji's 1936 biography of Soejima begins its supplement with a tribute from T ōyama Mitsuru. This alerts us to the fact that there is a straight line running from the Soejima foreign policy of early Meiji to the later activities of the Kokuryūkai (Black Dragon Society). Indeed, T ōyama informs us that when Soejima briefly replaced Shinagawa as Home Minister in 1892, the staff he brought with him were provided by Tōyama. Likewise, when Tōyama died, the mourners were to be led by ex-Prime Minister Hirata Kōki, who was to be the only civilian executed as a war criminal after the Second World War. Whereas Reischauer has popularized the thesis that the thirties represent an aberration, the Soejima–Tōyama–Hirata line suggests an essential continuity which, of course, goes back far beyond Soejima's time. It is this sense of continuity which is so lacking in both the so-called primary sources and in the standard histories – a lack that grievously distorts the events of 1873, the Beasley-type accounts of Japanese imperialism and also much of the writing on post-war Japan. Hirata, Matsuoka and Yoshida Shigeru were close FO colleagues who began their careers in China at almost the same time. When Hirata was appointed Prime Minister, his first act was to nominate Yoshida as his deputy and to delegate to him the task of assembling a Cabinet. Yoshida himself proved unacceptable, but this does not invalidate the closeness of the Hirata–Yoshida ties. Matsuoka was to die in Sugamo prison, Hirata to be executed, and Yoshida to become the symbol of the 'new' post-war Japan until forced out by that other 'new' man, Kishi.

When one comes to research the Japanese advance into Asia, one is confronted with a complex, even chaotic, tapestry of forces, events and personalities. At the same time there are no confidential government sources, Hansard reports or solid information from foreign correspondents and missionaries. Thus one has to rely on diaries, letters, etc. which may well have been 'cooked', and be somewhat intimidated by the *goyō gakusha*. The *goyō gakusha* is a worldwide phenomenon; but the fact remains that the Japanese are distinguished by the fervour, the extent and the durability of their efforts to serve the State, and the great weakness of the main body of Western writing on Meiji Japan is that it has remained overly dependent on Japanese scholarship and official 'documents'. It has not achieved that basic independence and freshness of approach so essential when historians approach the story of another country.

# 3

# EZOCHI, KOREA
# AND THE FOUR GREAT
# WESTERN CLANS

Though the furious 1881 *Seihen* was triggered by the 'sale' of Hokkaidō to a new Satsuma company, the Japanese tendency to separate political and economic history and to leave 'local' history to local historians has led Japanese historians to treat that *seihen* without making any real attempt to discuss the Hokkaidō background. They have managed to reduce it to a political crisis taking place in Tokyo. Yet not only in 1881, but even in 1873, the basic question was one of general overseas expansion – Korea, Manchuria, the Ryūkyūs, (Okinawa) Formosa and Hokkaidō and the northern islands. They must be fitted into an overall picture – a picture which revolves around trade. So before moving on to Korea, let us consider Hokkaidō, partly as a section of a trading network and partly as the scene of Japan's early expansion and the area where the colonial policies were largely developed.

## EZOCHI

The name 'Hokkaidō' (North Sea Road) was not adopted until 1869 and parallels 'Tokaido' (East Sea Road), the great highway from Osaka to Edo (Tokyo). For centuries it had been known as Ezo Island (Ezochi), and the small islands north-east as Ezo-ga Chi Shima (the Thousand Islands of Eso). The new name was meant to emphasize the fact that the large northern island was now an integral part of Japan.

The Japanese first came in strength in the first half of the fifteenth century to trade with the local Ainu (Kaiho 1974: 22ff.), the hairy black-haired people of Caucasian extraction who had once occupied much of Japan. They built *tate* (or *date*), which were fortified trading posts under *kannushi* (fort chiefs). Most of these trading post masters were from Hokuriku, and especially Wakasa, Kaga and Etsuzen. It seems they were merchants who came to trade but later gave themselves the names of true *bushi* (warriors) and rewrote the family tree to conform with their new status. The Akita clan settlement at Matsumae in the south-west became the major Japanese centre.

In the 1450s the Ainu and the Japanese began a war which was to last a hundred years (ibid.: 24ff.). The Japanese were driven out of their trading posts, even Hakodate, but rallied around Matsumae whose leader, Kakizaki, eventually went on the offensive. The war ended in 1550 with the treaty which in effect ceded the south-east corner around Matsumae to the Japanese. Matsumae also acquired a monopoly of trade with the Ainu, and as the trading posts demonstrably needed the protection of Matsumae, they were obliged to sell it all their furs and fish. Thus developed the *chigyo* system whereby their followers were granted trading rights in eighty-five scattered places. The Matsumae wealth was based not on rice or general agriculture, but on the taxes on this trade.

Until the end of the sixteenth century the Ainu struggle had merely been a local struggle against various northern Japanese clans, with Kakizaki ruling Matsumae on behalf of Akita's Andō family. But once Hideyoshi united Japan, Kakizaki Yoshihiro went to Kyoto to pay his respects and became his direct minister. In 1591 he helped Hideyoshi put down Kujō, who had usurped power in Nambu, and in 1593 he was made virtual ruler of all Ezochi; though his direct rule was confined to the south-west corner, all Japanese entering the island required his permission. On Hideyoshi's death, this power was confirmed by Ieyasu as part of the Tokugawa policy of settling its foreign relations. About the same time the Tsushima clan was made intermediary in relations with Korea and Satsuma was given control of the Ryūkyūs. Like Tsushima, Matsumae had no *roku* and, in place of rice and agriculture, depended on trade for its income. Likewise they were not obliged to perform as regularly as other clans the crushingly expensive *sankin kōtai* system whereby the local lords had to spend much of their time in Edo and were thus kept poor and submissive.

Once Matsumae became independent of Akita, its prosperity increased. Though products such as skins, fish, seaweed and fish oil remained most important, timber, birds and gold dust were added to this list. Its prosperity was of a kind not seen in Hokuriku and Tohoku. Its culture was also of a high standard, with its poets and painters known in Edo.

This prosperity was not achieved without serious clashes with the Ainu, notably in 1642 and in 1669. At the end of the sixteenth century, the Tohoku Ainu had been hard hit by contagious diseases, especially measles and smallpox, and this had led them to flee to Ezochi. But there they were soon brought under the control of the *chigyō nin* or trader-soldiers who were like independent rulers. The scattered trader-soldiers grievously abused the trading 'rights' conferred by Matsumae. This abuse, combined with ecological problems (ibid.: 55–6) and the fact that the Ainu were forming larger political units, led to full-scale war. The Bakufu responded by ordering Tsugaru to send troops and Nambu and Sendai weapons. Even then it took three years to restore peace and concessions had to be made.

## Reform of 1717–21

We may divide Hokkaidō history into three broad periods (ibid.: 34ff.): the first lasted from the entry of the *wajin* (Japanese) till the end of the hundred years war in 1550 when Matsumae was in effect ceded to the Japanese; the second period extended from 1550 to 1717 when the dual role of trader-soldier ended and we see the development of the *ukeoi* system whereby merchants bought monopoly trading rights in certain areas. After 1717 came the modern period of 'armed commercial capitalism' (ibid.: 169) when the Matsumae clan withdrew from direct participation in trade, and acted as military police guarding the southern capitalists against Ainu uprisings.

This change to modern commercial capitalism was largely due to merchants from Ōmi (Shiga). The famous early merchants of Ezochi had melted away as quickly as they had arisen, but the Ōmi merchants rose more slowly and surely and retained their postions even though they were disliked in Ezochi – 'Ōmi robbers, Ise beggars' (Nagata 1966: 30–5). From their central position adjoining Kyoto the Ōmi merchants often began their lives as peddlars, travelling far and wide. Indeed, before the policy of *sakoku* was enforced, they were even established in Annam. As early as the Genroku period (1688–1704), the Ōmi merchants had formed their own Ezo association to keep out other merchants. Their great merchants houses all had branches in Hakodate, Esashi or Matsumae, but their headquarters remained in Ōmi (see historical encyclopaedias under 'Ōmi merchants').

The change to modern commercial capitalism meant the completion of the enslavement of the Ainu. It was this combination of great capital from Ōmi and Ainu slave labour which led to the commercialization of the fishing industry and to a level of prosperity unknown even in Edo.

In the Tenmei period (1781–9), the Tohoku poor started going to Ezochi in considerable numbers as seasonal workers. This alternative labour supply made the conditions of the Ainu even worse. It would seem that their great decrease in population dated from about this time. Kaiho (1974: 173–4) gives the following estimates: in 1669 40,000, 1804 26,000 and 1854 18,000.

To recapitulate: by 1717 the Japanese had already been in Ezochi for 300 years. The main centre had been developed by the Akita clan and the trading posts were set up by the other Tohoku and Hokuriku clans. In times of great change, it was the Tsugaru, Nambu and Sendai clans which provided reinforcements of men and weapons. From the early eighteenth century, the Ōmi merchants brought about a change to modern commercial capitalism based on Ainu slave labour and seasonal Tohoku labour, and backed by the Matsumae clan's military police. Thus the story of Japanese penetration revolved around the Tohoku and Hokuriku clans plus the rich, well-organized Ōmi merchants.

However, this picture must be modified. A hint is provided by the key Ōmi town, Ryōhama, which consisted of two villages, Satsuma and Yanagawa, named, it would seem, after their founders (Nagata 1966: 30–5). This would suggest direct links between Ōmi and the Satsuma trading system running through the Ryūkyūs, west of China and south to the Philippines. Hokkaidō products such as seaweed were an important element in this trade.

In addition, at least from the beginning of the nineteenth century, Japanese goods were flowing freely to the Black Dragon (Amur) region via Karafuto (Saghalien) (Kaiho 1974: 248). The Chinese had entered Karafuto much earlier than either the Japanese or the Russians. From 1751 to 1763 the Japanese had made a limited attempt to administer part of Karafuto, but the first comprehensive attempt was not until the Kansei period (1789–1800) when explorers were sent and a trading post set up. They found that Japanese iron products were being taken by the Ainu to the mouth of the Black Dragon River whence they penetrated into the Asian mainland. Early in the century the Chinese withdrew their base from the mouth of the Black Dragon, and so for the first part of the century Japanese goods flowed freely to the mainland via its Karafuto settlement.

Thus the Ezochi trade was an important element in a trade system extending north to the Black River and south to Ōmi and thence to Hakata, Shimonoseki and Nagasaki and on to Kansai, Korea, Satsuma, the Ryūkyūs, China and the Philippines. In Ezochi, of course, there was no Rule of Law, the traders being a law unto themselves. The picture is not of frontiersmen trading with the natives, but (for at least a century and a half before the Restoration) of an extreme form of modern commercial capitalism. This system had three components: the wealthy, highly organized Ōmi merchants; the Matsumae clan's military police; and the labour supplied by Ainu conscripts and Tohoku seasonal workers.

After the Boshin War, the Matsumae clan was eliminated, so who would provide the military police? Ainu numbers were dwindling, so who would provide the labour? The whole island was now under the Meiji government, so what form of administration would be set up? Japanese historians have covered these three aspects in some detail, but they have skirted round the major story: what happened to the Ōmi merchants and to the long-entrenched commercial capitalistic trading system? Consult, for example, the historical encyclopaedias under 'Ōmi merchants', and one is told that by the middle of the Meiji period they had faded from the Hokkaidō scene because their commercial practices and organization were too conservative and not suited to the modern world.

The truth would seem to lie elsewhere. By far the largest of the Ōmi clans was Hikone, a *fudai* clan close to the Shogun. This was the clan of Ii Naosuke, the Bakufu minister who carried out the great crack-down on the enemies of the Shogun in the late fifties. He was subsequently assassinated but remained the subject of vilification. Hikone and the other small Ōmi clans managed to change sides in time to avoid the ignominy of being branded traitors, but they were complete outsiders in the Meiji scene, and so lost their position in Hokkaidō. For the four great clans – Satsuma, Chōshū, Tosa and Saga – the problem was how to get control of the rich Hokkaidō trade without becoming directly responsible for the irksome duties. Thus the story of Meiji Hokkaidō was to be one of a vicious power struggle between the four top clans for the high administrative positions and for control of the trade, while the defeated clans were called upon to provide the new militia and, together with the new urban poor and the remnants of the Ainu, the labour. Not only in 1881 but also in 1873 Hokkaidō was an integral part of the bitter, interlocking political and commercial struggles.

The fate of the Ōmi merchants illustrates the nature not only of the Satchō takeover after 1868 but also that of Japanese *goyō* scholarship. We shall later take up the story of the Ono-gumi in Kyoto and Murai in Nambu. They, too, were Ōmi merchants, and their fate and that of the Hokkaidō Ōmi merchants make it all too clear that they were deliberately brought down by the Satchō victors. This overall story has been virtually ignored by Japanese historians, and it should remind us of the fact that Japanese history is still heavily slanted in favour of the victors.

## KOREA

The Japanese advance into, and eventual absorption of, Korea must be seen as part of this same fierce struggle for commercial empire. Japanese plans to move into Korea were an integral part of both the 1873 and 1881 *Seihen*, but to understand those plans they must be regarded as part of an ongoing story stretching from 1340 down to the present day.

When dealing with the 1870s *seikan-ron* debate Japanese historians are strangely reticent when it comes to discussing objectives. Korean historians, however, have no such inhibitions:

> Japan, which succeeded in attaining modernization before any nations in Eastern Asia soon undertook the colonization of Korea to obtain raw materials and dispose of her processed commodities. Succeeding in this task, Japan expanded its aggression to the Chinese continent.
>
> (Hong 1973: 173)

Events subsequent to the 1876 opening of Korea would seem to bear out these conclusions. Japan moved quickly to buy up Korean grains, especially rice, and resisted Korean attempts to limit their export. They also flooded the country with Japanese textiles. Once Korea had been annexed, they instituted a land survey as a prelude to taking over vast tracts of land which were then sold off cheaply to the *zaibatsu* and to Japanese colonists. Unemployed Koreans migrated in droves to Vladivostok, Manchuria and to Japan itself. Others were brought to Japan as forced labour, while, within Korea itself, the cheap labour was utilized to develop munitions industries as Korea was turned into a base from which to attack China.

It does not necessarily follow that when the Meiji government forced open Korea in 1876 its objectives were to take over the Korean rice trade, make it a market for her textiles, appropriate great tracts of land for her *zaibatsu* and colonists, bring Korean forced labour to Japan, and use Korea as a base from which to attack China; but the historian should be aware of subsequent events and be on the look-out for evidence of such objectives.

Japanese and Korean histories differ substantially in their accounts of mutual relations. Many Japanese historians have argued that for much of its history Korea was a tributary state and that in the Meiji period Japan was merely seeking to restore its position. Korean historians respond by pointing out that from 1917 the Japanese made intensive searches in South Korea for early Japanese remains but found nothing. On the other hand, there is ample evidence that Korean civilization flowed into Japan from 300 BC onwards. It is even argued that Shōtoku Taishi (574–622), the famous royal statesman, was a Korean (ibid.: 52–3).

Just before the 1894 War, that most perspicacious of travellers, Curzon of India, described Korea as 'this shuttlecock among the nations' (Curzon 1894: 83). This description is applicable not just in the modern era but throughout most of its history. In the thirteenth century, the Koreans resisted the Mongol invasions and, as the Mongols were weak at sea, shifted their capital to Kōka-tō (Kangwha island). Eventually the Mongols prevailed and forced the Koreans to join them in their invasions of Japan.

The Mongol invasions so weakened Korea that it became an easy prey for *wakō*, especially after 1350. For Japan, this was seventy years after the Mongol invasions, but those invasions had helped to impoverish the *samurai* and bring on the downfall of the Kamakura Bakufu.

The Japanese internal wars disrupted normal trade and from about 1350 (Watsuji 1950: 160) led to a proliferation of *wakō* based mainly in North Kyūshū and the Inland Sea. Their fleets of dozens, and even hundreds, of ships stepped up their attacks on the Korean coast, and from 1369 on the coast of Ming China as far south as Canton. They seem to have had no plans to subjugate and colonize, but it is estimated that between 1375 and 1388 they attacked 400 places in Korea (ibid.: 161–2). This forced the peasants to move inland and to leave fertile coastal regions to lie fallow. Maritime traffic became paralysed, so grain could no longer be transported by sea and taxes in kind could not reach the capital. Even Kangwhatō came under attack (Ki-baik 1984: 162–3). Diplomatic representations to Japan proved fruitless, the Japanese authorities claiming they lacked the power to suppress the pirates. But Korean counterattacks, especially against their Tsushima lair in 1389, gave some relief.

Largely because it had been unable to prevent the Japanese attacks, the Wang dynasty fell in 1392 and the successful General Yi Song-gye (Taejo) became king. He moved his capital inland to Hanyang, the site of present-day Seoul, a place easy to defend, for the River Han leading up from the coast was difficult to navigate and passed four miles from the city which was guarded by a ring of unoccupied rocky hills. The origins of Seoul must be borne in mind when considering the pious protestations of early Meiji 'surveyors', Japanese and Americans, who tried to proceed up the river.

As the old aristocracy resented the upstart Yi, 'he was in need of authoritative sanction for his regime, and he chose to make political use of Ming China to this end' (ibid.: 189). Thus he sent tribute parties several times a year, and they became the medium of cultural borrowing and economic exchange.

### Wakō

In the succeeding centuries, the *wakō* tended to become legitimate traders, but when barriers were raised against trade, they would revert to their old piratical ways. Thus they were again to be an important element in bringing down China's Ming dynasty.

Japanese history tends to remain silent about these *wakō*, and most of our information comes from Korean and Chinese sources. However, it is clearly a mistake to regard them as pirates acting independently. In the civil wars of the 1340s pirate fleets were asked to come to the aid of loyalists in Kyushu. Their help made it possible in 1345 for the loyalists to consolidate their position in South Kyushu and to move up the coast to Higo (Kumamoto). In 1347 a pirate fleet attacked the coast of Chikuzen, and in 1348 we have references to a prince moving his headquarters 'under pirate escort' (Sansom 1963, Vol. 2: 74–5).

As the 'pirate' attacks on Korea proliferated from 1350, it would seem that there was at least a degree of connivance and co-operation on the part of the Japanese authorities. Japan was a highly mountainous country where internal communications were difficult. In times of great stress, such as civil wars, food supplies were bound to be interrupted. Korea, however, presented a vastly different picture.

As Curzon was to write: 'in the possession of an excellent climate, a soil of more than ordinary fertility, vast tracts of still virgin country, and a robust rural population, Korea possesses the four conditions of agricultural prosperity' (1894: 181). The 'pirate' attacks suggest that there was a supply and demand situation rather than spontaneous raids to meet temporary shortages. Sansom (1963, Vol. 2: 148–50) pointed out that Ōuchi Yoshihiro (1356–1400) of Western Honshu was a dangerous rival to Shogun Ashikaga Yoshimitsu:

> Yoshihiro's strength depended partly upon his influence over other western warlords and partly upon his close links with pirate chieftains in the Inland Sea, some of whom were engaged in freebooting in Korean and Chinese waters *on his account*.

By this time wholesale markets had developed in cities such as Kyoto and Sakai and a powerful clan of wholesale dealers had obtained a virtual monopoly. It seems clear that the *wakō* were not simple pirates but acted as agents for the great *daimyō* and as suppliers of rice for the wholesale merchants.

The role of the merchants has likewise been obscured. From 1570 Nobunaga sent several missions to Korea seeking the re-opening of trade. He seems to have been influenced by the great Hakata merchants (Okamoto 1969, Vol. 12: 162). Hideyoshi likewise had close merchant ties. When Hideyoshi himself left Osaka, he was accompanied by many Kansai merchants, and in Kyūshū he was soon using the great local merchants such as Kamiya Sōtan to rebuild Hakata as a base from which to attack Korea. Hideyoshi is too often depicted as a megalomaniac who single-handedly launched Japan into a period of aggression. Yet it would seem that the *wakō* were in effect an organ of state working closely with the great western *daimyō* and the Kansai wholesale merchants, and that these *wakō*, *daimyō* and merchants were urging Hideyoshi to invade Korea and thereby secure Japan's rice supplies.

This is probably the central feature in the relations between Japan and Korea in the period from 1340 to 1940: mountainous Japan wanted rice from fertile Korea, which was generally reluctant to export its rice. When she would not trade Japan would take the rice by force, the authorities keeping their hands officially clean by letting the *wakō* do the dirty work. This ongoing story of rice relations is vital to our understanding not only of the *seihens* of 1873 and 1881 but also of the origins and nature of Japanese imperialism.

The *wakō* continued to play a vital role in Japanese affairs for some centuries. Before attacking Shimazu, Hideyoshi had to defeat Odawara in the East. 'A large fleet of vessels, some carrying troops, others provisions, was provided by Mōri and Ōtomo and the freebooters under their control' (Sansom 1963, Vol. 2: 326). When Hideyoshi invaded Korea, his naval force 'was composed largely of craft manned by pirates who were under the control of *daimyōs* of provinces bordering on the Inland Sea' (ibid.: 354). These forces proved no match for the Koreans, and 'the pirate admiral Kurushima was driven to commit suicide'. Later their discipline was improved and they had some success.

## Slaves

Though rice was throughout Japan's main target in Korea, there was generally a second target: slaves. This again is a topic Japanese historians prefer to ignore, and there is little in the way of documentation.

Within Japan slavery seems to have been quite widespread and of a long duration. One of Hideyoshi's many charges against the Portuguese – and one which the missionaries found hardest to answer – was that they ran a lucrative trade in Japanese slaves (Watsuji 1950: 374ff.). However, the Portuguese, unlike the Japanese in Korea, were not raiders who simply carried off the locals as slaves, but traders. Quite obviously they operated within an established system and bought slaves with the connivance of the local *daimyō*. Though a trifle arrogant, it was not unreasonable of the missionaries to point out that the suppression of the slave trade was the responsibility of the Japanese government. It is, of course, impossible to give statistics for slavery, but Sansom (1963, Vol. 2: 270), for example, deals with slaves as 'booty' brought back by the *wakō*, and points out that 'Much of the diplomatic correspondence between Japan and Korea at this time deals with the repatriation of captives or fugitives held in either country.'

Despite his indignation at the Portuguese slave trade, Hideyoshi, too, regarded the taking of slaves as a legitimate form of booty. A sixty-year-old Usuki doctor named Keinen crossed to Korea in 1597. He left a diary, *Chosen Nichinichi-ki*, which gives a graphic account of his nine-months' stay and especially of the battle for Ulsan (Okamoto 1969, Vol. 12: 336–9). On getting to Ulsan he was disgusted to find groups of 'evil merchants' who had accompanied the army to Korea. They would follow up after each battle, rounding up people as slaves, binding them with a rope around the neck and driving them back to Pusan with a whip. It was, wrote Keinen, like a scene from Hell.

It is not so surprising that, at the start of the Meiji period, the idea of using Korea as a source of forced labour should be revived.

## The Hideyoshi invasions

By about 1587 a crisis had developed in relations between the two countries, and war was long seen as inevitable (Sansom 1963, Vol. 2: 361–2). Once he had united Japan, Hideyoshi was left with a huge experienced army which he feared to disband. The end of the civil wars caused a business slump and widespread unemployment. Though some business men were opposed to foreign wars, it seems the majority were urging foreign expansion (Hulbert 1905, Vol. 1: 352). Moreover, Hideyoshi was angry that Korea would neither send envoys nor grant access to China. In short, the situation was remarkably similar to that of 1868.

When war came in 1592, the Japanese enjoyed striking early successes due to their superior organization, their fine fighting spirit, and the fact that they had firearms and the Koreans did not. That the Japanese were eventually forced to negotiate a withdrawal was due mainly to three factors: the Koreans proved superior at sea; the Korean people formed Righteous Armies (*Uibyong* in Korean; *Gihei* in Japanese) which harassed the invaders; and Chinese troops, after being poised for some time beyond the Yalu, came pouring into Korea.

Though the Japanese were forced to withdraw, Korea had been devastated by seven years of warfare. The damage was physical, social, cultural and psychological. Almost all that was beautiful had been destroyed or carried off; it was necessary 'to restore order in the Korean social system' (Hong 1973: 113–14), and, for a quarter of a century after the war, the land under cultivation was only about 30 per cent of that of the pre-war period (ibid.: 127). The psychological damage was never repaired. On Hideyoshi's orders noses and ears were cut off, pickled in salt, and sent back to be stored in the Ja-bul-sa monastery in Kyoto. Estimates of the Korea mutilations usually range in the hundreds of thousands, and many of those thus mutilated remained alive for years, a grim reminder of the invaders' savagery. Thus even three centuries later, a pro-Japanese observer such as Curzon had to comment on 'the national race-hatred between Koreans and Japanese', and to contrast it with 'the amicable terms on which the Koreans and Chinese appear to subsist side by side' (Curzon 1894: 206).

In some ways Japan gained from the wars. Korean art treasures, including bells and lanterns, were taken back to Japan, as were 'living treasures'. Korean potters were to form famous industries in Satsuma, Hizen, Hagi, etc. It might also be argued that the war succeeded in wasting a huge army which would otherwise have posed a threat to the government. On the other hand, the war was a tremendous financial drain and led to widespread agrarian uprisings which proved to be another threat to the government.

Some historians have managed to misinterpret Hideyoshi's disastrous seven-year war. Thus the preface to Conroy's *The Japanese Seizure of Korea 1868–1910* claims that 'Hideyoshi had demonstrated in the 1590s that the conquest of Korea was militarily feasible'; as no further Japanese attempt was made until the Meiji period, the Japanese annexation 'cannot be judged to have been giving expression to a deep-seated historical urge'. Conroy ignores the four major lessons of that war – lessons which were not wasted on the Meiji leaders: control of the seas was vital; the invasion had to be carried out without bringing the Chinese streaming across the Yalu; care had to be taken to see that the war did not produce another Tokugawa Ieyasu who had craftily managed to sit out the war; and the war had to be ended quickly before the Koreans acquired modern weapons and its people organized Righteous Armies, and before Japan itself was rent by peasant uprisings brought on by savage wartime taxation.

An interesting summary of the Korean war legacy was provided by 'enlightened' Fukuzawa Yukichi (*Fukuzawa Zenshū*, Vol. IV: 600ff.) who, by 1878, was already suggesting the advantages of a war against the West – not against any specific country or on any specific issue, but a war which would serve countless generations to come, just as Hideyoshi's Korean war had done, by providing a traditional enemy whose very name would provide a rallying cry and make the Japanese people unite as one.

## Korea and China

The Korean wars weakened not only Korea and Japan, but also China, which became easy prey for the Manchus. When the Manchus attacked in 1618, the Chinese asked for and gained Korean support, but once the Manchus gained the upper hand, the Koreans changed sides, and it was a combined Manchu–Korean

Army which gained ultimate victory in 1637 (Hulbert, Vol. 2: 66ff.). Thereafter Korea settled down as the Hermit Kingdom, but kept its suzerainty relationship with China. Indeed, in some ways Korea was now more Chinese than China, for it kept, for example, the Chinese clothing now abandoned in China.

As Meiji Japan was to trumpet its attempts to 'liberate' Korea from Chinese 'control' it is important to understand what Curzon termed 'the historical tutelary position of China' (1894: 121). Right down to the 1894 war, that position was manifested in the following manner: every Korean king and queen received their patent of royalty from the Peking court; tribute missions continued; the name of the reigning Korean monarch was conferred by the Chinese Emperor; when the Imperial Commissioners arrived from Peking, the king was obliged to proceed outside the capital to receive them; Peking had to be notified of royal deaths; and the Korean king could not wear the imperial yellow.

Curzon also stressed the religious and cultural ties he found there even in 1894. Korean Buddhism was akin to the Chinese in all its outward forms (ibid.: 108), while Seoul was 'in most exterior aspects a Chinese city' as its founder was 'a monarch who in everything aped the Chinese model' (ibid.: 121). Even more important, 'among the upper and lettered classes, Chinese itself is the invariable vehicle both of speech and correspondence just as it is also the official language employed in Government publications, proclamations, examinations and decrees' (ibid.: 98). This was, of course, classical Chinese, and not contemporary colloquial Chinese.

The logic of this ritual suzerainty and cultural affinity is easily understood if one considers the Japanese connection. In the fourteenth century, the ceaseless rice and slave raids had brought down one dynasty and had led in 1392 to the setting up of a new dynasty which moved its capital to an inaccessible spot inland. It was the savage Japanese invasions of the late sixteenth century which devastated the country, produced an enduring race-hatred relationship and led Korea to become the Hermit Kingdom whose conscious cult of poverty told the world 'we have nothing and we need nothing, so please go away'.

## The role of Pusan

By 1400 Shogun Ashikaga Yoshimitsu was firmly in charge in Japan. As China and Korea had persuaded him that he had more to gain by regular trade than by piratical attacks he agreed to suppress the *wakō* and to institute regular trade missions. This system, however, soon broke down, and the *wakō* raids continued. The Koreans responded in 1419 by attacking their Tsushima lair.

> The Sō house, the rulers of Tsushima, now sent repeated missions to Korea to express their contrition, and in response the Yi government took a conciliatory position, granting the Japanese limited trading privileges. Three ports were opened up to them along the southeast coast of Korea, at Naeipo (Ungch'on) Pusanpo (Tongnae) and Yomp'o (Ulsan), and trading and living quarters (Waegwan) were established in each to enable the Japanese to conduct their business. In consequence, Japanese vessels fairly streamed into the three ports, carrying away with them large quantities of rice and cotton cloth. The Korean side then decided to work out a treaty that would limit the volume of goods given or traded to Japan, and such an agreement was reached in 1443.
>
> (Ki-baik 1984: 191–2)

Tsushima ships were limited to fifty a year, and the amount of rice and beans limited to supplies for about 100 people.

In 1510, as a result of Japanese riots in the three ports, trade was suspended, but in 1512, as a result of Sō entreaties, a new treaty was drawn up. It did, however, halve the number of ships and the exportable amounts of beans and rice.

Later in the century, the trade with both China and Korea again broke down, yet despite their mutual antipathy, Japan and Korea still needed each other's trade. Thus, after the Hideyoshi wars, Japan was soon pressing to have the three ports re-opened. After some time, they were allowed back into Pusan, but the number of annual ships was reduced to twenty (Hulbert 1905, Vol. 2: 59). They frequently protested that their quarters and port facilities were too restricted, and in 1678 they were given permission to move to the site of present-day Pusan. Their reception halls, houses, etc., were built by carpenters from Tsushima, this task taking three years. The Koreans undertook to keep the settlement in good condition, and repairs were made sixteen times between 1721 and 1864 (ibid.: 153). But Pusan remained essentially a Japanese settlement which must be equated with foreign cities in Japan such as Kobe and Yokohama.

Though the Tokugawas had soon assigned Korean trade and diplomatic relations to the lord of Tsushima, and this system continued till the Meiji Restoration, it must be remembered that Tsushima had strong Chōshū ties, while the traditional trading centres such as Hakata and Satsuma did not lightly abandon their traditional sources of wealth. Thus one encounters frequent references to secret trade, and once the Bakufu fell and Japanese seclusion was abandoned, it was inevitable that these western trading clans should seek to open Korea and to restore and expand the old trade. In short, the geographical position of the Korean capital and the suzerainty relationship with China were both due mainly to the need for protection from Japanese invaders. For Japan, it was necessary to destroy this relationship and to prevent Chinese troops from pouring across the Yalu before she could safely invade and occupy Korea. Hence the much trumpeted need to 'liberate' Korea from China. Once that had been done, she could pursue her centuries-old designs on Korean grain and labour.

## THE FOUR GREAT WESTERN CLANS

The Meiji charge into Asia and the fierce competition for commercial empire were to be dominated by the four great western clans, so let us look briefly at the history of these four clans, especially their relationship with the continent and with each other.

### Chōshū

The long Sengoku period of civil wars meant that the centre of gravity shifted away from Kansai to western Honshu even though that region lacked the centre's natural resources. By 1500 the great western barons such as Ōuchi of Yamaguchi and Kyūshū's Shimazu and Ōtomo were playing an important role on the national stage. Thus in 1500 a fugitive Shogun sheltered in Yamaguchi, and in 1508 Ōuchi restored him to office (Sansom 1963, Vol. 2: 261).

The Ōuchi empire expanded to include seven provinces stretching from present-day Okayama prefecture across western Honshu and into the two north-eastern provinces of Kyūshū, including the great trading city of Hakata. The possession of Hakata was particularly important for it had long been the centre of the China trade, and it was the wealth from the China and Korea trade which provided the basis for Ōuchi's expansion and subsequent power. Later the Ōuchi's wealth was to be supplemented by mining, for in 1530 the Iwami silver mines were discovered and in 1542 an even richer deposit at Ikuno in Tajima (ibid.: 257). The Hakata merchants likewise played a key role in this mining development, for it was they who brought skilled men from China and Korea to improve the smelting processes.

The civil wars and consequent decline of the national capital meant the cultural as well as the political and economic emergence of the provinces. Yamaguchi became a great cultural centre which attracted nobles, scholars, poets and painters. Throughout the Sengoku period, new ideas and learning continued to enter Yamaguchi from Korea and China. Thus it is not surprising that Jesuit Francis Xavier, after entering Japan at Kagoshima in 1549 and touring as far as Kyoto, decided that Yamaguchi was the most suitable place for his headquarters.

However, in 1551 the Ōuchi chief was assassinated, and in 1554 his domains passed to the Mōris who were based on Hiroshima. The Mōris were unable to maintain their grip on Hakata, which was devastated by rival Kyūshū lords. Due to the disturbances in both countries, 1548 saw the end of the official China missions, and with the fall of the Ōuchis there was no one capable of controlling the *wakō*. But once they seized Macao in 1557, the Portuguese, whose ships were strong enough to repel the *wakō*, entered the China–Japan trade as carriers and middlemen, mostly trading Chinese goods for Japanese silver (ibid.: 266). Thus this trade continued to form the basis of Mōri power.

At Sekigahara in 1600, the Mōris and Shimazus formed the backbone of the western army. The defeated Mōris were severely punished, being reduced to the two provinces which came to be known as Chōshū. They were forced to leave Hiroshima and make their castle town in the small Japan sea town of Hagi. Chōshū was still a clan of substance, but it had lost both the mainland trade and the Japanese silver mines. Most of the Mōri retainers followed their lord to Hagi, thus causing a top-heavy society, and making it impossible for all the *samurai* to retain their full rank and income. Inevitably, Chōshū also lost its status as a cultural Mecca, with the position tending to be reversed; for Chōshū students now trudged off to Kyūshū to study the new Western learning coming in through Nagasaki.

The Meiji Restoration was to be not so much the restoration of the Emperor as the restoration of Chōshū and Satsuma commercial and political power.

## Satsuma

The story of Satsuma's development as a commercial power revolves around its Ryūkyū links and the southern trade.

The Ryūkyūans, whose homeland consists of about sixty islands, are believed to have become culturally distinct about 2,000 years ago. Over the subsequent centuries Ryūkyūan and Japanese gradually became mutually unintelligible.

The first tribal mission to China was in 1372. Chinese families were brought to the Ryūkyūs to set up industries, and Ryūkyūan students were sent to China from 1392, so strong trade and cultural ties developed. By the fifteenth century the Ryūkyūans had already opened trade with Siam. The Kyūshū *daimyō* would then pick up these southern products which were largely sold in Korea. From 1430 Japanese ships were sailing direct to Siam and by 1450 Ryūkyū ships were going to Malacca rather than Siam.

In 1432, when the Chinese trade was suspended by the new Shogun, Ming China tried to revive the official trade by using the Ryūkyūs (Watsuji 1950: 165). A protracted struggle developed between the Ōuchis on the one hand, and the Sakai-based Hosokawas and Satsuma on the other, to control the China trade, with Hosokawa and Shimazu sending their ships to Sakai via Tosa in southern Shikoku.

Thus one is looking at a system of trade routes, with the Japanese acting largely as middlemen for about 150 years from 1425, bringing goods from Siam, Java, Malacca, etc. to the Ryūkyūs and then taking them west to Fukien in China or on to Korea or east via Tosa to Sakai. The Ōuchis, of course, used Hakata as its trading centre from which goods were taken via Tsushima to Korea or directly to north and central China. The main goods sent by Japan to China and Korea were copper, silver, sulphur, swords and the goods brought from the south.

In the second half of the sixteenth century, the Europeans penetrated South-east Asia and Ming sent its own trading ships, so the Japanese role as middleman declined sharply. This helped turn Japanese traders to the Philippines, a region familiar to the *wakō* in the fifteenth century. There they clashed with the Spaniards, who for their part were keen to break the Portuguese monopoly of trade and religion in Japan. Like the Ōuchi in Yamaguchi, Satsuma's Shimazu in the sixteenth century used their trading wealth to embark upon a policy of territorial expansion. It is highly misleading when Western historians such as Conroy (1960: 215) begin talking of 'Kyūshū-ites', for much of Kyūshū regarded Satsuma as their traditional enemy. The small neighbouring clans like Obi in Miyasaki, and the large northern clans, such as Chikuzen (Fukuoka) and Saga, were wary of Satsuma, for by the 1580s it had absorbed Kumamoto and was threatening to unite all Kyūshū under its banner. It was at the express invitation of the northern clans that Hideyoshi entered Kyūshū and drove Shimazu back south.

After Sekigahara, Satsuma was not treated as harshly as the Mōris, for this distant wealthy clan's power remained essentially intact. It was confined to the three southern provinces, but it was soon working harmoniously with the Tokugawas. Hideyoshi had demanded that the Ryūkyūs contribute troops for the Korean war, but Shimazu interceded on their behalf and their commitment was reduced to providing supplies. In 1609, on the pretext that it had not met its obligations, Satsuma conquered it with the approval of the Shogun, its fleet of 100 ships with modern arms meeting little resistance. The northern islands of Amani were placed under direct Satsuma rule, but the Ryūkyūs were permitted to retain their royal family and a façade of independence. China ties, both ritual and commercial, continued, for Satsuma wanted to profit from this indirect China trade, the Ming ban on trade with Japan having been a great blow. Satsuma also extracted a substantial annual tribute from the Ryūkyūs.

From the time Shimazu entered the islands the people suffered cruelly because of the double exploitation by Satsuma and their own king (Gabe 1979: 1–29). But this trading wealth enabled Satsuma to restore its fortunes, and by the end of the eighteenth century it was probably the wealthiest and strongest clan. Its lord, Shigehide, had resigned and gone to live in Edo, marrying a daughter to the Shogun and being 'the power behind the throne'. Unlike Chōshū, it was not an emasculated power brooding over past glories, but a wealthy one able to bide its time. Yet it shared with Chōshū the knowledge that its future, like its past, lay in overseas trade.

## Tosa

Wild and rugged country effectively separated Tosa from her nearest neighbours, yet it was no isolated outpost, for it looked out onto the Pacific and depended largely on the sea. In the Sengoku period, Satsuma ships sailing to Sakai could not pass through the Yamaguchi-controlled entrance to the Inland Sea, so they came via

Tosa. Its presence on this trade route meant it was in regular touch with two advanced regions, Kansai and Satsuma.

Nor was it intellectually isolated. Throughout the Sengoku period new learning entered Ōuchi territories from Korea, and, in 1548, an Ōuchi scholar, Minamimura Baiken, settled in Tosa bringing the newer Confucian teachings from Korea. He is generally regarded as the founder of a famous Tosa school of thought, Nangaku, though many regard its real founder as a disciple, Tani Jichū (1598–1649). (It is unlikely that Jichū was directly taught by Baiken.) Jichū's pupils included Yamazaki Ansai (1618–82), the son of a Kyoto *rōnin* who became a Zen priest, then went to Tosa to study under Jichū. He returned to open a *juku* in Kyoto, then also taught in Edo. His teachings aimed at combining Confucian and Shintō thought, and the *sonnō* aspects of his teachings were picked up by a disciple and carried to Mito, thus helping in the evolution of that clan's famous school of thought. Thus Tosa was not isolated either commercially or culturally.

Politically, too, it was a part of national movements. In the fourteenth century the Hosokawas were allotted the whole island of Shikoku for their part in helping the Ashikagas gain power, but in Tosa the land was virtually under the control of seven prominent families. After the Ojin no Ran, they engaged in a many-sided struggle, with Chōsokabe Motochika coming out on top. In 1575 he set out to bring the rest of Shikoku under his control, but, as with Shimazu in Kyūshū, he was defeated by Hideyoshi in 1585, and thereafter was confined to Tosa. He died in 1599.

As Tosa fought on the side of the western clans at Sekigahara, Motochika's heir, Morichika, was removed and retired to Kyoto. Later he joined the unsuccessful attempt to restore power to Hideyoshi's young son, Hideyori. He and seventy-two followers were executed and their heads displayed to the public gaze (Sadler 1978: 293). Tosa was then handed over to a Tokugawa supporter, Yamanouchi, who built in Kōchi a fine castle around which a town soon grew up. His successor, Tadayoshi, greatly developed his territory. His long-serving *karō*, Nonaka Kenzan (1615–63), was a disciple of Tani Jichū and applied Nangaku principles. New industries were developed, harbours improved, and large areas of land brought under cultivation. The Yamanouchi followers had become the upper *samurai* while the Chōsokabe *samurai*, now 'low class', were largely forced to occupy the newly developed regions, becoming half-*samurai*, half-farmer. This broad class division is clearly seen in the Meiji period. For example, Itagaki's forebears (Itoya 1974: 12–13) came to Tosa with Yamanouchi, and as the first Itagaki had no children, a Yamanouchi was adopted as his heir. On the other hand, Sakamoto, Nakaoka, Hijikata, Kōno Togama and most extremists traced their roots back to pre-Yamanouchi Tosa.

The two largest clans in northern Shikoku were *shinhan* (Tokugawa family clans), for they were assigned to sons Ieyasu produced late in life. Thus, in the Bakumatsu period, they were tightly bound to the Tokugawa cause. Tosa, on the other hand, had greater freedom of action, for its rulers were merely Tokugawa allies, while its lower *samurai* were generally anti-Bakufu. In the early Meiji period, Tosa was to flirt with the idea of uniting Shikoku under its leadership as one power block, but it was not the natural leader of Shikoku; and, as in northern Kyūshū, when Hideyoshi defeated Tosa, he was regarded as a deliverer rather than an oppressor. Thus it is not surprising that Meiji Tosa was soon to abandon the idea of a Shikoku league, in favour of closer Satchō ties. Her position on the key Satsuma–Sakai trade route, and the fact that she looked out onto the Pacific, caused her scholars and rulers to dream of overseas expansion, especially to the south; and this dream was embraced with great enthusiasm by 'low' *samurai* such as Sakamoto Ryōma, who sought to reverse the fate imposed by Sekigahara.

## Saga

In the sixteenth century, Satsuma united the south of Kyūshū and then went on to defeat Higo (Kumamoto) in the centre. In the 1580s it was planning to attack North Kyūshū when Hideyoshi arrived from the east, defeated Shimazu, and established control over Kyūshū.

Hideyoshi had grandiose schemes of world conquest. His first aim was to follow the Chinese model and to extract tribute from his neighbours. In 1587 through Tsushima's Sō, he sought tribute from Chōsen (Korea); in 1588 through Shimazu from the Ryūkyūs; in 1591 from Luzon and in 1593 from Taiwan (Takeno 1979: 57–8). In 1592 his troops crossed over into Korea, and when the Indian Vice-Consul sent a message, he replied by relating how he had united Japan and was about to take China, whence it would be easy to move on and occupy India. There he would teach Shintō and the true versions of Buddhism. Though Christianity was the 'false religion', he would permit traders to come and go. His letters to the Philippines were even more blunt in referring to conquest. He called on them to submit to 'the Will of Heaven'.


### Hideyoshi and Nabeshima

Saga had long regarded Satsuma as their traditional enemy. Thus their armies fought alongside Hideyoshi against Satsuma. Within two years of the Satsuma campaigns, Hideyoshi had taken over Nagasaki and entrusted it to the Hizen (Saga) General Nabeshima, a public declaration of the closeness of their relationship. Later he was responsible for Nabeshima succeeding as *daimyō* (ibid.: 128ff.).

When Hideyoshi heard that his forces had taken Keijō (Seoul) he at once announced that he would shift the Japanese capital to Peking and would receive the Japanese Emperor there. He himself would make his headquarters in Ningpo because of its importance as a trading centre. Land in China and Korea was to be distributed among Japanese nobles and *daimyō*, while armies were to be sent on into India and South-east Asia.

Readily embracing Hideyoshi's plans, Nabeshima crossed with his army to join the earlier generals such as Katō. Like Hideyoshi, he wished to switch his capital to the mainland, and earnestly begged that he be given new domains in either Korea or China. It should be noted that this desire for mainland territory was not just the personal whim of Nabeshima, but was shared by the faction loyal to the old *daimyō* (ibid.: 137). It was claimed that in Hizen, in every hamlet and village, the people knew that Hakata's wealth came from the China trade, so the common people right down to the lowest shared this dream of setting up an empire in Ming China.


### Nabeshima and the Tokugawas

Like those of Hakata, the Hizen merchants helped organize supplies for Korea, and the Japanese defeat came as a great blow.

Though Nabeshima was on the side of the western alliance at Sekigahara (ibid.: 149), he was neither replaced nor punished. The Nabeshimas responded by serving the Tokugawas faithfully. In 1642, Nabeshima and Fukuoka's Kuroda were made jointly responsible for the defence of Nagasaki, a task they performed conscientiously right down to the Bakumatsu period. Being thus responsible for Nagasaki, and situated between Nagasaki and the administrative centre, Hita, Saga was truly incorporated into the Bakufu system, and the Bakufu ties were strengthened by marriage alliances.

Four aspects of Saga's history must be made clear. First, its traditional enemy was Satsuma, and Nabeshima had in effect won his *daimiate* by fighting with Hideyoshi against Shimazu. Thus, when Saga rebelled in 1874 against the Satchō government and Ōkubo responded with great ferocity, it was the predictable culmination of centuries of history.

Second, Saga's responsibility at Nagasaki meant its officials were relatively familiar with dealing with the West. Hence it was, at least initially, well represented in the Meiji government, especially in positions dealing with foreigners.

Third, its position at Nagasaki alerted Saga to all the dangers posed by the West. It built up its own navy and navigation school, and these may be regarded as the forerunners of the Japanese Navy. The association with Nagasaki inevitably meant that Saga became one of the most progressive clans, and its schools attracted many outside students.

Finally, we must note Saga's interest in Ezochi. From his youth, Kansō, who was lord from 1830 till he retired for his son in 1861, dreamed of controlling Ezochi (see *Hokkaidō no Yoake* 1965: 14ff.). But defence and trade were to go hand in hand: he hoped to use the Amakusa products, especially sugar, to trade with the Ezo sea products (ibid.: 15–16). He also planned to develop Amakusa mines and timber to pay for warships, and these could then be used to back overseas expansion. Saga would be in a position to expand south from Amakusa and north from Ezochi; and, of course, Saga's close involvement with the Hideyoshi invasions had not been forgotten. The point to stress is that expansion into Ezochi was regarded as a part of, and not an alternative to, general expansion in other directions.

In 1840 Nagayama Sadatake was sent to tour Tohoku to investigate ways of Saga helping to develop and defend this region. This problem was made the subject of debate by the students of Kōdōkan, the clan school.

After the 1854 Treaty, Hori Toshihiro was appointed as Hakodate magistrate. Kansō sent Shima north with him to tour Ezochi and Karafuto. On his departure, Kansō had the Kōdōkan students write poems 'On Seeing Someone Off to Ezochi'. Shima kept a record of his travels which created considerable interest. Again, on Shima's return, Kansō had the students give speeches and hold debates on

Ezochi. All accepted the need to guard and develop Japan's north and west gates, and some such as Etō went on to argue that they should go abroad to trade and use the profits to develop Ezochi (ibid.: 18).

For the historian, concentrating on one man can be a convenient form of shorthand; but be it Fukuzawa, Saigō or Etō, it is a highly dangerous procedure. We have seen how, in Hideyoshi's day, the people of Hizen generally supported plans to set up a province in the mainland. In like manner, it was not a question of one or two Saga men like Etō suddenly becoming advocates of expansion. Here we have a clear picture of public debate being officially promoted and carried on with great vigour.

In the 1873 *Seihen*, a distinction is often made between the military and civilian factions (*bu* and *bun*). Probably a more important distinction is that between the military and commercial factions. The extreme Emperor party, typified by Maki (Kurume), Kusaka (Chōshū), Anegakōji (noble) and Takechi (Tosa), regarded it as Japan's 'holy mission' to expand. They envisioned military expansion, but they must be regarded as ideologues. There was another school of more modern and pragmatic men who sought to expand for commercial reasons. Of course, the division was not simple and clear-cut, for many of the latter claimed to be ideologues, while some of the Emperor party were not averse to commercial gain. Yet it remains a valid and useful distinction, and the Saga clan must be seen as belonging to this second school.

Late in the Ansei period, it looked as though Saga would obtain Amakusa from Ii, but his assassination ended such hopes. The clan did, however, obtain the Chishima Island of Shikotan as a result of Tanaka Yoshiemon's negotiations. This was used as a trading post, and Tanaka persuaded Hizen merchants to send ships to trade at Nemuro and Kushiro. Big shipowners such as Taketomi Heisaku and Taketomi Gihachi sent ships and made a great profit (ibid.: 19).

Thus Saga had long been interested in Ezochi and had developed significant trade. This it hoped to develop as part of a wider trade network. Thus it is not surprising that with the *ishin*, Kansō became the first *Kaitakushi Chōkan* (Development Office Chief) with most of the officials being Saga men. After Kansō's death, Shima and the other Saga officials were to be driven out and the *Kaitakushi* became a Satsuma preserve. Hokkaidō history was not a thing apart, but very much a part of the wider anti-Satchō struggle. When the *Kaitakushi* was wound up in 1881, Saga's Ōkuma and Sano led the opposition to the *haraisage* ('sale') of much of Hokkaidō to a mainly Satsuma company. Historians frequently bring their opposition down to questions of personal ambition, but it must be seen as the climax to a much longer story.

## Fukuoka

As well as the four great clans which dominated the Meiji government, special note should be taken of Fukuoka, for this prefecture was to be the home of Japan's most famous rightest organizations, and one of their protégés, Hirata Kōki, was to be the only civilian executed after the Second World War (see Takeno 1979: 226ff.).

Japan's Yayoi period (300 BC–AD 300) began in northern Kyūshū under influence from Korea and was characterized by extensive trade with both Korea and China.

In 663 Dazai-fu was made the administrative centre handling relations with Korea and China. Hakata was its port, receiving overseas envoys and acting as a trading centre for goods not only from Korea and China, but also from the south. For a millennium, Hakata was Japan's cultural and commercial gateway to Asia.

After being ruled by the Ōuchis then devasted by rival Kyūshū clans, Hakata was placed under Hideyoshi's direct rule in 1587. Hideyoshi also gave Kuroda, a Bizen (Okayama) general, territory in Kyūshū as a reward for his services in the Kyūshū wars. Kuroda made his capital at Nakatsu and his son married a daughter of the Shogun. The son fought well at Sekigahara while the father kept northern Kyūshū secure. They were rewarded with over 500,000 *koku* in Chikuzen. Hakata lies east of the Naka River, but from 1601 Kuroda drained the marshy land west of the river and built a strong castle. The name of this area he changed from Fukusaki to Fukuoka in honour of his forebears who came from Fukuoka in Bizen. Thereafter Fukuoka was a *bushi* town, Hakata a merchant town.

The Kurodas took no direct part in trade, but left it to the merchants, both the great old Hakata families and the new merchants who had followed them from Bizen. Of course the Tokugawa restrictions severely affected Hakata, and the larger merchants therefore set up branches in Nagasaki, and many of them responded to the restrictions by resorting to smuggling. There was 'almost a mania for smuggling', and only 'the plodders' stuck to regular trade, while 'the keen blades' all turned to smuggling. The officials also 'cooked' their books: 'trade accounts published by the Nagasaki Kaisho were false, and no credit could be given them at all' (Takekoshi 1967, Vol. 2: 181–3).

In 1667 Hakata's Itō Kozaemon, who was believed to have Kuroda backing, was caught smuggling by the Bakufu representatives and about twenty were crucified or executed (ibid.: 183ff.). Thereafter the Kurodas kept a tight rein on smuggling. But at Nagasaki it was never really stamped out. Shinseitō – Holy Isle or Isle of Silence – between Korea and Kyūshū became a famous base for smugglers, and right down to the Meiji period, people such as Ōkuma grew rich helping merchants subvert the laws they were paid to uphold.

The trading activities of people such as Itō were clearly to the benefit of Kyūshū and of Japan as a whole, but they constituted a threat to the Tokugawas and perhaps to the new warrior class brought in from the east. If the Tokugawa rule was to last, the great western clans had to be prevented from building up economic, and hence military, power.

With the Restoration, Satchō were likewise concerned with concentrating not only political but also economic power in their own hands. Tosa and Saga were able to challenge through normal channels, but Fukuoka was effectively excluded from the government. Even Nagasaki declined rapidly with the opening of Yokohama and Kobe. Fukuoka was to become famous for its rightists, but the ideological factors should be kept in perspective, and the unchanging geo-political factors clearly understood. A revival of Fukuoka, and of northern Kyūshū generally, could only take place if it could resume its traditional commercial and cultural role as the gateway to Asia. The real extremists were the Satchō clans which sought an unnatural monopoly of power, privilege and wealth.

# 4

# TOKUGAWA JAPAN

## SEVENTEENTH- AND EIGHTEENTH-CENTURY JAPANISM

Once the Tokugawas adopted a policy of seclusion, it became highly inconvenient still to regard China as 'the Middle Kingdom' or the centre of the world. As Buddhism had originated in India and Confucianism in China, seclusion meant that Japan was being cut off from its spiritual and intellectual roots unless these imported doctrines could be balanced out by a body of teachings originating in Japan. Hence there developed the teachings of the *Shintōsha* ('the Shintō people') and this term, with no real change in meaning, gradually gave way to the *kokugakusha* (the National Studies people).

*Kokugakusha* and Sinologists were united in their hostility to Buddhism. In the words of an Indian *kokugaku* scholar, S. A. Prasad, the *kokugakusha* not only rejected Buddhism, but regarded India as most lowly and its people as 'black, stupid and filthy' (Prasad 1984: 530) – an attitude which has survived to the present day.

Though the Bakufu and clan governments still relied heavily on Confucian doctrine, the *kokugakusha* saw 'the China heart' as a corrupting influence and sought to return to that fine 'Japanism' which had existed before the penetration of Chinese influence. Thus 'a whole brave new world of patriotism emerged in the seventeenth century: . . . patriotic men, parties, vocabulary, theory, ethics and psychology. The patriot profession was born' (ibid.: 471).

## *KOKUGAKU* PIONEERS

Motoori Norinaga (1730–1801) called his learning *kogaku* or Ancient Learning, and listed Keichū Ajari (1640–1701), Kada Azumamaro (1669–1736) and Kamo Mabuchi (1697–1769) as its parents.

Keichū was a Buddhist monk who studied the ancient classics, especially *Manyō shū*, in an attempt to return to the thoughts and ethos of antiquity (*fukko shisō*). He gave a rather routine acknowledgement to the myths contained in the ancient classics *Kojiki* and *Nihongi*, but did not push them dogmatically as an expression of literal truth.

Kada Azumamaro was anti-Keichū. His teachings were immature in that he dealt with the universal soul and did not concentrate on the unique Japanese soul; but historically he is important as the teacher of Motoori's teacher, Kamo Mabuchi.

Mabuchi was probably the first Tokugawa patriot to write habitually of Japan as 'the imperial country' (ibid.: 456). He wrote scathingly of Chinese customs such as deposing bad kings, and claimed that Chinese influence in Japan had made things elegant on the outside and rotten inside.

Whereas Mabuchi simply referred to Japan as 'the imperial country', Motoori aggressively insisted that failure to use this term was close to treason. He also insisted that the old myths should be regarded as literal truth. He repeats the familiar ideas that the Japanese Emperor, being born of the gods, is unique and is the emperor of the whole world. Just as there is only one sun in the sky, there can be only one emperor in the world. 'Motoori's originality lay not in any particular proposition, but in composing a systematic theory of the imperial country out of ideas that were already there, and in forcefully and seasonably publishing the theory' (ibid.: 459–60). One of Motoori's bitter regrets was that Hideyoshi wasted his time in Korea instead of attacking China directly (ibid.: 462).

Inevitably, as Meiji Japan began to move into China, there developed a boom in Motoori studies. Since the Second World War, scholars such as Maruyama Masaō have virtually ignored Motoori's rabid Japanism, and have concentrated on his *naimenteki shinjō* ('internal feelings and emotions'). But his historical significance surely lay in his development of the theory of international relations as being between one imperial country (Japan) and many barbarian tributaries – clearly an adaptation of the Chinese doctrine of the Middle Kingdom.

This question of terminology is of the utmost importance. When Motoori demanded that Japan be referred to as 'the imperial country' and the Japanese as 'the men of the imperial country' – *mikuni* and *mikunibito* – he was not merely concerned with etiquette but was issuing a constant reminder that the Mikado was the emperor over all other kings and chieftains in the world. At the start of the Meiji period, when the new government wrote to the Korean government, it was to refer to Japan as 'the imperial country', making it all too clear that Japan was claiming a superior position and was preparing to 'restore' its position in Korea. Korea's refusal to accept the Japanese messages was thus both rational and justified.

Neither Mabuchi nor Motoori were anti-Bakufu. Far from being political activists, they stressed loyalty to both Emperor and Shogun. However, there were emerging other schools openly hostile to the Bakufu. Yamazaki Ansai (1618–82) had founded Suika Shintō, and Takenouchi Shikibu (1712–67), one of his disciples, set up a school in Kyoto attended by some of the nobles. These included names prominent in the Bakumatsu struggles: for example, Iwakura Hisatomo (1737–99) and his father Iwakura Tsunetomo (1701–60), Tokudaiji Kinmura and Higashikuse Michitsumu. Shikibu taught a passionate imperialism with a sharp anti-Tokugawa edge until 1758 when he was banished from Kyoto. Iwakura Tsunetomo and Higashikuse Michitsumu were also forced into retirement.

Motoori's Japanism was an extreme form of racism and nationalism. It was probably inevitable that such feelings and teachings should develop once Japan was sealed off from the world. They cannot be attributed to pressure from Europe, for these widespread anti-foreign teachings were mainly directed at India and China, and aimed to justify *sakoku* by showing that Japan, the new Middle Kingdom, was independent of, and spiritually superior to, the rest of the world.

Motoori sought to change people's hearts but not to spur them into action against the government. The next great teacher, Hirata Atsutane, was to produce activist disciples, and even before Motoori's death, the move to 'restore' the Emperor may be said to have been begun by Takayama Hikokurō (see chapter 5). Such activists differed from Motoori, who was satisfied with the existing regime and frightened of change; but they all had in common one basic characteristic: their patriotism was a kind of religion.

## THE BAKUFU IN THE SEVENTEENTH AND EIGHTEENTH CENTURIES

By the end of the seventeenth century, the total income of the Tokugawa family was about 17 million *koku*, out of a national total of 26 million (Sansom 1963, Vol. 3: 4), whereas that of Konoe, the highest noble, was only 2000 *koku*. The 130 noble families were indigent, being reduced to teaching arts and crafts and marrying their daughters to rich *daimyō* (ibid.: 28). The royal family itself was effectively subordinated. Shogun Tokugawa Ieyasu married his daughter to the Emperor, then in 1629 forced the Emperor to resign for his own daughter, that is to say Ieyasu's granddaughter. She was the first Empress since the eighth century.

Ieyasu legislated to achieve a stable non-changing society. To encourage obedience and frugality, the Tokugawa Buke Sho-Hattō laid down laws against lewdness, gambling and selfish conduct such as choosing one's own wife. There was an elaborate system of checks and balances, with inspectors and spies touring the land. From the outset, opposition was crushed ruthlessly. After Osaka castle was taken in 1615, thousands were executed and their heads displayed on the road between Kyoto and Fushimi. 'Justice' was based on torture.

Under most Shoguns, monumental corruption became endemic to the system. This was partly due to the fact that many Shoguns were little more than figureheads. For example, Ietsuna ascended in 1651 at the age of ten, and for the remaining thirty years of his life his ministers ruled in place of this weak, dispirited Shogun.

In the eighteenth century, the Shogunate reached its peak under Yoshimune (1716–45), but he was succeeded by his weak, stammering son, Ieshige (1745–60). Under 'this imbecile Prince little was accomplished, and in 1760 he resigned office for his son Iehara who, though weak and nervous, was not a lunatic' (ibid.: 198). But by 1760, there was already considerable anti-Shogunate feeling, especially in Kyoto.

Under Iehara, the decline continued. The seventies and eighties saw a series of natural disasters including floods, fires and plagues. The great Temmei famine, which lasted from 1783 to 1788, was one of the three worst famines in Japanese history. Half the population of northern Japan was said to have died in seven years and there were many reports of widespread cannibalism (Takekoshi 1967, Vol. 3: 127ff.).

These disasters helped precipitate the downfall in 1787 of Chamberlain Tanuma, a man of most humble origins who was detested by the Sanke (Three Tokugawa Families). To get allies among the other great feudal lords, Tanuma had arranged a marriage between Ieharu's son, Ienari, and the daughter of Satsuma's lord, Shigehide.

The [Shimazu] family presented Tanuma with a silver ship eighteen feet long, loaded with gold and silver, in return for his services. In many such ways the clans that were previously kept out of Court circles now gradually encroached over the threshold.

(ibid., Vol. 2: 127)

The downfall of Tanuma in 1787 saw the introduction of the Kansai Reforms and the nomination of Matsudaira Sadanobu (1758–1829), the young *daimyō* of Shirakawa in Mutsu, as president of the Council of Elders. Sadanobu was benevolent, but his attempts to revert to the policies of his grandfather, Yoshimune, meant that 'he was in fact a reactionary in an era of inevitable change' (Sansom 1963, Vol. 3: 198). At first Sadanobu's relations with the Kyoto court were good, but when Emperor Kokaku sought to confer rank and titles upon his own father (see p.74) the Bakufu refused. The matter was eventually settled, but it seems that the anti-Bakufu feeling, clearly visible since around 1760, now extended right up to the Emperor.

In 1787 Sadanobu had helped Ienari, a minor born in 1773, to be elected as Shogun, but when Ienari attained his majority in 1793, he himself took over.

### Hayashi Shihei and coastal defences

The opportunity to oust Sadanobu was provided by his absence inspecting coastal defences.

Hayashi Shihei (1738–93), the Edo-born son of a Bakufu minister, went to study in Nagasaki in 1775, where he heard from the Dutch about Russian expansion north of Japan. Shihei became a noted Dutch scholar and mixed with leading Dutch scholars in Edo. In 1785 he wrote *Sankoku Tsuran* (*Illustrated Survey of Three Countries*) which gave a geographical account of three 'countries' – Korea, the Ryūkyūs and Ezochi – and also of the Ogasawara Islands. He drew particular attention to Russian encroachments, and urged the full development of Ezochi.

In 1786 Shihei finished *Kaikoku Heidan* (*Discussion of the Military Problems of a Maritime Nation*) which he published in Sendai in 1789 at his own expense. Again he stressed the Russian menace and the need to improve arms and coastal defences. In 1791 Sadanobu summoned him to Edo for questioning and imprisoned him for criticizing the

Bakufu and unsettling the people. All his books and his printing press were confiscated.

Shihei was soon to be vindicated, however. In 1787 two Russian ships had appeared near Nemuro and, through the Ainu, asked to open trade for there was a food shortage in Kamchatka (Takekoshi 1967, Vol. 2: 127). They were told to return the following year, but they were then informed there could be no trade save through Nagasaki. Five months after Shihei was arrested, they again came to Ezo to land two shipwrecked Japanese sailors and to seek trade. Sadanobu rejected their advances and kept the affair secret.

> Realizing too late that Shihei of Sendai had been right about the Russians, Sadanobu ordered the *daimyō* to look to the sea defences and in March, 1793, himself proceeded in war attire to the coasts of Sagami and Izu to see what was being done, but this sudden change of policy was inexplicable to the people, who, carefully lulled as they had been into security and kept in complete ignorance of outside affairs, saw no reason for the necessity of defence or preparation.
>
> (ibid., Vol.3: 163)

It was while he was in Izu that Sadanobu was deposed, though this was no consolation for Shihei, for he died that same year. His works, however, did not die, and *Kaikoku Heidan* was to re-appear in several new editions in the period 1848–53.

Post-war historical encyclopaedias mention merely that Shihei wanted to develop Ezochi, but it must be stressed that Shihei wanted a Japanese advance into all three 'countries'. In the words of Kata Tetsuzō, he urged geographical knowledge of these three countries as preparation for wars of offence and defence, so that they would 'be ready for the time when Japan's brave *samurai* raise troops and enter these three countries' (Kata 1940: 161). It is important to bear in mind that Shihei's ideas were widely disseminated in the middle of the nineteenth century, and that it was not unusual to lump together these three 'countries' as undeveloped regions vital for the defence of Japan and therefore suitable areas for absorption.

The year 1793 thus saw the deposition of Sadanobu, the death of Shihei, and the beginning of Ienari's long 'age of debauchery' (Takekoshi 1967, Vol. 3: 169). It also saw the *seppuku* in Kurume of Takayama Hikokurō, whose mission to Kyūshū is widely regarded as the start of a positive *sonnō* movement.

One must take note of the economic background to these political events. The 1930 three-volume economic history by Takekoshi, a noted journalist and politician, argued that 'the history of Japan for 250 years was a history of the struggles between the power of the sword and the power of the purse' (ibid., Vol. 2: 283). In other words, there was a three-way class struggle between the *samurai*, merchants and farmers. 'Benevolent administrators' in both the Hōjō and Ashikaga eras had periodically cancelled *samurai* debts, and, when the *samurai* got deeper into debt with the Tokugawa peace, the Bakufu revived this policy, cancelling debts in 1685, 1702 and 1706 (ibid.: 501–2). Though the direct protests of the merchants were unsuccessful, such laws so stifled lending that the merchants were able to fight back and finally prevailed. Most merchants

> were sprung from commoners who for hundreds of years had been oppressed, despised and insulted by the *samurai* class, and had patiently endured such treatment. Now with the power of wealth they waged war against the *samurai* for the honour of their fore-fathers who had suffered under *samurai* oppression.
> (ibid., Vol. 3: 72–3)

Takekoshi goes on to argue that 'the growing economic influences of the people conquered the military power of the Hatamoto and Daimyo, and, increasing year after year, finally crushed the Tokugawa Shogunate itself' (ibid.: 101). The Takekoshi thesis of the merchants fighting for the honour of their forefathers and finally crushing the Shogunate is, of course, highly debatable. But he is on firm ground in pointing out that Tokugawa problems were largely economic and that economic factors played a major part in their decline and downfall. The whole Tokugawa system was as much economic as political, and the same basic factors are to be seen at work in the Meiji period.

> The motive of the Shogunate in issuing the Act prohibiting the sailing abroad of the people was not simply its detestation of Christianity, but also the fear that, if left free to expand their influence abroad, ronins would eventually menace their own country.
> (ibid., Vol. 2: 129)

This same fear was to be a basic factor in the 1873 *Seihen*. The Ōkubo party was in general agreement with the attack-Korea school, but it wanted the attacking forces to be firmly under the control of the Satchō government, and was afraid that an attack led by the caretaker government would be dominated by the *rōnin* and the extremist clans of western Japan, and that once they had expanded their wealth and power abroad, they would be a threat to the central government. The 'documents' generally ignore these underlying, unchanging factors, and the arguments of the protagonists must largely be regarded as rationalization of their hopes and fears.

It should also be noted that the Tokugawa policies had strong racial overtones, for not only were all Japanese abroad refused permission to return, but all part-Japanese children were expelled from Japan and their parents were refused permission to communicate with them. When the Deshima Dutch went up to Edo on their annual visits they were treated with great condescension (Ledyard 1971: 115). Thus the racist teachings of the *kokugakusha* were not a thing apart, but went hand in hand with such practices.

Despite such posings of racial superiority, it would seem that, for a time at least, the Shogunate did believe that the Russians were a major threat. To provide coastal defences, it would have had to increase expenditure, but its income was fixed. Thus the new burden was mostly passed on to the clans; but they, too, had a long history of financial problems. Moreover, though military vassals of the Shogun, as far as trade and industry were concerned, the clans were virtually independent states which competed against the Shogun and against each other. They frequently adopted extreme principles of monopoly and state ownership, and would store their goods in Edo and Osaka to await the best prices. Edo and Osaka were two separate business worlds (Takekoshi 1967, Vol. 2: 430ff.), with the former on the gold standard and the latter, often in defiance of the law, on the silver. The clans' relation with the Osaka business world was a complex story of both co-operation and competition, with the great merchant families trying to make themselves indispensable and the clans striving to establish their independence (ibid.).

These factors, too, are fundamental to any understanding of the Meiji *Seihen*. Though political centralization was achieved in the years 1868 to 1871, old economic practices could not be simply brushed aside. Laws were soon passed to prevent them from trading, but the clans – now prefectures – did not cease to be economic entities, though their economic activities now centred around new companies and banks. The Meiji period saw an intensification of the old economic rivalries, while the 250-year struggle between 'sword and purse' may likewise be viewed as reaching a new dimension.

Finally, the plight of the farmers should be considered. An uprising of about 50,000 in Kurume against unfair taxation was followed in 1764 by an uprising in Kōsuke and Musashi involving an estimated 200,000 (Sansom 1963, Vol. 3: 179), while Hita was the scene of a major disturbance in 1773. The great Temmei famines led to rice riots which spread from Osaka, where the castle itself was attacked, to Edo, Nagasaki and elsewhere. Eventually they were quelled but the impotence of the Bakufu had been demonstrated.

In one sense, the real decline of the farmers went back to Hideyoshi's 1588 sword-hunts which deprived the farmers of weapons save for sticks and stones. With the Tokugawas, class stratification became more rigid and farmers could no longer move into other classes. Their rice had usually been divided with the *daimyō* 40–60, but under Yoshimune the *daimyō* share was increased to 50 per cent (Takekoshi 1967, Vol. 3: 134). 'The Kyōkō [1716–35] era was in fact a period when the farmer-class was most hard hit, and in spite of the law forbidding it, agricultural land changed hands widely' (Kata 1940: 161). Takekoshi's emotive words about the long-lasting oppression of the merchant classes might perhaps be better applied to the agricultural classes; and, in the early Meiji period, with feudalism formally abolished, it seems the government was more afraid of farmer uprisings than of the more spectacular *samurai* rebellions.

## HIRATA ATSUTANE AND SATŌ NOBUHIRO

Imperialist teachings did not, of course, die out with the deaths of Shihei and Motoori. Those who seek to date the Emperor system from about 1890 generally depict the Meiji Restoration of 1868 as a great watershed which divided the 'new Japan' from the old. Hence it must be stressed that the nineteenth century, both before and after 1868, saw a continuing, seemingly irresistible development of *kokugaku* ideas, with 1868 providing no great watershed.

Honda Toshiaki (1744–1821), an Echigo *samurai*, studied Dutch and Western science, travelled widely, especially round Ezochi, and in 1798 published *Keisei Hisaku* (*A Secret Plan for Governing the Country*) and *Saiiki Monogatari* (*Tales of the West*). Honda advocated the abandonment of *sakoku* and the institution of state-managed foreign trade and overseas colonization. He stressed the importance of islands as forts and as trading bases, and placed particular emphasis on the north, even advocating that the capital be moved from Edo to Kamchatka to share the same latitude as London. In Ezochi he wanted to start with fishing and sealing then later move into agriculture. A major feature of his programme was the use of convict labour (Kata 1940: 167) – a policy later adopted by the Meiji government. Again it should be stressed that for Honda, Ezochi was not the end of the line, but a base from which commercial and military expansion was to be launched into northern Asia.

Whereas Honda was something of an individualist, Hirata Atsutane (1776–1842) was essentially a *juku* head who, though lacking in great originality, played a major role as systematizer and propagandist. Atsutane was born in Kubota, Akita, the fourth son of a *samurai* (Tahara 1963: 84ff.). Perhaps because Akita had serious economic problems, he fled the clan at nineteen and made for Edo. Little is known of his early years in Edo, but at twenty-four he became the *yōshi* (adopted son) of a Bitchu *samurai*, Hirata Atsuyasu. At one time he practised as a doctor (ibid.: 124), but it was as a teacher that he made his mark. It is not clear whether he actually entered Motoori's *juku* (ibid.: 91) but certainly they became soul-mates, and Atsutane is generally regarded as the greatest of his successors.

Like Motoori, he wrote from the perspective of the governed, not the rulers. Thus though he drew close to the Kii and Owari clans, his attempts to approach Mito failed, for the Mito teachings revolved around the ruling classes (ibid.: 265ff.). Towards the end of his life he was virtually driven out of Edo by the Bakufu (ibid.: 272–4) because of his *sonnō* teachings. He had become a *samurai* of his native Satake clan in Akita and was recalled to Kubota in 1840 to teach, but he was given very little income and died there, a lonely old man, two years later.

In the Bakumatsu and Meiji periods, his disciples, led by Hirata Kanetane and Ōkuni Takamasa, once more became prominent and, with the *ishin*, obtained high positions in the government departments dealing with religion. They were soon to lose influence as the pragmatic Meiji leaders set out to establish a modern, secular state, but their ideas and influence did not die, and after the 1881 *Seihen*, Satchō, menaced by both Mitsubishi and *minken*, was to renew its old alliance with the Shintō–*kokugaku* forces. It should be stressed that Atsutane and his disciples stressed the universality of the religion and saw Shintō as a universal, world religion (ibid.:

145). For Motoori, the Emperor was a god and above criticism, but for Hirata he was a god but not above criticism (ibid.: 287–9). To demonstrate that he was the emperor of all the world, Hirata turned to foreign studies, especially of Chinese and Indian texts, to find supplementary evidence; but then he turned back once more to the Japanese classics (ibid.: 202).

It must be remembered that Atsutane was virulently anti-Buddhist, and that he regarded Indians as the lowest of the low (Prasad 1984: 430). His wider studies went hand in hand with a progressively harsher patriotism. Thus, as far as we know, 'treason' was not mentioned by Mabuchi, and perhaps but once in Motoori, though he often stops just short; Atsutane, however, was very strong on treason (ibid.: 530), and the charge of being 'un-Japanese' was taking on real force. Far from becoming more world-minded as a result of his wider studies, the Hirata school built up the idea that every Japanese was high class and that all foreigners were really their servants. Indeed, Hirata addressed the problem of the origin of the foreign species. The Japanese, of course, were descended from the gods; as for foreigners, Atsutane suggested that they might have been bred into existence in the manner of maggots or mosquito larvae. This bright idea was not completely original, for the ancient Chinese used *namban* (southern barbarians), for the people to the south, with the character for 'insect' figuring prominently in the word for 'barbarian'.

By the Bakumatsu period, *kokugaku* teachings had penetrated far and wide through Japan. 'Mabuchi turned out about six hundred disciples, who scattered themselves over forty provinces and were in great request as lecturers to various clans' (Takekoshi 1967, Vol. 3: 158). His disciple, Motoori, had sent even greater numbers of disciples to all parts of Japan; Motoori's followers broke into various schools, with Atsutane's students alone numbering in the thousands. Despite various doctrinal differences and Bakufu oppression, the basic *kokugaku* teachings had taken root far and wide: Japan was the centre of the universe; the Emperor was the emperor of the whole world; and all Japanese were superior beings. It was a religion based on racial supremacy, and tied in well with the imperialist teachings of practical men such as Hayashi Shihei, Honda Toshiaki and Satō Nobuhiro.

Kodansha's *Encyclopaedia of Japan* describes Satō Nobuhiro (1769–1850) as an agronomist born into a family of scholars in Akita. He travelled with his father to Ezochi then to Edo where he studied under Dutch scholar Utagawa Genzui. After brief service with the Tsuyama clan, he travelled around the country studying agriculture. He became interested in Shintō and entered Hirata Atsutane's *juku*. He also became friendly with Takano Chōhei and Watanabe Kazan, and narrowly escaped arrest in the round-up of *rangakusha*. As his fame spread, he was called by many *daimyō* to advise on agriculture and maritime defence.

It was in response to senior councillor Mizuno Tadakuni's request that he wrote his *Fukkohō Gaigen* (*Outline of How to Restore the Old*) in which he proposed unifying Japan under a single ruler and placing all land, production, commerce and transportation under direct government control.

(Kodansha)

Neither Kodansha nor the *Kawade Shobō* mention his *Kaibosaku* or his plans for world conquest. It is difficult to believe that this is the same Satō who gets eight pages – more than any other individual – in the 1940 book on colonialism by the highly respected, German-trained Keio professor, Kata Tetsuzō (*Shokumin Seisaku*). Satō's importance as an imperialist is also recognized by the Black Dragon Society's 1933 publication, *Tōa Senkaku Shishi Kiden* (*Records of the Men of Spirit who Pioneered East Asia*). It gives (pp. 13–16) a full three-page extract from Satō detailing the steps by which Japan should take Manchuria, Korea and China: the first attack should be launched at the mouth of the Black Dragon River (from which the Black Dragon Society took its name); as the Manchurians are impetuous and disorganized, and the Chinese cowardly, a great army would not be required. The first striking force should come from Aomori, the second from Sendai, both first wintering in Karafuto to become acclimatized. As these northern people were conquered, they should be treated well, so that they would become allies. This good treatment is something Satō stresses, but he does add that if there is any resistance to the Heavenly Troop they should, of course, all be killed, this being the Will of Heaven.

The Ninth Force should be *shinsei*, that is, led by the Emperor himself; it should, without fail, be accompanied by Kumamoto troops. It should first take Nanking and make it the provisional capital. Then, as the Japanese rule well – alleviating all people's poverty, incorporating Chinese officials into its government, building schools and shrines – the whole of China and Manchuria would gradually come under Japanese control. Backed by these resources, the Emperor would then be able to go on to force other rulers throughout the world to acknowledge his sway.

Kata's work (1940: 168–76) likewise concentrates on Satō's plans for world conquest. Satō argued that naval strength was required to counter the Russians, and this could be built up, as England had done, by trading overseas. Writing in 1809 he urged the taking of Kamchatka and Okhotsk to deprive Russia of its window to the East and thus 'remove these pirates from the sea'. Apart from this plan, Satō had another for 'the English problem'. This meant expansion to the south. 'How deeply moved must Satō-in-his-grave be now!' (ibid.: 172). His plans involved launching a sudden attack from the Ryūkyūs on Luzon and Parigia. Once these had been occupied and fortified, they could continue moving south, while Philippine products could be collected and sold to China, Russia and South-east Asia. From the South Seas they could go on to take the whole world.

Many of these ideas were developed in *Kaibo Saku* (*Plan for Naval Defence*), and it would seem that this is the real reason why this work is not mentioned in the post-war articles on Satō 'the agronomist'. These ideas were further developed in *Kondō Hisaku* (*Secret Plan for Unifying the World*). As Japan is *Shin-shū* there should be no difficulty in unifying the world and bringing all countries together as one. As Japan was the first country created in the world it was the foundation of all other countries, so this pristine state should be restored; all other countries should be made its prefectures and wards, and all other rulers should be made ministers and servants of Japan. This was Japan's duty and destiny.

It was important to take China first as, with her wealth and strength secured, no other country would be able to resist.

Satō, however, acknowledged one major problem in the carrying out of his plans: the Japanese people. After 200 years of peace, the Japanese people were prosperous and just enjoyed living their own lives. The idea of war preparations did not appeal to them. If they knew of his plans, they would think him crazy, or they would get angry and think of him as a criminal; thus a positive programme of education or indoctrination was required.

Satō, then, was not a typical agronomist. Kata's book quickly ran through several editions, for Satō was highly relevant in 1940. But he was equally as relevant in 1873. Doctrines of the honourable Saigō Takamori, wanting simply to reprimand Korea for her rudeness and then return to Japan, are so manifestly absurd that they would hardly be worth discussing were they not put forward so consistently by leading historians. Hayashi Shihei, who had stressed the need to have detailed geographical knowledge of 'the three countries', and then to occupy them, enjoyed a revival in the 1840s. With the Restoration, detailed Satō-style plans of conquest were put forward by special envoy Sada Hakuho. Saigō then sent his spies on long missions into China and Korea, and, like Satō, drew up fairly detailed plans for the conquest of Korea.

Satō was very much a disciple of Atsutane; his attitude to the Emperor and imperial expansion was in the *kokugaku* mainstream. He was employed in practical matters by progressive clans including Satsuma and Uwajima, but wherever he went he spread his gospel, and he personally seems to have helped link clans with extremist tendencies, such as his own clan in Akita, Tsuyama in Okayama, and Kurume whose leading dignitary, Honjō Ichirō, sent his son to study under Satō. Thus Satō can neither be dismissed as a crank nor re-clothed as an agronomist, but must be seen as an influential thinker in the *kokugaku* mainstream. The 1873 *Seihen* debate has been distorted beyond recognition by historians whose accounts begin with the year 1868, and the nature of Japanese imperialism by those who begin their account with the 1890s.

## THE BAKUMATSU PERIOD

Ienari, with his Satsuma wife, dozens of concubines and scores of children, remained Shogun till 1837 when he retired for his son, Ieyoshi; but he remained the real power till his death in 1841. Ieyoshi was to die in 1853, perhaps assassinated for capitulating to the Americans. His successor Iesada, 'was little better than an imbecile' (Takekoshi 1967, Vol. 3: 304).

He, too, was provided with a Satsuma wife. He died suddenly in 1858. Again there were strong suggestions that he had been assassinated for giving in to Western demands. He was succeeded by the weak, sickly thirteen-year-old Iemochi. Of course, these pathetic young men were personally insignificant. What must be noted is the growth of a more widely based government. Whereas the Bakufu had been run by the Tokugawa family and a few close associates, from the end of the eighteenth century Satsuma had played a major role. As the world became smaller, and the Opium Wars in China made the threat to Japan all too clear, the Bakufu turned increasingly to a policy of consensus. Not only the great *tozama* clans, but also the small *fudai* clans and the *hatamoto* (bannermen) were increasingly consulted, while, within the great clans themselves, a significant number of lower *samurai* were rising to positions of responsibility; thus there was a definite tendency towards a more widely based and representative government. There was growing pressure on Satsuma to defect from the Bakufu side and to establish a new government in the name of the Emperor, but Satsuma wanted neither to set up a more widely based and representative government, nor to hand over power to the Emperor and his Court. What Satsuma wanted was to step out, at the appropriate time, from the shadow of the Bakufu, and to assume control of the government in the name of the Emperor. Its first task would then be to divest itself of the Court and those clans which had long given the Court ideological and practical assistance.

It was essentially economic factors which were to lead Satsuma to defect. Under Ienari, the debauched, lavish life-style had apparently stimulated trade, but the prosperity was not firmly based, and in the last years of his rule (1832–7), a 'miserable sequence of disasters recurred. Famine and disease were followed by peasant uprisings and "smashings" in the towns. The Bakufu was again in a precarious situation' (Sansom 1963, Vol. 3: 208–9).

Both the central and most clan governments instituted programmes of reform based on austerity and development of trade and industry. Yet the Bakufu had but limited success. In the thirties, agrarian uprisings were chronic, especially in the small and middling fiefs which could not effectively legislate to control their own economies. There was also increased rioting in the cities, largely by the new urban poor who had poured in from the countryside (ibid.). Ieyoshi's main minister, Mizuno Tadakuni, tried to drive them back to the land and also to break up the power of the great wholesale dealers. But his policies were going against the tide of events; his residence was attacked, and he died in disgrace in 1844.

The failure of the Bakufu reform measures, and the ultimate defection of Satsuma, came down to one basic cause: the clans had independent economies which were in keen competition with each other and with the Bakufu. To maintain its power and to meet the threat of an encroaching world, the Bakufu had to increase its income; but its attempts to maintain control of trade put it increasingly on a collision course with the great western clans, especially once they obtained the backing of Great Britain which, like the clans themselves, wanted to see the end of *sakoku* and a full and open system of trade in friendly hands.

This intense economic competition between the various independent clan economies did not just spontaneously evaporate with the setting up of the Meiji government or even with the abolition of the clans in 1871. Indeed, that competition may even be regarded as intensifying, and Satchō moves to consolidate all power in their own hands were not to implement a particular ideology – ideology was a tool which, by 1871, had largely outlived its usefulness – but rather to enable them to monopolize internal wealth and power, and to lead the coming charge into Asia.

It should be noted that from Takayama Hikokurō onward a study of individual activists generally reveals merchant backing. That the merchants had good reason for seeking a new order is demonstrated, for example, by Satsuma's 1835 decision (see *Kawade* under 'Zusho Hirosato') that its debts in Osaka, Edo and Kyoto would be paid off over 250 years. Despite an uproar in Osaka, all its debts were thus virtually cancelled.

Two further points should be stressed. The first is the question of currency 'reform'. In the words of Takekoshi

> In the Tokugawa period, whenever the currency was revised, any profit that resulted was credited to the treasury as an item of extraordinary revenue, and in all cases of revision the main object of the Shogunate was financial profit to itself, with the natural result that there were considerable 'pickings' for officials and those engaged in the bullion business. The maladministration of currency by the Tokugawa Shogunate had been continuously practised from the Genroku era.
>
> (1967, Vol. 3: 226)

Control of the mint was to be one of the 'plums' of the new government and a good indicator of just who was closest to the centre of power.

The second point is that while we must inevitably turn to consider the four great clans which were to dominate Meiji Japan, a concentration on these clans automatically distorts the nature of the Bakumatsu struggle. Not only was Aizu, the clan most loyal to the Emperor, to be branded as 'traitorous', but clans which had provided much of the ideological impetus to the movement were soon to be branded as 'rebellious' or 'backward' and squeezed from the scene (ibid.: 208). To be a top Satchō man meant not only quick political, commercial and military promotion, but also a posthumous elevation in the hierarchy of saints and philosophers.

## The development of *seikan-ron*

As we have seen, the idea of attacking and occupying Korea went so far back into Japanese history that it is impossible to seek one date or one person to act as a landmark. However, in his authoritative study of Japanese–Korean relations, Tabohashi (1972, Vol. 1: 298) points out that though the idea of attacking Korea had long been discussed in abstract terms as part of *kokugaku* teachings, it was not till the Bakumatsu period that its immediate implementation was urged. According to Tabohashi, it was said that the first such advocacy came from the Matsuyama clan in Bitchu (Okayama). The clan chief, Itakura Katsukiyo, and his chief minister, Yamada Hōkoku, reformed their own clan. Itakura also served in the Bakufu government, and in 1861 he presented a paper urging that China should be attacked and occupied immediately – not a day should be wasted (ibid.: 299–300). He pointed out that in the previous autumn, the British and French had occupied Peking and the Emperor had fled to Manchuria, leaving China without a ruler. Hence Japan should send troops and move into this void. One army should be sent to Taiwan, a second to Korea, and a third to Shangtung. They should ensure the welfare of the conquered peoples, and issue an edict restoring old laws and customs, then perhaps most of the people would submit without a struggle.

It should be noted that Itakura's plan is essentially the same as that advocated by Satō Nobuhiro, and it likewise puts *seikan* in the context of far wider expansion. Japanese historians frequently claim that Japan was merely reacting to changing external situations, and it may be argued that this was a case in point; but the British–French occupation of Peking did not lead to the development of *seikan-ron*; instead, it merely led many to believe that the time had come to implement the *seikan* ideas which had long since been widely accepted in theory.

Tabohashi then traces the story (ibid.: 302–10) through a Tsushima man, Ōshima, who met Yamada Hōkoku in May 1863 and spoke of Tsushima's problems. Yamada's response was to demand to know why, if Tsushima's problems were so severe, they did not trumpet that Korea had broken her treaty obligations and then launch an attack. Ōshima soon expressed agreement, and became

69

a publicist for the *seikan* cause. Tabohashi claims that whereas Yamada really hoped for the successful implementation of these plans, Ōshima was more concerned with getting both the Bakufu and the great western clans to recognize Tsushima's special rights.

According to Tabohashi, among those converted by Ōshima was Chōshū's Kido, who got the backing of Ōmura. When Kido became a high official in the Meiji government, others rallied to this cause, so he became the centre of a *seikan* faction within the government.

Tabohashi postulates that there was another *seikan* faction which grew up quite independently from the Itakura–Ōshima–Kido line (ibid.: 301). It began with a Foreign Office official, Sada Hakuho, who, after studying the Korean situation on the spot concluded that it was necessary to send troops to punish Korea. Saigō and Itagaki were essentially an extension of the Sada line.

No objection can be raised to this last statement, but though Tabohashi is still highly regarded and his book is often treated as the definitive work, his thesis smacks strongly of 1940, the year of publication. Sada reached his conclusions long before he went to Korea, and the concept of two independent lines of *seikan-ron* development – one the result of objective investigation of the actual situation in Korea – soon starts to crumble when one looks more closely at the people involved. When introducing Sada, Tabohashi merely mentions (ibid.: 226–7) that he was a former Army Ministry official who was back resting in his native Kurume. He names the three other members of the mission but gives no details.

Though it seems objective, this approach distorts the whole picture. Broadly speaking, one may accept that the much vaunted 'Saigō *seikan-ron*' was an extension of the 'Sada *seikan-ron*', and that debate is better approached through Sada rather than Saigō. But it is grossly inaccurate to portray Sada as a Foreign Office official who became converted to *seikan-ron* after seeing the Korean situation on the spot. Sada's diplomatic career was very brief, and his whole life revolved around the fact that he was a Kurume man. Sada, his father and brother, were all disciples of Maki Izumi, so one must go back and look at Maki's *seikan-ron*. Maki himself was greatly influenced by *sonnō* activist Takayama Hikokurō, who committed *seppuku* in Kurume in 1793. So let us look at this Takayama–Maki–Sada line to demolish the myth that a *seikan* faction grew up within the Foreign Office as a response to what

70

their officials saw in Korea. Until that myth is disposed of, one cannot begin to understand the 1873 *Seihen*, or give a decent burial to the current Anglo-American *orthos doxa* which depicts Japanese imperialism emerging around 1890 in response to changing external conditions.

# 5

# KURUME: TAKAYAMA, MAKI AND SADA

## TAKAYAMA HIKOKURŌ

It is important to realize how late Satsuma joined the *sonnō* movement if we are to understand the 1873 *Seihen*. Carol Gluck (1985) has tried valiantly to prove that the Emperor system was created after 1890 and that it did not penetrate terribly deeply into the national consciousness. But to understand and assess the Imperial Rescript on Education, the Emperor system set up after 1890 and the earlier great political crises of 1873 and 1881, one must see them as a culmination of forces and movements extending over a long period of time, and not as something springing up within a few years. The story of Takayama Hikokurō is of great help in providing this sense of continuity.

Hikokurō was born in Kōzuke no Kuni (Gumma) in 1747 (Mikami 1940). His family were farmers who wore swords. At seventeen he went up to Kyoto to study. It was a period of great criticism of the Bakufu, and he came to know many *shishi* and nobles, most notably Dainagon Nakayama Naruchika. In 1789 he travelled to Edo, then on to Mito, where he developed ties with Nagakubo Sekisui, an authority on the north, and with Fujita Yūkoku. In 1790 he went on to Nambu, then crossed to Matsumae and into Ezochi proper. Thence he returned to Kyoto and began his travels west.

Backed by certain Kyoto nobles and merchants, he made his way to Satsuma to persuade that clan to move against the Bakufu. In this purpose he failed, and with the Bakufu spies closing in, he made his way back to Kurume, where he committed *seppuku* in 1793.

Pundit Tokutomi (ibid.: 4–5) dismissed Hikokurō as an ignorant man who was given to weeping and wailing and who achieved little, while post-war historical encyclopaedias give a revised, one-dimensional account of Hikokurō as an early exponent of the 'check Russia' school (see Heibon 1953). Yet there can be no doubting the nature and extent of his influence: he wrote of *kokutai ron* and preached restoring power to the Emperor. His major significance is as an opponent of the Bakufu and as a forerunner of *sonnō-jōi*. Maki Izumi was to be head official at Suitengu (Mikami 1940: 7) where Hikokurō was buried, and he revered him from his childhood. In 1842, Maki organized services to commemorate the fiftieth anniversary of his death, and in 1868–9 Lord Yorishige ordered that his grave be repaired and a shrine erected to both Hikokurō and Maki, and bestowed a stipend upon their descendants. The hundredth anniversary of his death was honoured, and in 1900 the Crown Prince visited his grave. Other royal visits were to follow and in 1911 Generals Ōyama and Yamagata planted a tree in his honour. Even in the post-war period (1959), a Takayama Sensei Society was formed, though now the emphasis would seem to be on building up Hikokurō as an anti-Russian symbol. But Sada Hakuho's younger brother, Gonnosuke, was closer to the mark in his 1909 recollections when he claimed that the *sonnō-jōi* movement began with Hikokurō (ibid.: 167–9).

Hikokurō's close ties with the nobles must be stressed, for we are dealing with the names familiar to us in the Bakumatsu and Meiji periods: Iwakura, Sanjō, Nakayama, Higashikuse, and also the forebears of Sawa. Like Iwakura Tomomi, Iwakura Tomonobu was a *yōshi*, having been adopted from the Yanagihara household. Hikokurō had stayed with Iwakura as early as 1783, and before his travels to Kyūshū, he made Iwakura's his headquarters, staying there for 200 days. It seems that he presented an opinion paper through Iwakura to the Emperor Kōkaku, then twenty, for his diary refers to asking a favour of Iwakura, then wondering about the opinion of the Emperor. We are not told the nature of the opinion paper, but he had just disposed of his family to go west, so surely the paper would be dealing with that *sonnō* mission. Biographer Mikami argues from the evidence that Hikokurō had an audience with the young Emperor himself (ibid.: 134–6).

Kōkaku was, of course, the son of an Emperor, but he did not become the son of an Emperor until 1884. The Japanese Royal Family was no different to other royal families. Officially, it had continued in unbroken line from early antiquity, and each Emperor was given his official serial number. Thus Kōkaku Tennō was officially Number 119. But the family had seen its share of dynastic struggles and usurpations, and in the eighteenth century it had sunk very low indeed. If we use the *Kawade Encyclopaedia* to trace its fortunes, we are struck by the fact that the potted histories tell us little more than serial number, date of birth, childhood name, mother's maiden name and place of burial. These potted histories are a striking testimony to the irrelevance of the Emperors in the life of the nation.

The century opened with Higashiyama (Eastern Mountains) Tennō number 113 (1675–1709). He succeeded to the Emperorship at the age of twelve and reigned for twenty-two years. He was followed by his fifth son, Nakamikado (1701–39), who ascended at nine and resigned in 1735 in favour of his son.

Sakura Machi (Cherry Town) Tennō (1720–50) reigned from 1735 to 1747. He sought to restore some dignity to his position by reviving certain offices and ceremonies but this invoked the wrath of the Bakufu which in 1747 forced the indignant Emperor to resign for his son, little six-year-old Momozono (Peach Park) Tennō. Sakura Machi is best remembered as a poet, but perhaps his reign should be seen as sparking the first stirrings of the anti-Bakufu movement.

The problem, however, was not to be solved simply by removing the Emperor. In the 1750s a great impact was made by the radical teacher Takenouchi Shikibu, son of a Niigata doctor. His Kyoto *juku* was so crowded, largely with young nobles, that he sometimes gave the same lecture eight times a day. His message was that the nobles must give up their idle ways and become worthy nobles, that they should educate the Emperor so that he would be a worthy ruler, and that all should revere the Emperor. It has been argued that Shikibu's objective in elevating the Emperor and preaching *sonnō* was to form a rallying point against the Bakufu (*Kokumin no Rekishi*, Vol. 16: 192 *et seq.*). His students included members of the great noble families such as Ogimachi Sanjō, Koga, Tokudaiji and Iwakura. These higher nobles undertook the instruction of young Momozono, and found in him a most willing student. In 1758, however, Shikibu was arrested and subjected to a lengthy interrogation. He startled his interrogators by openly criticizing the Bakufu. He was consequently exiled from Kyoto and noble followers such as Iwakura Tsunetomo were forced to resign.

Momozono died in 1762, leaving behind a four-year-old son. Most recent Emperors had ascended as children, but the four-year old was considered rather too young. So the throne passed to an aunt, Sakura Machi's second daughter, who reigned as Gosakuramachi Tennō. She was to live until 1813, but retired in 1770 for her nephew. The Kyoto-centred anti-Bakufu agitation had continued in the 1760s, leading to a major crackdown in 1767 (ibid.: 203 *et seq.*). Those arrested included Shikibu, who was now exiled to a distant island.

Gomomozono (later Peach Park) Tennō likewise died young in 1779, leaving no issue. Quite clearly, the weak constitutions and early deaths of the Emperors posed a problem. So in 1779 the eight-year-old sixth son of Kanin no Miya Sukehito was 'adopted' as Gomomozono's son and succeeded as Kōkaku Tennō. It is now permissible, of course, to write freely of the Shoguns, and to use words such as 'weak and imbecilic'. Yet articles on the Royal Family still reek of official court chroniclers and are remarkably free from political analysis. Thus it is not easy to find simple answers to questions such as, 'Did Gomomozono "adopt" Kōkaku before he died or after? What was their exact relationship and who decided that this adoption and succession should take place?' One must surmise it was a Bakufu decision.

The fact that Kōkaku was 'adopted' surely shows that he was not next in line of succession. At least on the father's side, he must have been about a fourth cousin. The Kanin princely family dates from 1718. Previously there had been only three princely families, of which Fushimi was the most noted, from which consorts could be chosen or emperors adopted. It would seem that it was partly to stop excessive inbreeding, and partly to spare some of the royal children from the religious life, that Higashiyama's eighth son was allowed in 1718 to form a fourth princely family and given the name Kanin. Kōkaku was Higashiyama's great-grandson, but he was fairly distant from the main line of succession. Of course, his son, grandson and great-grandson (Ninkō, Kōmei and Meiji) were also descended from this junior princely family.

Not unnaturally, despite the 'adoption', Kōkaku still regarded Kanin no Miya Sukehito as his father, and in 1788 he sent Nakayama Naruchika – whom Hikokurō had got to know well – up to Edo to get the Shogun's consent to confer upon Sukehito the title of Emperor in retirement. The Shogunate refused and continued to refuse right up to Sukehito's death in 1794. The decision was a bitter blow not only to Sukehito but also to Kōkaku, for it would seem to emphasize his own vulnerability and somewhat qualified legitimacy. It was now nearly half a century since Sakura Machi had been forced to resign for his little son, and Kyoto had become the centre of a well-developed anti-Bakufu movement. It is not difficult to picture Hikokurō, a friend of Nakayama and Iwakura, having an audience with Kōkaku before travelling west. Kōkaku was to live until 1840 but he resigned in

1817 in favour of his son, Ninko. In 1884, when the Emperor system was being put together and the 'unbroken line' myth was becoming a holy writ, Sukehito was given the title Emperor Kyōkō, thereby reinforcing the family tree of Kōkaku's great-grandson Meiji.

Like Maki after him, Hikokurō had strong merchant backing, 'borrowing' his expenses for the Kyūshū trip from rich Kyoto merchant Ōmura Hikotarō (ibid.: 157–8) and staying with local merchants such as Hirose Tansō's father in Hita. This would support the view that merchants played a significant role in the *sonnō* movement from the very outset. Though the movement was later to be taken over by Satchō, Hikokurō's career would also suggest that it was more grassroots in origin than is usually accepted. Hikokurō travelled throughout Japan, going from village to village, and he was distressed at the economic, spiritual and military decline he observed. It was this grassroots knowledge and his picture of Japan as one entity, rather than mere Shintō or Mito teachings, which provided his motivation.

Again, it should be stressed how widespread and deep-rooted was the opposition to the Bakufu. In 1791, when Hikokurō travelled to Kyūshū, it was already well over thirty years since Iwakura Tsunetomo had been forced to resign because of his association with the radical teacher Takenouchi Shikibu, so Hikokurō's patron, Tomonobu, was carrying on a well-established Iwakura family tradition. At the start of the Meiji period, the capital was shifted, stealthily and by stages, from Kyoto to Edo. This was partly to facilitate control of the east and north-east, but it was also to enable the pragmatic, newly emerging Satchō leaders to shake off the shackles of Kyoto, where the *sonnō* movement had its origins, and of those clans such as Kurume, which had strong spiritual and diplomatic ties with Kyoto.

Hikokurō travelled via Okayama, Fukuyama, Hiroshima and Kokura, staying with friends from his Edo and Kyoto days – friends who would seem to have shared his aspirations (ibid.: 160ff.). Indeed, a look at Hikokurō's hosts illustrates quite dramatically that the main outlines of the *sonnō* movement were visible by 1790, and that Satsuma, and even Chōshū, were latecomers to the scene.

## Kumamoto and Shimei

Hikokurō spent 100 days in Yanagawa and Higo (Kumamoto). There his main contact, and one of his hosts, was Takamoto Shitagau (1738–1813), better known as Shimei (ibid.: 219–22).

The sixth son of a certain Harada, he was descended from a Korean captured during the Hideyoshi invasions and he often signed his name as Rhee Shimei or Rhee Shitagau. He was adopted by the clan doctor Takamoto, but as a young man went to live the life of a stoic in a hut at the foot of Mount Asō. Many young men came to study under him, and he dreamed of setting up a school of Imperial Studies. This did not eventuate, but one of his disciples, Nagase Miyuki, went up to study under Motoori, and one of Nagase's students Hayashi Ōen (1798–1870), a doctor, military teacher and *kokugakusha*, is generally regarded as the father of the Higo Emperor party. Many of the *Shimpū ren* members who rebelled in 1876 had studied at Hayashi's *juku*.

Shimei himself wrote extensively and kept in close contact with both Hikokurō and Motoori. There is thus a straight line from Hikokuro–Shimei–Motoori, through Nagase to Hayashi Ōen and the young Higo extremists of the Bakumatsu and early Meiji periods. Meiji education was virtually taken over by the Higo men, who were mainly responsible for the Imperial Rescript on Education. Not long before the 1881 *Seihen*, this group, including Sasa Tomofusa and Inoue Kowashi, formed a rightist, imperial organization they later called the Shimeikai (*Kokudō Sasa Kikō* 1936: 55 *et seq.*; Introduction, 6 *et seq*). It is fashionable to write about Inoue Kowashi in terms of his 'German ideas' but, though clothed in Western garb which gave a cloak of modernity, his basic ideas must surely be traced back to Shimei and beyond.

Hikokurō did not introduce *sonnō* ideas into places like Kumamoto and Kurume, but found them already firmly established. It is manifestly inadequate to start an analysis of the Emperor system, the Imperial Rescripts on Education, etc. as late as the year 1792, but it becomes quite indefensible when Gluck depicts them as dating from around 1890 and consequently not penetrating deeply into the national psyche.

## Fukuoka and Kamei

Motoori's influence extended to most parts of Japan. Thus one of his disciples was a poor Fukuoka *samurai*, Aoyanagi Tanenobu (1766–1835), who returned home to win recognition as one of Kyūshū's three great *kokugakusha*. But even earlier than Aoyanagi was Kamei Nanmei (1743–1814) (Mikami 1940: 314–15), a famous teacher at the clan school. Hirokurō's close friend and fellow *sonnō* activist, Karasaki Hitachinosuke, stayed with Kamei in 1791. Karasaki, a Takehara man, went to Kurume in 1793 and burst into tears at Hikokurō's grave. In 1796 he was to commit *seppuku* in Takehara after burning all his papers, apparently to avoid implicating his lord. His 1791 stay with Kamei was soon followed by that of Hikokurō, and these visits seem to have been responsible for the fact that in 1792 Kamei was driven out of the clan school and thereafter endured hard times.

An interesting testimony to Kamei's importance was to be provided by Sugiyama Yasumichi, writer son of the noted Fukuoka rightist who was the power behind Katsura Tarō. Sugiyama described Kamei as 'the forefather of the Genyōsha' (Mikami 1940: 315–17), the forerunner of the Black Dragon Society. Indeed, Kamei's influence can be traced down not only to Fukuoka's notorious Black Dragon Society, but also to the development of extreme *sonnō* thought in Chōshū. Earlier than Yoshida Shōin, and more radical, was the priest Gesshō (1817–58), who was greatly influenced by an uncle who had studied under Kamei and had returned home to become a *sonnō* activist (Misaka 1979: 42ff.). But Gesshō, the first noted *sonnō* teacher in Chōshū, was active about sixty years after Hikokurō stayed with Kamei, Shimei, etc., thus reinforcing the picture of Satchō as latecomers to the *sonnō* movement.

## Nakatsu

While in Edo, Hikokurō stayed freely with the famous doctor Maeno Ryōtaku (1723–1803) in the Nakatsu compound. There he met and debated with the clan's leading scholars, and also the lord, Masataka, then still a boy. When he visited Nakatsu, he also had as contacts from his Kyoto days Watanabe Shigena and Nomoto Hakugan, then teachers in the clan school (Mikami 1940: 169–72). Though the clan lords, the Okudairas, were closely related to the Tokugawas, the blood lines had died out, and young Masataka had been adopted from the Satsuma Shimazu family. Obviously, Hikokurō was received sympathetically, and it is not surprising that this progressive clan should produce a Fukuzawa Yukichi.

## Tosa

Among Hikokurō's Edo friends was Tani Bankei. The genealogy does not seem all that clear, but according to Mikami (ibid.: 186), Bankei's grandfather studied under Yamasaki Ansai, while his grandson was Tani Tateki, who played a distinctive educational and spiritual role in Meiji Japan. Mikami gives the poems exchanged by Bankei and Hikokurō (*Heibon Sha: Dai Jimmei Jiten* 1953). Again it must be stressed that Tani Tateki's role cannot be understood simply by looking at the Meiji period, but must be defined by reference to his grandfather, the friend of Hikokurō, and to even earlier Tosa *kokugakusha*.

## Hikokurō and Satsuma

Like all visitors, Hikokurō had trouble in entering Satsuma, but he eventually succeeded and stayed for 100 days. He was helped by two teachers (Mikami 1940: 263ff.) of the clan school, Akasaki Kaimon and Kuroda Kaneyama, and on his departure Lord Narinobu presented him with clothes, a personal gift and money to cover his expenses. However, he had been unable to meet Narinobu to urge that Satsuma move against the Shogunate.

When Shigehide resigned in 1788 in favour of the fifteen-year-old Narinobu, he left a debt of five million *ryō*. He went up to Edo, married a daughter to the Shogun Ienari, and lived in great splendour as 'the power behind the throne'. There was no hope of persuading Shigehide to abandon this new-found eminence for an alliance with the anti-Bakufu elements. Back in Satsuma, Narinobu's ministers took measures to restore the economy, but the retrenchment angered Shigehide. Thus when Hikokurō arrived, the position was an explosive one, so inevitably he was kept at arm's length. Eventually, Narinobu had to resign and the leaders of his faction to commit *seppuku*. This *Chichibu kuzure* was similar to the Bakumatsu *Takasaki kuzure*. In both cases the losers had great support among the lower *samurai*. Already one can see the genesis of the 1873 struggle; for on the one side many of the frugal lower *samurai* in Satsuma itself wanted to restore their fortunes by making common cause with the *sonnō* activists of the other clans, while the Satsuma leaders in Edo, enjoying new-found glory and power, had become alienated from the *samurai* back home.

## Death in Kurume

In mid-1793, hemmed in by Bakufu scouts and spies, Hikokurō returned to Kurume to die. He again stayed with his old friend, doctor Mori. In his last few days he was feverish, and, while in a fever, he destroyed most of his diary. However, this would seem to have been a rational move to protect others. Mori's description of his last days is reproduced in *Sennin no Omokage* (1961: 74) together with his last verse:

> The body has grown old,
> And now becomes earth.
> But even though it have no grave,
> My spirit will guard this land

This last verse, like his suicide, was very positive: he was issuing a challenge to future generations. It was a call which would not go unheeded.

It should be stressed that the *sonnō* movement was not brought to Kurume by Hikokurō. That he should spend so much time there, and choose it for his *seppuku*, was due to the fact that he found there so many soul-mates, as he did in Nakatsu, Hita, Fukuoka, Nagasaki and Kumamoto. They were not so much fields in which he pioneered the *sonnō* message as regions where he found spiritual brothers ready to be integrated into a national movement orchestrated from Kyoto.

The only exception was Satsuma. Hikokurō's determination to penetrate Satsuma was due not to the presence there of many spiritual brothers, but to the fact, well understood by the Kyoto nobles and *shishi*, that the Bakufu could not be overthrown till Satsuma could be persuaded to move. For the nobles and the progressive clans, the problem was how to involve Satsuma without having it betray the movement by simply replacing the Tokugawa Shogunate by a Satsuma Shogunate.

The Kurume to which Takayama Hikokurō came in 1792 was no isolated backwater. It was close to Hita, the Kyūshū administrative centre, and also to Saga and Nagasaki, so even in the eighteenth century it was already advanced in various aspects of Western learning such as mathematics, astrology and map-making (ibid.: 580–1). Moreover, it had been involved in major national movements ever since Hideyoshi subjugated Kyūshū. As he planned to use northern Kyūshū as a base from which to attack Korea, he sent five followers to rule key areas, one of which was Kurume. Its new ruler was Kobayakawa Hidekane, one of the Hiroshima Mōris.

Kurume duly contributed 1,500 troops to the first Korean invasion and also supplied rice and coolies (*Kurume shi-shi* 1982, Vol. 2: 3–4). At Sekigahara, however, these five Hideyoshi lords were all on the side of the west, and so were replaced. The defeated Mōri clan had to abandon Hiroshima and move to Hagi, and Hidekane's family followed them there. Hidekane became a priest but soon died, and his ashes were also transferred to Chōshū, the new Mōri domains.

Kurume thus began its modern history as *seikan-ron* and inevitably the Korean invasions loomed large in Kurume memory. The other point to bear in mind is that Kurume had personal ties with the Chōshū from the time the Mōri clan moved from Hiroshima. In the Meiji period we talk of Satchō but it must be remembered that Satsuma and Chōshū had been traditional enemies and Kurume's early ties had been with Chōshū.

## MAKI IZUMI

This, then, was the clan where Hikokurō found many soul-mates and where he ended his life. He was buried in Suitengu shrine where the Maki family had been head officials for twenty generations. In 1813, Maki Toshiomi had a son, Yasuomi, who became known as Maki Izumi. Toshiomi was raised to *samurai* status by Lord Yorinori and permitted to visit the castle. He was so grateful that he trained his sons with extreme severity, but he died suddenly leaving eleven-year-old Yasuomi (Izumi) as head of the temple and of a family of five.

From his childhood, Maki Izumi revered Hikokurō. His *sonnō* beliefs were fostered by his teacher, *kokugakusha* Miyasaki Awa no Kami, who had studied under a noted *kokugakusha* in Kyoto. Miyasaki had been invited to teach by many lords, but he would not respond, for his temple was directly attached to the Royal House. This spirit of direct allegiance he imparted to young Izumi (*Sennin no Omokage* 1961: 193–4). At eighteen Maki married the twenty-seven-year-old daughter of Ishihara, a rich merchant who had been given *samurai* status (Yamaguchi 1973: 22–3). They had four sons and a daughter who first married a rich merchant related to her mother, and later a rich landowner, also related to her mother. It would seem his wife's people helped him during his long period of confinement. The Maki story, like that of Hikokurō, thus raises the question of to what extent the rich merchants were behind the anti-Bakufu movement.

In 1832 Maki went up to Kyoto and was made an official of the fifth rank with the title *Izumi no Kami*. Of course, he was a fervent *Sonnōka* and after a period of study at the clan school, he began to attract students of his own. His closest friends included Kimura Saburō, Sada Shūhei (father of Hakuho) and Ikejiri Mochisaemon, a clan teacher who was to die in battle. In 1841 the clan heir, Yoritō, sent Kimura to Mito, and he was followed in 1842 by Murakami Shūtaro (*Kurume shi-shi* 1982, Vol. 2: 658–9). This was the beginning of the so-called Tempo Gakuren, for they brought back the teachings of Fujita Tōko and Aizawa Yasushi. In 1844 Maki also travelled east for six months. He is sometimes described as studying under Aizawa in Mito, but in fact he stayed there for only seven days (Yamaguchi 1973: 40), and though the Tempo Gakuren was based on Mito teachings, their ideas were greatly developed by Maki. Other prominent members of their group were Mizuno Masana, Ikejiri Mochisaemon, Sada Shūhei, and the Fuwa brothers, Magoichi and Mimasaka (*Kurume shi-shi* 1982, Vol. 2: 659).

The group based their hopes on the young heir, Yoritō (1822–46). His father, Yorinori, lord from 1812 to 1844, had been noted for his flamboyant extravagance which, combined with the nationwide Tempo famines, caused severe currency problems. Connections had been established with the great Osaka merchants to get backing for their currency, but eventually Koike, etc. would give them no more credit and their paper money lost all value (ibid.: 440ff.).

Young Yoritō had studied Yōmeigaku under Satō Issai. His succession in 1844 coincided with the arrival in Nagasaki of a Dutch warship bringing a letter from their king urging the opening of the country. Yoritō instituted a five-year plan both to restore the clan finances and to modernize and Westernize its defences. He also sent *kikiyaku* to Nagasaki (Yamaguchi 1973: 48), one of their functions being to gather information about foreign countries.

The varied strands in Kurume history are now clearly visible. The old pro-Bakufu conservatives, typified by *karō* Arima Kenmotsu, were still a major force. The Western influences, coming in from Nagasaki and Saga, may be seen, for example, in the introduction around 1830 of a Western-trained doctor (*Kurume shi-shi*, Vol. 2: 580–1). Young men were sent up to Osaka to study under Ogata Kōan, and a fierce rivalry built up between the Chinese and Western doctors. Saga was the first clan to introduce vaccination and Kurume followed in 1852–3 (ibid.: 584). To institute his reform programme, Yoritō made Murakami his main minister. Murakami was a strong advocate of building up not only coastal defences but also a modern navy (ibid.: 594–5) to patrol and defend as far as Ezochi and the Ryūkyūs. His desire for a modern military system led to the sending of many students to study Dutch and English, especially after 1861. In 1866 Aston led an English party to Kurume, and in 1867 Kurume exhibited at the St Louis Exhibition (ibid.: 590).

Murakami was joined in the government by other Tempo Gakuren members such as Imai Sakae, Nosaki Heihachi and Fuwa Mimasaka. Maki and Kimura remained outside the government, but bombarded the lord with opinion papers, notably on the danger from the West and the need to set up an Emperor-based system (Ogawa 1983: 12).

However, a split developed between the Tempo Gakuren group inside and that outside the government. Yoritō became seriously ill, and Murakami, Fuwa, etc. discussed the succession. This angered Maki, especially as they wished to by-pass the next brother for a younger one. Yoritō died in 1846, and was duly succeeded by the next brother, Yorishige, but his wedding plans further split the clan, for the Shogun ordered him to marry the daughter he had adopted from the Arisugawa-no-miya house. Despite strong opposition to this crippling expense, the wedding took place in 1849 (*Kurume shi-shi*, Vol. 2: 575–6). Over half the expenses had to be borrowed.

By this time Murakami was completely alienated from Maki and the Tempo Gakuren group outside the government. Once entrusted with responsibility, he had had to compromise with the conservative members of the government and could not push straight on with the Maki programme. His isolation seems to have affected his mind, and in 1850 it seems he launched an attack on a government leader but was himself overcome and killed (Yamaguchi 1973: 58–60; Kawashima 1911). The Murakami family lost their *roku* and his colleagues Imai and Fuwa were dismissed but soon reinstated (*Kurume shi-shi*, Vol. 2: 661–3).

Though not in the government, Maki had great influence. In 1847 he had gone up to Kyoto to witness the inauguration of Emperor Kōmei. This strengthened his *sonnō* spirit and love of the past, and enabled him to make allies of nobles such as Sanjō (Ogawa 1983: 12). In 1852 the Maki–Kimura party convinced Lord Yorishige that the conservatives were plotting to replace him with a younger brother. The Arima Kenmotsu group were imprisoned, but they were soon released as Yorishige was persuaded that the charges were groundless. In their stead, Maki, Kimura and Mizuno were all placed under house arrests for fomenting trouble. They remained confined for ten years, thus sparing Kurume involvement in the Ansei troubles.

During his long period of confinement, Maki was permitted to teach. By 1859 his students were so numerous that he was allowed to use the main hall in Temmangu, where he conducted two sessions daily. Few of his followers were full *samurai*, most being *shōya*, doctors, temple officials, etc. (Yamaguchi 1973: 76). From 1858 his writings had become more extreme, for he was not only earlier than Shōin in advocating the overthrow of the Bakufu, but was describing the Emperor as the Emperor of the whole world. Through the Dazai-fu temple chief, he sent a copy to Sanjō, who burnt all his correspondence at the time of the Ii crackdown (ibid.: 87).

Maki's hut was now a *sonnō* planning centre, but his own movement to direct action seems to have been inspired by the secret visits, on 26 September 1860, 11 December 1860 and 15 October 1861 (*Kurume shi-shi*, Vol. 2: 676), of Hirano Kuniomi, the Fukuoka 'organizer' of Kyūshū's extreme *sonnō* party. Like Hirano, Maki rested his major hopes on getting Satsuma to move. When Hirano's attempt to enter Satsuma failed, Maki himself fled the clan with just two followers. They left in broad daylight, and were trailed by officials, but no attempt was made to arrest them. Though the clan was still *sabaku* (support the Bakufu) it would seem it was taking out insurance by letting Maki loose. Many of Maki's students wished to flee with him, but Maki refused, partly because, not being true *samurai*, their only sword practice had been with wooden swords, and partly, it would seem, because Maki himself was class-conscious (Yamaguchi 1973: 103–4). Maki's plan called for converting Satsuma's lord and also for assassinating high officials in Kyoto and Edo.

Though allowed into Satsuma and interviewed by Ōkubo, Maki was unable to meet Hisamitsu or Saigō. Instead, Hisamitsu left for Kyoto with a force of 1,000 men on 16 March 1862. Maki's request to accompany him was refused, for Hisamitsu's objective was to bring the Kyoto-based extremists under control. Maki was allowed to leave on 1 April 1862. Three weeks later he entered Kyoto where he organized attacks, including one on the *Kampaku*. However, the Teradaya plans were discovered, and Maki was arrested and sent back to Kurume.

In early 1863 he was pardoned, for the Kurume lord was bending in the wind. Early in 1863 he accepted Maki's plan for a Satsuma alliance, and sent him on a mission with Fuwa as the nominal leader. Again Maki failed, for he was distrusted by Satsuma, which was still *kōbu-gattai* and which was preoccupied with the Richardson slaying. A wide gulf also opened between Maki and Fuwa.

Sanjō's nobles and the Chōshū extremists were now dominant in Kyoto. It was decided to form a Royal Guard (*shimpei*) (ibid.: 144–6). From Kurume, a force of twenty-one Maki disciples, including Sada Sōichirō (Hakuho) and Honjō Kanae were chosen, with Maki in command. Five were soon replaced by people even closer to Maki, including his brothers and a son. Mizuno and Kimura were still in prison, but Sada and a certain Katō petitioned that they be released.

With Maki in the ascendant, Arima Kenmotsu was placed under house arrest, but within a week the situation was reversed (ibid.). Convinced that Maki was planning to flee, Lord Yorishige agreed to the arrest of his faction members – the so-called 'Maki hunt'. Kenmotsu was restored to power and a squad of full *samurai* was sent up to Kyoto, for it had been argued that it was an insult to the Emperor to have temple officials, etc. as Royal Guards. Maki was grilled about the young people whom he had urged to be given a role in government. As all but Sada were *heimin* or *ashigaru*, Maki could merely reply that all responsibility rested with himself. The fact that Maki's other followers were of low rank helps explain why Sada was given a high position in 1868 (ibid.: 146–52).

Once more, Maki's allies in Chōshū, Kyoto and Tsuwano secured his release, and he and twenty followers were allowed up to Kyoto as Royal Guards. He proceeded via the merchant Shiraishi in Shimonoseki to Chōshū, where he pointed out to Mōri that Chōshū alone could not drive out the barbarians, and urged the need for an imperial edict to unite the country (ibid.: 155). He arrived back in Kyoto after a year's absence, but now he had the blessing of the clan and the backing of the Chōshū Army. He met with Katsura, etc., and presented a five-point plan which included a *jōi* edict. This was agreed to by all, including the Kampaku, and the radical nobles. Through Sanjō and Tokudaiji, the plan was presented to Kōmei, who agreed to issue the edict and to rally national support by making a pilgrimage to Yamato. That Maki was now the dominating figure, guiding both Chōshū and the nobles, is confirmed by Aizu documents (ibid.: 161).

On 19 June 1863 Arima Kenmotsu entered Kyoto with the Kurume heir. That same day Maki met Sanjō and advocated setting up cannons in Dairi to help Chōshū destroy foreign shipping. Sanjō summoned Kenmotsu and ordered that this be done, and directed the Kokura clan to assist. The Yamato trip was proclaimed on 13 August 1863. In accordance with Maki's plan, many *daimyō* were ordered to attend the Emperor, and Chōshū, Higo, Tosa and Kurume were directed to provide troops.

At this point, however, Satsuma and Aizu staged a *coup d'état*. Kōmei's trip was cancelled and the radical nobles confined. Maki urged Sanjō to lead the 2,000 Royal Guards to the palace to query the orders but he refused and instead the seven nobles fled to Chōshū, denying the Royal Guards permission to go along, for they were the Emperor's troops. But in addition to the main Chōshū force of about 400 troops, Maki, Mizuno, etc., and also Tosa's Hijikata, went along with about thirty men (ibid.: 168–70).

On 5 September 1863 the Royal Guards were disbanded. Sawa (with Hirano), staged an uprising in Ikuno, and Nakayama Tadamitsu, the young uncle of the future Emperor Meiji, led a force in Yamato; but both were crushed. Maki blamed the crafty Satsuma men for the *coup* of 18 August, but he still needed Satsuma. Though he had never met Saigō, he sought his help in turning Satsuma around, sending a letter dated 13 September 1863 to merchant Shiraishi Shōichirō asking him to get a letter to Saigō.

On 11 October 1863, after a meeting at Yuda with Katsura, Kusaka, Mizuno and Hijikata, etc., Maki composed his letter to Saigō. One must assume that the others were in fundamental agreement with this letter which urged that Japan take Korea, Manchuria and the South Islands. 'They should make their country's authority shine in all four directions' (ibid.: 181).

As the moderates had gained the ascendancy in Chōshū, twenty-five of the Kurume guard returned home. But the Kyoto *coup* had given the Kurume conservatives heart, so the returnees, including Sada, Kimura and Ikejiri, were promptly arrested. They were to remain in prison until the Restoration (*Kurume shi-shi*, Vol. 2: 696). They were in considerable danger, especially when Fukuoka killed fourteen imprisoned *sonnō-ka*, but Mizuno, who had remained in Chōshū, got a message to Satsuma's Ōyama, and his good offices helped get them spared (ibid.: 700).

Leaving Mizuno and Hijikata to guard the nobles, Maki and Kusaka went up to Kyoto with 1,500 men, but they were defeated by the Satsuma–Aizu forces. Maki and sixteen followers, mostly from Higo, Tosa and Kurume, are said to have faced towards the palace and committed synchronized *seppuku*. However, the bodies were burnt beyond recognition, and Japanese history tends to prettify its most sordid epidoses, so it should be recalled that throwing live prisoners on a bonfire was one of the atrocities practised around this time (see Miura 1925: 368ff.).

## Maki's place in history

Maki, like Hikokurō before him, aimed at putting *kokugaku* and Shintō ideas into practice.

Sada was so fond of writing of 'Sada's seikanron', and so much has been written of 'Saigō's seikanron', that one must stress that both Sada and his father were Maki followers and that ten years before the *seikan* dispute Maki was writing urging Saigō to attack Korea.

Because of the foreign threat Maki wanted to occupy and colonize Karafuto (Saghalien) (Ogawa 1983: 25–7). As Japan could not fight the big four simultaneously, he advocated that Japan should trade and avoid conflict with America; but this was merely tactical: all citizens, young and old, male and female, had to share the defence of Japan which, when ready, would then expand overseas.

Nariaki of Mito preached *sonnō*, but his *sonnō* revolved around the Shogun, and was essentially feudal: the Shogun was to revere the Emperor, the *daimyō* revere the Shogun, the *samurai* revere the *daimyō* and the *heimin* revere the *samurai*. For the *samurai* or commoners to swear direct allegiance to the Emperor was tantamount to disloyalty, even rebellion. The Mito ideas were developed by Aizawa, who briefly taught Maki and continued to correspond with him. But whereas Aizawa opposed extremism, Maki broke with the feudal order and spoke of *tenka*. Thus he was not greatly distressed at having to go against his own clan (Yamaguchi 1973: 217ff.). Mikami, for example, claims that Maki was the real Commander-in-Chief of the Chōshū forces, but though this may be disputed, there can be no doubt of his importance as a spiritual and political leader.

Whereas men such as Yokoi Shōnan and Hashimoto Sanai were moving towards a modern state, Maki was going back to the ancients (ibid.: 241ff.). Whereas Shōnan and Sanai were operating within the Bakufu framework, Maki wanted to sweep away the Bakufu and go back to the golden age before Nara. He was quite happy with a strict class system, and even advanced elaborate clothing rules to make the distinctions still plainer. Yamaguchi argues that Maki, who did not wish to set up a modern state, paradoxically did more than the progressives to push Japan in this direction for that was the inevitable result of sweeping away the Bakufu.

Likewise, Maki was not intentionally part of a social revolution, but he had close ties in Kurume with rich merchants and landowners such as his wife's people, and his own followers were almost exclusively *heimin* or *ashigaru*. He also relied heavily on Shiraishi, for example, at Baseki. The fact that his faction was composed of doctors, temple officials, rich landowners, etc. meant that he was, in practice, leading a bourgeois revolution.

Maki's major contribution is all too clear: namely, the concept of holy wars, internal and external. Of course, he did not originate this concept, but he played a leading role in its propagation and development. His insistence that foreigners defiled the soil of Japan (*Nippon o kegasu*) was in sharp contrast to his doctrine that Japan itself should occupy Korea, Manchuria, the Philippines, etc., and turn them into vassal states.

Of course, not all Japanese people were in Maki's corner. The majority, even in Kurume, clearly regarded him as a dangerous fanatic. Yet it remains true that this element of religious fanaticism is central both to the story of Meiji Japan and to the longer story of Japanese imperialism. Because religious fanaticism and paranoiac self-righteousness were never far below the surface, it is impossible to treat the 1873 *Seihen* simply as a constitutional crisis.

## SADA HAKUHO:
## A STUDY IN MEIJI DISINFORMATION

After the Satsuma-led *coup* of 18 August 1863 and the subsequent death of Maki and the imprisonment of his followers, the conservatives remained in power in Kurume until the Restoration, when the Maki faction members were released and, led by Mizuno, took over the clan government. Like Maki, Mizuno had been confined for most of the fifties, and later stayed with the nobles as confidant and guard in Chōshū and Dazai-fu Kyūshū. They were bitter men, committed to Maki's programme of setting up an Emperor system within Japan and of 'restoring' the Emperor's position in the world.

The clan was awarded a certain number of positions in the new Meiji government. As the Maki followers included few men of rank, the position made available in the Foreign Office went to Sada Shōichirō, now known as Hakuho. Both he and his father had been prominent followers of Maki. His appointment was not the recognition of individual merit so much as an allocation to the Kurume clan, or, more specifically, the Maki faction.

At the Foreign Office, his chief was Sawa, the most extreme and impetuous of the young nobles. *Goyō* histories tell us little about Sawa, but it should be remembered that there was no love lost between Satsuma and the nobles, apart from Iwakura. It was widely believed – and probably correctly – that Satsuma had been behind the assassination of Anegakōji Kintomo (1839–63) who with Tosa extremist Takechi riding by his side (Sasaki 1970, Vol. 1: 512), had gone up to Edo as Sanjō's deputy bearing the edict demanding that the Shogun drive out the foreigners. Sawa (1835–73) had also been born an Anegakōji, his father having preceded Kintomo's as head of the family. Thus Sawa had particular reason to be hostile to Satsuma, but all the young nobles blamed Satsuma for frustrating their plans and forcing them to flee to Chōshū. It was also widely believed that Satsuma and Iwakura were responsible for the assassination of the Emperor Kōmei (Sasaki 1970, Vol. 2: 365–8), so when news reached Dazai-fu of the proposed Satchō alliance, the hostile young nobles had to be persuaded. No doubt the argument stressed what had been realized at least since 1790, namely the fact that the Shogunate could not be overthrown unless they enlisted the support of Satsuma. Thus they would have to lay aside their fears of a Satsuma Bakufu; but victory won, there would come, inevitably, the showdown with Satsuma.

As we have seen, Kōkaku lived till 1840, but in 1817 he retired for his son Ninkō (1800–46). Towards the end of his life, Kōkaku stressed the need to improve the education of the children of the Kyoto nobles. Ninkō was about to build a school when he died, and the project was taken up by his son and successor, Kōmei (1831–66). The school developed into the famous Gakushū-in.

It would be interesting to explore the relationship of Kōmei and his grandfather Kōkaku. From the outset of his reign, Kōmei demonstrated his resolve to play a positive role. In 1846 he sent the Bakufu an imperial edict on the subject of coastal defences, pointing out that they should be regarded as matters of great urgency and importance. In 1850 he ordered the seven shrines and seven temples of Kyoto to pray for deliverance from the foreign evil. He also sent the Bakufu another edict – something unprecedented in Court–Bakufu relations. Kōmei was not yet out of his teens, which rather suggests that, like his great-grandson Hirohito, he received early and intensive training – that he was familiar with the previous hundred years of history and knew well the story of Kōkaku and also Hikokurō.

In America assassination tends to be good for the reputation, but in Japan physical assassination is likely to be followed by character assassination. There still seems to be no authoritative, impartial biography of Emperor Kōmei. In Japanese history the Kōmei assassination has never been granted more than a furtive footnote. Yet unless we recognize and examine that assassination, it is quite impossible to give a fair assessment not only of activists such as Sawa and Sada but also of virtually the whole of non-Satchō Japan. Indeed, the whole of the story right down to the present day becomes blurred and out of focus.

The simple fact is that there never was a Meiji Ishin. The term should be scrapped or put in inverted commas and allowed to stand as a symbol for the blackest cynicism, hypocrisy and betrayal. Rather than highlighting one year – 1868 – the emphasis should be on the years 1866–73 as a whole, and instead of using the mythical 'Meiji Ishin' as a title, we should be writing of 'The Satchō Usurpation of Power, 1866–73'. The 1866 assassination of Kōmei was followed in quick succession by the enforced resignation of Shogun Keiki and the transfer of the capital, stealthily and by stages, to Tokyo, then in 1871 came the military coup, followed in 1873 by the showdown which left the regicides Ōkubo and Iwakura firmly in control. Of these various episodes, clearly the key action was the assassination of Kōmei. What followed was essentially consolidation, and once their position had been consolidated in 1873, the regicides were able to push on quickly in 1874 with their grab for Japan's wealth, and in 1875 begin their charge onto the Asian Mainland.

Despite the fact that the *Meiji Ishin* was never more than a sedulously propagated myth, one may make out a strong case for a *Kōmei Ishin*. Blurred though the outlines be, surely Kōmei was both strong and capable. *Fukko Ishin* (restoring the old and thereby making the spirit new again) contained the idea of taking power from the Shogun and restoring it to the Emperor. During his reign Kōmei did much to re-assert the position of the Emperor. Outraged that Westerners had established a physical presence in Japan, he issued an edict demanding that the Shogun expel them. Later, however, he came to realize that a civil war would be a disaster which would threaten the nation's independence, and so he refused to allow the extremists to push him into an armed conflict with Yoshinobu (Keiki), the new, youthful Shogun. Instead he adopted a policy of *Kōbu Gattai*, or co-operation between Court and Bakufu. Under these two capable, youthful leaders – Keiki and Kōmei – the process of national reconciliation, so vital in view of the perceived external threat, was proceeding apace, with both central and clan governments becoming more widely-based in terms of both class and geographical representation. At the same time young men were being sent abroad – future 'Meiji' thinkers like, for example, Fukuzawa and Nishi Amane, and future business leaders like Shibusawa and Masuda – to acquire the skills and techniques of the West.

Surely we have here all the essential elements of an *ishin*: a restoration of power to the Emperor and Court, a Shogun once more serving the Emperor, scholars searching antiquity to discover and preserve the national essence while at the same time the nation was rapidly acquiring the new knowledge necessary to 'restore' its position in the world.

Yet this *Kōmei Ishin* was rudely shattered by the assassination of the Emperor. If Kōmei had lived, there was no way Satchō could have acquired their subsequent vast power, wealth, land holdings and aristocratic titles. That crime set Japan along the road to the Boshin Civil War of 1868 and subsequent armed conflicts such as the Seinan Civil War of 1877. It was those civil wars which were largely responsible for Japan's economic problems, and those economic problems, together with the Satchō desire to defend their monopolies, which helped propel Japan along the road to imperialistic expansion. Rather than being consigned to a furtive footnote, the Kōmei assassination must be seen as a central event in Japan's modern history. Not the least remarkable of Satchō achievements was getting the term *Meiji Ishin* written into Japanese history. The new Meili rulers had assassinated the legitimate Emperor and replaced him with a frightened sixteen-year-old puppet; they had shattered the process of national reconciliation and they went on to impose a policy of helter-skelter modernization. Surely in no other country in the world would these events be described as a Restoration of the power of the Emperor and a return to the old ways. Japanese history has two major myths: the ancient myth of divine origin and the modern myth of the 'Meiji Restoration'. It is this modern myth which still confers legitimacy on the Japanese 'Establishment'.

At the time of the Kōmei assassination rumours of poisoning were widespread. Sasaki Takayuki, for example, noted the rumours in his diary (Sasaki 1970, Vol. 2: 365–8) and pointed out that mourning clothes were worn for only three days as against fifty for Emperor Kōkaku. These rumours refused to die away, and in 1909 Korean An Chong Kon gave the assassination of anti-western Kōmei as one

91

of his fifteen reasons for assassinating Itō Hirobumi (Nakano Yasuo 1984: 6 *et seq.*).

Also significant is the contemporary British witness. Journalist Black's *Young Japan 1858–1879* summed up Kōmei as 'the bigoted barbarian-hating Mikado', while Mossman (1873: 278–9) referred to 'the inferior character and talents of the deceased Mikado' and described him as 'avaricious and irresolute'. Neither Black nor Mossman would have had access to Kōmei. Fairly clearly they were quoting members of the Meiji government, and it is most odd to have Japanese maligning their recently-deceased Emperor to foreigners. Such conversations, however, become understandable if Kōmei were assassinated.

In December 1979, the *Rekishi Dokuhon* (1979: 91 *et seq.*) summed up the modern verdict of guilty. It is always difficult for judge and jury to decide how much weight should be attached to the testimony of scientific experts, but in this case a team of modern doctors were unanimous in declaring that the evidence showed that Kōmei had been poisoned when well along the road to recovery from smallpox. There are various theories as to how the poison was administered. One has Iwakura's eldest sister, who had borne Kōmei two short-lived children, as the agent while another has Iwakura presenting Kōmei with poisoned writing brushes, knowing he was in the habit of sucking his brushes.

Another important witness brought forward by Rekishi Dokuhon was Ernest Satow, the young Bakumatsu diplomat who had a close relationship with many of the future Meiji leaders. In late life Satow declared that he had it on very good authority that Kōmei was indeed assassinated.

The *Kawade Encyclopaedia* agrees with the above verdict, and helps flesh out the picture in its entry '*Kōmei Tennōki*' (the Records of Emperor Kōmei). In 1891, the Miya-Nai Sho, presided over by Tokutaiji Mitsunori, elder brother of Saionji Kinmochi, began work on the voluminous Kōmei records. They were finally published in 1905, but there were only a limited number of copies and they were not to be shown to third persons or quoted. With the end of the Second World War, they were thrown open to full scrutiny. The conclusion has been that this Tennōki is not reliable history, for there are numerous signs of tampering and deletions. It gives the official Satchō account of Kōmei's death but this does not accord with the diary of Nakayama Tadayasu, the maternal grandfather of the future Emperor Meiji – it was Tadayasu who was entrusted with the upbringing of both Meiji and Meiji's son Taishō.

The *Kawade Encyclopaedia* gives no further information about Tadayasu's diary. Nor does it elaborate on another vital piece of information: a damning account of Kōmei's death sent to Rinnōji no Miya by the high priest of a leading Kyoto shrine. Here we are again entering a grey area where clear illumination would be greatly appreciated.

It would seem that during the Boshin War there was for a time a dynasty struggle with the boy Emperor being challenged by a rival claimant. The many wives and progeny of the Royal Family and leading aristocrats, plus the cryptic, still somewhat reverential manner of telling their story, makes it difficult to present a clear picture.

The third Tokugawa Shogun, Iemitsu, built a shrine in Ueno and stipulated that the abbot must always be a son of the reigning Emperor, probably as a kind of hostage. In 1866 this abbot, Rinnōji no Miya (1847–95), was the ninth son of Fushimi no Miya Kunichika Shinnō. It will be recalled that the Fushimi family was an older royal house than Kanin, the newer Fushimi branch from which Kōkaku and Meiji were descended. The first Fushimi prince, Yoshihito (1351–1416), was the eldest son of the reigning Emperor. Thus the Fushimi had been a royal family for three hundred years when one of its sons first formed the Kanin royal family. That was a time of civil war and of rival claimants to the throne and the son of the third Fushimi prince was able to ascend the throne as Gohanazono Tennō. It is hard to find a detailed pedigree for the 1866 Rinnōji no Miya, but his closeness to the throne and the degree of legitimacy of his claim could hardly have been less than that of Gohanazono or of Kōkaku in 1779 (*Kawade Encyclopaedia*; *Fushiminomiya*).

Rinnōji no Miya had lived in Edo since 1858 and when the Satchō forces advanced to Edo in 1868 he tried to negotiate the safety of the city (*Fukushima Ken Dai Hyakkajiten*). Then he fled north with the Tokugawa forces who proclaimed him Emperor. It was he who issued the Sendai and Yonesawa fiefs with orders to attack the Satchō forces.

This dynastic dispute has, of course, been virtually obliterated from Japanese history. Significantly, I first encountered it in the local *Fukushima* encyclopaedia. Where it is mentioned, for example by Lloyd (1909: p.24), this prince is usually depicted as a child and the dupe of the 'rebel' forces. However, as the *Kōmei Tennōki* entry points out, his religious counterpart in Kyoto had sent him a letter on Kōmei's assassination. Thus it would seem this twenty-one-year-old prince quite freely made his claim to the throne.

Rinnoji no Miya was captured and was pardoned. He was given the title Prince Kitashirakawa, became a military man, and died of illness in Taiwan in 1895. He had many progeny. One son married a Meiji daughter, whilst another married a Shimazu and produced a daughter who was to become Hirohito's consort. Thus the dynastic dispute was papered over. Yet this ongoing struggle should be borne in mind when we view the frenetic activities of Sada and Sawa and consider the exiled young nobles in Dazai-fu having to face up to the fact of a Satchō alliance.

With the *ishin*, Satsuma maintained its friendly relations with many ex-Bakufu officials. Its marriage of convenience with Chōshū was widely regarded as an unnatural one which would soon be dissolved, setting the stage for an ultimate trial of strength to decide the successors to the Tokugawas. But before this could happen, Satchō had to throw off the shackles and restraints imposed by the ideologues with their *kokugaku* ideas of a semi-religious state. The ideologues' headquarters were in Kyoto and the nobles were, if not their leaders, at least their patrons and organizers over a period of 100 years. These ideologues were doubly dangerous in that virtually every clan, including Satchō and Tosa, had their own extremist factions.

Sawa then, like Sada, should not be viewed as one who was put in charge of foreign affairs because of his ability and experience. It was an appointment which acknowledged the century-long role of the nobles. As Sawa has been virtually written out of the Meiji story, it is difficult to give a reliable assessment of the man and his work, but it would seem that he was as extreme as Maki and Takechi. Instead of proceeding to Chōshū with the other six nobles, he put a dummy in his bed and sneaked away in the dead of night to join Hirano's Ikuno uprising (Sasaki 1970, Vol. 3: 158). With the Ishin Sawa was put in charge at Nagasaki. Among his attendants was Sada's younger brother, who had served the nobles at Dazai-fu. From Kyūshū, Sawa returned to Tokyo to take charge of foreign affairs.

As the Kurume clan was soon under Mizuno, who had been with the nobles throughout their exile, and as Sada had been a significant follower of Maki and Mizuno, the relationship of Sawa and Sada cannot be viewed simply as that between Foreign Minister and subordinate official. Instead, they were essentially fellow conspirators, dedicated activists of long standing. They were also equally incensed at the way Satchō had taken over the government, opened the country and 'betrayed' the Restoration. Sasaki (1970, Vol. 4: 275 fn.) goes as far as to suggest that Sawa was behind all the major disturbances in 1870, including the Toyama–Atago affair, the Chōshū Irregulars uprising and the Maruyama affair (see chapter 6). Sada was also clearly involved in the Maruyama affair, which again emphasizes their relationship as being one of fellow conspirators. Sawa was forced to resign over the Maruyama affair, but in 1873 he was appointed as Special Envoy to Russia. He died suddenly just before his departure. Again there were rumours of assassination.

It was Sawa who appointed Sada to lead the first full Meiji mission to Korea. They were not experienced career diplomats, but fanatical *sonnō* activists not long free after years of confinement, sharing the same ideology, privy to each other's thoughts and plans, and heirs to Maki, Anegakōji, Takechi and generations of noble activists and *kokugakusha*.

In 1903, Sada Hakuho, then seventy-three and ill, dictated his *Seikan Ron Reminiscences* to a disciple, Itō Akira (Sada 1903). He described himself as the major promoter of *seikan-ron* – Sada's *seikan-ron*. He had spoken of it constantly during his nearly five years in prison, explaining to his fellow prisoners that Korea was really a tribute nation and that Japan's position there had to be 'restored' as a prelude to a wider campaign of expansion. Whenever he lectured on the subject, his voice would rise and it was wonderful for driving away the gloom. Later, during the military campaigns in the north, he constantly preached *seikan-ron*, and on returning from the war, he presented the Dajokan with an opinion paper urging that Korea be attacked.

When the capital was moved to Tokyo, Sada, like many Kyoto-based officials, lost his position. He returned to Kurume but was soon up to Tokyo on clan business. He again presented an opinion paper on *seikan-ron* (ibid.: 39). It seems these two papers are no longer extant, and we are given few details, but Sada told his recorder they were in all essentials the same as his 1870 Report.

In October 1869, he received a letter from the Dajokan appointing him to lead a mission to Korea. He was summoned by Sawa who explained that no reply had been received to a message sent the previous year through the Lord of Tsushima. For 200 years, only Tsushima men had gone to Korea as Japanese representatives, so now Sada could not present himself as being on an official mission: he would either present himself as a Foreign Office official there on business, or he could say he was a Tsushima man.

As he was also to investigate the trade situation, it was at first intended that a merchant should accompany him, but it was decided instead to send Saitō Sakae, an official versed in commerce. His deputy was another official, Moriyama Shigeru, and they were also accompanied by two servants. Before departing, Sada tried to read up on Korea, but the only books he could find were three volumes of Korean poetry presented to him by Miyamoto Shōichi.

They left Tokyo in November, but in Nagasaki Sada had to enter hospital. The doctor, Hirotsu Shunzō, was interested in Korea, and asked to accompany them. As Sada was not fully recovered, he discussed the matter with Saitō and Moriyama who agreed to take him along. Later, Hirotsu was to join the Foreign Office, and, like Moriyama, to make many trips to Korea. Sada, however, was never to go back for he had vowed not to return save at the head of an army.

From Nagasaki they proceeded to Tsushima. There Sada narrowly escaped being shot by a Tsushima man. It seems the Tsushima people were desperate at the thought of losing their trade monopoly (ibid.: 42). They sailed from Waninoura in the north, taking four hours by local boat to Pusan. Just before sailing they ran into a Chōshū man, Kuriya Tasuke, who was just back from a secret visit to Pusan, and he provided much useful information. Chōshū had strong links with, and influence on, Tsushima so Sada was not sure whether Kuriya had gone to Korea privately or on clan business.

The Pusan trading post was now down to 100 inhabitants. Though all Japanese were generally confined to the post, twice a year they were permitted to visit the graves of the Hideyoshi dead. Thus the Sada party did get to see something of the countryside. However, he had trouble catching the Korean officials who deliberately dodged him. Eventually, he received an answer as to why they had not replied to the Japanese correspondence, but finding this answer unacceptable, he returned ahead of his colleagues to Tsushima where he stayed to write his report. As he then had to re-enter hospital in Nagasaki, Moriyama and Saitō took his report up to Tokyo.

Sada's 1870 Report was aggressively *seikan*, advocating occupying Korea then moving into central Asia and also expanding to the south. He boasted in 1903 that if his Report had been adopted Japan would by then stretch into the Philippines, and *sekai dai-ken* (world supremacy) would be hers. Sada referred to a Berlin linguistic conference about 1900 where one speaker recommended Japanese as the most suitable universal language. The dream was clearly of the whole world united under Japan and using the Japanese language.

Sada's reminiscences went on to refer to the interference to 'Sada's *seikan-ron*' by Satsuma's Yokoyama and Terashima (ibid.: 48–9). Then he discussed the Maruyama affair (ibid.: 49–50) and the Saga uprising, and concluded by relating a conversation with Itagaki on 18 February 1899, at a meeting of a historical society. They held a long discussion on the authenticity of certain unspecified Korean documents. Itagaki pointed out that Soejima had vigorously defended their authenticity, but Sada bluntly stated that these so-called 'Korean statements' had been made up by Japanese officials.

Sada's 1870 Report on his mission to Korea was, predictably, little more than an exposition of 'Sada's *seikan-ron*', which might also be described as 'Maki's *seikan-ron*'. Sada used a classical Chinese expression to compare Japan and Korea to lips and teeth: if the lips are lost, the teeth get cold. France, Russia and America were all wanting to attack Korea, so if Japan let the opportunity slip, it would lose out to these Western countries.

His Report quite explicitly urged the sending of a special envoy, but made it quite clear that this was merely part of the ritual before declaring war. If the Emperor was insulted, his ministers should be prepared to die. Thus if no apology was forthcoming, the envoy should be withdrawn and the troops sent in. Of course, there was not the remotest chance of the Koreans apologizing, so the sending and subsequent recall of an envoy was merely to provide a cloak of legality for the subsequent invasion. He gave detailed plans of campaign, and claimed thirty *dai-tai* would be enough to conquer the whole Peninsula, for the Korean government was corrupt, oppressive and highly unpopular.

Like Korea, Ezo, the northern islands, Luzon, Taiwan, Manchuria and China would all come under the imperial sway. Sada stressed that, far from there being a shortage of troops, there was such an abundance that they were arousing fears of internal rebellions. 'Fortunately', there was Korea.

He compared Korea to Ezo, hammering home the point that Korea was much to be preferred to Ezo, which had been a great drain on the Treasury. Korea, on the other hand, was rich in rice and wheat and would be a veritable goldmine. To attack Korea was to implement a policy of *fukoku kyōhei*. Indeed, the conquest of Korea would enable them to collect Korean wealth and Korean people to use in Ezo.

Though Sada spoke of conquest, not occupation, it is quite clear that he was advocating not mere punishment and withdrawal but permanent occupation. Japan was to grow rich and strong on Korean rice and grains; Korean people were to be conscripted to work in Ezochi, and Korea was to be a base from which to launch further expansion. As we have seen, these ideas were similar to Hideyoshi's which, in the intervening years, had never been allowed to die out.

As it had for centuries, Japan still felt the need for Korean rice. *Wakō* could no longer be employed, though many such as Maruyama proposed the use of irregulars who would have approximated to *wakō*. Once Korea had been occupied, many Western observers, such as Keio teacher Lloyd (1909: 286), were to attest to the fact that the Japanese 'carpet-baggers' were little better than the pirates of old. But in 1870, for newly emerging Japan, some proper justification had to be provided before Korea could be invaded, and Sada felt that the answer could be provided by sending an envoy who would fail and be withdrawn. Sada's plan was publicly debated and later repeated by Saigō, who set it out as his own line of reasoning. Saigō merely paraphrased Sada, and yet, contrary to all the evidence, Japanese historians cannot usually bring themselves to accept that Saigō wanted to occupy and exploit Korea.

Sada's deputy, Moriyama, also put in a report to the Foreign Office. Kemuyama described Moriyama's proposals as more peaceful than Sada's, but this is debatable. Moriyama agreed that the Koreans had been rude without reason, but he placed greater emphasis on the need to negotiate before sending in troops. However, as he must have known no apology would be forthcoming, it would seem he was not more moderate than Sada but merely more concerned with *taigi meibun*. He recommended that 50,000 troops be sent, and gave the standard argument that the *samurai* were disaffected and should be sent overseas to forestall internal uprisings. Like Sada and Saigō in 1873, he provided fairly detailed military plans, including a description of what routes the invaders should follow (Kemuyama 1907: 147–8).

Again like Sada, Moriyama made it quite clear that Korea was to be permanently occupied. He wrote of unemployed *samurai* being transplanted to the Peninsula (ibid.: 142). Though the 'management' of Korea would at first involve some expense, this could soon be recouped by selling Karafuto to 'any nation but Russia' and soon Korea would be contributing to both the wealth and the strength of Japan (ibid.: 148).

Sada's *Reminiscences* are a valuable document which deserves to be labelled a 'primary source', for though they cannot be accepted as history, they do provide an authentic example of studied disinformation. Kemuyama interviewed Sada while writing his pioneer study (ibid.: Intro.), and Sada's version of events has been incorporated into official Japanese legends. Though it is difficult to present reliable documents to discredit Sada, the internal evidence and the logic of the situation clearly indicate that, at the very least, he was guilty of half-truths and distortions.

Sada's constant proselytizing is worth noting, for it demonstrates that he was wedded to this policy long before he went to Korea and before the Koreans 'insulted' Meiji Japan. But his attempt to build up a picture of 'Sada's *seikan-ron*' is simply ridiculous. Sada was preaching to the converted, for his prison-mates were fellow-followers of Maki, who had likewise been preaching this policy – one widespread long before his own day. His description of Sawa calling him in to explain the purpose of the mission also beggars belief. Sada was the highest ranking member of Maki's twenty Royal Guards who went up to Kyoto; he was also a prominent member of the party of thirty who were allowed to escort the nobles to Chōshū. The impetuous young Sawa escaped in the dead of night to fail at Ikuno, which rather suggests that Sada had an *aniki* relationship with Sawa. Moreover, Sada's young brother served the nobles at Dazai-fu and accompanied Sawa to Nagasaki. These two old comrades-in-arms and fellow extremists, after years in the wilderness, were working together in the Foreign Office to bring about a true 'restoration'. Each must have known every detail of the other's thoughts on Korea. The formal picture Sada paints of the Foreign Minister summoning him to explain Japan's policy towards Korea is therefore ludicrous. This is not a mere question of style or presentation; for it was a case not of a Foreign Minister and his officials making a considered, measured response to a changing external situation, but of two extremists, having captured office, proceeding to implement plans they had nurtured for years.

The account of the accidental meeting in Tsushima, just before they sailed for Pusan, with Kuriya Tasuke of Chōshū smacks of evasion. Like Satsuma and Tosa, Chōshū had been trying to get into Korea to trade; Waninoura was a tiny place; both Sawa and

Sada had strong Chōshū ties; Kuriya, recently returned from a secret trip to Korea, was able to give much useful information; and Sada's party had planned to leave earlier for Pusan but had been delayed by his 'illness'. It all adds up to a somewhat unlikely story. Surely the timing of Sada's arrival in Waninoura was deliberately co-ordinated with that of Kuriya. This, of course, would put Chōshū in on the launching of the *seikan* activities, which is what the Sada mission amounted to. Failing the unearthing of documents on Kuriya, the historian must either take Sada at face value or engage in speculation. The former course is so manifestly unwise that constant speculation is called for. One must note, and attach significance to, the fact that he met the recently returned Kuriya. As private trade presented such problems, it would seem likely he was an experienced Chōshū clan spy, especially as he was so well informed about Korea; and, this being so, it would be more logical to believe that this was a carefully arranged meeting designed to provide Sada with the latest information. Whoever or whatever he was, it is most unlikely that Kuriya was his real name.

The dubious nature of Sada's account emerges more clearly if we examine his account of Hirotsu, 'the Nagasaki doctor'. Here he has distorted the picture, partly by omission, and partly by a series of little lies which add up to a major untruth. He did not lie when he described Hirotsu as a Nagasaki doctor, but he failed to mention that Hirotsu was not only a Kurume man but his own relative. Hirotsu was descended (*Sennin no Omokage* 1961: 35–8) from Hirotsu Rankei (1709–94), a noted scholar and teacher whose *juku* developed into the clan school, *Meizendō*.

Rankei married a Sada and had four children. One of his sisters also married a Sada, so obviously the families were very close. Rankei's writings include many essays relating to Korea; for example, one deals with the plans to transfer huge rice supplies and store them in Pusan the year before Hideyoshi's invasions (Hirotsu 1911: 39–40). Thus the Hirotsu–Sada family interest in Korea goes back at least as far as Rankei.

Rankei's second son, Shochō, became a doctor in Nagasaki, but he also made a name for himself as a writer, his novel *Asagao Nikki* (*Diary of a Morning Flower*) being turned into a Kabuki play. He died in 1818 (not 1804 as recorded in *Kurume Jimbutsu Shi* 1981: 444) before the birth of his son Shunzō. The fact that Shunzō lost both parents at an early age probably made him closer to his Sada cousins.

In 1853, at thirty-four, Shunzō went to Nagasaki to study Western medicine under Pompei and Smidt, an American doctor. There he took the name Tomita Nanrei. In Nagasaki, he maintained his ties with the clan, and would submit opinion papers. One urged the abolition of feudalism and the establishment of a *gun ken* system. According to information provided orally by Kurume's senior historian, Koga Yukio, his name appeared in the clan records in 1870 as clan *kikiyaku* in Nagasaki – literally 'an official who hears'. His work included translating articles on the West, spying on other clans, and, probably, giving the latest information on Korea.

On his return from Korea, Shunzō joined the Foreign Office and became something of a specialist on Korea. He also did some writing – not fiction like his father but more in the line of Rankei. Thus in 1873 he published *Jishu no ken* (*The Right of Self-Determination*). This echoes Rousseau and precedes Nagae Chomin's translation of *The Social Contract*. Shunzō was delighted that the Eta had been given full legal rights, arguing that it was ridiculous for Japan to cling to such discrimination in the age of steam and electricity. Though he maintained that it was necessary to give equality to all her citizens to build a strong and prosperous Japan, he did not extend the ideas of equality and independence to Koreans, even though he wrote part of the book while in Pusan. Despite this limitation, Shunzō clearly differed greatly from his cousin, Sada, for he was not an extreme ideologue but a modern, Western-trained scientist with enlightened views which had been fostered by his many years in cosmopolitan Nagasaki.

Shunzō was to die in 1883. His second son, Ryurō, a noted novelist, wrote essays which throw further light on Shunzō (*Sennin no Omokage* 1961: 327–8). One mentions that he joined the Foreign Office because he wished to 'manage' Korea (ibid.). He also recorded how military men such as Nozu and Ōnuma were frequent visitors to their home in the middle and late seventies and how they, too, had their hearts set on 'managing' Korea. Clearly the talk was not about a punitive expedition but about occupation and control. The repeated use of 'manage' would perhaps suggest that economic control was of prime importance.

Ryurō's son, Kazuo, was also to become a leading literary figure in the Shōwa period. Thus the Hirotsu were a highly literate family, with Shunzō's father, son and grandson all being noted writers of fiction, while he harked back to the more serious writings of Rankei.

Once one understands the Sada–Hirotsu relationship, much of

Sada's story becomes suspect. Hirotsu was on the Kurume clan payroll in Nagasaki and also while in Korea. On his return he would have had to report to the clan. Though a Foreign Office official in the young government, Sada was still very much a Kurume man and would certainly have kept Mizuno and the clan informed of developments. It is inconceivable that he would have invited Hirotsu to Korea without prior consultation with the clan.

It should also be recalled that, with the *ishin*, Sawa himself was put in charge in Nagasaki, and that he was accompanied there by Sada's younger brother who had served the nobles during their long years in exile. Inevitably, the younger Sada would have renewed acquaintance with his cousin, Hirotsu. Further, it seems reasonable to speculate that young Sada introduced this professional *kikiyaku* to Sawa, himself a great conspirator. It will be recalled that Sasaki Takayuki credited Sawa with being behind every uprising in 1870. His diary references to Sawa are very brief, but he does give one seemingly innocuous letter from Sawa to Sasaki which ends with the injunction, 'Without fail burn this letter' (*Sasaki Takayuki Nikki* 1970, Vol. 4: 19–20). Sada's account is deliberately evasive and misleading and it is far more logical to believe that Hirotsu was quite well known to Sawa, that Sada and Sawa in Tokyo planned his inclusion, that the question was discussed and cleared with Mizuno, that correspondence on the subject passed between Tokyo, Kurume and Nagasaki, and that this correspondence was duly burnt.

Sada may have been sick, as he claimed, both before and after going to Korea, but he was a vigorous man who lived to a ripe old age, and being conveniently ill was an established custom. Kurume affairs were in a climactic state, and it would seem more likely that the delays were due to the situation in Kurume and to a desire to liaise with the returning spy in Tsushima. Sada's little asides – he needed a doctor in Korea, Hirotsu happened to be interested in Korea, he got Saitō and Moriyama to agree – merely serve to remind us that Meiji disinformation could be quite elaborate.

Why, then, should Sada disguise his close relationship with Hirotsu? Nepotism was too widespread to be much of a problem. The answer lies partly in the nature of his relationship with Sawa, and partly in the fact that Sada and Hirotsu were both from Kurume which was under the extremist Mizuno, and which was a clan viewed by Kido and Ōkubo with deep distrust. Half the mission was from Kurume; Hirotsu would be reporting back to that clan, and Sada and Sawa were not so much responsible diplomats as conspirators actively engaged in launching *seikan*. To have announced that Sada was taking along his cousin, a Kurume clan spy, as their fourth member, would have been to advertise the true nature of their mission.

Tabohashi (1940, Vol. 1: 229) claimed that when the mission returned, its recommendation that Korea be attacked was not taken seriously but was regarded as *shosei ron* (mere student theorizing) and was consequently buried by the government. Sada (1903: 49–50) himself related how on their return he and Moriyama called on Ōkubo at his office. Ōkubo was very stern and would not give an inch. He merely replied that the question would be studied in due course. Sada attributed this negative response to the fact that Ōkubo was against an invasion, but the answer would seem to lie in Japan's internal struggles. Here was a plan pushed by the people who had inherited the mantle of Maki and Anegakōji. Had it been carried out, the discontented *samurai* of western Japan would have found employment in Korea. The new Meiji government was not yet in effective control of Japan itself. Had the disaffected *samurai* of Kurume, Higo, Fukuoka, etc. been able to settle in Korea under leaders committed to further imperialist expansion, the government would have been faced by the same problem Ieyasu dreaded, namely that overseas Japanese would 'cross the Rubicon' and threaten the home government. It was also going to be manifestly impossible to stop the Korean settlers from advancing further afield – the sort of situation which developed in the 1930s. Ōkubo was not opposed to expansion, but he wanted it controlled and directed by a Satchō government in firm control of Japan, and not by the likes of Sawa, Sada and Mizuno. There was no way that the government would move in 1870.

Let us consider Tabohashi's thesis that there were two *seikan-ron* schools – the Itakura–Ōshima–Kido line which grew out of *kokugaku* teachings, and the Sada–Saigō–Itagaki line which developed as a response to the actual situation in Korea. This is a distinction which cannot be sustained. As we have seen, Sada was very much in the Takayama Hikokurō–Maki line, with its own strong links to the Mito school and to Hirata and the *kokugaku* mainstream. Tabohashi could reach such a conclusion only by ignoring Maki.

Likewise it is too simplistic to regard Ōshima Tomonojō as meeting Matsuyama's Yamada Hōkoku in May 1863 and becoming an instant convert to *seikan-ron*. Ōshima remains a somewhat shadowy figure. Kemuyama (1907: 148) claimed that he was as important as people like Moriyama, but as he operated 'behind a curtain', he was never widely known. He was born in Izuhara, Tsushima in 1826. He became a *jōi* activist usually operating under the name Nakayama Shinzō. In all probability, he also used other aliases, making it difficult to chart his network of contacts. His activities led to his being placed under house arrest for some time, but he was later appointed as clan representative in Osaka. There he got to know the activists from other clans and became a close friend of Kido. The dates are not all clear, but he presented an opinion paper to Anegakōji Kintomo, who was assassinated in 1863, so in the turbulent early sixties it would seem that he was not so much a Tsushima man as an independent *sonnō* activist and a member of the wide circle which included Kido, Katsura, Takechi, Hirano, Maki and the young nobles. It would also seem that, as happened in so many clans, once the pendulum began to swing in favour of the *sonnō* party, Ōshima was promoted to high office by his own clan and he became their spokesman on Korea. But as the clan was related to Chōshū, Ōshima's own close ties to Kido and Chōshū provided no conflict when, for example, he and Kido called on Katsu to discuss the Korean question.

After being recalled to serve in a high post he was sent to Korea in February 1869 (Tabohashi 1940: 157). He entered the Foreign Office in 1870 and in 1871 he was sent back to Korea. Kemuyama (1907: 148) states that he crossed to Korea to study the country and wrote a long account which he presented to the Foreign Office, but it is not clear whether this was before or after he became a Meiji official.

If Ōshima knew Anegakōji, it would almost certainly follow that he also knew Sawa in the early sixties. As he was so close to Kido, and as he was in Kansai during those turbulent years, he, too, must have known Maki and his leading disciples such as Mizuno and Sada. As Sada and Ōshima were both leading proponents of *seikan-ron*, and as both had such strong Chōshū links, it would seem inevitable that they met and discussed attacking Korea. Relations with Korea were conducted through Tsushima, and though Ōshima was depicted as being sent to Korea in February 1869 by his clan, it is highly likely that the Foreign Office was involved. Ōshima was pushing his clan's interests, but for years he had been advocating an attack on Korea. The Sada mission was intended as a prelude to such an attack, and as such would surely have had Ōshima's support. Sada stayed in Nagasaki and Tsushima for some time both before and after going to Korea and wrote his report in Tsushima. Surely the logical inference is that Ōshima's trip to Korea was linked with Sada's mission, and that 'Kuriya', who gave him such valuable information at Waninoura, was a Chōshū agent working with Sawa, Sada and Ōshima.

These are not trivial matters, but are highly relevant to our understanding of the nature of the Sada mission and of Japan's subsequent relations with Korea. Conroy (1960: 26) has referred to the Sada mission as 'the fact-finders' and this sets the scene for his thesis that Japan had no long-range plans to occupy Korea. Quite clearly the members of the Sada missions were not 'fact-finders', but were a party of *sonnō* activists, long-time advocates of attacking Korea, who would seem to have sent their spies on in advance and to have acted in conjunction with at least sections of the Chōshū extremists. Their real aim was to prepare the way for an attack on Korea. Kemuyama would seem to be on safe ground in linking Sada's *seikan-ron* with that of Saigō and Itagaki, for the crisis of 1873 revolved around Saigō's desire to go to Korea to provide the pretext for an invasion, and once again the Ōkubo side refused because Saigō was allied to the 'extreme clans' of north and central Kyūshū. Had his men conquered and formed settlements in Korea, they would have posed a constant threat to the Japanese government.

# 6

# MARUYAMA, DAIRAKU, KURUME'S CONVULSIONS AND SHINTŌ'S 'BRIEF HISTORY'

'Sada's *seikan-ron*' can be understood more clearly if we look at events in Kurume after the Restoration. Its fierce internal struggles cannot be separated from similar struggles elsewhere, and become entwined with the anti-government activities of Shimabara's Maruyama and Chōshū's Dairaku. Kurume affords an excellent example of the sort of explosive situation which existed in many clans, and throws into sharp focus the potentially destructive forces which helped impel Sada in 1870 and Saigō in 1873 to press so urgently for an invasion of Korea.

Many historians have tended to be casual in their use of the words 'conservative' and 'extremist', so let us look more carefully at the eight most prominent Kurume figures: Arima Kenmotsu, Fuwa Mimasaka, Imai Sakae, Honjō Chūta, Mizuno Masana, Kimura Saburō, Furumatsu Kanji and Ōgawa Mabuchi. They can be divided into four broad groups.

Arima Kenmotsu (1822–68) (Yoshikawa 1981), who became clan *karō* in 1846 shortly after Yorito's death, may be regarded as a true conservative. Apart from brief periods in 1852 and 1863 when the Maki faction placed him under house arrest, he remained in power until the Restoration.

Fuwa, Imai and Honjō are more difficult to classify. Though opposed to the Maki–Mizuno group, they cannot be branded as conservative, and are better thought of as progressive, enlightened and responsible. Fuwa and Imai were originally members of the Tempo Gakuren, but they went into the government to help Murakami institute reforms. They had to compromise with the conservatives, and the realities of office gave them a sense of responsibility. They became completely estranged from Maki, and Fuwa emerged as the strong man in Kenmotsu's government. Honjō Chūta (*Kurume shi-shi*

1982, Vol. 2: 590ff.), second son of Meizendō professor Honjō Ichirō, in an important 1861 opinion paper, pushed ideas then becoming common in many parts of Japan: the need to buy modern ships and weapons and to trade with the West to build up Japan's wealth and power. He also advocated the training of farmer-soldiers. Imai Sakae (ibid.: 614–15) spent many years in Edo, and had a clear understanding of the national and international situations. He returned to the clan in 1863, and was largely responsible for persuading Kenmotsu and Fuwa to change the clan policy from *jōi* to *kaikoku*. He himself studied English and made a secret trip to Shanghai to buy a ship for the clan.

Mizuno was also a high-ranking *samurai*, but he and Kimura represented what was by 1868 an older generation of ideologues – the men who had been close to Maki, were generally outside the government and had spent long years in confinement. Sada Hakuho and his father belonged to this group, as did Mizuno's younger brother, Yoshida Tamba. They were close to the nobles such as Sanjō, and this perhaps would have made them responsive to some degree to the demands of the central government.

Their struggle, however, had been going on for some decades, and by 1868 a new generation of extremists had grown up more independent and less likely to be restrained by the likes of Sanjō or even Mizuno himself. They are typified by Furumatsu Kanji and Ōgawa Mabuchi, a sickly young man whose own imminent demise gave a cutting edge to his extremism.

Furumatsu (*Kurume Jimbitsu Shi* 1981: 427ff.) was born in 1834, the second son of a doctor named Shimizu Senryū. In 1845, when the clan chose twenty to enter the new Meizendo dormitory, he was the only commoner chosen. Unhappy with the strict social distinctions between *samurai* and *heimin*, he soon resigned and went to study medicine in Higo. Later he went up to Edo for three years of study. He returned to the clan in 1862 to practise medicine with an older brother, but he was already a political extremist and in 1863 he fled the clan for Kyoto. There he participated in an unsuccessful Mito-led uprising, escaped to hide in a fishing village, and later returned to Kyoto with a new name, Furumatsu. He tried to enter Chōshū when it was attacked by the Bakufu in 1866, but was arrested and imprisoned in Hiroshima. Freed in 1868, he went up to Kyoto. Bitterly opposed to the plan to shift the capital to Edo, he had a furious debate with Kido – an indication, perhaps, that he had known him for some time. Becoming increasingly hostile to the Meiji government, he returned to Kurume in 1869 and was appointed lecturer in the clan school. As the clan authorities must have anticipated, his lectures expressed great hostility to the central government. The life of Furumatsu, like those of Hikokurō and Maki before him, raised the question of to what extent the Bakumatsu struggles were class struggles.

## ELIMINATING THE OLD GUARD

On the night of 26 January 1868, Fuwa Mimasaka, a famed swordsman, was overcome and slain at his own front gate by a gang of twenty-four led by Ōgawa Mabuchi (*Kurume shi-shi* 1982, Vol. 2: 701). It was no sudden rash decision but had been planned with Mizuno while he was still at Dazai-fu. Mizuno had gone up to Kyoto with Sanjō, but with the assassination of Fuwa, he returned to Kurume and took over the government with his brother, Yoshida Shikie (Tamba).

Various reasons were advanced as justification of the assassination: the invitation to Aston's English party to visit Kurume was an insult; the failure to ally fully with Satchō had cost the clan dearly; and the various bodies set up to promote trade had been a great burden on the people. This last explanation brings to mind the reasons behind the assassination of Yoshida Tōyō in Tosa (see chapter 11). But it would seem the immediate reason was that Yorishige planned to take a Kurume force to assist Shogun Keiki.

With Mizuno in charge Arima Kenmotsu was, of course, forced to retire and died that same year, and the clan rallied to 'the Emperor's cause'. A force of 500 was sent to Hakodate, and Imai Sakae assembled a fleet of six ships which acted mainly as transports. Despite these services, on 25 January 1869, Imai, Honjō Chūta and seven others were ordered to commit *seppuku* (*Kurume shi-shi* 1982, Vol. 2: 703–4). The reason given was simply that 'this was inevitable as they had interfered with national policy'. Imai has left an account of his trip to Shanghai to buy a ship (Imai 1866). It reveals him to have been an enlightened modern man whose comments on social, economic and international questions were consistently sound and objective. That such a rational, modern man, who had served his clan so well, should be, as it were, taken back in time, and forced to line up and end his life in such a barbaric manner, comes as a tremendous shock to any reader of his rather charming work, *Dream Story of an Autumn's Night.*

Much has been written about the pro-*seikan* faction wanting to head-off rebellions against the government. Sada seems to have left no comment on the *seppuku* of the Imai group, but he could not have remained unmoved. For years many clans had been torn apart by the conflict between the *sonnō* and *sabaku* forces. These clashes did not simply end with the *ishin*. The Kurume clan illustrates the point that the urgent advocacy of an attack on Korea seems to have been not just to head-off uprisings against the central government, though this was clearly one of the factors involved, but also to prevent clans like Sada's Kurume from continuing to tear themselves apart.

Though it had sent forces in the Boshin War, Mizuno's Kurume and the central government soon became mutually disillusioned. The Kurume lords were related to the ex-Shogun, for Yorishige had married a Shogun's daughter; they also had marriage ties with Satsuma, Yoritō having married a Shimazu. But this did nothing to endear Satsuma to the lower *samurai* and *heimin* who now dominated Kurume affairs. Satsuma was still the self-centred wealthy clan which Hikokurō and Maki had tried in vain to move. Now the signs were that it would, as had been feared, try to set up a second Bakufu. It seemed more at home with the old Bakufu officials than with the successors of its old enemies like Maki and Takechi.

This basic hostility solidified around four issues: the choice of the capital; the establishment of an effective state religion; the degree of local autonomy; and the failure to 'restore' Japan's position in the world. Maki's strong ties had been with Kyoto, and his followers had been anticipating the setting up in Kyoto of an Emperor system based on antiquity and the semi-religious teachings of the *kokugakusha*. Alternatively, some had urged Osaka as the capital, and the move to Tokyo automatically meant that Kurume was far from the seat of power. When the young Emperor first travelled up to Edo, Kurume was ordered to provide part of his escort, but Yorishige, pleading illness, returned home, and his 'leave' then dragged on. The ritual execution of progressives like Imai, and the prominence of Furumatsu, etc., meant that the government had every reason to be on its guard. The *seikan* question was part of this overall picture. Mizuno, Furumatsu and their supporters are often pictured as both backward and fanatical, whereas people like Itō Hirobumi and the other Satchō oligarchs are usually depicted as enlightened. Yet what these Kurume extremists wanted was basically what the Satchō oligarchs forced on the country after 1890: namely, the Emperor system and expansion into the mainland.

People like Furumatsu had, of course, been conspiring for years with extremists from other parts of Japan, and it was inevitable that their own hostile reactions to the new Meiji government should see them again caught up in wider conspiracies. Two in particular, those of Maruyama and Dairaku Gentarō, were to prove a tragic link to the outside world.

To back Mizuno's power, a special 'support force' (*Ōentai*) of about 1000 men had been formed (Maruyama 1899: 23). It was modelled on the Chōshū Irregulars – in itself enough to cause the central government concern. Mizuno had trouble controlling this force which, hearing it had been criticized by a townsman, executed the critic and put his head on display. Ōgawa and Furumatsu also formed their own military group apart from the *Ōentai*. It was an explosive situation and outsiders Maruyama and Dairaku provided the spark which, in 1871, produced what is commonly known as Kurume's *nanki* (difficult period).

## MARUYAMA SAKURA (1840–99)

Maruyama, the son of a Shimabara *samurai*, was born in Edo. At nineteen he entered the Hirata Kanetane *juku*, where he became acquainted with many students who were to be his fellow *sonnō* activists. Likewise his Mito contacts were 'not shallow' (ibid.: 23ff.), for Tadakazu, the Shimabara lord whom he served, was the sixteenth son of Mito's Rekkō. Thus Maruyama should be pictured not as a country *samurai* but as a product of the Hirata and Mito school, and his story again emphasizes the absurdity of ignoring Hirata Atsutane and the other *kokugakusha* when analysing the 1873 *Seihen*.

He had started to study Dutch at Hirata's *juku*, and in 1861 he went to Nagasaki to continue his studies. In 1863 he moved up to Kyoto, where he engaged in *sonnō* agitation, operating mainly with former comrades from the Hirata *juku*. The picture is somewhat blurred, but his close contacts included Maki, Mizuno and Tosa's Takechi (ibid.: 31). When, at Maki's suggestion, Sanjō and Anegakōji obtained the *jōi* edict from the Emperor, Maruyama returned to his clan with orders that it carry out the edict (ibid.: 38). The clan agreed, but with the *coup* of 18 August 1863 these plans were cancelled. Maruyama stayed on in Shimabara, opening his own *juku* and presenting various opinion papers urging reforms. In April 1864 he visited the nobles at Dazai-fu, and in 1865 he helped rally Kyūshū support for Chōshū. When they lost, he was arrested and confined till the Restoration. When Sawa arrived to take control of Kyūshū, he secured a pardon for Maruyama and offered him a position in Nagasaki (ibid.: 53). Sasaki Takayuki noted (1970, Vol. 3: 272) how the appearance of this Shimabara *kinnō ka* aroused comment when he arrived at Sawa's official residence for an interview. He claimed his uniform was a replica of that worn in the days of the legendary Jimmu Tennō who is alleged to have become the first Emperor in the seventh century BC. Obviously Sasaki was not exaggerating when he commented that 'he looked exceedingly different'. Jimmu Tennō's Korean associations should also be noted.

As Maruyama had close ties with Maki and Mizuno in 1863, it is inevitable that he also knew Sada. Moreover, as he was in Nagasaki in 1863 and 1868 and had visited Dazai-fu where Sada's brother was serving the nobles, it is highly probable that the Sada cousin, Hirotsu, was also included in this network.

Early in 1869 he transferred to Kyoto then on to Tokyo where he worked briefly in the Ministry of Religion before moving into the Foreign Office. He soon submitted his resignation, however, because the government refused to implement the proposal of the *Kaitakushi* official, Shima, that the Russians be driven from Karafuto. Instead of accepting his resignation, Sawa urged him to go to Karafuto to investigate. He finally agreed, on condition that he could take a party of forty-seven *shishi* at government expense (Maruyama 1899: 64–5). His plan was to train them for future action. He received farewell presents of *sake* from the Emperor and cloth from Sawa.

Failing to settle the Karafuto problem on the spot, he returned to Tokyo and urged strong measures. When he received no backing he turned his attention back to Korea and began to organize a private military expedition.

In his *Reminiscences* (1903: 49–50), Sada took great pains to dissociate himself from Maruyama's projected private army. His protestations of innocence are not terribly convincing. One day, he claimed, Maruyama called him to a quiet office, told him that he was now working for 'Sada's *seikan-ron*', and asked for his co-operation. Sada rebuked him for the lack of *taigi meibun*, and refused to commit himself. Maruyama accepted his refusal, but then swore him to secrecy and specifically asked that not even Moriyama be informed.

Maruyama was arrested for suspected involvement in other uprisings and for planning a private invasion of Korea. A Foreign Office colleague, Mizuno, warned him (ibid.: 50ff.) that he was about to be arrested, so he had time to burn all his incriminating documents. Mizuno was subsequently dismissed. The most incriminatory fact was that Maruyama had borrowed 200,000 *ryō* from a German and eventually he had to confess that this was for the Korean expedition. Sada admitted that this money had been borrowed before Maruyama spoke to him, but claimed that, as he refused to join the conspiracy, Maruyama never mentioned it to him.

The Sada version cannot be taken seriously. Sawa, Sada, Maruyama, Moriyama, etc. were members of a movement going back many years. Their long list of martyrs includes Maki, Kusaka, Takechi, Anegakōji, etc. Central to their movement was the concept that Japan's position in Korea should be 'restored'. One cannot expect to find conclusive documentary proof, but the circumstantial evidence is strong enough. Sawa's own son was involved, and Sawa was forced to offer his resignation. Sasaki Takayuki noted that Sawa was believed to be behind all the uprisings in 1870, and Maruyama Masahiko (1899: 56) remarked simply that his father 'was to present himself as a sacrifice for Sawa'. Sawa was very much involved in sending the Sada–Moriyama mission to Korea with the object of launching *seikan*. When Sada's report was not acted upon, it seems clear that Sawa and others within the Foreign Office began to plot action which would force the government's hand. The picture is not of a body of professional diplomats but of extreme activists, who had long been comrades and had all seen their leaders killed and had themselves been imprisoned for years – activists who now saw their old enemy, Satsuma, 'betraying' their revolution. The warning to Maruyama came from within the Foreign Office, and bearing in mind that Sada's own impassioned *seikan* plea had been ignored, it is simply inconceivable that he was not involved with his old 1863 comrades now working in the same office.

It should be noted that for Maruyama, as for generations of *kokugakusha* and activists, Korea and the northern islands were not alternatives but part of an overall programme of imperial expansion. A long paper setting out his political opinions made it clear that he was still the *sonnō* fanatic who had appeared in Sawa's office wearing ancient garb: 'Our Emperor is not just the Emperor of these islands but the Great Emperor of the six continents. . . . If you don't have the spirit to swallow the six continents, how can one really revere that one Person?' (ibid.: 111). Put simply, he was advocating a war of religion to conquer the world – the basic creed of the Hirata school. He also dealt with practical questions, arguing that there should be no laziness in the nation (ibid.: 115), and that the unemployed should be rounded up and set to work in Hokkaidō – a nice complement to the Sada plan of Korean forced labour. He also indulged in swipes at Satchō, saying that the *ishin* had taken place in name only and that government posts had gone to a pack of unknowns (ibid.: 102). This view, of course, was held also by Sawa, Sada, Mizuno and all those who had carried the *sonnō* banner for years while Satsuma propped up the Bakufu.

As we are dealing with subversive activities where the participants covered their tracks and burnt all correspondence, and as there were uprisings in many parts of Japan, it is impossible to reduce this disorderly period to a nice, orderly narrative; but a few salient facts stand out. Maruyama's deputy (Tsuruku and Koga 1970, Vol. 2: 51), in charge of gathering information and jointly in charge of accounts, was Furumatsu Kanji. Also on Maruyama's ten-man committee was another Kurume man, Shinomoto Kenzō, one of the group which had assassinated Fuwa Mimasaka in 1868 (*Kurume Jimbutsu Shi* 1981: 285). When the *Ōentai* was established in 1869, he was made an officer. As Furumatsu and Ogawa with their private army had established themselves as the power behind Mizuno, it seems reasonable to say that the Kurume clan was deeply involved in Maruyama's plans. Thus Sada's non-involvement becomes even more unlikely.

The full story of these 1870–1 uprisings cannot be told here, but one should note that, apart from Kurume and Shimabara, those playing important roles included the nobles, Akita clan, the disaffected Chōshū Irregulars and the Tsuwano clan. Of course, this by no means completes the list; for example, Maruyama's committee of ten included three from Tōyōtsu (Nakatsu), two from Tokyo and Okazaki Kyōsuke from Tosa (Tsuruku and Koga 1970, Vol. 2: 51).

The nobles most clearly involved were the twenty-five-year-old Odagi Michiakira (also called Atago Tsukyoku) and Toyama Michisuke. They were indignant at the shifting of the capital and the general tendency to play down both the role and the talents of the nobles. Japanese historians are fond of quoting contemptuous references to the nobles by Itō and others, but it would seem fairer to say that what these young nobles lacked was not talent or dedication but a firm power base.

Both Odagi and Toyama were arrested in March, and at the end of the year were forced to commit *seppuku*. Though it is difficult to confirm the degree of his involvement, there can be little doubt that Sawa was a leading conspirator. There were widespread rumours that he and Arisugawa were personally to lead the invasion of Korea, and, when arrested, Maruyama was taken to the Etsuzen clan residence by a 100-troop escort – in itself a probable indication that it was believed that bigger fish were involved (Maruyama 1899: 121–2).

## AKITA PREFECTURE

The above rumours suggested that many of the invasion troops were to come from Akita, a geographically isolated northern clan. Akita had never been close to the Tokugawas, for its lord, Satake Yoshinobu, had formerly been lord of Mito, but because he stayed neutral at Sekigahara (Imamura 1969: 71), he had his *roku* reduced and he was transferred to Akita. Of course, he was accompanied by his *samurai*, and by numerous merchants. Thus, as in Tosa, many of the *samurai* of the former lord had to return to the land, providing an alienated, non-submissive element. Because of the climate, it had few crops other than rice, but it had mines which produced gold, silver and copper, notably Anin mine, which, till the end of the eighteenth century, ranked alongside Besshi (ibid.: 104ff.).

Akita played an important role in the *sonnō* movement, for it produced both Satō Shinen and Hirata Atsutane. The 1830s were a time of great distress due to the Tempo famine and the subsequent epidemics (ibid.: 137). The fragile clan finances were further strained by the need to provide coastal defences, and by the 1855 Bakufu order to help garrison the northern islands. In 1840 the Bakufu had ordered Hirata back to Akita and he died there in poverty in 1843, but not before collecting a great number of disciples, including *samurai*, *gōno* farmers and merchants. His Akita *juku* continued to keep in close touch with Atsutane's heir, Kanetane, a clan official in Kyoto. Kanetane was deeply involved in the *sonnō* movement, and especially with the Chōshū extremists (ibid.: 145ff.).

In the Boshin War, Akita played an ambiguous and undistinguished role, eventually coming down on the side of the government, but being then invaded by neighbouring Shōnai and suffering heavy losses. The big merchants and farmers were ordered to raise armies, but it was difficult to find recruits. These 'grass-roots' soldiers received little for their services, while the abolition of the clans caused the lower *samurai* great hardship. Thus in 1871 the disaffected elements tied up with similar factions elsewhere. A Kido letter to Makimura described the Akita clan as being in the conspiracy up to its neck, along with Kurume and Shimabara, while a Yamagata letter to Kido named Hatsuoka Keiji, adviser to the clan heir, as the main conspirator (ibid.: 156). The six leaders were arrested and sent to Tokyo where Hatsuoka was executed and the others given long sentences. The loss of its leaders was a great blow to the clan which henceforth was disliked and boycotted by the Satchō government.

In 1873 its Anin copper mine was taken over by the government (ibid.: 169ff.). This is sometimes defended as a wise policy move, but it must be noted that 1873 – the year of the *seihen* – was when Mitsubishi, Godai and Inoue-Chōshū all got their hands on rich mines (see chapter 11). This cannot be dismissed as an incidental by-product of the *seihen* but must be viewed as one of its underlying causes. The *haraisage* of Anin took place in 1884 and, as usual, the petitions of the wealthy local merchants and farmers were ignored, and the mine was sold off to Furukawa who was inextricably involved with Mutsu, Shibusawa and various government officials.

## DAIRAKU

The story of Dairaku Gentarō is likewise a complicated one. He was a disciple of the Chōshū priest Gesshō, who was earlier and more extreme than Shōin. At the end of the civil war, the Chōshū Irregulars were treated very badly and many refused to disband. Kido and Inoue had to return to the clan to break their power, being careful to reject offers of assistance from Satsuma. Dairaku became one of the leaders of these disaffected irregulars, and was generally believed to have been behind the assassination of Ōmura. When their forces were defeated, the leaders fled to Kyūshū and Dairaku eventually made his way to Kurume. There it was Furumatsu who arranged his hiding place, moving him from village to village.

The central government was increasingly suspicious of Kurume, and, in August 1870, and again in January 1871, Mizuno was summoned to Tokyo and grilled by Sanjō (*Kurume shi-shi* 1982, Vol. 2: 706). He was informed of plans to abolish the clans and set up prefectures; but the Kurume *Ōentai* were implacably opposed. Only when Lord Yorishige was placed under house arrest and powerful government forces were assembled in Hita, was it possible to restore order in Kurume. Dairaku, who had been singularly unimpressed by suggestions that he should commit *seppuku*, was tracked down and

115

despatched by a party of fourteen led by Shimada Sōtarō (*Kurume Jimbutsu Shi* 1981: 427ff.). Nor did this please the government, for it deprived them of the opportunity of submitting him to the traditional interrogation. Thus the Shimada party were among the many arrested and sentenced, Shimada getting ten years. The loss of so many leaders was a great blow to the clan. Ogawa was executed, but Furumatsu had his sentence commuted to life. He was imprisoned in Tokyo's Ishikawashima prison, where he spent his time writing and teaching the other prisoners. He died treating them during a prisoner cholera epidemic in 1882. Mizuno was likewise given life, and died within a couple of years. Shinomoto, the other Kurume man on Maruyama's committe, was given seven years which he served in Kumamato prison. He was pardoned in December 1877, and died in 1885 (see Kurume Jimbutsu Shi entries for Shinomoto, Furumatsu and Ogawa).

Maruyama was tried by Kōno Togama who in 1874 was to preside over the farcical trial of Etō Shimpei. He admitted that he was *seikan*, for if Japan did not take Korea, some other country would. He also admitted that he was frequently visited by Furumatsu, Okazaki, etc., and that they planned to send spies to Korea. However, he denied that they planned to send an army and thus break the law of Japan. The court was not impressed by these denials and gave him life, which was to be served on the island of Takashima near Nagasaki (Maruyama 1899: 127). While still in the Justice Ministry prison, Maruyama and his comrades cut off their hair. In a poem dated 3 March 1872 (ibid.: 148), Maruyama referred to this hair being entrusted to Kumamoto's Sasa Tomofusa.

Before summarizing the significance of these 1870–1 upheavals, and their relation to the 1873 *Seihen*, let us look briefly at Maruyama's later career and at that of Sasa.

## MARUYAMA'S LATER LIFE

Maruyama was pardoned in 1880. On coming out of prison, he was helped by the Shintō officials in Nagasaki, and on his way up to Tokyo, he visited the Dazai-fu and Ise shrines. On 27 January 1881 he was made consultant to the Shintō head office (ibid.: 228ff.). The Shintō world was then split into factions. Iwakura asked Maruyama to act as conciliator, and he seems to have continued in this role for some time.

On returning to Tokyo, he was soon active again as a rightist. The 1881 *Seihen* was looming, and to counter the popular tide he helped found the *Meiji Nippo*, an anti-*minken* paper (ibid.: 193ff.). In April 1881, he helped form the Chūaisha, and with the formation of the Imperial Party in 1882, he represented the Chūaisha in this new party, and travelled widely preaching the anti-*minken* cause. The Chūaisha played an important role in promoting militarism (ibid.: 241ff.). Military education was not then popular, and there was no great rush to enrol in officers' school. So Chūaisha money was used to promote a kind of preparatory school for the army. At one stage, Kawakami Soroku was principal, Maruyama superintendent, and Kodama was in charge of accounts. It was Kawakami Soroku who, as Army Chief of Staff, built up the intelligence network on the mainland and laid the detailed plans for war. Kodama is remembered as Governor of Taiwan and as Japan's most capable general in the Russian War. But it should also be noted that Kodama formed a close alliance with Fukuoka rightist Sugiyama, and they later brought Katsura into this alliance which was essentially devoted to promoting war on the mainland. Thus Maruyama fits nicely into this little group.

In 1886 Itō appointed him as assistant to Inoue Kowashi, and he played a role in setting up the Emperor system. He travelled widely in Europe, and in 1890 was made *Genrō-In Gikan*. When the 1894 War broke out, he was ecstatic. With the warm approval of the army, he crossed to Korea to lecture the troops on history, and to hold a ceremony for the fallen so that, even though buried in foreign soil they might become gods protecting Japan. A mass ceremony was held in front of Envoy Torii, Army Chief Nozu, journalists, etc. Maruyama was resplendent in his shrine outfit, and behind the great crowds, Koreans looked on dumbly (ibid.: 331–3).

In 1899, at the age of fifty-nine, Maruyama died of 'softening of the brain' (ibid.: 257). There is a chilling consistency about his life story: the *jōi* activist of the sixties; the 1870–1 organizer of the private invasion of Korea; the school superintendent of the eighties who harangued his students on the glory of dying for the Emperor; and the Shintō dignitary consecrating Korean soil. Certain names keep recurring. It seems he kept his ties with Sada (ibid.: 339–40), and a strong, on-going relationship with Soejima and Sasa.

## SASA TOMOFUSA

In 1936, thirty years after Sasa's death, a collection of his letters and articles was published (*Kokudō Sasa Sensei Kikō* 1936) by a committee headed by fellow rightists Toyoma and Sugiyama. It provides further proof that we are dealing with a continuous story and that Maruyama should be seen not as an eccentric who flourished briefly but as a link from Motoori and Hirata down to the rightists of the thirties.

Sasa was born into a Kumamoto *samurai* family in 1854 (ibid.: Intro.). He was taught first by an uncle who was a friend of Yoshida Shōin, then at fifteen (ibid.: 573) he entered the *juku* of *kokugakusha*, Hayashi Ōen (1787–1870), who taught many of the Shimpūren members. In 1871, when the clans were abolished, the clan school was also abandoned. This led to a boom in *juku* and Sasa and some friends formed a society called Sekiinsha. The Hayashi *juku* had also been broken up following his death in 1870, and the fact that Maruyama and company should entrust their hair clippings to the teenaged Sasa probably indicates that he was already regarded as a major Hayashi disciple. (It might be noted that Sugiyama was even younger when he decided to do something for his country and went up to Tokyo to assassinate Itō.)

Sasa later visited Mito. Like the rebels of 1870–1, he was convinced that Satsuma had set up a second Bakufu, and so he sought to bring about a second *ishin*. When the Shimpūren rose in 1876 he restrained his followers, however, for he realized that the rebels faced certain defeat. He regarded the rebels as basically religious, while he was a practical man whose main object was the penetration of Korea.

In the 1877 War he was wounded and sentenced to ten years imprisonment, but he was released in the spring of 1880 (ibid.: 558). He and some friends started a school named Dōshin Gakusha. Very soon it was giving lessons in both Korean and Chinese, but before the end of the year it had to close partly because of financial problems, partly because Sasa spent most of 1881 in Tokyo, and partly because many of the students were turning to Rousseau instead of the old *kokugaku* teachings.

We have seen how in 1792 Takayama Hikokurō stayed in Kumamoto with Shitagau Shimei. In 1881, while Sasa was agitating in Tokyo, he and his Kumamoto friends formed the group which became known as Shimei-kai (ibid.: 6). The main persons involved in Tokyo were the bureaucrats Inoue Kowashi, Yamada Shingo and Yasuba Yasukazu, while at the Kumamoto end were Sasa and Tsuda Seiichi. Their immediate purpose seems to have been to support Satchō during the 1881 *Seihen*, but their long-range plan was to work to set up the Emperor system. The whole nation was then debating the question of where ultimate authority lay. The Shimei-kai argued that it lay with the Emperor – an unfashionable view then supported publicly in Tokyo only by Fukuji Kenichirō's Nichinichi Shimbun, the fashionable view being that authority lay with the people and the law. Sasa's group therefore formed a political organization, Rikken Jiyutō, to fight for *kokken*, but in the spring of 1882 this was dissolved and replaced with the Shimei Gakukai which concentrated on education and propaganda. They were to start their own newspaper with Inoue Kowashi as the main (though anonymous) writer.

Sasa's school, thus re-opened with Shimei-kai backing, concentrated its teachings on the Emperor as the centre of all authority, and in an age when such things were virtually unheard of, it ranked moral education and military-style physical education as equal in importance to the formal subjects. In May 1883 the Emperor gave the school his stamp of approval in the form of a 500-yen donation (ibid.: 557–8). It became a Meiji *meibutsu* with many exalted visitors such as Mori Arinori, who in 1887 pronounced it the best school he had seen. Indeed, its principles were incorporated in the Imperial Rescript on Education and it became the model for the national system which reproduced its moral education and military training.

In politics, as in education, Sasa continued to work with Kumamoto men within the government, especially Inoue Kowashi and Motoda Eifu. Kowashi is generally pictured as an enlightened bureaucrat trying to introduce ideas he brought back from Europe, but he must be understood as a leader of the Kumamoto rightists. Sasa's closest ally, however, was Fukuoka rightist Tōyama Mitsuru. In 1889 they opposed Ōkuma's Treaty plans (ibid.: 21ff.), calling together on various ministers and presenting joint opinion papers. At the same time Sasa was in close contact with Motoda and Inoue Kowashi, visiting their homes in strictest secrecy.

Sasa was elected to the first parliament. In the notorious election of 1892, he and Tōyama helped Home Minister Shinagawa intimidate would-be *minken* voters, and barred their entrance to the polling booths. Sasa also moved closer to Yamagata, with Inoue and Kiyoura acting as go-betweens (ibid.: 19–20).

Of course, Sasa and Tōyama also worked together to force Japan into war on the mainland. As early as 1882 (ibid.: 22–4), some of Sasa's ex-students were sent to Korea to conspire with Korean

119

factions. The people Sasa and Tōyama sent were usually part-spies, part-merchants, but they also set up three newspapers in China (ibid.: 584–6). In 1894, the Hiroshima Headquarters tried to assemble interpreters from all over Japan, but the great bulk – 120 – came from Kumamoto. Their intelligence network put Sasa and Tōyama in a position to both lead and coerce the governments. Sasa's 1936 editors have considerable justification for their claim that Sasa and Tōyama played a leading role in bringing about the wars against China and Russia.

Again it is the continuity of the story which must be stressed, from the early *kokugakusha*, through Takayama Hikokurō, on to Maki, Takechi, Kusaka and the young nobles in 1863, then to the troubled years of 1871–4 and on to the period ushered in by the 1881 *Seihen* with Kumamoto and Fukuoka in the forefront of the rightists. It is one continuous story, down to the thirties and the Second World War.

In 1870–1, the 'extremist' leadership was still provided by a wide range of relative outsiders: Sawa and the other young nobles, the Mizuno–Furumatsu Kurume, the Chōshū Irregulars and the men of Hirata's Akita. That these various elements were linked at least loosely is clear; for example, Furumatsu was both Maruyama's deputy and also the person who arranged Dairaku's hiding places.

It is important to realize that, though theirs was a many-sided movement, its general aim can be summed up as the achieving of a genuine Restoration. Thus much of their activity was directed against Satchō, especially Satsuma, which was seen as setting up a second Bakufu. They also wanted a semi-religious state – along the lines of the subsequent Emperor system – whereas the pragmatic Satchō leaders wanted a modern secular state. Of equal importance, they wanted to 'restore' Japan's position in the world. The Satchō leaders could not be viewed as opposed to an invasion of Korea, but they could not allow it to be carried out by western clans such as Kurume and led by the likes of Sawa and Maruyama. So in 1870–1 the rebellious elements were crushed and the *seikan* debate postponed, while Satchō went on to carry out their own *coup d'état*.

The Satchō and various assorted 'enlightened' elements were to stay together for the remainder of the seventies and were to achieve the opening of Korea in their own way. But the internal commercial warfare between the great *zaibatsu* – especially Mitsubishi versus the Satchō companies – led them to break ranks. The embattled Satchō forces were compelled to look for new allies, and this led them back to their erstwhile allies, the ideologues, whom they had abandoned in 1871. From 1881 one sees men like Maruyama, Sasa and Tōyama largely working in harness with the Satchō government. Much of Japan's history for the following sixty years flowed from this renewed alliance of 1881.

To understand the 1873 *Seihen* one must appreciate the great confusion and vicious cross-currents of the early Meiji period. Too often we are given a picture of men of principle calmly discussing matters of state when the true picture should be one of savage battles for survival. The very word 'alliance' is misleading. The great histories of Ancient China, which were well known to the Meiji leaders, described how alliances were made against a specific enemy and were apt to be a mere prelude to the final showdown between the two allies. The Satchō alliance against the Bakufu seemed to be a classic case: there was little feeling of having formed a permanent alliance based on mutually held principles.

## THE 1871 *COUP D'ÉTAT*

In 1869, Yokoi Shōnan and Army Chief Ōmura had both been assassinated, and 1870 saw many uprisings in which, it would seem, Sawa and other Foreign Office officials were involved. It was a vicious circle, for the widespread discontent led Satchō to introduce administrative changes strengthening their control, while these changes in turn helped provoke fresh uprisings.

At the start of 1871, Kido, Ōkubo and Iwakura were all in western Japan, leaving Hirosawa in charge, but on 9 January 1871 he, too, was assassinated. This sent a cold chill through the government which now suspected all bureaucrats save those from the four big clans, and the clan system itself came to be regarded as incompatible with a modern state (Miyaji 1985). March saw a great crackdown with a purge of both bureaucrats and army personnel, including Sawa Nobutane. The clan and *sōmō* troops in Tokyo were steadily disbanded and disbursed, and Satchō and Tosa troops were brought up to guard the capital. At first Satchō alone had planned to start a national army, but Tosa's new strength enabled her to join the club (Hirao 1935: 326–7). Much to Etō's indignation, Saga was not asked to join, but clearly the events of 1867–8 had not been forgotten. In the Boshin War, Satsuma had lost 514 dead, Chōshū 427, Tosa 106 and Saga only 75 (Matano 1914, Vol. 1: 546–7). Thus the new

*Konoe-hei* attached directly to the Emperor came only from the other three clans.

With all under control, on 14 July 1871 the clans were abruptly abolished. As Miyaji (1985: 116) points out, it was literally a *coup d'état* which firmly established the *hanbatsu* monopoly of power. It is often argued in justification that such a monopoly was necessary to create an enlightened modern state. The argument is a specious one. The Bakufu had been moving rapidly in that direction, and nearly all the outstanding people associated with 'the Meiji Enlightenment' had been sent abroad by the Bakufu which was then defeated by forces preaching *sonnō jōi*. 'Meiji Enlightenment' was the product of neither the Boshin War nor the *coup* of 1871, both of which must be attributed to the Satchō desire to monopolize wealth and power.

Though excluded from the *coup*, Etō and Ōkuma were able to maintain for Saga at least nominal status as one of the Big Four. Etō was placed in charge of the newly created Education Ministry, which he handed over after a month to his Saga friend, Ōki. He then became President of the Council of the Left, an institution set up on 28 July 1871 at the instigation of Etō and Gotō. They sought a Separation of Powers along Montesquieu lines, with the Dajōkan in charge of the executive branch, the Council of the Left as a council to initiate legislation, and the Shihō-sho (Justice Ministry). There had been three earlier councils, but all had quickly degenerated into debating chambers (Matano 1914, Vol. 1: 626ff.). Thus Etō now sought to make the Council of the Left a body which could stand up to the Executive. He persuaded a reluctant Gotō to transfer from the Construction Ministry with its bottomless supply of patronage to become its President.

An important question rarely addressed by Japanese historians is to what extent, even in these early years, the great merchants were pulling the strings behind the scenes. As Saigō well knew, in 1871 Inoue – 'Mitsui's *bantō*' – was living in a Mitsui residence (*Ōkuma Kō 85 Nen Shi* 1925: 436). Ōkubo's diary records that when the reforms of 8 July 1869 gave Ōkuma great power at the Treasury, Godai came day and night to express his alarm, and on 22 July 1869 Ōkuma was duly shifted to the *Minbu-Sho* (ibid.: 285). Ōe Taku, Gotō's future son-in-law, got to know Iwasaki in Nagasaki in 1867. When he went up to Tokyo in 1870, he carried a letter of introduction from Iwasaki to Ōkuma and went to stay in Ōkuma's home (*Sukumo Jimbutsu Shi* 1968: 101). Although Ōkuma and Inoue were often fierce rivals, they were, as Saigō and Itagaki well knew, 'a fox and a badger in the same hole' (*Ōkuma Kō 85 Nen Shi* 1925: 470). Well before the *ishin*, Ōkuma was close to the clan's *goyō* merchants and to the wealthy trader and smuggler Furukawa Hikobei, who used him to recruit *rangakusha* for his activities (ibid.: 91ff.). On coming up to Tokyo, Ōkuma, Itō and Inoue all quickly became familiar, for example, with Yokohama's somewhat shady Takashima Yoshiemon (ibid.: 295ff.) who was to play a leading role in railway construction. The ties with Itō became so close that Itō's heir, Hirokuni, married his daughter. Even by 1871 Itō's activities had made him conspicuous enough for the *Mail* to single him out: 'he is by no means a popular man with the best class of Japanese officials. His too easy accessibility to foreigners of inferior standing is not calculated to raise his reputation' (*Japan Weekly Mail* 21.10.1871). The *Mail* message became blunter with subsequent attacks urging the government to 'deal remorselessly with the corruption which . . . infects it from top to bottom' (ibid.: 20.1.1872 and 11.5.1872).

The 1871 *coup* was carried out not by reforming zealots but by a very corrupt government which went on to ride roughshod over the law. Though the evidence is somewhat sketchy, it is clear that even in the early Meiji years, the great commercial figures – Mitsui, Iwasaki, Godai, Ōkura, Takashima, etc. – were already working very closely with the government or some of its officials. When we come to consider Korea, we must not take literally statements about the government 'asking' the *zaibatsu* to help. It seems fair to say that from 1868 onwards the great commercial houses had a hand in each and every major political struggle. That was certainly true of the 1873 *Seihen*.

The role of the *sōmō* forces also needs to be stressed. At the start of the Meiji period, each clan still had its own regular troops and usually *sōmō tai*, or 'grassroots irregulars'. As we have seen with Maki, those with *sōmō tai* connections, such as Arisugawa, Nakamikado Tsuneyuki and Sawa, found themselves in opposition to Satchō rule (Miyaji 1985: 34–6). The Irregulars had virtually been excluded from the fruits of victory. They were not represented in the new government, for its members were nominated by the clans pretty much along class lines – lower *samurai* came to the fore, but not *heimin*. This seems to have been a factor in the assassinations of Yokoi and Ōmura, which coincided with an uprising of the disbanded Irregulars. Kido and Inoue were unable to restore order until February 1870. They had averted their greatest fear – that the *sōmō tai* would combine with the farmers in a widespread *ikki*, a somewhat variable term which included full-scale peasant revolts, with the rebels being urged on by all the elements such as doctors, priests and rich landowners, who had provided *sōmō tai* backing. These *ikki*, especially in Chōshū, were highly relevant to the 1873 *Seihen*. Kido, like Shōin, had been an early advocate of a Korean invasion, but if the Irregulars from Chōshū and Kyūshū had been able to swarm into Korea, they would have posed a constant threat to the established governments in both Tokyo and Chōshū. This sort of danger was well understood by the Tokugawas. On the other hand, were Japan denuded of troops for a Korean invasion, the added taxes would almost certainly have led to widespread *ikki* – a danger understood by some of Hideyoshi's generals. The almost inevitable upshot would have been that a triumphant Saigō would have re-established order on returning home – and then, perhaps, with an appropriate show of reluctance, have allowed himself to be made Shogun. Whether the Korean invasion was undertaken by the new national army or entrusted to Irregulars, the outlook for the Ōkubo–Kido faction was a gloomy one.

One must also note the religious struggle. Gluck (1985) would have us believe that the Emperor system ideology emerged gradually only during the late Meiji period (1890–1912), and that consequently it did not penetrate deeply into the Japanese psyche and was thus easily jettisoned after the Second World War (ibid.: 284–5). She refers to Shintō having had only a short-lived heyday in the early seventies, a view which was already being espoused by Griffis in 1876: 'The enterprise of establishing Shintō as the national faith has failed vastly and ignominiously.'

Curiously Westerners have generally praised 'the shrewd warriors of Satsuma and Chōshū' (Chamberlain 1905: 237ff.) for their duplicity in taking over leadership of the *sonnō jōi* movement and then abandoning both the policy and its *sonnō* allies. Thus Chamberlain declared that 'history has never witnessed a more sudden volte-face. History has never witnessed a wiser one' (ibid.). One must ask, of course, what was the purpose of the Boshin War? The Bakufu was proceeding as quickly as possible with a policy of modernization. Satsuma was not opposed to the policy, just to the fact that it was being carried out by the Bakufu. Akita carries the Chamberlain argument further, dismissing the government's opponents as 'outs' and praising Satchō for being concerned at the dangers of sharing power with 'irresponsible and selfish elements' (Akita 1967: 3). Satsuma joined the opposition to the Bakufu for its own economic and political advantage, then blatantly adopted its policy of modernization. This cynicism and duplicity must be borne in mind when we look at the 1873 *Seihen*. Ōkubo and Iwakura brought down the caretaker government over its Korean policy, then cynically adopted that policy, sending an expedition to Taiwan in 1874 and opening Korea in 1875.

The same 'flexibility' is seen on the religious question. Shintōism suffered a set-back in 1871, partly because it complicated treaty revision, partly because the modern young men preferred *bummei kaika* and partly because its devotees were mostly anti-Satchō. But the century-old movement did not just fade away, and by 1880 the Shintō activists were making a come-back. Rather than regard the period 1868–71 as 'a short-lived heyday', the middle and late seventies should be regarded as a brief reversal for Shintōism. Though the religious question did not surface directly during the 1873 *Seihen*, it was this widespread feeling of betrayal and of *heimin* disillusionment and discontent – this combined religious and popular factor – looming menacingly in the background, which made the 1873 *Seihen* not just a political crisis occurring in Tokyo but a major crisis involving and affecting the whole nation. The whole Meiji leadership had a credibility problem, and it was that credibility problem which was largely responsible for leading it into the Emperor system and into foreign wars.

Let us look for a moment at Shintō's 'short-lived heyday'. The fate of the ideologues may be illustrated by the story of Ōkuni Takamasa (1792–1871) (see Ōsaki 1943), the son of a Tsuwano *samurai* who had been a Bakufu minister in the Tenmei period. Takamasa's mother was from Kurume as was the clan lord, Kamei Koremi, a brother of the Kurume lords Yoritō and Yorishige. He studied under Hirata Atsutane and at the Bakufu's *Shōhei-juku*, then later he undertook Chinese and Dutch studies in Nagasaki. He fled the clan to teach independently in Kansai, his hundreds of students including Iwakura Tomochika (ibid.: 94). Later he accepted a position in the clan Yōrōkan on condition that he be allowed to live in Kyoto, merely going to teach in Edo and Iwami in autumn and spring. The clan lord, as well as the main ministers, would sit in on his lectures. He also enjoyed the patronage and protection of Mito's Nariaki (ibid.: 103–4).

Takamasa's teachings were in the *kokugaku* mainstream, revolving around *kōdō sekai ishin rinen* (theory of the restoration of the world to the Imperial Way). This, of course, involved the restoration of the old, original world order where Japan was the centre of the universe. This *kōdō sekai ishin* would bring the whole world into eternal harmony under the Emperor. Takamasa objected to the term *kokugaku*, substituting *hongaku* (fundamental studies), an expression taken from the *kojiki*. He did not feel overwhelmed by the coming of the Westerners; instead, his writings became highly inflammatory, emphasizing Japanese racial superiority and the importance of taking over the whole world.

His disciples included Fukuba Bisei (1831–1907), a Yōrōkan professor who established links with the Chōshū extremists (Yoshikawa 1981), and Tamamatsu Misao (1810–72) who taught and wrote papers for Iwakura while he was under house arrest. These papers later formed the basis of the *Jimmu Fukkō* proclamation. In 1868 Shintō was installed as the State Religion and a Council of Spiritual Affairs was given equal rank with the Council of State (Chamberlain 1905: 422).

Takamasa, Fukuba Bisei, Tsuwano's Lord Kamei, Hirata Kanetane and Tamamatsu were all given high positions. Naturally, they expected to play an important role in a government with a strong ideological commitment. They were soon to be disillusioned.

Part of the early struggle revolved around the shift of the capital. When the Emperor went up to Edo, the Kurume lord refused to provide an escort and returned home (ibid.: 422). At that time it was merely announced that the Emperor was on tour, and by the end of 1870 the question had still not been publicly settled (see chapter 5). A related issue was the education of the Emperor. Here the conservatives were on top, the appointments revolving around the Hirata school, with Hirata Kanetane and the Tsuwano members prominent. But for many years the common dream of the *kokugakusha* had been to set up a university of national studies in Kyoto. With the *ishin*, it seemed that this dream would be realized. In 1869, however, Tokyo was made the centre of education, and Hirata and Nishikawa Yoshisuke were ordered up from Kyoto (Miyaji 1985: 54–60). The hardliners protested to Sawa, but the two main schools in Kyoto were abolished.

In June 1869, the first set of education guidelines stressed nationalistic aims such as the need to foster a sense of national purpose and character. Miyaji (ibid.: 80–4) believes that Hirata and Maruyama had a big hand in drawing up these guidelines, but in February 1870 a new set of guidelines watered down their approach.

By this time, hardliners such as Tamamatsu and Yano Motomichi had been appointed to positions in Tokyo, but this merely led to these hardliners forming a committed brotherhood. The Sinologists also settled their differences with the *kokugakusha*, and became their allies against the government. Of course, both Confucianists and Shintōists had common enemies in the Buddhists and Christians. About this time, there was widespread destruction of Buddhist shrines, while the Christians had soon become an issue in both Nagasaki and Hakodate (*Japan Weekly Mail* 11.5.1872).

Sawa had taken a hard line in Nagasaki imprisoning hundreds who refused to recant (*Ōkuma Kō 85 Nen Shi* 1925: 9–11). This had led to a confrontation in Osaka with Parkes and the other envoys, and though victory on that occasion probably belonged to Ōkuma, the Westerners continued to hammer home the theme that an anti-Christian Shintō-based state would find it difficult to achieve treaty revision. This factor, combined with the fact that these elements were anti-Satchō and were perhaps incompatible with the setting up of a modern secular education system, led to a confrontation with the government. Within the Education Department, Saga's Shima had been giving his strong support, while Soejima was also secretly in close contact (Miyaji 1985: 80–4), but on 13 July 1870 most of these top officials, including Shima, were dismissed, and the leading *kokugakusha* and Sinologists were unceremoniously thrown out. Thereafter Western-trained scholars were steadily added to the Emperor's tutors (ibid.: 101). By this time the Council of Spiritual Affairs had ceased to exist, having been progressively reduced to the rank of a department, then a bureau and then a sub-bureau (Chamberlain 1905: 422).

Tamamatsu had soon retired and died in 1871. Though he continued as a consultant on religious affairs, Ōkuni Takamasa had also soon retired, largely because of age, and died in 1872. Even so, a look at this group suggests the fallacy of Gluck's argument (see Heibon 1953 under 'Fukuba', 'Ōkuni' and 'Tamamatsu'). Fukuba's career is highly suggestive, for it took off again after the 1881 *Seihen* when he was made Sanji-in Gikan; in 1887 he was made a viscount, and in 1890 Genro-in Gikan. Tamamatsu also received posthumous recognition after the 1881 *Seihen*, for his son was made a baron in 1884. As the Emperor system took root, honours were, of course, bestowed on Hirata and Satō Shinen, and, somewhat later, in 1915 Ōkuni Takamasa duly received his posthumous honours. The years 1872–80 must be regarded as an aberration – a 'brief depression' – for Shintō and national learning.

Sasa and Maruyama, of course, further drive home this point. As we have seen, Sasa in the early seventies was entrusted with the hair of Maruyama and his fellow prisoners. He went on to establish a school emphasizing moral education and physical training – a school which became a prototype for the Meiji national system. Meiji education was largely Higo education. There is a straight line back not only to the activists of 1869–71, but also to Shimei, Kamei, Hikokurō, etc. 100 years earlier. One simply cannot talk of the Emperor system 'gradually emerging' only after 1890 and then dissolving away, leaving nary a trace, after 1945.

It is probably Maruyama who gives us our most vivid pen-picture: student of Hirata; a weird figure appearing in Nagasaki dressed in Jimmu Tennō garb; organizer of a private army to invade Korea, then taking the blame for Sawa; freed in 1880 and soon helping to run an anti-*minken* paper and act as conciliator in the Shintō world; organizer of a *juku* to provide students for officers' school; and resplendent in his Shintō gear conducting a mammoth ceremony to consecrate Korean ground. How can one take 1890 as a starting point?

One final point should be emphasized. Maruyama first entered the Religious Department, then switched to the Foreign Office. The close ties between the Religious Department and Sawa's Foreign Office are as clear as those between Kurume and Tsuwano. Sada was the disciple of Maki; he also shared the views of Ōkuni, Takamatsu, Hirata, etc. at the Religious Department. He went to Korea, not to bring back a treaty of friendship, but to launch the process whereby the whole world would be 'brought into harmony under the Emperor'. This fact must be central to our understanding of the 1873 *Seihen* and of modern Japanese imperialism.

# 7

# JAPANESE PERCEPTIONS OF THE 1873 *SEIHEN*

The movement to restore power to the Emperor began in the second half of the eighteenth century when it was already centred around Kyoto nobles such as Iwakura, Sanjō and Nakayama. But as they lacked a real power base, even by 1790 they realized that they could not overthrow the Shogunate without the backing of the great western *han* (fief), Satsuma. Though there was a clear danger that the Tokugawas would be replaced by a Satsuma Shogunate, the Emperor party had little option but to accept this risk. Satsuma, however, had become comfortably entrenched in Edo as the power behind the Tokugawas, and so refused to move. There were sharp divisions within the fief between the upper *samurai* living in luxury in Edo and the hordes of lower *samurai* living spartan lives back home. We must be careful not to think of Satsuma, and its 'foreign' policy, as one single entity, for whereas the Shimazu, the Satsuma lords, like the Shoguns, built up a network of marriage and adoption alliances with the rulers of other fiefs, many of its lower *samurai* were to conspire with their activist counterparts from other clans. Once Perry had opened Japan, the movement to restore the Emperor became entwined with that to drive out the foreigners and so became known as *sonnō jōi*. Though many lower Satsuma *samurai* were part of this extremist movement, it was not until the mid-1860s that the Satsuma leaders decided that the time was ripe to combine with Chōshū, their old political and commercial rivals, to join the *sonnō jōi* activists and overthrow the Tokugawas.

With the Restoration the role of the nobles and other *sonnō* activists was recognized, the 119 councillors (*sanyō*) appointed by the first Meiji government coming from nineteen *han* (fiefs) (Hackett 1968: 70–1). These activists naturally expected the government to set up a system based on the Emperor and on Shintō ideology. Instead it made a dramatic volte-face, moving the capital to Edo and speeding up the process of Westernization and centralization. The dominant clans also moved quickly to consolidate their own control, and in the reorganization of June 1868 the number of councillors was reduced to twenty-two from only seven fiefs. When the Dajōkan (Council of State) system was set up in 1869, the title *sangi* was substituted for that of *sanyō*, and of the twenty-six *sangi*, nine were from Satsuma, seven Chōshū, four Saga and five Tosa, the only outsider being Katsu.

Within the government, opposition to Satchō was largely concentrated in the Foreign Office and in the Ministry for Religious Affairs. The Foreign Minister was Sawa, perhaps the most extreme of the young nobles, and it was said that Sawa was the guiding figure behind a wide network of anti-Satchō conspiracies and uprisings. Several government leaders were assassinated, including Ōmura, the Chōshū military leader, and his death left Saigō Takamori, the Satsuma general, as the undisputed military leader. In 1871 the assassinations and constant conspiracies led Satchō, backed by Tosa, to concentrate their own forces in Tokyo and to execute a *coup d'état*. There was now a vicious circle, for this increased concentration of power inevitably provoked even more bitter opposition.

As much of this opposition sprang from the relations with the West, the government decided to send a Mission abroad to prepare the way for revision of the Unequal Treaties. It was led by the noble Iwakura, with Satsuma's Ōkubo and Chōshū's Kido as his deputies. It sailed in December 1871, leaving behind a caretaker government under Sanjō, a noble closely tied to Chōshū, and backed by the mighty Saigō. It was pledged to introduce no major initiatives, and with Chōshū men Yamagata Yoritomo at the Army Ministry and Inoue Kaoru deputizing for Ōkubo at the Treasury, it was felt the Satchō dominance would safely survive the absence of the Iwakura Mission.

Saigō, however, had long-established ties with *sonnō* activists from other fiefs. He continued to be, or to play the role of, the simple, upright *samurai*, and was contemptuous of the corruption prevailing in both the army and the Treasury, then a vast ministry combining the functions of three or four modern ministries. For Inoue Kaoru he had a special contempt, and at the Iwakura Mission farewell party he addressed him loudly as 'Mitsui's bantō'. One report also had him declaring that it would be a good thing if the ship carrying the Mission members sank to the bottom of the ocean. Clearly he was not the ideal defender of the Satchō *batsu*. Indeed, his own closest ties within the government were with Itagaki, the bluff, honest Tosa military leader.

Another important factor was the major role now being played by Saga. For much of the Bakumatsu period, it had straddled the fence and had been too late in entering the fray to claim a position equal to that of Satchō in the new Meiji government. Saga, however, had avoided debilitating internal struggles, and its wise ruler, strong economy and modern fleet gave it significant advantages. Moreover, Saga and Fukuoka had long been responsible for the defence of Nagasaki. Thus it had become a centre of Western learning, and the experience its officials had gained in dealing with the West led to their rapid promotion in the Meiji government. Notable among them were Ōkuma Shigenobu, a young go-getter already on the way to making a fortune; his cousin, the pragmatic, self-serving Ōki Takatō; the stern, scholarly Soejima Taneomi, who had taken over as Foreign Minister; and Etō Shimpei, a radical activist who had developed a close relationship with both Saigō and Tosa's Gotō.

With the departure of the Mission these four Saga men and their Tosa allies stepped onto the centre stage, introducing sweeping reforms including the abolition of *samurai* stipends and special privileges, the introduction of conscription, the granting of full citizenship to the Eta (untouchables), the outlawing of the sale of girls to houses of prostitution and the setting up of a national system of compulsory education. These reforms aroused widespread resentment, especially in the countryside. In May 1873, in Minosaku-kuni alone, tens of thousands rose up and attacked the local officials (Taniguchi 1964: 155ff.). It should be noted that these reforms could not have been carried out without the backing of Saigō. The 1873 *Seihen* is sometimes summed up as a *bun* versus *bu* (civilian versus military), with Saigō depicted as an unenlightened soldier trying to prop up feudalism and Ōkubo as a modern, enlightened bureaucrat. This interpretation ignores the fact that the caretaker government was a progressive, reformist administration which perhaps proceeded too rapidly.

Etō Shimpei emerged as the key figure in the caretaker government. In the first years of Meiji, he had been involved in the immediate problems of administering a poverty-striken Tokyo, but in mid-1871 he was placed in charge of the newly created Mombusho (Education Ministry). He supervised its inauguration, then after a month handed over to his clansman, Ōki, while he moved to the Sa-in

(Council of the Left), which was set up on 28 July 1871 (Matano 1914, Vol. 1: 624). There had been earlier legislative bodies, but they had soon degenerated into debating chambers. Now Etō and Gotō sought to establish the Sa-in as a strong legislative body, and to establish the Separation of Powers along Montesquieu lines. That the dilution of Satchō power was a major objective is shown by the fact that of the thirty-four appointments they made to the Sa-in, only five were from Satchō.

In April 1872, however, Etō switched to the Justice Ministry which had been set up in July 1871, but had failed to take root. He proceeded vigorously to establish a nationwide system of courts responsible to the central government, and to bring the country under the Rule of Law. This brought on a bitter confrontation with Satchō central and provincial officials who sought to remain above the law.

Yamagata and 'the Chōshū Army' had already been involved in major scandals. Saigō had rescued Yamagata but had then had himself raised to Field-Marshal. This brought agonizing cries from the Chōshū camp and others who suspected that Saigō wanted to become Shogun. As Etō's law reforms brought him into conflict with Chōshū on many fronts, Inoue at the Treasury, while meeting all the demands of the corrupt army, claimed that there were no funds to meet the expanded demands of the Justice and Education Ministries. When Etō and his colleagues resigned in protest, Sanjō asked Ōkuma to investigate the financial situation. He found in favour of Etō and Ōki. It was now the turn of Inoue and Shibusawa to resign. Inoue promptly led a party north to Nambu where he set up a sign saying that the rich Osarisawa mine, which had been taken over by the Treasury then sold off cheaply to a Chōshū man, was his own private property. An outraged Etō responded by taking Inoue to court. At stake was the fate, not only of Inoue but of the Chōshū *batsu* as a whole and, consequently, the survival of Satchō dominance. This situation, plus the widespread unrest caused by the progressive reforms, led Sanjō to urge the Iwakura Mission to return post-haste.

By this time the Mission had degenerated into a Grand Tour. In America it had been led to believe that if it had the correct papers of accreditation it could negotiate directly to have the Unequal Treaties revised. Ōkubo and Itō therefore hastened back to Japan for the necessary papers. They received, however, a very cold reception, especially from Foreign Minister Soejima. After a fifty-day delay they were given papers of a sort but these did not permit them to sign any treaty, but merely to lay the groundwork. They had lost considerable 'face'.

Itō had become alienated from his highly sensitive clansman Kido, and was now virtually a follower of Ōkubo. This and other factors meant that the Mission broke into factions, and so it returned to Japan in dribs and drabs, Ōkubo arriving back on 25 June, Kido on 23 July and Iwakura on 13 September. By this time the caretaker government was firmly entrenched, and the returnees were outsiders. Thus instead of rejoining the government Ōkubo and Kido left Tokyo to await the return of Iwakura.

It was at this stage that *seikan-ron* became the dominant issue. The historian must decide whether the two sides were really deeply divided over Korea, or whether the returnees were in essence seeking a convenient issue on which to attack and overthrow the caretaker government. The idea that Korea should be attacked and occupied was already commonplace long before the Restoration. In the early Meiji years frequent attempts were made to restore diplomatic relations with Korea, but it maintained its own policy of seclusion, merely permitting a small Japanese trading station at Pusan.

Things came to a head at about the time when Ōkubo arrived back in Japan. In February 1873 Foreign Office official Hirotsu Shunzō had been sent back to Korea, and in May he was joined by a close colleague, Moriyama Shigeru. In June Moriyama returned to Japan with what he claimed was a Korean notice which had been stuck up outside the Japanese post. It was highly offensive, describing the Japanese as 'monkeys'. Soejima was then in China, whence he had gone partly to negotiate over some Ryūkyūan fishermen who had been slaughtered in Taiwan, and partly to sound out the Chinese attitude in the event of a Japanese attack on Korea. Moriyama therefore presented 'the monkey poster' to Soejima's deputy, Ueno Kagenori, who urged the Sei-in to send troops to Pusan to protect their citizens and then to move on Keijo (Seoul) to negotiate. The matter was debated in the Sei-in by Sanjō, Itagaki, Gotō, Ōki and Ōkuma. It should be noted that the sole Satchō representative was Saigō. Sanjō supported the sending of a force to Pusan, but Saigō proposed that he himself should go unescorted as envoy and proceed alone to Keijo. If he were insulted or killed, the righteousness of their cause would have been established before the world, and Japan could then invade.

It was eventually agreed that no decision could be reached until

Soejima returned. When he arrived back in August he argued vigorously that he, not Saigō, should go to Korea. Saigō countered that the envoy would probably be killed and that the nation could not afford to lose Soejima. Saigō ultimately prevailed, and on 17 August a formal decision was made to send him as envoy. This decision was then approved by the Emperor. The best Sanjō could achieve for the Satchō side was to have Saigō's departure delayed until Iwakura's return.

Meanwhile, the Satchō forces, especially Itō and Kuroda, had been urging Ōkubo to rise up and regain control. But it was not till 10 October – nearly three and a half months after his own return and a month after Iwakura's – that Ōkubo agreed to give battle. On 13 October, both Ōkubo and Soejima were made *sangi* (councillors) and a meeting called on the following day saw Saigō, Itagaki, Etō and Soejima pitted against Ōkubo, Iwakura, Ōkuma and Ōki. With Kido absent due to illness, there was no Chōshū representative. This first meeting achieved little. Iwakura spoke of the Russian 'menace' and of their conflicts in the northern island of Karafuto. Saigō replied that the dispute in Karafuto was essentially one between private citizens, whereas that in Korea affected the honour of the Emperor. He added that if they wanted to send an envoy to Russia, he himself would go. Iwakura replied coolly that the Foreign Office was handling negotiations with Russia.

Itagaki then spoke in support of Saigō, and Ōkubo in opposition. (Ōkubo's argument was set out in an opinion paper to Sanjō and Iwakura. It is analysed in Mōri 1978: 142ff.) Ōkubo argued what has become known as the *nai-gai* case; that is, rather than engage in foreign adventures, the government should concentrate on settling the internal political and economic problems. He claimed that a Korean war would not only work to Russia's advantage, but would also lead to a heavy debt to England, which would then use that debt to bring disaster to Japan. Ōkubo's whole argument was based on the belief that a Saigō mission would lead to war, and though he was not opposed to a Korean war as such, he held that Japan's domestic problems had to be solved first.

When the meeting resumed on 15 October, Saigō absented himself. According to the account in Iwakura's diary, there was further debate, then Sanjō and Iwakura retired to consider their verdict. They found in favour of Saigō. Thereupon Ōkubo stormed out, declaring he could not remain in the Cabinet.

Ōkubo not only resigned as *sangi* but also handed back all his awards and ranks. This deeply shocked Iwakura who also resigned, as did Kido, Ōkuma and Ōki. There was then a flurry of activity, with Itō and Kuroda at the centre. Sanjō took to his sickbed – whether he had a stroke or was feigning illness as part of a deliberate plot is not clear. The Emperor, the trump card, was now brought into play: on 20 October he visited the ailing Sanjō then he called on Iwakura and commanded him to take over till Sanjō recovered.

As the re-instated Iwakura seemed to be stalling on Korea, Saigō, Etō, Gotō and Itagaki called on him on 22 October. The polite greetings soon gave way to a furious confrontation. Iwakura offered to hold a further Cabinet meeting to consider the question, but Etō replied brusquely that the matter had already been decided, and that he, a mere stand-in for Sanjō, had no right to change accepted policies. Deeply stung by these attacks, Iwakura responded that he had his own ideas and that he intended to carry them out. The visitors stormed out, and the rupture was now complete.

Since direct access to the Emperor was barred, Saigō, Gotō, Itagaki and Etō all resigned. Great numbers of officials and soldiers followed suit. The Ōkubo side, of course, all cancelled their resignations. Ōkubo was now firmly in charge, and raised men of second rank to fill the vacancies. His clansman Terajima was made Foreign Minister, and the two Saga men Ōkuma and Ōki were rewarded with the Treasury and Justice Ministry respectively, while Itō and Katsu were also made ministers.

The progressive reforms of the caretaker government were not reversed, nor was its imperialistic foreign policy. An expedition was to be sent against Taiwan in 1874, and Korea to be forcibly opened in 1875–6. Of the losers, Soejima was to remain in the political wilderness; Etō returned to Saga in 1874, led an unsuccessful rebellion, and was beheaded; Saigō led a larger uprising in 1877, but he too lost and committed *seppuku*. Itagaki became one of the leaders of the democratic movement and, very briefly, Prime Minister, before subsiding into a lonely old age. Gotō largely concentrated on business and married his daughter to the Iwasaki (Mitsubishi) heir. The Mitsubishi wealth was then used against the Satchō government and played a central role in the 1881 *Seihen*.

Japanese writing on this vital crisis of 1873 often has a strange air of unreality. This is seen most clearly if one looks at the accounts in high school textbooks, all of which have to be approved by the Ministry of Education (ibid.: 56–66). They take the year 1868 as their starting point: when the new Meiji government sent its representatives, the Koreans refused to receive them and insulted the Japanese nation and the Japanese Emperor. Thus many in Japan wished to punish Korea for its rudeness, while others argued that Japan had too many internal problems to embark upon foreign adventures. The writers of these officially approved textbooks are literally *goyō gakusha*, that is, historians serving the government. Their simplistic accounts cannot be taken seriously as history, and are little better than the myths and legends which served as history in pre-war Japan.

These nationalistic accounts indicate that the central thread of Japanese history writing was not broken by defeat in the Second World War but has continued down to the present day. At least from the Restoration onwards, the central concept has been that of *taigi meibun*. This may be translated simply as 'justification', but it is better understood as 'historical justification'. It was important to justify their actions not only to their contemporaries, but also to posterity and to their gods. There should be no stain on the *kokutai*. This expression could mean 'the national structure', as in Matsudaira Shungaku's September 1867 opinion paper (Sasaki 1970, Vol. 2: 514) which referred to bringing about a complete revolution in the centuries-old *kokutai* and replacing it with a restored imperial rule and ancient order. *Kokutai*, however, could also assume an almost mystical meaning, conjuring up images of national essence and identity.

Where generations of politicians are obsessed with historical justification, the task of the historian becomes extremely complicated. Thus when Inoue Kaoru wrote at great length on some contentious subject to his good friend Itō Hirobumi, giving all sorts of arguments and details which must have already been familiar to Itō, and that letter was then carefully preserved, the letter should be regarded not as a private, spontaneous expression of true belief, but as a case presentation set out for posterity. The situation is somewhat akin to that of modern American presidents who set up their own presidential libraries; if it is ear-marked for preservation, even a guileless little note from the president to his wife should be regarded as a historical public relations exercise.

Japanese historians covering the 1873 *Seihen*, like the principals themselves, have been largely concerned with *taigi meibun*. In the context of their own age, they have generally provided historical justification for the nation or for its ruling faction. Histories of the 1873 *Seihen* may be divided into four main periods. Until the end of the nineteenth century, government censorship resulted in the *seikan* faction being depicted as reckless and ambitious adventurers, and the Ōkubo faction as high-minded patriots; then, once Korea had been taken, Saigō and company were restored to favour, and down to the Second World War both factions were portrayed as patriotic men of principle whose differences were mostly on matters of timing and method. With defeat came a reaction, largely Marxist led, and both factions tended to be portrayed as grasping imperialists. In recent years, the pendulum has begun to swing back. Mōri Toshihiko's excellent 1978 study, *Meiji Rokunen no Seihen no Kenkyū*, is now widely regarded as the definitive work. It analyses virtually everything ever written on the subject, and gives a balanced appraisal of motives and objectives. Yet even Mōri concludes that Saigō did not really want to attack Korea, and that he would have been happy with an apology. *Taigi meibun* has been restored: if Saigō did not wish to attack Korea, then neither did Japan, and the subsequent seventy years of Japanese aggression can be explained away as Japan reacting to changing external situations.

Though most Japanese historians generally agree in their broad narrative of the 1873 *Seihen*, there are great gaps when it comes to seeking detailed accounts of what was said and done, while the motivation and objectives of the participants remain obscure. Was the Ōkubo side really anti-*seikan*? Did Saigō merely wish to obtain an apology from Korea or did he plan to occupy Korea and use it as a base against China? Was the Russian 'menace' a real issue or just a red herring? Was the whole Korean debate just a cover for a bitter power struggle between Satchō and their enemies? These and similar questions have been debated down the years, and that debate still continues.

In Japan there was no tradition of objective history writing, and Japanese historians generally wrote for the edification of the people. Thus the new Meiji government, which was sadly lacking in credibility, was merely carrying on established custom when it imposed a tight censorship and sought to mould public opinion. As a consequence, documentary evidence for the early Meiji years is flimsy and unreliable. Various key figures stored their correspondence or kept diaries but these were not published till decades later, and there was a distinct tendency for politicians and others to amend or falsify these personal records. It was not until the twentieth century that the government arranged for the collection and publication of selected documents and official histories. Both must be regarded as being in essence 'victor's history'.

## BRITISH WITNESS

For thirty years there were no serious histories written by objective contemporaries, but merely official legends which were largely handed down orally. The gist of these legends was that Ōkubo and company were true patriots, enlightened men of principle, while the Saigō faction were backward relics of the feudal age and Saigō himself a vainglorious, would-be Napoleon.

The absence of proper understanding and serious debate is attested to by the writings of foreign observers (see chapter 2). In view of the local tendency to amend or falsify personal records, the Western historian naturally tends to feel a degree of relief on turning to the evidence of contemporary British observers. Probably the most quoted is *A Diplomat in Japan* by Sir Ernest Satow, English gentleman, scholar and distinguished diplomat.

Satow does indeed provide valuable pen pictures of persons and events. Sanjō was 'a pale, effeminate-looking, undersized man of 33' (Satow 1968 edn: 359); Higashikuse, as a Japanese envoy, impressed by the cool way he handled a battery of questions from foreign representatives (ibid.: 324); while Sawa, when first encountered in 1868, 'wore a rather forbidding expression of countenance, not to say slightly villainous, but for all that had the look of a good companion and, a year or two later, when he was minister for foreign affairs, we liked him greatly' (ibid.: 343).

Satow also gives a cool appraisal of the role of 'the Chief' (Parkes) – 'If he had taken a different side in the revolution of 1868 the outcome would have been very different' (ibid.: 141) – while his vivid portraits of Meiji's early exposure to the public gaze are a great help in putting the subsequent Emperor system in perspective. When he first met Parkes (ibid.: 358) it was arranged that his speech should be written down for him. But he never got past the first sentence, and it was over to Itō who took centre stage with an English translation. Parkes was later to develop the habit of lecturing both the Emperor and his ministers (Daniels 1967: 219–20) and to engage in outrageous acts of bullying, but by 1880 he was a spent force. Itō, on the other hand, even after the construction of the Emperor system and Meiji's mid-life deification, always remained very much the self-confident, senior partner in his relationship with the Emperor.

As we have seen in chapter 5 (p.92) Japanese historians have placed great store on Satow's corroborating testimony that Komei was indeed assassinated so, in view of the unsatisfactory nature of contemporary Japanese witness, let us look more closely at the account of this concerned English gentleman and scholar. He reports that some traders 'conveyed to me the news of the Mikado's death which had only just been made public. Rumour attributed his decease to smallpox, but several years afterwards I was assured by a Japanese well acquainted with what went on behind the scenes that he had been poisoned. . . . I certainly never heard any such suggestion at the time. But it is impossible to deny that his disappearance from the political scene, leaving as his successor a boy of fifteen or sixteen years of age, was most opportune.'

At this point in time it is impossible to criticize the Japanese for failing to discern that Satow's tongue was firmly planted in his cheek. Here is, indeed, a major problem. Over the years historians, like most people, lose the ability to laugh even when, as here, a good chuckle is clearly called for.

In his introduction to the 1968 edition Daniels warns us to approach Satow with caution: he is not averse to boasting, he writes with the advantage of hindsight, and he is not unfamiliar with the arts of evasion. For example, he successfully concealed that he had a Japanese *de facto* and two sons – not the done thing for a young diplomat.

Perhaps the key to Satow is the fact that he was not quite an English gentleman, for his father was a Continental and the family were 'in trade'. In the 1950s I met two distinguished diplomats who both opened up to me, a young 'colonial', about matters which had gnawed at them for years. One was Vere Redman, a prominent, permanent fixture on the Tokyo diplomatic scene. He had obtained excellent results in his modern languages degree at London University and that got him into the diplomatic corps, but he had done his degree externally – not quite the right background for a top-ranking diplomat – so he became a linguist and a Japan specialist and though in time he had acquired a definite aura, the pre-aura Redman carried quite a chip. In like vein Purtell, who wrote the definitive studies on the Chinese in South-east Asia, was also very conscious of the fact that he was essentially a mere linguist and that his linguistic qualifications circumscribed his diplomatic career. He had made himself a leading British authority on Cantonese and one of his students obtained a Chair at London University. Purtell himself later tried to obtain an academic post, only to be told that he had no formal qualifications. It was suggested that he do a course at London University.

The Satows, Redmans and Purtells must be regarded as the pillars of the diplomatic corps, but they were not from quite the right circles and were expected to remain pillars propping up their betters. Such a situation perhaps mitigates against the officer being always 'a servant of the state', and encourages a secret life and a larrikin streak. Satow was still a teenager when he arrived in Japan as a junior officer. By the time Parkes arrived on the scene Satow had already acquired a considerable knowledge of Japanese language and society. With many young Japanese, including future Meiji leaders, he had achieved that sort of intimacy, transcending race and nationality, which develops when young men habitually go 'brothel creeping' together. Bearing in mind this degree of intimacy and the widespread nature of the assassination rumours it is simply inconceivable that Satow heard nothing at the time. The little touches, such as hearing about Kōmei's death from a group of traders, have a familiar ring. It might have been scripted by Sada Hakuko or Sasaki. The above account was written not by a rather wild, pig-headed young man in his early twenties, but by a dignified, retired senior diplomat. We are right back with Sasaki, Masuda and all the other eminent old men who manufactured carefully amended versions of past events. Any relief felt at turning from Japanese to English cooking must arise from the fact that we have here evidence that human response does not vary all that much from race to race.

Satow, we may surely take it, heard about the Kōmei assassination 'from a reliable source' back in 1866. The interesting question is whether he heard about it before or after the event. Daniels has suggested that Satow tended to exaggerate his own role, but it is also possible that the reverse is true. Take Satow's account of an article he wrote for the *Japan Times* (ibid.: 159), calling for a revision of the treaties and a remodelling of the Constitution to provide for a confederation of *daimyōs* under the headship of the Mikado, with the Shogun descending to 'his proper position' as a great territorial noble. 'It was doubtless very irregular, very wrong, and altogether contrary to the rules of service, but I thought little of that.' The article was later translated with the help of his Japanese teacher and 'copies got into circulation'. Indeed they were sold in all the bookshops of Osaka and Kyoto under the title '*Eikoku sakuron*' ('English policy'), and it was believed that they represented British policy. Satow added that as far as he knew the article never reached the ears of 'the chief'.

This is questionable but the printing, translation and circulation of the article are historical fact. Later Parkes met and was impressed by Shogun Keiki. 'I hinted to Saigō that the chance of a revolution was not to be lost. If Hiōgo were once opened, then goodbye to the chances of the daimyōs' (ibid.: 200).

Here we merely have Satow's unsubstantiated statement, but if he were capable of publicly urging that the Shogun be overthrown and of privately 'hinting' to Saigō that he should start a revolution without delay, surely one must also consider the possibility that the suggestion that Kōmei be eliminated emanated from Satow. In recent times the many admirers of the CIA have built up for that organization an image of cute originality, but any empire, be it American, Japanese or British, inevitably has men 'in the field' who conceive it as their duty to cut vast swathes off every visible corner. The authoritative account of British involvement in Bakumatsu politics has yet to be written. But there were clearly three elements: the Foreign Office, representing the government and Parliament; the British envoys in Japan, representing not only the government but also the local British community; and the field-workers, such as Satow, who tend to represent their own instincts and view of the cosmos. What can be said with confidence is that the overriding British interest was trade, and this involved the promotion of Satsuma. The countless British travellers' tales and the like must all be viewed through the prism of this overriding concern, and we must accept the fact that contemporary British witness does not take us far, and, as for Satow, he should be allowed, in his public as well as his private life, to cross racial lines and be lumped squarely with Sasaki, Masuda *et al.* In 1873 the Japanese leaders clearly did not divide over Korea. One may perhaps wonder whether they did not divide basically along Kōmei lines – assassins to one side with Iwakura and Ōkubo, non-assassins to the other with Etō, Itagaki and Saigō.

## FUKUZAWA YUKICHI

One of the few 'contemporary' articles on Saigō was that written by Fukuzawa Yukichi, 'the sage of Mito'. Not long before Fukuzawa died in 1901, the *Jiji* began the serialization of *Teichū Kōron* (Teichū is the name for the year 1877), an essay defending Saigō (*Fukuzawa Zenshū* 1960, Vol. 6: 529ff.). Fukuzawa further claimed that it had been written in 1877, but because it was impossible in those days openly to attack the government, he had put it away in a drawer to be kept for his descendants so that they could understand the events of 1877 and keep alive the spirit of resistance.

This essay argued that it was not wrong to overthrow a tyrannical government. The Bakufu had been a case in point. Such a bad government could be opposed with arms, or with the written word (*bu* and *bun*), or again money could be used as a weapon. Saigō chose to resort to arms; Fukuzawa's method was different, but in spirit there was no difference between him and Saigō.

If the government provided no leadership, and the people had no means of expressing their opinions, then popular explosions were inevitable. Thus the government was responsible for the troubles, and Saigō was the victim.

Unfortunately, Fukuzawa's veracity must always be open to question. His own autobiography brands him as one with little regard for the truth. We have only Fukuzawa's word that he wrote this in 1877 and put it away until the end of the century. When the Constitution was promulgated, there was a Great Pardon, and Saigō's name was removed from the list of traitors. By 1901, the work of rehabilitation was well under way.

It should also be noted that the day after Ōkubo was assassinated, Fukuzawa wrote an editorial (ibid., Vol. 19: 655–6) in the *Minkan* which was frostily cold, if not callous. There was no praise for Ōkubo's work or sympathy for his death. His assassination was compared to that of Ii. An examination of various countries showed that such killings were common in dictatorships, rare in democracies. Hence to eliminate assassinations, the people should be given a share in the government.

Such an article the day after the assassination, when passions were at their height and the government most vulnerable, would suggest that Fukuzawa was far from intimidated. When the government demanded an apology from the editor (ibid., Vol. 17: 243fn.), he simply closed down the magazine, thereby wrong-footing Ōkubo's successors. It would probably be fairer to conclude that Fukuzawa did not publish a defence of Saigō in 1877–8 because he was still co-operating with the government and hoping to extract a subsidy for Keio (ibid.: 261ff.). Again it should be noted that the reference to people using money as a weapon against the government does not sound like 1877, but would suggest a date subsequent to Mitsubishi's assault on the government.

One can accept the general thrust of Fukuzawa's argument,

namely that in the seventies it was quite common to criticize Saigō as a traitor and dangerous, if not impossible, to publish a detailed defence. At the same time, one must be ruthless in examining sources, and Fukuzawa is a case in point. Craig (in Ward (ed.) 1968: 103) put it nicely when he described the Fukuzawa autobiography:

> The real Fukuzawa bears little resemblance to the Fukuzawa described in the Autobiography. At least in political matters, the latter is an old man's imagining years later at the turn of the century, of what he ought to have thought and felt as a youth.

The same is probably true of *Teichū Kōron*. However, Fukuzawa's claims to have written it in 1877 seem to have gone unquestioned, largely because the historians have grasped at straws in their attempts to obtain contemporary accounts.

Fukuzawa's own position was full of paradoxes. Though usually associated with progress and 'enlightenment', he was probably Japan's leading warmonger, and his son-in-law, Momosuke, became Japan's greatest war-profiteer. As early as 1878, his *Tsuzoku Kokken Ron* (*A Popular Introduction to State Rights*) (*Fukuzawa Zenshū* 1960, Vol. 4: 600ff.) described war as inevitable (*gaisen yamu o ezaru koto*) and stressed that national might depended on economic power and the ability to buy weapons. He also advocated an extreme form of national unity – a call which he frequently repeated. For example, the *Jiji* editorial of 28 October 1882 declared:

> If you must show a liking for the expression 'party', let us turn the whole of Japan into one party, one faction, and turn our blades outward and fight together against the Western party, the Western faction thousands of miles beyond the sea.
>
> (ibid., Vol. 8: 362–3)

This is a fair description of what was to happen in the 1930s. It also coincides quite closely with the objectives of the post-war education system, except that the war after 1945 became economic. Needless to say, when war came in 1894, Fukuzawa was beside himself with joy: 'My happiness is so intense there is nothing I can do but shed tears' (Kiyooka 1985: 237). No addled-brained jingoist or religious fanatic could have put it better.

Despite his credentials as an imperialist, Fukuzawa remained *persona non grata* with the government because of his 1881 attempt, in conjunction with Ōkuma and Mitsubishi, to bring down the

Satchō government. The 1881 *Seihen* led Satchō to reactivate its old alliance with the ideologues and this led in turn to the recall of the old-style instructors to teach *moral education* and an extreme form of patriotism. In 1886 the inspection of all textbooks was instituted, and in 1893 it was carried one step further with a system of approval and recommendation. In 1903 the system was taken to its logical conclusion when the use of government-compiled textbooks was made compulsory in all schools, including private institutions. The Fukuzawa camp could merely deplore these trends (ibid.: 223ff. and 255ff.), especially as all Fukuzawa's writings were deemed unsuitable.

This textbook question ties in with the failure to develop the writing of objective history. Though the self-proclaimed apostle of enlightenment, Fukuzawa was an arch-imperialist who advocated a one-party, national unity government to prepare for war against the West and who taught that it was Japan's duty to wage war to take 'civilization' to the Asian mainland. Japan entered the Meiji period encumbered by a heavy burden of racist and nationalist *kokugaku* teachings. It desperately needed its enlightened, Western-trained scholars to clear the air. Instead its outstanding Western scholars taught that to wage aggressive wars on the mainland was a moral course of action which was Japan's duty and destiny. Apart from its effect in promoting imperialism, this 'enlightenment' teaching, far from encouraging the writing of objective accounts of Japan's recent history, helped the forces pre-empting its development.

## THE ESTABLISHMENT OF PARLIAMENT

With the approach of the opening of parliament, the situation changed to some extent. To mark the promulgation of the Constitution, there was a Great Pardon, and Saigō was among those whose name was removed from the list of traitors. The government, however, was not about to let Saigō be fully rehabilitated and used as a weapon against them. In other words, it was not yet prepared to turn Meiji history over to impartial historians. An interesting account of its stonewalling is contained in the official biography of Inoue Kaoru – a biography whose compilers included men such as Shibusawa, Masuda and Kaneko (*Segai Inoue Kō Den* 1933, Vol. 5: 329ff.). It relates how Kaneko had spent over a year studying the Western parliamentary systems and procedures. In each country, the experts consulted emphasized the need to collect and publish the records on recent Japanese history. Kaneko therefore drew up a plan for collecting source material on the Restoration, and presented it to Prime Minister Yamagata and imperial household Minister Hijikata. Itō, however, scotched the plan, arguing that the timing was bad. It would lead to the re-fighting of old battles, break up the Satchō harmony, provide ammunition for their enemies, and burst the delicate bubble of constitutional government. Thus the bodies working on collecting and publishing historical sources continued to confine themselves to earlier ages, and the century closed with still no attempt having been made to collect and publish the source material which would make possible a serious history of the Restoration years.

Events in parliament soon bore out the wisdom – from his viewpoint – of Itō's caution. Inoue Kaoru in particular became the target of attacks relating to the early Meiji years, and these attacks, of course, were calculated to undermine the whole Chōshū *batsu*. In 1894, for example (ibid., Vol. 4: 322ff.), fifteen Yamaguchi men from Sanami-gun petitioned to have surplus tax money returned. From 1873 to 1875, the Chōshū *Kyōdō sha*, a prefectural body, collected the prefectural rice tax, then sold it in Kansai at a considerable profit. The petitioners therefore demanded the return of this surplus money to the tax-payers, and a committee was set up to investigate their demands. In effect, they were accusing Inoue of having conspired with his protégé, Governor Nakano, to defraud the tax-payer. The charges then moved on to 1876 when Inoue, as Construction Minister, was said to have conspired with Fujita on trade matters.

A minority report did find him guilty of conspiring with Nakano over rice and with Fujita over trade, but the majority committee report eventually decided that the case against Inoue had not been proven, and that even if he had broken regulations by engaging in trade while a government official in the years 1872 to 1878, this should not be made an issue in 1894 (ibid.: 327–8). What must be stressed is that Inoue was not exonerated – it was merely impossible to obtain enough evidence to convict him.

In the late seventies, Fujita was also embroiled in a notorious counterfeit money case. While his home was being searched, certain telegrams were discovered. They had been sent by Yamagata during the Seinan War, and were mostly addressed to Torio Koyata, advising him of the state of the war. The obvious inference, which was soon drawn, was that Yamagata had been leaking information to Fujita-kumi, the semi-official Chōshū company, to assist its trading.

In defence it was claimed that Torio had been busy rushing around Kansai in the course of his army duties, and that he had merely entrusted the telegrams to Fujita for safe-keeping.

Another parliamentarian to query Inoue's activities was Haseba Sumitaka who declared that he had often heard not only that Inoue engaged in trade from 1871, but then when he went to Korea in 1875–6, he deliberately sent back a telegram, after agreement had been reached, saying that negotiations had broken down. This telegram was said to have forced up the price of rice and to have made a fortune for Fujita. Did the parliamentary committee find any evidence to support these stories? The committee replied in the negative (ibid.: 349).

As they were dealing with trails twenty years old, and as the Bakumatsu *shishi* had been trained in the art of burning correspondence, it was not surprising that the trail had gone cold. What must be stressed is that the opening of parliament did not help the cause of objective history writing. Etō Shimpei's attempt to set up a strong, independent judiciary had failed, so the corrupt oligarchy remained above the law. The setting up of parliament, however, opened a Pandora's box. Questions could be asked, not just about the present but about events and issues going back to 1868. The last thing the government wanted was to follow the gratuitous advice of the various foreign authorities and collect and publish source material on the Restoration and Meiji years. Indeed, the picture which emerges is not merely the negative one of the government refusing to act but one of the government engaging in what perhaps can best be described as the 'pressure cooking' of history. Its vulnerability in the face of parliamentary interrogation inevitably meant that, as far as possible, the slate was wiped clean, and that there would never be any real danger of historians uncovering a solid body of documentary evidence on which to judge the government.

## TORIO'S CONVERSATION WITH SAIGŌ

Because of the extreme paucity of contemporary accounts, source-starved historians have grasped at straws and have then used those straws to build an imposing edifice. Though intrinsically of little value and often palpably false, these stories cannot be ignored for they have assumed a central position in the historical debate. Perhaps the best example is the conversation that General Torio Koyata is purported to have had with Saigō in 1873.

Torio claims that, in the summer of 1873, he presented Saigō with a plan to revive the *samurai*. They were to be put in charge of the *chintai*, their stipends were to be restored, and two-thirds of the taxes were to be used on the *samurai* and army. The Ministers of the Left and Right also had to be army men. Torio claimed that Saigō had agreed with him on every point. There were, of course, no witnesses to this conversation, nor anyone who came forward to declare that he had heard Torio discuss this important conversation in the years between 1873 and 1891.

At the best of times, such unsubstantiated claims made long after the event and after the death of the other party to the conversation must be treated with the greatest caution. At most they can be used only as supplementary evidence to a fairly well-established case. In Torio's case, his claims must be dismissed as worthless. Their only value has been in showing how desperate many historians have been in building up a case.

Torio (1847–1905) was no simple, bluff soldier. A Chōshū *sonnō* activist, he entered the Army Ministry in 1871 (*Kawade*) and the following year was put in charge of the Ōsaka *chintai*. He became known as a conservative who combined with Miura to form an anti-Itō–Yamagata faction within Chōshū, and with Tani and Soga to form a nation-wide conservative group. He wrote extensively on Buddhism and later became a member of the House of Lords and of the Privy Council. In his excellent 1978 study, Mōri Toshihiko pointed out that especially after the 1881 *Seihen*, Torio was an anti-mainstream leader. He became a leader of the anti-Yamagata Monday Club within the army, and in 1889 he was placed on reserves along with Miura and Soga. The following year the Monday Club was disbanded. Thus, once Saigō had been re-instated, Torio clearly stood to gain by invoking his name (Mōri 1978: 103ff.).

Many have used Torio's professed conversation to build up a picture of Saigō as a feudal reactionary. Yet as Mōri and others have pointed out, Torio's account of Saigō is completely at variance with the actions of the caretaker government, such as abolishing stipends and introducing conscription, while as Haraguchi (1968) has argued, if Saigō were such a reactionary, he would hardly have nominated Itagaki, a fervid supporter of a parliament, as his successor.

Indeed, the very idea of Torio being close to Saigō seems ludicrous. Saigō was contemptuous of both Inoue and the Chōshū army corruption. Yet Torio had a very special relationship with Fujita. Inoue was closely involved in the formation of the Fujita-kumi, which acted as a semi-official Chōshū company. Inoue and many other Chōshū leaders continued to profit from its activities. Essential to its early development were the army contracts passed its way by the Osaka *chintai* under Torio. Masuda (Nagai 1939) has left an account of how Torio used Fujita's Osaka residence as his own home, how they regularly played *go* and how Torio, a very blunt man, would, for example, roughly chastize Fujita for filling up his homes and storehouses with junk. The 1894 parliamentary attacks relating to the Yamagata telegrams to Torio which were discovered at Fujita's are all part of the overall picture: in the seventies at least, Torio was very much a part of the corrupt Chōshū military clique which made fortunes from working in with people like Fujita. It is highly unlikely that the professed conversation ever took place or, if it did, that Saigō responded with more than a non-committal grunt. Thus Torio's testimony must be regarded as worthless save as an illustration of the sterility and narrowness of much of the historical debate.

Two other sets of reminiscences should be noted. In 1903 Sada Hakuho, who led the 1869 Mission to Korea, dictated his *Seikan Ron Reminiscences* to a disciple, Itō Akira. It is a fascinating document, but it hardly qualifies as history. Perhaps it should be regarded as Sada's last dying effort to help promote a war against Russia.

Whereas Sada's *Reminiscences* occupy but one slim volume, those of Tosa's Sasaki Takayuki (1970) occupy twelve volumes. They are probably the most quoted of contemporary chronicles, and have generally gained unquestioning acceptance. But it should be noted that the original diaries and papers were not sorted through till the years 1903 to 1907 when Sasaki was already an old man. As many were torn or moth-eaten, Sasaki and his *shosei* frequently had to both edit and re-write. There must have been a tremendous temptation to edit out or to amend facts which had become unpalatable. In addition to the diaries, a volume of reminiscences, *Kinnō Hishi, Sasaki Rōkō Sekijitsu Dan* (*A Secret History of the Emperor Party – Sasaki Rōkō's Tales of Olden Days*) (Tsuda 1915) was dictated over a period of six years; but they were not brought out till five years after his death. Though they closely follow the diaries, they read like the careful compilation of a case rather than as a simple spontaneous outpouring.

Indeed, a closer examination of Sasaki would suggest that his diaries were fairly extensively doctored. He has generally been pictured as a somewhat distant sympathizer of the socially inferior

Takechi, who assassinated Tosa leader Yoshida Tōyō in 1862. But this is merely Sasaki's own self-serving portrait. He was instead one of a handful of high-ranking *samurai* who were produced by the same schools as Takechi, shared his ideals and obsessions, and helped formulate his strategy. Again we get the rhetorical device of a police report from 1862 coming into his hands in 1893, and he then learnt 'for the very first time just what a heavy cloud of suspicion he had been under' (Tsuda 1915: 251–2).

Once the historian has rejected Sasaki's account of his own role in 1861–2 he must become sceptical about much of the 'diaries'. They smack of hindsight when dealing with Saigō and Etō, and one must view with scepticism entries such as that dated 8 August 1871 which states that 'a certain priest' claimed that Saigō was a *kinnō ka* but did not understand *kokutai*: 'this seems strange, but when you think about it, it has a deep meaning, so I'll record it here just as I heard if for the sake of later years' (Sasaki 1970, Vol. 5: 183; also 119).

There is a danger of confusing form with substance. Just because Sasaki's work is in the form of diaries and Masuda's of reminiscences (Nagai 1939) one cannot simply classify the former as a primary source and the latter as secondary. Once we reach the twentieth century, works dealing with the major figures – Ōkubo, Kido, Inoue, Shibusawa, Etō, etc. – were published with increasing frequency. They might be in the form of a diary or journal, of collected letters or writings, or simply an official biography based on the above. But whatever the form, they must be regarded as case pleading, and the authenticity of their evidence can never be assumed without question. In particular one must examine the internal evidence and the logic of the situation.

## MORALITY AND DUTY

Another development which should be noted was the discovery of the efficacy of cloaking one's actions with protestations of high moral intent. Here a notable pioneer was a leading Christian, Uchimura Kanzō, who published (1932–3, Vol. 15: 201ff.) in English to convince the world of the righteousness of Japan's 1894 War against China. Uchimura expressed regret that Japan had not gone to war in 1873, describing this failure as 'a spiritual loss' (ibid.: 210–12). Japan was, of course, a highly moral nation: 'New Japan was moral product. . . . Heaven made New Japan through its own son and reverer. . . . The nation conceived in Righteousness, should it not be called a Christian nation as well?' (ibid.: 224).

Japan's righteousness was best understood by looking at Saigō whose 'thinking was that of a saint and a philosopher' (ibid.: 218). Saigō personified Japan: 'he was Japan etherialized into a soul' (ibid.: 204). 'Saigō was too much of a moralist to go to war merely for conquest's sake. . . . To crush the weak was never in him; but to lead them against the strong and so crush the proud, was his whole soul and endeavour . . .' (ibid.: 210).

In other writings, Uchimura continued his plea: 'Let Japan have this opportunity of serving the world' (ibid., Vol. 16: 35), for 'savagery and inhumanity reign there [Korea] when light and civilization are at its very doors' (ibid.: 31). Japan's righteousness, he claimed, would become evident at the end of the war when it was seen 'nothing of material profit shall accrue to us from helping her.'

Within a few years Uchimura was expressing his deep shame at having tried to justify the Korean War (ibid.: 337), and was suggesting that the only salvation for the Japanese people would come from without: 'What the Japanese people may fail to do, because of their powerlessness, these foreign fleets may accomplish by their pressure upon the tyrants' (ibid.: 350).

Despite his recantation Uchimura had sown seeds which would come to fruition. His picture of Japan's heaven-sent career smacks strongly of the *kokugakusha*, but in a country where scientific history writing was not even in its infancy, his substitution of passionate belief for objective reasoning was to provide an unfortunate precedent. His picture of Saigō as Japan personified, and the rhetorical trick of equating Japan's righteousness with that of Saigō, were to become canons of Japanese history writing which survive to this day. It should be stressed that his 'moral' approach bore little relation to that of 1873 when Korea's weakness and the advantages of conquering her weak neighbour were the aspects stressed. It had been seen as important to depict the invasion as fully justifiable, and as a restoration of Japan's historical position, but there had been little attempt to picture aggression as morally correct in that it was good for the invaded. Uchimura's impassioned and repetitive insistence on the righteousness of Japan's cause in 1894 and his linking of that cause to his picture of modern Japan as conceived in righteousness and heaven made had helped set a precedent, and this synthetic moral cloak was going to make it even more difficult to establish history writing as an objective science.

## THE EARLY HISTORIES

With the turn of the century, straight histories of the Restoration years began to appear. By 1908 four noteworthy studies had been published, but like the biographical works, none was objective history.

In 1901, Volume One of the *Jiyū-tō* (Liberal Democratic Party) history was published. It was supervised by Itagaki, who wrote the preface in which he rejected the traditional view of the 1873 crisis as a struggle between the civilian and the military party, and depicted it as a power struggle between Satchō and the anti-*hanbatsu* forces from which were to develop the *minken* movement and the Jiyū-tō. *Seikanron no Bunretsu Shimatsu* (*A Complete Account of the Split over the Attack-Korea Debate*) (see Mōri 1978: 62ff.) appeared in 1906 under the name of Naganuma Kumatarō, a former official of the Great Council of State who became a *minken* journalist after the 1881 *Seihen* but never achieved prominence. It was claimed that this account was dictated by Naganuma in 1881 to a certain Seisatsu Itsujin. Naganuma was dead by 1906, but Matano Hansuke, Etō's biographer, later revealed that 'Seisatsu' was really Haseba Sumitaka who went on to become Education Minister in Saionji's Second Cabinet.

While accepting Naganuma's authorship, Mōri found the work subjective and inaccurate. The *seihen* was depicted as a power struggle and not one over policy, but the differences over morality were also stressed. Mōri grouped this 1906 book with the 1901 *Jiyū-tō* as a *minken* production, but further clarification seems called for.

To attribute the book to Naganuma is to twist the normal concept of authorship. Surely it was written by Haseba, though perhaps based on interviews twenty-five years earlier with Naganuma. There were obvious practical advantages in having the authorship attributed to someone beyond the reach of the law. It will be recalled that Haseba had been a leading figure in the bitter 1894 parliamentary attacks on Inoue. He was a Satsuma man – hence *nishisatsu* – who served in the early police department (*Kawade*) but resigned and returned to Satsuma with Saigō in 1873. He served in the Seinan War, was wounded and imprisoned till 1880. He joined the Kaishintō and later the Jiyū-tō and Seiyūkai, and had a distinguished parliamentary career. He would seem to have been quite capable of writing his own book but would not have been writing as an impartial historian.

In 1907 a Waseda professor, Kemuyama Sentarō, published

*Seikan-ron Jissō*. Kemuyama was a competent historian, and most subsequent historians acknowledge this work as their starting point. Yet Kemuyama was very much a product of his times. The successful occupation of Korea made it impossible to be too critical of Saigō and Etō, so Kemuyama set out to restore Saigō's reputation. Yet he may perhaps be said to have been interested in achieving a national consensus over past and future expansion on the mainland. He had the somewhat dubious advantage of interviewing both Sada and Ōkuma. Though Ōkuma and Ōki stuck with Ōkubo during the 1873 *Seihen*, after Ōkubo's assassination in 1878, Ōkuma was to combine with Mitsubishi in an attack on the Satchō oligarchy, and this attack brought on the 1881 *Seihen*. Thereafter he took a leading role in founding the Progressive Party to wrest power from Satchō. Ōkuma was the founder-benefactor of Waseda University, so Kemuyama's strong Ōkuma connections means that his book must also be regarded as representing one of the major elements of the Satchō opposition.

Kemuyama made a considerable impact, as did the 1908 *Seinan Chronicle* of the extreme right wing Kokuryūkai (Black Dragon Society). They depicted themselves as the spiritual heirs of Saigō, but took the line that both factions in 1873 were imperialists who differed only on timing. The preface by Uchida Ryōhei stressed the links between Saigō and their own Greater Asia policy, for *seikan* was not just about taking Korea but was a plan for setting up a Greater Asia under Japanese rule.

Mōri's 1978 study contains a summary and an analysis of virtually everything ever written on the 1873 *Seihen*, and one cannot quarrel with his treatment of the *Seinan Chronicle*. Mōri's approach – a perfectly legitimate and useful one – was to classify writers according to their school of thought rather than chronologically; yet it is of equal importance to get the time sequence fixed firmly in mind, and to make sure that the state of history writing is perceived against the events of the day. So let us digress for a moment to look at Uchida Ryōhei.

Uchida (1877–1937) was a Fukuoka activist whose father had been one of the major founding fathers of the Genyōsha, the forerunner of the Black Dragon Society. Much has been written on the Fukuoka and Kumamoto rightists, but let us base our summary on Hitomata's fascinating biography of Sugiyama (Hitomata 1975) and the study of Uchida by Kyūshū University professor Hatsuse.

Sugiyama, an early would-be assassin of Itō, was close to Tōyama, to Kumamoto's Sasa and Inoue Kowashi, and also to Gotō Shimpei with whom he co-operated in Taiwan and Manchuria. He also drew close to the Chōshū General Kodama, a Governor of Taiwan, and the two were said to have formed a secret society to bring on war with Russia. They promoted Katsura as Army Minister, and initiated him into their secret society. When Katsura became Prime Minister in 1901, Kodama stayed on as Army Minister, with Sugiyama as the power behind the scenes.

Hitomata's account (Hatsuse 1980) of the absorption of Korea is based largely on the Kokuryūkai's 1935 *Nikan Gōkoku Mitsu Shi* (*A Secret History of the Amalgamation of Japan and Korea*). Sugiyama and Uchida both wrote forewords in which they praised each other's role.

At the end of the Russian War, when Itō was sent to Korea as special envoy, Sugiyama had Uchida attached to him as 'special adviser', but he could be better described as a bodyguard or 'minder' directly responsible to Sugiyama. Itō had little option but to take him, though he knew his history: he had been involved in the Tōgaku-tō disturbances in 1894 in Korea; had gone to live in Vladivostok in 1895 to spy for the Genyōsha (Hitomata 1975: 187ff.); had made a return overland trip to St Petersburg in 1896–7, diagnosed Russia's internal weakness and returned a firm advocate of war; in 1900 he had gone to China with Sun Yat Sen but had clashed with him over his assassination plans; and he had then helped found the Kokuryūkai, one of the earliest and strongest advocates of war with Russia. He was certainly not an 'adviser' that Itō himself would have chosen.

Soon after arriving in Korea, Uchida began to support, and to gain financial control over, the Isshin Kai (Go Forward Together Society) which had been founded in 1904 by old Japan collaborators such as Sō Heishun. Itō was made Viceroy in 1906, but things did not go smoothly. The king was forced to abdicate in July 1907, and a new Treaty was signed. Itō summoned the various foreign consuls and made a speech proclaiming that Japan had no territorial ambitions in Korea. It was widely reported and warmly applauded, but Sugiyama regarded it as a betrayal of the Russian War. Sō had become Home Minister and had been urging the advantages of annexation. When Itō refused to listen, Sō resigned and went to Tokyo with Uchida for talks with Katsura, Terauchi and Yamagata. Uchida sat in on the talks. Sugiyama himself now crossed to Keijō (Seoul) and demanded Itō's resignation. Outgunned, Itō gave him a letter addressed to Yamagata expressing his intention to resign at some unspecified date, but he stayed until July 1909. Four months later he went to Harbin to meet Russian leaders in a last-ditch attempt to arrange a treaty and thus forestall the Japanese annexation of Korea. There he was shot by a young Korean, and, as Saigō had argued in 1873, the assassination of the Japanese representative provided the perfect *taigi meibun* for the annexation of Korea.

Sugiyama later wrote a biography of *Yamagata Gensui*. He refrained from going into details about the Korean annexation, but simply noted (see Hitomata 1975: 192) that it had been planned by five people: the three Isshin Kai leaders, Uchida, and Kikuchi Tadasaburō.

It is unlikely that the full story of the Itō assassination will ever be known, but it is fairly clear that by around 1907 Itō was largely a spent force fighting a desperate rearguard action against the army, the *zaibatsu* and the Kokuryūkai, all of which were pressing for the annexation of Korea. Significantly, Uchida had finally broken with him earlier in 1909 and so did not accompany him to Harbin. Like the death of Kōmei, that of Itō came at a wonderfully convenient time and helped change the course of history. The suspicion that his Japanese enemies plotted the assassination remains strong. Certainly what can be stated with confidence is that in 1908, when the Black Dragon Society's *Seinan Chronicle* came out with a foreword by Uchida, Itō was fighting a desperate battle, if not literally for his life, then at least for his political life. At long last he accepted that the Satchō government had to supervise the collection of documents and to write its own histories if it were not to lose the vital propaganda war with the rightists, the army and the political parties. The collected documents and the official histories published after 1909 should not be viewed naively as the manifestation of a noble desire to discover and propagate objective historical truth; rather should they be seen as the products of, and weapons in, a fierce political struggle, the viciousness of which is clearly illustrated by the Uchida story.

## THE OFFICIAL COLLECTION OF SOURCES

To flesh out this picture, let us return to the official Inoue Kaoru biography and its account of the official collection of source material on the Restoration period.

It will be recalled that around 1890 Itō had scotched Kaneko's plan to collect source material as likely to provide ammunition for the government's enemies. In 1908 (*Segai Inoue Kō Den* 1933, Vol. 5: 331ff.) the British Ambassador, Sir Claude MacDonald, asked Inoue if there was a reliable history of the Restoration. When he replied in the negative, MacDonald urged that a complete Japanese history be published in English, and also pointed out how important it was for people to understand their own history. Thus Inoue again took the matter to Itō. Though worried lest people should think they were writing history from the Satchō standpoint, Itō was now more favourably inclined. However, he was soon to leave for Harbin, and so asked that Inoue wait till he returned. Itō's assassination meant further delays, but in 1909 the Satchō leaders set up Shōmeikai (Society to Make Bright and Clear) and it eventually settled down to the task of collecting source materials relating to the Restoration. It finally met in the Kazoku Kaikan with Inoue as Chairman. Those present included the other Genrō plus Hijikata, Higashikuse, etc. (ibid.: 336).

The task was soon seen to be too big for the Shōmeikai, and it was decided that it should be transferred to a government department. A popular proposal was that it should be undertaken by the imperial household Ministry, but Yamagata argued that Satchō would then be seen to be hiding behind the Emperor. Thus the task was entrusted to the Education Ministry. Inoue, however, stayed on as Chairman of the History Committee, and his advisers consisted of Yamagata, Ōyama, Hijikata, Matsukata, Tanaka Mitsuaki and Itagaki – that is, two each from Satsuma, Chōshū and Tosa. The full committee consisted of thirty-three members, but it was a top-heavy group of ministers, nobles, *zaibatsu* heads, etc. or the heirs of the above group. The Shōmeikai also continued to work independently collecting material.

In 1913 Yamamoto's Treasurer refused to appropriate money for the History Committee but Inoue went directly to the Prime Minister and had the funds restored. A year later, after the clash with the imperial household Minister, Inoue resigned as Chairman, but he remained a committee member until his death.

Let us recapitulate: for three decades after the Restoration there was little attempt to produce a serious history of those years. Instead, victors' legends, largely handed down orally, were accepted and reproduced by Western observers. With the setting up of parliament, Itō scotched attempts to collect source materials. Satchō, and especially Inoue, came under repeated attack in parliament for their past misdeeds, and the government's concern was to see that records were destroyed. But attacks on Satchō continued from four main sources: the *minken* movement, the Fukuzawa–Ōkuma forces, the Kokuryūkai and the palace officials such as Hijikata and Sasaki.

By 1908 all four groups had become actively involved in writing 'histories' as a way of discrediting the government: the Jiyū-tō had brought out its 1901 history of their party, and in 1906, Haseba, who had taunted Inoue in parliament, produced 'Naganuma's' history; Fukuzawa in 1901 had suddenly rediscovered his '1877' essay on Saigō, while Kemuyama, a professor of Ōkuma's Waseda, had produced his 1907 history; Sasaki was working on editing his own version of Bakumatsu and Meiji history; and in 1908 the Black Dragon Society had produced its *Seinan Chronicle* in which Itō's 'minder', Uchida, had vigorously argued that Saigō's *seikan ron* was identical with the doctrines of the Kokuryūkai. One may accept that the British Ambassador spoke to Inoue in 1908, but that was hardly a major factor. What does stand out is that by 1908 it was all too apparent that Satchō could no longer stonewall. They, too, would have to get into the business of writing 'histories'. That Itō finally acknowledged this necessity just before he went to Harbin forms a sad little epilogue to his life story.

Of course, the nature of the History Committee is self-evident. The forty years which had passed since the Restoration had seen no real attempt to collect sources or to produce objective histories, and the setting up of the History Committee can hardly be regarded as the beginning of history writing as an objective science. It was designed as an official organ in the narrowest sense of the word. That the History Committee should be chaired by Inoue was the ultimate irony.

## THE MOVE TO CONSENSUS

Thus history writing down to the Second World War must be regarded as a branch of politics. *Goyō gakusha* presented the governmental and the national case, but the main point to note is that it was the tight control of source material collection which enabled the government to mould history.

The fact that Japanese history was essentially the servant of Japanese politics did not mean that no fine histories were written. Whatever the country, the finest histories have not inevitably been objective and impartial. Matano's 1914 biography of Etō, for example, though written with fire and conviction, is a work of great scholarship and insight. Matano drove home the message that Etō was fighting to establish the Rule of Law, while Satchō were fighting with equal determination to remain above the law. This fight must be seen as one of the central issues of the 1873 *Seihen*.

Yet despite these fine individual works, it must be said that history writing, and history research, as objective sciences were virtually non-existent. Like education as a whole, history writing was made to serve 'the interests of the state' as conceived by those in power. As the century advanced, and Japan moved deeper into Asia, the movement was towards consensus. Just as political parties were abolished for a one-party state, so the conflicting claims of the rival factions of the Meiji era were retrospectively reconciled till they all fitted snugly under the umbrella of Greater Asia under Japanese rule.

Here the best example is provided by the works of Tokutomi Iichirō (Sohō), who wrote and spoke almost non-stop for many decades. The identity of his researchers and speech-writers has never been conclusively established, but Tokutomi is better regarded not as a historian but as a pundit ever willing to pontificate on a good national cause. Here we must part company with Mōri (1978: 73–9) who highly recommended Volumes 86 and 87 of Tokutomi's *Kinsei Nippon Kokumin shi* (*Modern History of the Japanese People*) which was apparently written in 1941 though not published till 1961.

Mōri argued that during the writing of this 1941 history, Tokutomi changed his stance as he became more familiar with the material. In the early sections he stressed the *nai-gai* debate, though claiming they were not really incompatible, for the expansion into Korea was meant to settle Japan's internal problems, while the settling of her internal problems was intended to clear the way for expansion. As the work proceeded, Tokutomi stressed the various personal conflicts – an approach already commonplace – but towards the end he again changed and depicted Saigō as mostly concerned with the Russian 'menace': 'Others may have used Russia as an excuse, but for Saigō Russia was already a black cloud hanging over our land' (ibid.: 349–50). To back his case, Tokutomi drew upon the testimony of a Shōnai man named Sakai Gendan. According to Tokutomi (ibid.: 131–2), a Sakai letter dated 9 January 1874 recorded that Saigō had told him that war with Russia was inevitable. They must therefore first provide for the defence of Hokkaidō, next settle the Korean question, then extend their sway to Nicholai and guard 'this territory'.

Mōri's work falls away at this point and becomes highly inconsistent. He accepts Tokutomi's assurance that Sakai was a most reliable witness. Yet we have again merely the unsubstantiated testimony of a passing acquaintance from another clan. If the Russian 'menace' was central to Saigō's thinking, it is remarkable that we do not have full and verifiable witness from his own close associates. In any case, Sakai's account mentions no time span. There were many who believed that Japan should combine with Russia to carve up the Asian mainland and then, at some time in the future, these two dominant powers would have to fight for ultimate supremacy. Again, even if Saigō did speak as Sakai claimed, and was thinking of war in the near future, it hardly supports Mōri's major conclusion that Saigō's aim in his projected mission to Korea was not to bring on a war but to obtain a peace treaty. Surely Sakai is reporting Saigō as saying that he wanted to occupy Korea, whence they would not only invade Manchuria but also move north and drive the Russians out of Asia.

Mōri must be regarded as distorting the role of both Tokutomi and Saigō. Instead of viewing Tokutomi as a profound thinker who reached his conclusions after viewing the full body of evidence, one should go back to two earlier works of Tokutomi, a 1926 essay on Saigō and a 1927 study of Ōkubo. The Saigō essay is a brief but wordy portrayal of Saigō as 'a nearly perfect hero' (Tokutomi 1926: 86). It was originally delivered as a eulogy on the fiftieth anniversary of his death. Saigō's purity was stressed, and Tokutomi insisted that in 1873 there had been no power struggle (ibid.: 75–6), for Saigō was incapable of mean thoughts, and the two sides were comprised of patriotic, high-principled men who simply disagreed on what was best for the country (ibid.: 80): Saigō's *seikan-ron* was not about Korea; their *aite* was Russia. For an island country like Japan, with a large population, imperialism in one form or another was inevitable (ibid.: 66–7). Saigō 'opened the door for Japanese imperialism' and his teachings were carried out in 1894–5 and 1904–5.

Tokutomi's thesis was further developed in his 478-page study of Ōkubo which pointed out that Saigō should be described not as a supporter of *taigai ron* but as an advocate of *Nippon teikoku hatten saku* (plans to expand and develop the Japanese Empire) (Tokutomi 1927: 153). In other words, he wanted permanent possessions. Indeed, Saigō, Ōkubo and Kido were all 'splendid imperialists'.

This is vastly different to the picture painted by Mōri who argued that Saigō merely wanted an apology from, and a peace treaty with, Korea, and that his main motivation was that Japan itself was under direct threat from Russia. Tokutomi was defending and encouraging Japanese imperialism. His mid-twenties eulogy on Saigō was not a serious political study but a highly political, nationalistic harangue. Saigō and those other 'splendid imperialists', Ōkubo and Kido, had wanted to occupy both Korea and Manchuria, and when their imperialistic expansion brought them into conflict with Russia, they would drive her out of Asia.

One must agree with Tokutomi in that both sides in the 1873 struggle were 'splendid imperialists'. But it is impossible to accept either that there was no power struggle or that both factions were composed of high-principled patriots. Such a struggle was simply not in the national interest.

Tokutomi, then, was essentially a publicist for the government and for imperialism. He was defending past imperialism, arguing away the clashes which had occurred, and preparing the way for future imperialism. In one sense, his position by the mid-twenties represents an advance, for whereas Inoue's 'history committee' represented the ultimate in partisanship, the stage had now been reached where internal differences had largely been set aside and 'history' had been formally embraced as an instrument of national consensus.

There was, of course, some dissent. Mōri (1978: 39ff.) has suggested that in the thirties, as Saigō became the patron saint of the militarists, the Marxists made him their target in an oblique attack on the military. Mōri cites Hara Heizō as an example of the Marxists portraying the 1873 *Seihen* as an inevitable class struggle, with Ōkubo and Kido representing modern capitalism, the central bureaucracy and the bourgeoisie, while Saigō represented feudalism and the old military classes. One must commend Hara's courage, but not his history.

Another major thirties history was Tanaka Sōgorō's *Seikan Ron, Seinan Sensō* (1939) which argued that *seikan* was a last dying effort by the *shizoku* to re-establish their position in the face of a world changing rapidly and moving towards capitalism. Though he described them as just the orchestral accompaniment to the *samurai* feudal struggle (ibid.: 3–4), he admitted that there were other factors: an instinctive reaction to foreign pressure; a need for Japan to exert herself diplomatically to get established on the international stage; and a need for an expansionist policy to compensate for the fact that *jōi* had been abandoned for *kaikoku*.

Tanaka cited Honda Toshiaki, Satō Nobuhiro and Hirata Atsutane to demonstrate that 'in resisting this [Western] oppression, the various people who dreamt of developing Japan, without exception envisioned a League of Asian nations, of which invariably the first step was the conquest and occupation of Korea' (ibid.). The expressions (Western) 'oppression' and 'a League of Asian nations', of course, nicely cloak the fact that the writers quoted all advocated world conquest. Tanaka was using the language of his day. Inevitably, so too did Kikata Sadao (see Mōri 1978: 44ff.) who won a 1940 *Mainichi* competition for the best work on *seikan ron*. His account reads like a Chinese epic, with Ōkubo and Saigō both great and noble heroes.

The end of the Second World War meant the emancipation of the Japanese historian. It might seem that he was then free to sit down and set the record straight. This, however, is an illusion. Sources remained a gigantic problem, and some decades would have to be largely devoted to the painstaking task of collecting and evaluating source material. Even then, practical problems would remain. Deciphering Godai's handwriting, for example, remained a task for the specialist, and when, for example, Ienaga came to write about Ueki Emori, just tracking down his scattered writings required years of foot-slogging.

But there were psychological as well as practical problems. In the thirties, Sansom warned the British government that Japanese policy was 'national' in the sense that it enjoyed the support of all sections (Trotter 1975: 172). The only differences related to time and method. The Treasury head, Warren Fisher, dismissed Sansom as 'a pedantic ass' (ibid.: 128), but, with qualifications, Sansom's assessment would seem to have been a correct one; and Japanese historians must be included in this judgement. For thirty years it had been impossible to write seriously about the 1873 *Seihen*, then for the next forty years history had been written by people who were united in their support of *seikan*, the occupation of Korea and Japan's further imperial ambitions. Thus though 1945 meant emancipation for the historian, and the open, often jubilant, embracing of democratic and Marxist doctrines, the ingrained thought processes were not to be cleared away overnight. Even those bitterly anti-military would not, generally speaking, arrive overnight at the conclusion that *seikan* was, from the outset, morally and politically unjustifiable. It should be noted that the Emperor's speech at the end of the war was a re-affirmation of *muzai ron*:

> We declared war on America and Britain out of our sincere desire to ensure Japan's self preservation and the stabilisation of South-East Asia, – it being far from our thought either to infringe upon the sovereignty of other nations or to embark upon territorial aggrandizement. . . .
>
> We cannot but express the deepest sense of regret to our Allied nations of East Asia, who have consistently co-operated with the Empire towards the emancipation of East Asia.
>
> (Craig 1967)

Japan accepted defeat, not guilt. The Marxists might set out to re-write history, but the historians of the previous forty years had not been officially disowned. The immediate post-war era saw bitter, emotionally charged battles, largely along class lines. This atmosphere, the official *muzai ron*, and the ongoing sources problem meant that conditions were far from perfect for objective history and that the reforming historians would almost inevitably veer to extreme positions. For reasons of space, let us merely note the work of five post-war historians.

Tōyama Shigeki (1950) pictured Saigō as feudal and reactionary and therefore embarrassed about the caretaker government reforms, and this turned him to *seikan*. In his eagerness to depict both sides as reactionary, Tōyama included Etō and Itagaki under this heading. Though he cleared Japan of the charge of economic imperialism, he still accepted the basic position that Japan's expansion was defensive in nature. His revisionist history became very unbalanced, especially when describing Etō as feudal and reactionary. Tōyama seemed to lack Etō's ability to handle modern political concepts, especially in relation to the judiciary.

Historical debate still tended to centre around Saigō. Tanaka Sōgorō brought out a 1958 biography which continued his 1939 argument, while a 1960 biography by Tamuro (see Mōri 1978: 44) painted an even more extreme picture of Saigō as a feudal reactionary. Inoue Kiyoshi provided interesting variations on this theme, notably in his chapter 'Seikanron to Gunkoku Shugi no Kakuritsu' ('The *Seikan* debate and the establishment of militarism') in his 1953 work *Nippon no Gunkoku Shugi* (*Japanese Militarism*), and in his 1970 biography of Saigō. Inoue also accepted that both sides were *seikan*, but with Saigō wanting a *shizoku* dictatorship and Ōkubo a bureaucratic dictatorship. As Mōri pointed out, this argument falls down if it can be demonstrated that Saigō was progressive, and Inoue was on slippery ground in arguing from Torio's testimony. However, Inoue made a valuable contribution in stressing how the people had been alienated by the reforms of the caretaker government, so that a civil war was a real possibility if the government proceeded with war against Korea. Thus the two sides split on the question of which should be placated, the *shizoku* or the *heimin*.

Again, it must be noted that Inoue was very much a product of his age. He not only concluded that Saigō was *gunkoku shugi* but he strongly urged that the true nature of his career should be made known to present-day (1970) Japanese who were faced by a revival of militarism and imperialism.

As Inoue feared, 1970 provided something of a watershed, for the rehabilitation of Saigō – and of Japan's imperialism – was once more under way. Mōri's thorough-going and penetrating 1978 study, *Meiji Rokunen no Seihen no Kenkyū*, is likely to remain the definitive study for some time to come. Mōri made three main points: Ōkubo's faction was concerned with getting back power from the caretaker government, and a successful Saigō Mission would have made this impossible; the Chōshū faction was trying to recover ground lost because of its corruption, and to push on with fresh extortion; and Saigō did not wish to attack Korea, but hoped to come back with a peace treaty. The main value of Mōri's book lies in his analysis of almost everything written on the 1873 *Seihen* and on his treatment of Chōshū corruption. Its great weakness lies in his treatment of Saigō. We are virtually back to Uchimura and Saigō as Japan 'etherialized'.

Predictably, Mōri's work caused considerable controversy. Let us take just one critic, Y. Iechika (1981: 30–62), who examined Ōkubo's role and concluded that Ōkubo's rivalry with Etō and his protection of Inoue were not the great issues Mōri had made them out to be. He came back to the belief that Ōkubo was, at least in the closing stages of the crisis, genuinely afraid that Saigō's mission would lead to war, and that he wanted a decade or two to settle Japan's internal problems. Thus we are back with the *nai-gai* school.

Though concluding that 'Mōri Toshihiko kun got too bogged down in considerations of Saigō's true heart' (ibid.: 60), Iechika accepted

Mōri's argument that Saigō did not want war, and noted that it had found general acceptance.

Finally, let us note a lightweight offering by a major historian, Tanaka Akira (1984), who re-traced the path of the Iwakura Mission. Tanaka pictures the Mission reacting to what they saw abroad. From Bismarck they learnt that Might is Right, and from the sight of many small states huddled together they absorbed the lesson that you must give yourself breathing space and avoid border problems. Hence the move into Karafuto, the Ryūkyūs, etc. It is *muzai ron* at its sloppiest, implying that Japan was merely imitating the West and was therefore essentially guilt-less.

No historian can simply write in isolation. He must acknowledge and confront current perceived wisdom. The known facts clearly indicate that Saigō, Satsuma and Japan wanted to attack Korea in 1873, and that for reasons of personal or group advantage, that attack was delayed for two years. Yet, as we have seen, Japanese historians now generally support Mōri's contention that Saigō – and, by extension, Japan – did not want war. Foreign historians are thus confronted with a dilemma: they must deal with current Japanese doctrine, but must avoid getting bogged down in areas such as 'Saigō's heart' which have dominated the debate but have obscured the major issues.

Sources provide historians with another daunting problem. It would be possible to write a book on the 'documents', discussing their authenticity and analysing their true import. This, indeed, is what much of the writing on the 1873 *Seihen* amounts to. But we must start with the realization that the documentary evidence is flimsy, unreliable and either 'doctored' or simply 'cooked'. Any work based on such documents is unlikely to do more than help perpetuate 'victors' history.

Thus we are brought to another great problem. What constitutes 'evidence'? Here the answer is both simple and complex: find out what happened. The events themselves are the best evidence. Questions of motivation and character must come later. To find out what happened, the historian must ask the right questions, and not settle down to a diet of red herrings. To illustrate these simple truths, let us look again at Mōri and his treatment of evidence.

He discusses at length what purports to be a transcript of Saigō's argument to the Cabinet. It has Saigō speaking in *Satsuma ben* (dialect) and telling Sanjō bluntly that he was not a Dajōkan of old but a Meiji Ishin Dajōkan:

> If things continue as at present, Japan will never be able to escape from being just an island country. It is *a good chance, a fine opportunity*, for Japan to enter and establish herself upon the Mainland, which is six times the size of Europe. If we let that chance pass, that lost opportunity will be deeply lamented by Japan. Defeating *Korea and China* presents no great problem. Though Russia is trying to lead her people on an expansionary course, her own internal situation is dangerous, and it is *simply impossible* for her to send a great force to conquer Japan. No matter what you say, it is Japan's *holy mission* to make Chosen its outer wall and base (for future expansion). Then it could link up with Russia for their mutual good.
>
> (Mōri 1978: 133–5 [my italics])

Whether authentic or not, this 'transcript' puts the standard *seikan* argument in a nutshell. Mōri, however, concludes that the chances of this transcript being authentic are only about three in ten. He admits that it is consistent with the statements of Sakai and Kabayama, but points out that there is no evidence to corroborate that this speech was ever delivered. He therefore equates it with Torio's 1891 recollections.

Mōri had encountered the transcript in a collection of documents published by Nakano Keigo. In a footnote, Nakano explained that the famous Fukuoka scholar, Satsuga Hakuai, had found it in Kurogi Yachirō's *Dai Saigō no Ikun to Seishin* (*Great Saigō's Posthumously Handed down Teachings and Spirit*). Apparently it was originally in vaults containing Cabinet records. Satsuga had planned to include it in the sixth volume of his work on Saigō, but it was towards the end of the war and there was no paper, so he died before he could do so. Nakano, however, stencilled and retained six pages.

Mōri approached the question of verifying its authenticity in three ways. In 1974 he visited Nakano in Matsuyama to see the stencilled copy. This proved nothing, as it was not, of course, in Saigō's own spidery writing. Mōri was inclined to dismiss it altogether, but as his own researches progressed, he began to think that it might possibly be authentic. His next step was to consider the verdict of other historians. He had been particularly impressed by Sohō Tokutomi who had portrayed Saigō as obsessed with the Russian 'menace'. But as we have seen, Tokutomi was already painting both

Saigō and Ōkubo as 'splendid imperialists' by the mid-twenties, and acting as propagandist for that imperialism. It was inevitable that he would dismiss as a fake evidence which purported to show that Saigō favoured linking hands with Russia. All Tokutomi's support does is to alert us to the fact that Mōri, and the present generation of historians who back him, are likewise living in an age which would generally be disappointed to learn that Saigō favoured friendship with Russia.

Mōri's third approach is to argue from the internal evidence. It is here that Mōri falls down most badly. He concentrates on the expressions 'good chance' and 'base of operations', insisting that they are not like Saigō, a highly moral man who would do no wrong. In other words, he concludes that the transcript is not authentic because it does not accord with his concept of Saigō's character. Surely Mōri has reversed normal procedure. One should be establishing what Saigō said and did to form a picture of his character, and not vice versa.

There would seem to be little hope of verifying the authenticity of such a transcript. It suggests the practice of Herodotus who, when lacking documentation, would invent speeches for his characters to deliver – speeches which gave in dramatic form the speech as the historian imagined it would have been delivered. Perhaps the best we can do is to accept the transcript as a Herodotus-style speech, then ask whether it gives a reasonable precis of Saigō's position.

Mōri would seem to have misinterpreted Saigō's concept of *taigi meibun*. This may be translated as 'historical justification' – the providing of a reasonable pretext so that present and future generations need not feel ashamed of their country. Saigō, at least, seems to have believed in the authenticity of the 'monkey poster' which Moriyama brought back from Korea. To Saigō it represented the ideal excuse for acting: no one could blame Japan for responding to such an insult. Hence Saigō's stressing that this was 'a good chance, a great opportunity'. Surely the whole concept of *taigi meibun* was, in a sense, opportunist. This would suggest that Saigō is better regarded not as a man bound by high, rigid moral standards, but as an alert opportunist, for a man bound by high moral standards would not act just because a suitable pretext had come along.

That Saigō really planned a war is strongly indicated by the fact that he and Itagaki sent off four young men on an intensive spying mission, two to Korea and two to Manchuria. Mōri (1978: 97) bravely argues that as a responsible statesman, Saigō had to prepare for war even though he hoped for peace. But that does not explain sending spies into Manchuria. If the object was simply to chastize Korea, there was no need to enter Manchuria. Surely it supports the view that Saigō wanted to use Korea as a base for further expansion. Even more telling is the fact that, when Saigō's mission was called off, his young spies tried to assassinate Iwakura (Teraishi 1976: 317–20) and suffered torture and ignominious death. Obviously, they had been carefully briefed about their own spying mission, and believed that they were preparing the way for an invasion.

Saigō, like Sada (see chapter 5) went to the trouble to prepare detailed maps, setting out the routes to be taken by the various divisions. Surely the picture is of Saigō thinking like a military man. This is further borne out by the fact that Saigō asked Ichiji Masahara to study a hypothetical Korean campaign (Mōri 1978: 85). In December 1872 Ichiji sent Saigō a long letter containing his analysis. His main conclusion was that it would take 40,000 men to conquer Korea. 'So it seems,' concedes Mōri, 'that it was not the case that Saigō had no connection with Seikan advocacy.' This cautious double-negative concession does not, of course, go nearly far enough. It is patently clear that Saigō was deeply involved in planning an invasion of Korea.

In considering the authenticity of the above transcript, one should consider not merely Saigō but also his colleagues, particularly Kurino, Itagaki, Gotō, Etō, Soejima and Kataoka. Were they sincere *seikan* advocates, or were they merely following Saigō's lead? Mōri admits (ibid.: 205–8) that the Satsuma men who were closest to Saigō, such as Kirino, were fanatical imperialists, but added that 'Kirino was not Saigō'. Gotō belonged to a Tosa school which had long advocated expansion (see chapter 11). Itagaki, Etō, Soejima and Kataoka were all the subject of very competent biographies. In each case the biographer stressed that his man had advocated *seikan* before Saigō, and deserved more of the credit for the eventual annexation of Korea. Maruyama (1936) pointed out that an integrated foreign policy had begun with Soejima, and one of his major themes was that it was Soejima who had introduced Saigō to *seikan*. Itagaki's biographer stressed his man's *seikan* credentials (Itoyo 1974), while Kataoka's biographer (Kawada 1939) roundly declared that it was Kataoka and Hayashi who introduced Itagaki and Gotō to *seikan*. Etō Shimpei's *seikan* credentials need no stressing; Matano (1914, Vol. 1: 127ff.) gives a long extract from a most vigorous 1856 Etō paper in which he argued that Japan should learn from the West then attack the 'immoral' nations until she made the whole world tremble and Japan became the number one country in the universe. For Etō, Korea was clearly a stepping stone.

Yet to concentrate on Etō as an individual is just as dangerous as concentrating on Saigō. As was shown in chapter 2, Saga was a progressive maritime state long interested in expansion, as well as a clan that was pro-*seikan*. With the 1873 *Seihen*, both Saga and Tosa were to split into opposing factions, but that does not mean that one side was pro-*seikan* and one anti-*seikan* (see chapter 9). Both sides were in favour of imperialistic expansion.

Thus in analysing Saigō's true intent one must note that his closest associates were fervent *seikan* advocates, and that these associates must not be thought of simply as individuals but as representatives both of clans and of forces and movements which cut across clans. Trying to determine the order of precedence in the ranks of the *seikan* advocates is a sterile exercise, for *seikan* teachings had long since been nation-wide. Certainly Saigō was not among the early advocates and it is nonsense to talk of 'Saigō's *seikan-ron*'. Hence when one comes to seek evidence to support the authenticity of the above transcript, the 'character' of Saigō and the opinion of Tokutomi cannot be regarded as significant evidence. Far more importance should be attached to the following four factors: Saigō was in no sense the originator of *seikan-ron*, but merely one who adopted a firmly established doctrine of Japan's 'holy mission' to expand; his close associates were all fervid supporters of that doctrine; he himself was directly involved in preparations for an invasion of Korea; and when he was prevented from going to Korea, he and his friends all resigned from the government. These facts do not prove that the so-called transcript is a genuine copy of Saigō's actual speech to the government leaders, but they strongly suggest that he would have spoken along the same lines. If it were not a genuine transcript, one must at least applaud the author as a competent modern-day Herodotus.

The art of history writing is not so much to find the correct answers as to ask the right questions. It is an indisputable fact that the movement or faction to which Saigō belonged wished to attack Korea. There is also fairly wide acceptance that the Ōkubo faction wished to attack Korea, though under its own leadership. Surely the most important question which must be asked is why they wished to attack Korea. Most strangely, Japanese historians studiously avoid this question, so one winds up with the kind of impression left by the Mombusho high school textbooks that Japan merely intended to chastize Korea.

The debate over 1873 is also a debate over 1945 and is an important element in determining the degree of guilt. Exonerate Japan in 1873, and you have gone a long way towards exonerating Japan in 1945. So let us look briefly at the nature of Japanese imperialism.

# 8

# THE NATURE OF
# JAPANESE IMPERIALISM

The Emperor system set up in Meiji Japan, and the concomitant militarism and imperialism, were monstrosities. Japanese schools still teach that in wartime unfortunate incidents happen, and that Japan was no different to other nations. The 'enlightened' Western Japanology establishment personified by Reischauer has helped this image recasting by taking the spotlight away from political history and focusing on social history – lots of women, peasants and 'daily life' – and by arguing, for example, that America and Japan were natural allies, with the thirties just a temporary aberration. Despite the inherent value of the social histories, the sum effect has been to encourage a state of amnesia and to produce a whitewash which might be compared to that of the lunatic fringe which maintains that there was no holocaust.

Two things must be stressed: the dual role of the Japanese people as accomplices and victims, and the essential continuity of the story from 1868 to 1945. The wartime atrocities were not a thing apart, incidental sidelights that the 'serious' historian can ignore; instead they must be seen as an integral and inevitable part of the story of modern Japan, and unless they are recalled and analysed, modern Japanese history becomes surgically sanitized and grossly distorted. Second World War atrocities should be borne in mind when considering the cryptic scholarly accounts of the repressive regimes imposed on Meiji Japan and subject peoples such as the Koreans. Yet so gigantic are the sins of omission of the historical fraternity, Japanese and Western, that if one confines oneself to the 'serious' histories, one becomes hopelessly lost, at one moment enveloped in a thick fog and at another wandering through a bleak and almost empty landscape. For example, at Oxford in around 1980 I attended an academic seminar on the 'idealistic and charismatic' young Japanese officers who controlled South-east Asia during the Second World War. The guru most quoted was Joyce Lebra, a Reischauer disciple whose biography of Ōkuma praised him for the interest he took in China. It was Ōkuma, of course, who presented China with the notorious Twenty-One Demands during the First World War. Thus it is quite therapeutic to turn to the simple comments of casual observers such as actor–writer Dirk Bogarde, who served in both Europe and the East. Bogarde has thus recorded a conversation with an 'old hand': 'Remembering Belsen I said: "The Germans weren't actually Fairy Twinkle Toes." "These are worse. Unfathomable. Savages. Bound four of our chaps with bailing wire into a tidy bundle, head to feet, doused them with petrol and set 'em alight. Alive." '(Bogarde 1988: 615). Bogarde later gave a succinct summary of feelings shared by countless millions: 'Everything I had been told by old hands had horrified me into incomprehension of so barbaric an enemy'. (ibid.: 639).

Burning prisoners alive was not something which originated spontaneously in the Second World War. The 'serious' histories gloss over the barbarity of the Bakumatsu and Meiji struggles, but, as we have seen in chapter 5, garrulous old General Miura – best remembered as the honoured perpetrator of the Queen Min massacre – has recorded how Satsuma men celebrated victory with a jolly, rollicking bonfire of live Aizu prisoners. We have also seen how the standard histories describe the defeated Maki force committing synchronized *seppuku* and then lighting a fire so that the Satsuma soldiers found nothing but charred corpses. Bearing in mind the Miura witness, and the difficulties involved in thus disposing of one's own body, one must question whether the scene was not in truth similar to that described by Bogarde. Either way – incineration or *seppuku* to avoid torture and mutilation – the story emphasizes the fact that modern Japan was conceived and born in a period of 'unfathomable savagery'.

So much of Japanese history has been papered over or beautified that one needs the scepticism of the criminal lawyer, the skills of the investigative journalist and the intuition of the historical novelist to explore it fully. In recent years, several distinguished, investigative journalists have turned their attention to Japan, and though the work of these non-Japan specialists will almost inevitably be flawed and limited, this does not negate their considerable value in breaking the mould and bringing a fresh approach. In view of the still prevalent feudal divisions into political historian, social historian, etc., and the ineradicable deference to 'authority' and hierarchy, it is also important for

Westerners to familiarize themselves with the work of Japan's many fine historical novelists. Before venturing to write on Japanese history, they should first immerse themselves in Japanese society for several years, then choose their *Virgil* to guide them through the labyrinths of the Japanese historical underworld. For many years, two historical novelists, Matsumoto Seichō and Shiba Ryōtarō, contested the number one spot as Japan's best-selling author. Matsumoto Seichō made his reputation as a writer of detective stories – a not inappropriate training for one determined to get below the surface of Japanese history. He has the resources to employ a body of researchers and is perhaps better thought of as the chairman of a hand-picked committee of emancipated young academics prepared to dig deep into the vast seamy side of things.

Shiba Ryōtarō does his own painstaking research. Though his work comes under the heading of fiction, he does everything humanly possible to be factually accurate when dealing, for example, with battles. Thus when researching the great naval Battle of the Tsushima Straits, he assembled a group of distinguished ex-navy men, and together they considered the available accounts and, where discrepancies arose, jointly decided the most likely scenario. Though a good nationalist, Shiba, like Matsumoto Seichō, is prepared to open up areas shunned by the academic historian. Thus his long novel, *Tobu ga Gotoku* (Shiba 1975), on the Seinan (or Meiji year 10) Civil War of 1877 contains a section which helps illuminate the nature of the modern Japanese army.

After the Saga uprising of 1874, large numbers of the Saga men had gone to great lengths to avoid falling into the hands of the enemy. The new Western swords were of little use for *seppuku*, so they assisted each other with hangings, stranglings, etc. (Matano 1914, Vol. 2: 458–60). The leaders were captured and despatched after a brief, meaningless farce of a trial far from Tokyo (see chapter 10); so to avoid such ignominy Saigō committed *seppuku* in 1877. However, despite the widely reported wartime atrocities, Saigō had apparently believed that the government forces would show some respect for the basic canons of international law. Thus at the final battle the three field hospitals were clearly marked with large white flags. However, Nagata Hachirō-tei field hospital was attacked and the wounded all butchered and incinerated.

Shiba suggests that though some of the atrocities were no doubt perpetrated by Satsuma's old enemies, the worst offenders were the new conscript forces:

For some reason or other, great numbers of the Satsuma corpses were stripped naked by the government forces, and some of these corpses had the penis cut off and stuffed in the mouth. It was as though these Satsuma men, who had been taught that war was lofty and noble, were being shown the real nature of war by these conscripts from the farms.

(Shiba 1975, Vol. 7: 305–6)

After centuries of repression, the farm lads had shown the *samurai* that they were equally as good, and the mutilations must be seen not as momentary excesses due to the pressures of war but as an obscene gesture reflecting centuries of fear and frustration. As these acts went unchecked and unpunished, they augured ill for this new-born 'modern' Japanese army.

In their generally admirable work on the Japanese *samurai*, Ratti and Westbrook reasoned as follows:

Even before the Meiji Restoration, the military tradition had permeated the whole of Japanese life to the extent of having lost its primary identification with a single class. That it had become the sole tradition of every Japanese subject was proven by the fact that when the military class tried once again to seize power from the emperor, the armies of the 'sword-wielding samurai' were crushed on the battlefields by an imperial army whose ranks were filled with conscripts from every class, including many farmers. . . . Thereafter, bowing to expediency, the leaders of the military class gradually acknowledged that every Japanese subject was heir to the tradition they had considered their own for so many centuries, and began to exhort their fellow countrymen to think of Japan as a nation of warriors.

(Ratti and Westbrook 1973: 34)

Here the authors are about as wrong as it is possible to be. To state that Saigō was trying to seize power 'from the emperor' is ludicrous, and to claim that the government forces defeated Saigō's *samurai* because they too were imbued with the *samurai* traditions is on a par with attributing Hideyoshi's early victories in Korea to the higher Japanese morale without mentioning that the higher morale was largely due to the fact that they had guns and the Koreans did not. In 1877 the government forces triumphed because they were the Emperor's forces and because they had superior power and resources. Farmers as a class hated conscription ('the blood tax') but the many farmer uprisings it helped provoke were brutally suppressed. The 1877 war merely demonstrated that it didn't require generations of breeding and martial spirit to produce conscripts able to handle a gun and follow orders. Subsequently, it was not a case of 'bowing to expediency' in *admitting* the farmer lads to the army but of continuing to force a highly reluctant rural population to serve in the army.

Indeed, it is quite impossible to understand the 'unfathomable savagery' of the modern Japanese army if one is seduced by such fanciful pictures of a whole nation permeated with *samurai* traditions. A common lament of Takayama Hikokurō, Satō Shinen and Yoshida Shōin had been the decline of *samurai* traditions and virtues – they were hard to find even among the *samurai*, much less the farmers and merchants – and though Saigō left little in the way of documentation, there can be little doubt that he wanted an overseas war to cleanse the *samurai* 'spirit' which was then typified by the gross greed and corruption of the new army department (see chapter 10).

Ratti and Westbrook are on safer ground in arguing that the scarcity of large-scale battles the Tokugawa peace

> actually made it possible for many masters of the art of combat to delve quite deeply into the mysteries and techniques of violent confrontation and to test their findings within the repressed, hence extremely virulent and explosive, reality of individual combat.
>
> (Ratti and Westbrook 1973: 22)

In the Bakumatsu period, as the anti-Shogunate struggle intensified, this 'virulent and explosive' individual combat became a dominant and highly visible factor. The *samurai* 'code', at least in practice, was no model of medieval chivalry. Even in the early Meiji period, what was tangible and plain for all to see was the 'extremely virulent and explosive' personal combat – an ongoing scene which highlighted the need for a national army based not on these violent individuals but on disciplined conscripts; and what these conscripts took from the *samurai* was not vague traditions so much as this model of 'virulent and explosive' individual combat. The Japanese army was to be largely modelled on the German, but even back in 1740, on ascending the throne of Prussia, Frederick the Great inherited a highly disciplined army of 83,000 professional soldiers. The 'modern'

Japanese army, on the other hand, was historically shallow: the instant 'modern' army of 1877 was essentially a conscript peasant army with no historical role model other than the *samurai*'s 'virulent and explosive' individual combat.

Indeed, Watanabe Shoichi (1980) has advanced the provocative concept of modern Japan as being essentially a peasant state. For most of the Tokugawa and Meiji periods, peasants probably constituted 80 per cent of the population. Moreover, with the Tokugawa peace, many *samurai* were forced back onto the land, and even where they maintained their *samurai* status, they lived the lives of peasants. This was especially so in Satsuma and Chōshū, which had lost much of their territory after Sekigahara. Thus traditionally most of Japan had literally been a peasant society. Watanabe uses the pejorative term, 'Don Peasant' – a narrow, down-trodden community given to sudden explosions such as those protesting the granting of legal equality to the *hinin*. If we are to begin to understand the 'unfathomable savagery' of the modern Japanese army we must set aside the romantic picture of a whole nation imbued with the spirit of *bushi* and picture instead this Don Peasant army of 1877 which was launched to lay to rest the power of their traditional oppressors, the *samurai*. This they did, and the 'modern' Japanese army born in this vicious, nasty civil war, was on its way.

It may be argued that the modern Japanese army was thus a people's army, and that some of the greatest armies of modern times have been people's armies. But the American revolutionary army, for example, fought for independence, and its soldiers had been accustomed to a large degree of autonomy and equality, and to traditional British civil rights, while the French revolutionary forces fought under the banner of 'liberty, equality and fraternity'. The Meiji revolution, however, had been in essence a power struggle. The country had been moving towards consensus, but Satchō wanted dominion, not consensus.

The Battle of Sekigahara in 1600 had essentially been between east Japan and west Japan, and east Japan had won. Now Satsuma and Chōshū were to reverse Sekigahara and establish their own domination of the political, economic and social life of the nation. They had rallied support under the slogan 'Drive out the foreigner', but once entrenched in power they cynically adopted the policies of the Shogunate and fully opened the country. Farmer attempts to participate in the Meiji revolution had been rudely rebuffed, and they were given no place in the Meiji government. Satsuma, Chōshū and Tosa donated troops to form a national army (see chapter 10), and though others were recruited later the 'Chōshū Army' and the 'Satsuma Navy' remained instruments of Satchō domination.

Japan's security problems were essentially internal. Not only in 1945 but also in the mid-nineteenth century was Japan treated with a generosity rare in international affairs. The Western nations wanted trade, not dominion. Had they been bent on conquest, little Japan would have been powerless. She displayed great skill in playing off one country against another and in avoiding the too ardent embrace of her new 'friends', but the fact remains that she was able to pass and enforce laws preventing foreigners from acquiring Japanese land, mines, railways, etc. and thus maintained a level of economic independence which would be the envy of much of the world today. The security problem was not the threat of foreign invasion but the threat posed by the constant activities of *samurai* who felt that their revolution had been betrayed, who bitterly resented the Satchō domination and who threatened to begin the charge into the mainland independently of the government.

The Meiji revolution had come complete with the slogan *seikan* and foreign aggression was clearly on the agenda; but for the Satchō government the immediate task was to break the residual power of the hostile *samurai* groups. This was the first task assigned to the new 'modern' Japanese army. The farm lads, already highly indignant that the *hinin* had been declared their equal, were dragged from their farms, and forced to fight for Satchō against their old oppressors, the *samurai*, in a civil war. They had been given shoes, taught how to eat exotic dishes like curry rice and trained to handle a gun. But this conscript Don Peasant army had little in common with the great people's armies of history; devoid on the one hand of tradition, bonding and true professionalism and on the other of ideology, motivation and role models (save for the *samurai*'s 'virulent and explosive' individual combat and perhaps the ghoulish deeds of Hideyoshi's armies 300 years earlier), this 'instant army' soon lapsed into barbarism.

A mere seventeen years after this 1877 war, this 'modern' Japanese army was sent overseas to attack Korea and China. Oblivious to the international conventions of war which had developed over centuries in the West, they committed appalling atrocities which went unreported in the Japanese press and have in effect been written out of Japanese history. These atrocities were thus described in J. Creelman's short cable of 11 December 1894 to the *New York World*:

The Japanese troops entered Port Arthur on November 21 and massacred practically the entire population in cold blood. The defenceless and unarmed inhabitants were butchered in their houses and their bodies were unspeakably mutilated. There was an unrestrained reign of murder which continued for three days. The whole town was plundered with appalling atrocities. It was the first stain upon Japanese civilisation. The Japanese in this instance relapsed into barbarism. All pretence that circumstances justified the atrocities are false. The civilised world will be horrified by the details. The foreign correspondents, horrified by the spectacle, left the army in a body.

(Knightley 1975: 58)

Even today this story remains virtually unknown in Japan. Thus after years of researching Japanese accounts, Shiba, in his best-selling novel (1972a) on the Russian War of 1904–5, concluded in good faith that the Western correspondents had been prejudiced and that the Japanese were therefore justified in keeping them at arm's length in 1904–5.

Whether one is talking about 1877, 1904–5 or any subsequent incident or war, these atrocities were an integral and inevitable part of Japanese militarism. In his fine 1989 book on Emperor Hirohito, journalist Edward Behr quotes a Nanking veteran, Azuma Shiro, who returned to China in 1987 to apologize for the 1937 Rape of Nanking.

He, like his fellow-soldiers who impaled babies on bayonets, buried prisoners alive and then ran over them in tanks, gang raped women aged from twelve to eighty and executed them when they were beyond satisfying their sexual needs, did not do so in a sudden fit of uncontrolled, undisciplined rage: all acted on orders handed down from on high. This is the message several veteran Japanese ex-servicemen have courageously and stubbornly imparted recently to tiny audiences of concerned Japanese citizens – mostly peace groups and anti-nuclear lobbies.

(Behr 1989: 197ff.)

The rationale repeated by Behr is that the Chinese were terrorized to discourage further resistance. This explanation, however, is far too simple. There is something inherently odd in the assertion that soldiers who raged through a city raping half-dead women tied to lamp posts were simply obeying orders. The atrocities were routinely committed over a long period, regardless of the state of the war. For example, in 1894–5 Chinese resistance was pathetically weak and in both 1877 and 1894–5 many of the worst atrocities were committed after victory had been assured. Hence this 'unfathomable savagery' must be analysed more deeply. But first let us carry the story on to the Second World War, and consider three of the most significant forms of atrocity.

In the Second World War Korean girls were rounded up, ostensibly as medical assistants, etc., to serve at the front. The irony of the name Jongshin Dae (or Teishin Dai in Japanese) is lost in the standard translation 'Volunteer Force', for *jongshin* literally means to offer one's body, and the actual role of these girls, some as young as eleven, was to 'serve' the Japanese troops. These unfortunate women have been the subject of at least one book (*Jongshin Dae* by Yim Jong-Han) and several recent articles. Obviously, it is impossible to give statistics, but Korean estimates range around the 200,000 mark. Again, of course, we have the problem of evidence. At the end of the war, not only were all documents burnt, but it would seem most of the girls were also disposed of. Yim gives an account, for example, of the girls in Burma being herded into caves which were then dynamited. A young monk, Seu Nam Hyun, has spent much time tracking down survivors in Japan itself. He claims to have found some hundreds shut away for mental problems, but instead of being in a regular mental institution they are in a leprosy sanatorium to make them inaccessible (*Hoju Tōa* 12.10.1990).

Of course, nationals of other countries also committed rape, and in Hiroshima, for example, one sometimes hears whispers of how, at war's end, Koreans about to be repatriated ran amok at Hiroshima station and raped schoolgirls. If true, such incidents are deplorable, but they cannot be equated with the systematic gang rape of conquered peoples as part of a policy deliberately instituted by the central government.

Vivisection of POWs and conquered peoples was likewise not merely the work of a few sadistic individuals, but was a part of the system. After the war, the story was fairly effectively buried, and it is only in recent years that writers such as popular novelist Morimura Seichi have rolled back the curtain. A balanced summary is given by court-watcher Kawahara Toshiaki in his somewhat syrupy 1990 book on Hirohito.

The unit in question consisted of a number of doctors and scientists gathered under the cover of the Kwantung Army Veterinarian Division. In addition to research into biological and chemical weaponry they also carried out inhumane and immoral experiments on thousands of Chinese and Allied prisoners-of-war, including such atrocities as injecting victims with germs and vivisecting them.

Obviously it was a matter that the Far Eastern Tribunal should have investigated, but due to strong objections from the U.S. Army the matter was dropped. The U.S. side quickly gathered up all the secret data available on the subject for fear that it might fall into the hands of the Russians.

(Kawahara 1990: 172)

The matter is put even more bluntly by Behr:

The story of 'Unit 731' is probably the darkest single chapter in Japan's immediate pre-war history – and as we shall see later, it is an equally dark chapter in American history too, an indelible stain on Macarthur's reputation, adding to the farce of the 'Tokyo Trials'.

(Behr 1989: 202)

Quite obviously a deal was made with the perpetrators of these hideous crimes against humanity: they got their freedom and America got their scientific data. The thirties as a 'temporary aberration' was not a historical judgement made by impartial academics but rather an 'inspired' policy imposed with savage cynicism by the US Army.

The notorious Unit 731 began its life in Japan, but later the headquarters were shifted to Ping Fan, 40 miles south of Harbin in Manchuria, presumably to be near the supply of *maruta* ('round-logs' – the POWs). After the experiments, the organs of the *maruta* were regularly bottled and flown back to Tokyo and used to illustrate lectures to the trainee army doctors, thereby establishing the injection of deadly germs and vivisection as normal, acceptable procedures. Of course, the scientific aspect was stressed. How much lung does a person need to survive? A US airman was strapped to a table, and, without anaesthetic, his chest was opened up and, at carefully regulated periods, his lungs were sliced away until eventually he died. Experiment ended. Data obtained. But one must recall the constantly recurring theme of widespread atrocities involving mutilations, and one can only suspect that there is a connecting link between these officially condoned mutilations and the officially arranged vivisection.

War-time cannibalism may not have been an official part of state policy, but it arose as a response to that policy. Towards the end of the war, especially in New Guinea, Japanese soldiers ate both natives and prisoners. Then when the supply of 'black pork' and 'white pork' ran out they turned to 'yellow pork', devouring their own men of most tender years. It was done in the name of the Emperor – the military caste system gone mad. Cannibalism as a theme made a considerable impact in post-war Japan. For example, Ōoka Shōhei, who had served in the Philippines, wrote a widely acclaimed novel, *Nobi (Fire on the Plain)* which gives a gruesome account of the disintegration of all normal human bonds. Another ex-soldier devoted many years to tracking down some of the culprits, then forced himself into their homes accompanied by relatives of the victims. He extracted confessions as the cameras whirred. In 1986 I saw his riveting documentary at a small theatre in Shibuya. The exclusively young audience waited quietly in long queues and afterwards left amid a most deathly hush. It is still incredibly difficult for them to find out about their past.

War-time cannibalism, like war-time rape, was not confined to the Japanese. But there were two distinguishing features: they partook to please the Emperor and they dined along class lines, the officers and NCOs eating the most junior privates. Duty to the Emperor excused any conduct.

As it is sometimes claimed that the Emperor system originated in the 1890s, we should note how the Emperor's name was already being used in the Bakumatsu and early Meiji periods. One may instance the young officers Saigō sent to reconnoitre in Korea and Manchuria – a fair indication, as the Black Dragon History (Kokuryūkai Hen 1966: 37ff.) points out, that Saigō had grander plans than just taking Korea. On their return, these young officers found that Saigō and his allies had resigned and *seikan* had been shelved. Infuriated, they made an unsuccessful attempt to assassinate Iwakura (Matano 1914, Vol. 2: 424–5). Betrayed by a lost sandal, eight were captured and interrogated. Seven soon confessed, but one, Shinomura Yoshiaki, refused, and was subject to the traditional 'interrogation'. When he proved stubborn, 'interrogators' stressed the pain the interrogation was causing the Emperor. Shinomura was likewise feeling a certain amount of discomfort, as the stones loaded onto his legs had broken every bone. Eventually, to save the Emperor further pain, he confessed and was allowed an honourable death.

Just as one must reject the romantic picture of a whole nation imbued with the *samurai* spirit, so too one must be careful not to take the Emperor system at face value. One must never lose sight of a few basic facts: the Meiji revolution was a power struggle, not an ideological war; the Meiji government was a corrupt military dictatorship or oligarchy; Satchō not only grabbed political power, but went on to turn much of Japan into a Satchō colony and themselves into the new 'aristocracy'; and Japanese imperialism was essentially economic imperialism. These questions will be dealt with later though, of course, they cannot be covered fully in the space of one volume. What we must do here is to deromanticize the story, to stress the continuity and to lay bare the utter brutality, ruthlessness and cynicism involved. Only then can one begin to comprehend not only the 1868–1945 saga, but also the story of post-war and contemporary Japan.

The documentary on war-time cannibalism was not just about war and cannibalism. Perhaps 'sincerity' should be regarded as the central theme. As one looked at these well-fed, well-housed, company director-type cannibals, it was a little difficult to take seriously the idea that they had dined on their young men to please the Emperor. It might have been more convincing if, after the war, they had shown deep remorse – adopted, perhaps, a religious way of life, or tried to help the families of the devoured. Instead they apparently felt that they had 'got away with it', thanks to the Emperor.

This atrocity might be taken as a metaphor for the Emperor system. Emperor Kōmei, Meiji's father, was most probably assassinated, and the finger is usually pointed at Iwakura and his sister. Thus an attempt to assassinate Iwakura was not necessarily all that displeasing to Meiji. Satchō had used the Emperor party and their slogan *sonnō jōi* to gain power. They then turned their backs on their Emperor party allies and cynically adopted the policies of the Shogunate. In 1873 they opposed the projected expedition to Korea, but having forced out Saigō and Etō over this issue, they promptly sent a party to force open Korea.

After the 1881 *Seihen* and the Mitsubishi-led attack on their prerogatives, they found themselves isolated, and so turned back to their erstwhile allies, the Emperor party. The outcome was the Emperor system. That system owed nothing to the personal wishes of the Emperor Meiji, a sincere statesman who strove to play the role of a constitutional monarch. Those who imposed the system on the Emperor and on the nation were able to maintain their power and to reward themselves with the highest titles and great wealth in the forms of mines and land holdings, both in Japan and overseas. There were, of course, some 'true believers', but few such could be found among the pragmatic men who took over in 1868.

It must be stressed that the Satchō–military–*zaibatsu* rule of the Empire and of Japan itself constitutes one story – assimilation in the worst sense of the word. In Japan, daughters were in effect chattels – goods which could be sold to brothels (for the benefit of the family). There they were virtually prisoners, let out only on rare occasions and then under an armed escort. Once the factory system started up, the position of the factory girls was little better, for they too were closely confined. The life expectancy of the girls in the brothels was not great and tuberculosis was rife, but they were made to work till the end. Sending such girls to the front was an accepted practice. Though even more brutal and degraded, the treatment of the Korean women was essentially an extension of the way Japanese girls were treated. Nor is it surprising that the captured Australian nurses found that conditions in the women's camp were far worse than in the men's, though there is, perhaps, some mitigation in the fact that the men who were massacred were bayonetted, whereas the nurses were driven into the sea and shot (Simons 1954).

Indeed, the imperial story generally highlights the horrors of the Satchō rule of Japan itself. One major reason for 'taking civilization' to Korea was to get hold of Korean rice, not just to sell in Japan but also in order to make a killing in the world market. Inoue Kaoru was one of the founding fathers of the present Japanese Establishment, and even now the upwardly mobile academic sees little profit in challenging his reputation. Inoue was to form the companies which gained control of Korean rice, completely dislocating their economy and causing untold hardship. When Korean representatives came to Japan to protest, the minister they had to approach was Inoue (*Segai Inoue Kō Den* 1933, Vol. 3: 436 *et seq.*).

Earlier Inoue and his group had secured control of Chōshū rice – a shady business which has never been completely unravelled. Later it was Inoue at the Treasury who made the decision to replace the old rice tax with a money tax. He and his colleagues at the Treasury foresaw that this would cause problems, for in many regions there was a shortage of money. They therefore made their contingency plans. Resigning from their posts, key officials hired a ship, sailed north to the most troubled regions and bought up the rice very cheaply. Masuda, for example, later wrote gleefully about what a killing they had made (Nagai 1939: 167). Of course it also stimulated the supply of girls to the brothels, and led to a wave of *ikke shinjū*.

The simple fact is that this early Meiji government was a corrupt military government of the type to be seen in many newly emerging Asian and African countries. The story of Korean rice was essentially an extension of the story of Japanese rice – the sort of vicious story invariably ignored by Western historians writing fulsome nonsense about 'the quality of Meiji leadership'.

The role of the secret police deserves special mention. The Tokugawas relied heavily on torture and on spies who toured the land disguised as pedlars, priests, etc. The Meiji government likewise used spies, and an elaborate spy network was built up on the mainland (Kokuryūkai Hen 1966, Vol. 1). Once Korea was annexed the spy network was extended, and the role of the secret police within Japan itself was also expanded. This traditional combination of spies and torture was to help define the nature of Japanese imperialism.

We must later look in more detail at the unsuccessful struggle to establish the Rule of Law. Here let us merely stress the continued widespread use of torture. As in most countries, torture had been systematically used since ancient times, but it had been made worse by the Bakufu (Tezuka 1956: 110–13). With the *ishin* it was, if anything, intensified. 'Justice' revolved around using torture to gain confessions. The four most popular forms seem to have been the rack, water torture, loading the victims' legs with stones, and stringing them up by the thumbs. Until the end of 1870, each region was allowed to continue its old legal practices, so the Bakufu system of torture remained in place, even though there were early attempts to moderate its use: it was not to be applied to the sick, to women within 100 days of giving birth or to those over seventy and under fifteen, while the four days of the year relating to imperial deaths were set aside as torture-free days. But even these modifications did not make Western residents any keener to submit to Japanese 'justice'.

This torture was not something affecting a tiny minority but was an essential part of the social fabric. Noted liberal, Osaki Yukio (Isa 1951: 47–8), the son of a low-ranking police officer who served in Takasaki, Ise and Kumamato, recalled how one of his father's duties was to 'interrogate' prisoners. To make his somewhat weakly son strong, he would drag him along to watch the tortures and subsequent executions and *seppuku*. Squeamish young Yukio received many a paternal lecture, for often he would hardly watch at all, and he did not join the other children when they poked about inside disembowelled bodies with sticks.

Long-continued practices seem to enter the national psyche, to resurface at times of crisis. Stringing people up by the thumbs and leaving them to gurgle till they died was a practice used in the seventeenth century to test the faith of Christians (Endo 1982). It resurfaced in the 1960s when the Red Army dealt thus with the followers whose fighting spirit was declining (Yomiuri 1972: 257). In the nature of things, there is no record of what torture was used in Japan's own prisons and in those of her Empire but there can be little doubt that its use was widespread.

Contemporary Western criticism of Japanese imperial excesses tended to be muted. For example, Hamilton wrote in 1904 urging Britain to stick with Japan, but he noted 'the wave of colonisation that lapped' Korea's shores after 1875 and admitted that none was as detested as the Japanese. 'Nor is the prejudice remarkable when it is considered that it is the scum of the Japanese nation that has settled down upon Korea' (Hamilton 1904: 96, 135–6). In their 'extravagant arrogance' they had produced 'an abominable travesty of the civilisation which they profess to have studied'.

Another pro-Japanese writer was longtime Keio teacher, Lloyd, who confessed that 'if half the rumours that come from that unhappy land are true, it would seem as though Japanese adventurers in the peninsular were deliberately setting themselves to destroying the fair name of Japan by the most reckless and unscrupulous behaviour' (Lloyd 1909: 66–7). Such muted criticism is better understood if we bear in mind the traditional forms of torture, the old doctrine of *hinin*, and the Second World War atrocities.

## THE JAPANESE AS VICTIMS

A realization that Japanese internal and external rule constituted one integrated story brings us to the question of the Japanese people as victims. In 1894 the new, 'modern' Don Peasant Japanese army became the full-scale instrument of the growing war machine. The Japanese people were now the accomplices of the imperialists. The Chinese were defeated with ridiculous ease. Territory was won and fortunes made. This war marked the first flowering of genuine popular Japanese nationalism.

Then came the so-called Three Power Intervention. Germany, Russia and France demanded that Japan hand back the territory gained on the mainland. She kept Taiwan, maintained her dominant position in Korea and was compensated with larger reparations, but she felt that she had been discriminated against and victimized, especially as those three powers soon carved out Chinese territory for themselves. Thus egged on by Britain and America, she used her reparations for military expansion. The 1895 victory had led not to joy but to a decade of cruel austerity.

The Russian War of 1904–5 is often referred to as the first modern war. Losses on both sides were horrendous (Warner 1974: 659). Towards the end, Japan was relying heavily on reservists. Though she had gained spectacular victories both on land and at sea, she was exhausted, as Russia well knew, so at the peace table she gained but little. As this was utterly incomprehensible to the average Japanese, the peace settlement was greeted with widespread rioting. Again there was the feeling of having been cheated and victimized. Of course, some fortunes had been made, a son-in-law of the 'enlightened' Fukuzawa Yukichi being without peer as a war profiteer (Miyadera 1953). Korea was retained and soon annexed. An Iwasaki (Mitsubishi) son-in-law was made the Korean Minister of Agriculture and Commerce. The ruthless policy of driving the Koreans off their land was accelerated and Mitsubishi became Korea's largest landowner, while other major *zaibatsu*, in which the Japanese political leaders were deeply involved, were rewarded with Korean mines.

Yet that brutal, exhausting and profitless war hung like a dark shadow not only over the generation that fought it, but also over the generation not yet born. It is probably no exaggeration to say that the psyche of Japan had been changed. Japan was becoming a dark and brooding nation. Social security was virtually non-existent and the plight of widows, orphans and bereaved parents was a blight upon the land. The whole nation had been loaded with a heavy material and psychological burden. The war had settled little, save perhaps to establish Russia as a 'traditional' enemy. Now Korea was being built up, as had been urged since Tokugawa days, as a base for further expansion, and, as had occurred with Britain, the possession of empire was soon changing the motherland. But whereas in the case of Britain the effects had been salutary, for Japan they were calamitous.

Akashi Motojiro (1864–1919), a shadowy figure, is dealt with in the historical encyclopaedias but he seems not to have attracted a biographer. Born in Fukuoka, the home of the Black Dragon Society, he studied in Germany then returned to Europe during the Russian War to set up what was in effect a one-man spy network. His main task was to contact the 'freedom fighters', be they Finns, Poles or Russian Jews and Communists, Lenin included.

Ironically, this underground experience was to be used in Korea, but there he was consigned the task of leading the campaign *against* the Korean freedom fighters. The refinements which were developed there were carried back to Japan itself and Japan likewise degenerated into a virulent type of police state. The wartime atrocities are not 'war history'; rather they are the key which unlocks the history of Japanese 'colonial' rule in all its brutality, ruthlessness and cynicism. They also give a good indication of the chains which were being drawn ever tighter around the Japanese people themselves.

Thus though the conscript forces became almost overnight the tools of the growing war-machine and accomplices of the imperialists, not only the young soldiers but also their families back home lived under a heavy shadow which did not lift when 'peace' came. Shiba Ryōtarō (1972a) has captured the pathetic plight of the young conscripts in his description of the scene outside Ryojun (Port Arthur) as General Nogi addresses these youths before sending them off on yet another suicidal and pointless frontal attack. The world knew Nogi as the victor of Port Arthur, for he was photographed riding into the city once it finally fell. In truth, Nogi was a fine poet and a man of outstanding 'spiritual' qualities, but he was a highly incompetent general who owed his promotion to the fact that he was a Chōshū man.

At Ryojun the Russians had modern machine guns embedded in thick concrete fortifications overlooking a large, open square. Time and again Nogi launched frontal attacks – vast waves which advanced, crashed and fell. Eventually, Nogi was rescued by his clansman General Kodama, who took Hill 203 (*Ni-rei-san*) overlooking the city, and from there he launched a decisive bombardment. Nogi's main positive contribution was a small gem of a poem, *Ni-rei-san*. The Japanese language lends itself to double meanings, and *Ni-rei-san* means not only 203, but also 'the mountain of your spirits' – a moving epitaph to those who died there.

In earlier ages, the *samurai* had been free to abandon an unsuccessful general but these modern conscript youths were free neither to move a muscle nor to utter a sound. Nogi's references to the loss of his own sons left them unmoved, and they listened numbly, mere specks of humanity caught up in a giant machine. Inevitably, their thoughts turned to the homes and families they would never see again, and though they may have died with '*banzai*' ('May the Emperor live 10,000 years') on their lips, it is ridiculous to picture them as fanatical warriors imbued with the spirit of *bushido*. They were simple, conscripted farmer lads and died as such.

During that same war, a young woman, Yosano Akiko, had the temerity to publish a remarkable poem (Yosano 1970: 34–7) urging her brother not to get killed in the war – a shocking affront to the Emperor. Around 1970, I watched a televised concert in which a leading actor suddenly launched into the opening lines of that poem – 'Shini tamau koto nakare' ('Don't you die'). I have never witnessed a more spontaneous and deeply moving response from an audience. The chord struck went beyond a simple anti-war feeling. The deep gut reaction sprang from the utter helplessness of those youths and the palpable futility of their sacrifice – a feeling of helplessness and futility which sank deep into the national consciousness.

## EMPEROR HIROHITO

No summary of Japanese imperialism can avoid the question of Hirohito's role. His approaching death inspired a spate of articles and various books debating his war guilt. Journalist Behr turned in an impressive work with a general verdict of guilty. It is hard to find fault with this verdict. For the historian, however, it is perhaps better to avoid words such as 'guilty' and to look dispassionately at Hirohito's role: true believer, ruthless cynic or helpless victim? If one accepts the proviso that strict consistency is not a normal human attribute, it is reasonably clear that Hirohito was a true believer.

In their systematic 'exhumation' of the history of the thirties (Matsumoto 1965, Vols 7–13), the Matsumoto Seichō team worked through the many extant letters of the young officers who terrorized the Japanese government and helped drive it along the road to war. In these letters, the name which recurs with remarkable regularity is not that of Kita Ikki, the leading Japanese fascist, but Yoshida Shōin, the young Bakumatsu teacher whose little Hagi *juku* was attended by most of the Chōshū men who were to become leaders in the Meiji government. In the 1850s Shōin was already advocating (see chapter 11) that Japan not only attack and occupy Korea and Manchuria, but also take over the Russian territories in

the north and Taiwan and the Philippines in the south, as well as
setting up colonies in Australia. When his extremist teachings led
to his execution in Edo, the small group who collected, washed and
re-assembled the body included Kido Takayoshi and Itō Hirobumi,
later Japan's first prime minister. The small town Satchō men were
to elevate themselves to the status of the new aristocracy, and a Kido
descendant, Kido Kōichi, was to be the longtime Keeper of the Privy
Seal and confidant of the young Emperor Hirohito. Kido's diaries
are perhaps the most important source on Hirohito.

Shōin had been taught by his uncle, Tamagi Bunnosuke, his
father's youngest brother, who had opened a private school, Shoka
Sonjuku, in 1842. There were no buildings or fees and the pupils
were mostly farmers and fishing lads.

Bunnosuke, a fanatical exponent of *kokugaku* teaching, was Shōin's
teacher from the age of five to eighteen. It was mostly classical
one-to-one teaching, with any self-indulgent movement, such as
brushing away a fly, provoking a savage slap or the cancellation
of the lesson. Bunnosuke was to outlive Shōin, and after the *ishin*
his pupils were to include another relative, Nogi Maresuke. The
closeness of the ties with the Nogi family is indicated by the fact
that Bunnosuke adopted Maresuke's younger brother Masayoshi as
his heir. In 1876 Masayoshi took part in the Maebara uprising and
was killed. It seems that Bunnosuke himself was involved, or at least
that he had inspired Masayoshi's participation. On 6 November
1876 Bunnosuke climbed to the mountain grave of his ancestors
and committed *seppuku*. It was a most unusual *seppuku* in that he
had a woman, Shōin's eldest sister, perform the *kaishaku*.

For some time, Nogi and his brother had been Tamagi's only
live-in students. Thus they were subject to the same emotional and
doctrinal pressure as Shōin had been (Shiba 1972b and 1972c). After
the Russian War Nogi became headmaster of the Peers School and
private tutor to the future Emperor Hirohito and his brother. The ties
between Nogi and Hirohito went deep. As was usual with imperial
babies, Hirohito was sent to live outside the palace. Satsuma's
General Ōyama was first approached (Kawahara 1990: 14) but
he declined the honour. Then another Satsuma man, Vice-Admiral
Kawamura Sumiyoshi, accepted, and Hirohito was moved into his
Azabu home. The second son, Chichibu, born a year later in 1902,
was also despatched to Kawamura's, but in 1904 Kawamura died,
so the children were removed and a special kindergarten was set
up within the palace. Two years later they were sent to the Peers

School. Thus Hirohito's contacts with the unstable, dissolute man who sired him were minimal, and Nogi became teacher, spiritual guide and father figure.

Nogi at and after Ryojun presents the figure of a man suffering from complete, irreversible nervous exhaustion. As his poems indicate, he was a man of great sensitivity – not the person to oversee such brutal slaughter. Having lost his own sons, it seems he long yearned for death and was sustained only by his 'faith' and his worship of the Emperor. Thus when Meiji died in 1912, he and his wife followed in a ceremonial suicide. Two days before this *junshi*, Nogi visited the eleven-year-old crown prince and explained his 'military duties':

> He also gave Hirohito two books, traditional works on the duties of the throne, the important parts of which he had marked in red for the crown prince's benefit, with instructions to have his attendants read the difficult passages to him until he was old enough to read them himself. It was clear that the general had come to bid him farewell.
>
> (ibid.: 22)

Apparently the boy took the news of the double suicide quite calmly. The picture surely is of a little boy already playing a larger than life role. In 1914 a special school was set up for him and five classmates. Again a Satsuma man, General Tōgō, was put in charge. However, Hirohito seems to have found Tōgō coarse and gluttonous, and he never approached Nogi's influence. In those years (1914–21) the major influence was Sugiura Jūgo, his ethics teacher. (The word 'ethics' is somewhat misleading. In post-war Japan, it was largely the government's desire to re-introduce a course in 'ethics' or 'moral training' that caused a deep and lasting rift between the Education Ministry and the teachers' unions, for traditionally 'ethics' meant indoctrination centred on complete obedience to parents and state and on the glory of dying for the Emperor. In other words, 'ethics' was taught to produce an obedient and unquestioning nation at a time when all dissent was being even more brutally suppressed.) It is worth noting that Tōgō sometimes sat in on these ethics lessons and nodded approvingly – that same Tōgō who in 1894 had sunk the Chinese troop ships before war was declared, then rescued all the British advisers and calmly watched every last Chinese drown. For 'ethics' we should read 'religious instruction' – intensive indoctrination in the religion which taught that both Japan and its emperors were divine and destined again to rule the world.

Sugiura had been born in 1855 into the family of a clan Confucian scholar in the small Zensho clan in Omi, a region with strong Tokugawa ties. After studying in Tokyo as a clan student, he spent the years 1876–80 in England majoring in chemistry. Back in Japan, he held a succession of distinguished education posts and also became a regular contributor to the leading newspapers *Yomiuri* and *Tokyo Asahi*. He seems to have developed ties with Toyoma and the Black Dragon Society, and was involved in the opposition to Ōkuma's Treaty Revision plans which were to be shelved when a bomb thrown by a Black Dragon fanatic blew off one of Ōkuma's legs. In 1890 he was elected to the first parliament but resigned the following year.

It is unlikely that a study of Hirohito's actions, or even his words, will ever reveal conclusive proof of the role he played or his own thoughts about that role. In her classic *Chrysanthemum and the Sword*, American anthropologist Ruth Benedict gives the case of the American housewife who, in autumn, daily remarked to the housemaid, 'Just look at all those leaves!' The maid soon fled and, when found and questioned, she explained that her ex-mistress had ordered her to rake up all the leaves every day. The Emperor's comments and orders would usually have been even less direct. The 'Just look at all the leaves' sort of order does not stand up very well in either the law courts or the historians' court, and as the post-war articles on Sato Shinen (see p.63 *et seq.*) indicate, Emperor apologists would have used it as proof that the Emperor was environmentally conscious.

Surely the key to Hirohito lies in the fact that he was a religious leader. The Pope's position does not afford irrefutable proof that he actually believes the Christian doctrine, but it is strong circumstantial evidence. Hirohito may be compared to the infant chosen to be Dalai Lama. Given the intense indoctrination and programming from birth, it is difficult to conceive of Hirohito not being a believer. The cornerstones of that religion were that Japan and its emperors were holy and that the world must be restored to 'harmony' under the Emperor. For Hirohito to have opposed 'the forward policy' would have been tantamount to his declaring, 'I am no longer a Believer.' It is almost inconceivable that this highly programmed, brain-washed young man ever seriously entertained such an idea, and even if he had done so he had no real outlet for such thoughts. Bearing in mind Hirohito's enforced remoteness, and the fact that he was surrounded by Satchō, military and *zaibatsu* 'advisers', the idea of his renouncing his divinity and his 'mission' is simply bizarre. For him, dissent was even more unthinkable than it had become for the average citizen. His role was to urge caution and to sustain the Faith. Questions such as 'Was Hirohito guilty?', and 'Could Hirohito have prevented the war?' are somewhat barren exercises if not quite meaningless.

Instead of concentrating on Hirohito's words and deeds, one should be examining his thoughts; and those 'thoughts' should be seen not as the product of an individual brain but as the almost inevitable response to a system of ideas going back far into Japanese history. A reading of the Kido Kōichi diaries (1984) should remove all doubts about Hirohito being in the *kokugaku* mainstream. He talked much about his desire for peace, so on the face of it Kawahara (1990: 206) is being quite reasonable in concluding that 'his honest virtue as a champion of peace and international harmony stood out for over sixty years'. Hirohito also repeatedly expressed to Kido his concern that the people did not fully appreciate the efforts he was making for peace. But this must all be dubbed pure *kokugaku-speak*. Kido's entry for 13 October 1941 reads as follows:

> The Emperor said the following: At present there is practically no hope for the successful conclusion of negotiations between the U.S.A. and this country. And we will have to issue an imperial proclamation of war on the morrow of our declaration of war upon the U.S.A. As for the attitude of the people toward such an imperial message, there remains much to be desired, for they have always ignored his intention of emphasising world peace and the hearty cooperation of the pen and the sword to that end. These intentions were especially stressed in the message issued upon Japan's withdrawal from the League of Nations, and the one issued when the Tripartite Pact was signed. It is very regrettable that these messages were interpreted as a challenge to both the U.S.A. and England. He said that it was his earnest desire that with the aid of Prince Konoye and myself, his real intention be expressed in the message of the proclamation of war.
>
> (Kido 1984: 311)

In other words, the 'peace efforts' in question were taking Japan out of the League of Nations, signing the Axis Pact, and declaring war on America – all very consistent when one remembers that lasting peace would come only when the whole world had been brought into 'harmony' under Japanese rule. These 'peace' initiatives would have been applauded by Sugiura, Nogi, Shōin and Tamagi. Any further progress in understanding Hirohito is likely to come from research not on the man himself, but on his teachers and his teachers' teachers, going back well beyond the Bakumatsu period.

The question of Hirohito's 'guilt' should not be allowed to distract attention away from those who forced the Emperor system upon the nation – from power groups which still form the backbone of the Japanese Establishment. There can be little doubt that the average Japanese regards Akihito, his wife and family with respect and affection, yet they know that Meiji, a wise, sincere and kindly man, was turned into the symbol of the iniquitous Emperor system. Not unnaturally, therefore, many still worry about 'the people behind the throne', and the use which might yet again be made of the royal family.

Once more it must be stressed that Japanese imperialism was essentially economic imperialism. The Emperor system and the Emperor himself were tools, as, indeed, were the Japanese people. Important though they were as tools, the Emperor system and the Emperor must not be allowed to dominate our thinking. The major purpose of this work is to reveal the origins of Japanese economic imperialism and to chip away at the myths which still underpin the mystique of modern Japan. Despite an initial post-war flurry, the power of those who masterminded Japanese expansion was not broken, the economic aggressiveness remained, and the Emperor system 'ethos' of Japan as Number One did not just evaporate and fade away. Yet the Emperor factor continues to bedevil our thinking. Thus Behr ends his incisive analysis with the following pat conclusion: 'Part of the Japanese "uniqueness" has been the ability not only to accept over the years, a version of history and of the Emperor's role, which is palpably, demonstrably false, but to impose it on the rest of the world' (Behr 1989: 466–7).

This is as false as the Mombusho's version of Japanese history. It was the Americans who decided that the Emperor should remain, and, generally speaking, not only the army but also academia and the media took their cue from this decision. The Emperor, of course, had to be not guilty, the war had to be downgraded to a temporary disagreement between two natural friends and Japanese militarism had to be shown to be not really so bad and in any case irrelevant to the post-war period. Rather than Japan imposing its palpably false version of its history on the world, it has been a case of America, determined that Japan should re-arm, attempting to impose its version on Japan. Though a uniformity of 'thought' was imposed in the thirties, it is highly misleading to write of post-war Japan as one identity 'accepting' a version of history. There is great diversity. The battle over history teaching still rages. Most post-war Americans writing about Japanese history have striven to be 'Japanese people friendly'. But the ultimate verdict will probably be that collectively they have failed. They have strayed too far from the ivory tower.

## THE MODERN IMPERIAL CLUB

One further question should be addressed: namely, the common Japanese claim that modern Japan was born into an imperialistic world and that Japan's imperialism differed little from that of other powers.

If a division is to be made, it should be between the older, experienced imperial powers and the new arrivals – Germany, Belgium, Japan and America. A detailed comparative history would no doubt prove instructive. Here there is clearly some justification, at least for some decades, of the Reischauer thesis of Japan and America as natural allies, for America was quick to 'appreciate' the Japanese position in Korea, in return for a similar 'appreciation' of the American position in the Philippines. The methods, too, were not all that different, especially during the revolt of 1899–1902:

> Wholesale and indiscriminate killing by American troops had depopulated large sections of the country. There were complaints that the troops had on one occasion been ordered 'to kill everything over ten years old' and that the Twentieth Kansas had swept through a town of 17,000 inhabitants leaving not one native alive. In a defence that foreshadowed the attitude of many Americans to Vietnam more than sixty years later, Hearst's New York Journal said 'The weak must go to the wall and stay there. . . . We'll rule in Asia as we rule at home. We shall establish in Asia a branch agent of the true American movement towards liberty.'
>
> (Knightley 1975: 58–9)

Britain, France and America did, of course, all make major contributions of substance to newly emerging Japan. They also made significant contributions of style. The Japanese had their own highly refined dress sense, but the French, as advisers to the Shogun's army, gave them a nice taste in modern uniforms, and when they went off for a day of barbarity, they were usually impeccably turned out. The Japanese also had a fine native brand of arrogance, but the British taught them how to refine it for the international stage. When Elgin's party made its way up the river to Edo the band (naturally enough) played 'Rule Britannia, Britannia rules the waves' – even waves of their own making on someone else's rivers. It was superb arrogance. Japan soon acquired military bands of its own and was before long making waves on Korean rivers to a chorus of approval from America and Britain.

Likewise none would deny the Japanese a native talent for hypocrisy, but in its modern international manifestations it was coached along by America or individual Americans. But whereas the Americans were more inclined to depopulate a region to introduce 'liberty', with the Japanese the slaughter was more likely to be in the name of 'civilization'. In nineteenth-century Japan one can see too the working-out of the 'indefinable' Anglo-American relationship. It was clearly that between a dominant imperial power and an aggressive young competitor. Thus well before the Perry expedition reached Japan, *The Times* (20.4.1852) was using heavy sarcasm to point out the blatant hypocrisy of the stated aims – 'just surveying' – and to sound a warning about the new threat to Britain's China trade: having 'finished up' America and absorbed the Mexican booty, American 'aggressions and conquests of the Asiatic coast are beginning' (*The Times* 8.4.1852). Undeterred by such criticisms the Americans sailed full steam ahead to convince the Japanese that they had arrived to save Japan from the British and the French.

Thus when it did begin in earnest, modern Japanese imperialism, naturally enough, was a pastiche of styles: the nattiness of the French, the superb arrogance of the British and the blatant hypocrisy of the Americans. But this question of style should not blind us to an overriding fact: 'modern' Japanese militarism and imperialism were straight out of the seventeenth century. It was an anachronism. Japan had been caught in a giant time-warp. In 1868 it was back to where it had been when Hideyoshi united the nation: it had large, excitable, unemployed armies which threatened the stability of the new regime; there was a business depression; and the agrarian classes, shut out from the *ishin*, posed a constant threat to the whole system. Hideyoshi and the Meiji leaders arrived at the same solution.

We have seen in chapter 6 how in 1868, Imai of Saga was forced to line up with eight comrades and commit *seppuku*. Even ten years earlier such an act would not have been so shocking. But the 1860s was the decade of Lincoln, Karl Marx and J. S. Mill. Imai was a modern man at home in this wider world, and it is this which makes his death seem such an act of barbarism. So with Japanese imperialism as a whole. Had it been perpetrated by Hideyoshi in the early seventeenth century, there would have been nothing remarkable in the story.

For all the 'romance' associated with their names, sixteenth- and seventeenth-century European empire builders were likely to have been pirates and slave-traders. Though the progress had been uneven, by the mid-nineteenth century the world had moved forward; Japan however, had remained rooted in the past. When it re-emerged after its long period of isolation, it did not join a modern imperial club, but carried straight on with the policies and attitude of Hideyoshi.

In the light of *kokugaku* teachings it was surely predictable that, once Korea had been absorbed, the Korean language and culture would be suppressed and the Koreans would be forced to adopt Japanese names and to worship the Japanese Emperor. It is sometimes suggested that this policy, being one of assimilation, was essentially the same as the French. But France had produced Rousseau, 'liberty, equality and fraternity', the Napoleonic Code and a language which had gone a long way towards replacing Latin as the lingua franca of Europe. Though one may quarrel with the whole doctrine of assimilation, one cannot dispute the fact that France had much to offer. On the other hand, there were neither cultural nor practical reasons to justify the imposition of the Japanese language and civilization.

To put Japanese imperialism in perspective, let us look briefly at both the First and Second British Empires, and note the fundamental differences. Though the First Japanese Empire was contemporary with the later stages of the Second British Empire, it had (not surprisingly) far more in common with the First British Empire.

## JAPAN'S IRELAND

The story of Japan in Korea from 1875 to 1945 has no parallels in modern British history. The comparison must be with the murderous Irish story of the sixteenth and seventeenth centuries. Korea was Japan's Ireland.

In the sixteenth century, when England emerged from baronial anarchy, it

> lacked the means and man-power to imitate the Spanish con-
> quistadors, but the acquisition of fertile Irish land was scarcely
> less tempting to the adventurer and certainly less costly than
> piratical attacks upon Spanish 'flotas' or voyages to discover
> the rich markets of Cathay. The enormous confiscations of
> land, the murderous revolts, and the retaliatory campaigns
> of extermination in the reign of Elizabeth were not different
> in kind from the Spanish exploitation of Mexico and Peru.
> (Harlow 1952, Vol. 1: 503)

In other places, the British were to deprive natives of their hunting lands, but only in Ireland did they plant 'colonies' by the systematic eviction of the tillers of the soil. In the seventeenth century, the planting of Ulster by Presbyterians gave the anti-Irish movement the emotional appeal of a holy war against Popery. The proprietorship of Ireland was vested in a small Protestant minority which controlled the land, parliament and trade in the so-called Protestant Ascendancy – and this entrenched oligarchy was backed by an imperial garrison.

Japan also emerged from 'baronial anarchy' in the sixteenth century. Soon it set its sights on Korean wealth and land. For sheer barbarity, the Spanish in Mexico and Peru, the English in Ireland and Hideyoshi in Korea were on a par – contemporaries who trod the world's stage at a certain phase stage in its development.

Hideyoshi, however, was defeated, and soon both Korea and Japan became hermit kingdoms and remained so till the mid-nineteenth century when a shrinking world forced them to re-open their doors. In the meantime the world had moved forward. Thanks partly to the support of powers such as Britain which wanted their trade, the Spanish South American colonies had gained their independence; and though Ireland remained a black spot, Britain had built up an impressive record as a colonial power. Japan, however, had been caught in a giant time-warp, and it re-emerged with the same problems, thought-processes and solutions, as it had in 1600. It was too weak immediately to imitate the great imperial powers, but Korea was still there, adjacent and vulnerable just as Ireland had been for England.

To blame the Koreans for the subsequent Japanese penetration is as outlandish as shifting on to Mexico, Peru and Ireland blame for their conquest, yet that is what official Japanese history still contrives to do. Meiji Japan simply carried on where Hideyoshi had left off. As with seventeenth-century Ireland, it was a shameless story of huge land confiscations, with murderous revolts followed by fierce retaliatory campaigns; the national treasures were plundered; the mines parcelled out among the *zaibatsu*; and the proprietorship of Korea vested in a small foreign minority backed by an imperial garrison. There were a few basic differences and modern refinements: Korea was to be used as a base for further expansion; there was a sophisticated secret police; and emphasis was placed on control of banking and currency. Yet overall the generalization stands: Korea was Japan's Ireland, and the story belongs more properly to the seventeenth century.

'Modernization' involves far more than science and technology, dress and social customs. Japan had experienced neither the eighteenth-century Age of Reason nor the nineteenth-century humanitarian movement. There was simply no concept of civil or human rights, and consequently no Rule of Law. The paraphernalia of modern civilization was mastered with surprising speed, but concepts of civil and human rights take far longer to absorb. This process had barely begun when Japan acquired its empire. In essence, its forces were seventeenth-century 'conquistadors'.

## THE FIRST BRITISH EMPIRE

The First British Empire revolved around North America and the West Indies. It was 'a sort of mutual-benefit society' (ibid.: 17). West Indian rum and sugar, Virginian tobacco and Newfoundland fish enabled the parent State to acquire the gold of Mexico and Peru, which purchased the teas and spices of the East, while the subtropical plantations grew rich under the protection of the Navigation Acts. But New England produced little that Britain required and became a rival to Britain especially in ship-building and in the carrying trade.

It was largely in North America that British colonial precedents were worked out. The Atlantic seaboard was 'peopled for the most part by migrants whose political thinking was saturated by the tradition of Westminster and English local government' (ibid., Vol. 2: 25). Well before independence they enjoyed a large degree of local autonomy. However, one must be careful not to romanticize this picture of empire for the First British Empire was based on slavery and on the broad general principle that colonies existed for the benefit of the Mother Land.

The loss of the American colonies precipitated the break-up of the First British Empire. Why have colonies if they break away as soon as they become a source of strength and profit? Yet the disintegration of the empire had already been well under way, for England herself had been turning against the idea of empire. Colonies such as the American were now feared as potential industrial rivals, and whereas they had once been welcomed as places which might absorb the superfluous population, it was now feared they would drain off the best artisans. Moreover, it had once been deemed expedient to have colonies as a safety valve – a receptacle for political and religious dissenters. Now, however, there was a brisk inflow of New World political writings which threatened to disrupt the political fabric of both England and Ireland.

The defeat of the French in 1763 had precipitated the crisis. Thereafter the colonists wanted neither to contribute to defence nor to be restricted to the Atlantic seaboard. Speculation had locked up so much land within the existing colonial borders that widespread colonization beyond the Appalachians had become imminent and that would be the signal for ferocious Indian resistance. Britain, which already had clear treaty obligations to a great number of Indian nations, favoured restricting colonization and establishing a huge Indian land reserve where their traders might go for furs. The settlers, however, insisted on their own imperialism, and the so-called War of Independence was essentially 'the clash between British and American imperialism in relation of the exploitation of the West' (ibid., Vol. 1: 179). Tragically for the American Indians, American imperialism emerged victorious. At the peace negotiations Britain's Shelburne fought a bitter rear-guard action for Indian land-rights, but by the final treaty 'a vast area between the Lakes and the Ohio had been thrown away and twenty-one Indian nations who lived there and whose hunting grounds Britain had pledged by treaty to protect had been basely deserted.' (ibid., Vol. 1: 433).

By 1849 the American Empire had reached California. Almost immediately, it began to cast its eyes across the Pacific where it would resume the bitter imperial rivalry with Britain. The sedulously propagated picture of little Japan against the rest of the world disguises the reality of fierce Western rivalry. For Britain and France, the Bakumatsu struggles were a continuation of their wars in Canada and India, with France backing the Shogun and

Britain supporting Satchō, while fear of Russian penetration south was for many English a major obsession.

A perusal of early Meiji English-language newspapers shows that the most venomous articles and letters related to the Anglo-American rivalry in Japan. America at some stage or other displayed four major aims: to have Japan as a client state whose foreign policy would be 'guided' by America; to control Japanese mines, shipping and railways; to use Japan as a staging-post, and later as a partner, in cutting into the rich China trade; and opening up Japanese waters to American whalers and sealers. The Japanese, however, astutely maintained control of their own mines, shipping and railways and ultimately decided to go it alone in China – the real turning point in Japanese–American relations. The only major American diplomatic victory related to the islands to the north. The Russians and the Japanese had been in both the Kuriles and in Karafuto (Saghalien). In the 1870s the Americans persuaded Japan to effect an exchange, Russia taking all of Karafuto and Japan the Kuriles. With Russia out of the way and the infant Japanese navy impotent, the American sealers, who had exterminated the seals along the Pacific coast well before Perry set sail, had a free hand north-east of Japan until those waters were also 'worked out'.

Much of modern Japanese 'history' is little more than sedulously propagated myths. The 'Meiji *ishin*' for example, never existed. The very term is an insult to our intelligence, and it should always be written in inverted commas. But this process, whereby myth becomes more real than reality itself, must not be seen as something peculiar to Japan. Let us take a homely example.

In his delightful autobiography, *A Ragman's Son*, Kirk Douglas (born Danielovitch) tells how when he came to make his 1959 movie *Spartacus*, he solved the accent problem by having all the slaves (the freedom-fighters) speak with an American accent and all the Romans (the oppressors) with a British accent. To an American, what could have been more natural? Little matter that the United States began its life as an aggressively imperialistic nation which destroyed the Indian nations and drove them off their land, or that the new nation was based on slavery. The British Empire abolished the slave trade in 1807 and slavery in 1833. The abolitionists had been opposed by powerful commercial interests, and it is doubtful if they would have prevailed had America still been part of the empire. This son of Russian Jewish immigrants had absorbed the essence, not of American history, but of the American myth.

## THE SECOND BRITISH EMPIRE

The Second British Empire aimed at 'trade, not dominion'. Colonies of settlement were neither planned nor desired; but a trading empire required fuelling depots and naval bases which were sought to provide protection against their European rivals. This trading empire revolved around India and the China extension. Thus during the Napoleonic Wars, Cape Colony and Ceylon were taken and later retained, then in turn Singapore, Penang and Hong Kong were all occupied. But though unplanned and unwanted, colonies of settlement did eventuate, for it proved impossible to restrain settlement to the area around Cape Town or to the Atlantic seaboard of Canada. With the Industrial Revolution came large-scale unemployment which led to mass migration. As with the American colonies, these new colonies of settlement inherited the traditional British civil, legal and political rights which led quite rapidly to the granting of responsible government.

Likewise with the 'trading posts' it proved impossible to restrain expansion, with the Colonial Office often fighting a vain rearguard action against the local planters and traders. These local Europeans inevitably demanded the traditional British rights, and where these territories remained under British rule, the same rights were then extended to the indigenous population.

The corner-stone of this trading Second British Empire was India and its China extension, so let us look at that story in a little more detail.

### The British in India

For most of the period 1599 to 1833, the British East India Company enjoyed a British trade monopoly extending far beyond India itself, and most notably to China (and Japan). Their object was 'trade, not dominion', but around their 'factories' in Bombay, Calcutta and Madras large cities grew up. In 1684 it was found necessary to fortify Bombay, and with fortifications came the beginnings of an administrative and fiscal system. As the great Moghul Empire disintegrated, the Indian population became the prey of unscrupulous adventurers and 'John Company', like the French, began to intervene in native affairs, partly to protect their 'legitimate interests' and partly as a ruthless bid for personal profit. The victory at Plassey in 1757 placed Bengal under Clive's control and in 1764 an agreement was reached placing revenue collection in British hands while leaving native administration under the nominal authority of the Nawab.

What followed was perhaps the most disgraceful twenty-year period in British history. When 'the great famine' of 1769–70 began, the anarchy in the administration immensely increased its horrors. The sufferings of the peasants were exploited by company servants who made a corner in rice, selling it at high prices, and enforced the continued exaction of land tax with cruel severity. It has been estimated that 10 million people died, about a third of the total population (ibid., Vol. 2: 47).

Reports from India reached the British press and were taken up in parliament. 'It was realised that the prevailing misconduct was a disgrace which was injuring the national interest' (ibid.: 157). There was genuine moral indignation, and Burke's passionate anger still makes stimulating reading. Of course, far more was involved than simple moral indignation. Company employees had gone to India to make their fortunes by private trading. Clive tried in vain to build up an honest Civil Service by increasing their salaries and stopping their private trade. The temptations, however, were too great and Clive's 'lofty condemnation of oppression and corruption, which was perfectly sincere, tended to lose its cutting edge in view of his own immense accumulation of wealth' (ibid.: 39–40). The basic fact was that Britain itself lacked an experienced professional Civil Service, and, without one, effective imperial administration was manifestly impossible.

It was widely known that the rival Dutch East India Company had been grievously weakened by corruption. The returning nabobs, though detested for their arrogance, vulgarity and ostentation, were able to buy landed estates, parliamentary seats and influence in the Company. Moral outrage and national and class interest all demanded that the disgraceful situation in Bengal be brought to an end.

Lord North's Regulating Act of 1773 set up a Supreme Court in Bengal 'to discipline the European population' (ibid.: 68). It was specifically to protect the native population against oppression. However, it was laid down that in all suits involving marriage, inheritance, caste and other religious usages, Hindu and Moslem law was to be adhered to.

Pitt's Act of 1784 intended to be, in the words of Burke, 'the Magna Carta' of Hindustan. It addressed the fundamental question of separating sovereignty and law from trade. The Company maintained its trade monopoly in India until 1833, but the 1784 Act set up a government department, the board of control for India, to govern British India. Among the most vexatious questions which had to be addressed was to work out an equitable land tax and thus relieve the iniquitous centuries-old oppression of the peasants.

Though the British government had thus become directly involved, there was a steady determination to pursue trade without dominion. The Dundas Resolutions of 1782

> had been adopted by the Commons with general assent. Resolution 44 had declared 'that it is the opinion of this Committee (of the whole House) that . . . to pursue schemes of conquest and extent of dominion are measures repugnant to the wish, the honour, and policy of this nation'. The frequent repetition of this affirmation of policy in later years illustrates the long rearguard action at home against the expense and hazards of 'imperium'.
>
> (ibid.: 139)

In the long run, however, the idea of limitation proved an illusion, and the power vacuum left by the fallen Moghuls was gradually filled by Britain. 'A metropolitan state cannot halt a moving frontier: it can only disengage by abdication' (ibid.: 156).

For India, the year 1784 may be conveniently taken as the start of the Second British Empire. Though inconsistencies and black spots remained, the achievements were tremendous, for they must be measured against the enormous complexities of tasks such as codifying Hindu and Moslem customary law and systems of land tenure. It may fairly be stated that for well over 100 years, Britain's main export to India was brains. Let us take just three examples.

The possession of colonies is a two-way street, for it affects the colonizing power socially, politically and culturally. It was the discovery of Sanskrit as taught in ancient India that gave the impetus to modern linguistic studies in the Western world. The pioneer was Sir William Jones (see Arberry 1946 and Cannon 1964), a classics student who taught himself Hebrew, then read Persian and Arabic at Oxford. After writing a Persian grammar and translating pre-Islamic poetry, he took up law and in 1783 sailed for Calcutta as judge of the supreme court. He was already known for his 'belligerent liberalism' (Arberry 1946: 15), being a vigorous opponent of both slavery and 'the fratricidal war' in North America. Indeed, he was a friend of cleric Shipley, a noted opponent of that war, who argued that 'I look upon North America as the only nursery of free men left on the face of the earth' (ibid.: 12). It seems that Jones became Shipley's active intermediary with Benjamin Franklin in seeking to end that war.

Well before going to Calcutta, Jones was acknowledged as England's foremost Oriental scholar. In 1773 he was elected as a member of 'the Club', Samuel Johnson's immortal coterie which included Gibbon, Sheridan, Burke, Garrick and Sir Joshua Reynolds, and in 1780 he became Club president. His Calcutta appointment was no chance decision. For five years he campaigned to get such a position, publishing a treatise in 1781 in Arabic, with an English translation, on the Shafiite law of inheritance, helping to convince the authorities that a knowledge of Islam (and Hindu) law and languages was necessary for the administration of the Asiatic territories.

In 1834, when the Crown took over the main responsibility for India, the historian Macaulay was appointed to the supreme council of India. He was already renowned as a champion of emancipation and of parliamentary reform. In India he vindicated the liberty of the press, maintained the equality of Indians and Europeans before the law, and inaugurated a modern system of national education. He also drafted the penal code which became law in 1860.

A contemporary of Macaulay's in India was the famous social and political reformer J. S. Mill, whose 1859 essay *On Liberty* was to be widely studied in Japan. For twenty years, Mill was in charge of the East India Company's relations with the Indian States, and then until the Company's dissolution in 1858 he was head of the examiner's office.

It is important to bear this wider background in mind when considering the origins and nature of Japanese imperialism. The system of education which was set up in India was based on English, mainly because India had no lingua franca. But it went hand in hand with a scholarly fascination with the great Indian civilizations and languages, and due to the efforts of British scholars Indian studies underwent a renaissance. These scholarly traditions were later transferred to Japan by young diplomats and academics such as Satow, Aston and Chamberlain.

As one could easily predict from a study of the *kokugakusha* and of Bakumatsu activists, the Japanese in Korea would seek to impose the Japanese language and culture. Far from experiencing a renaissance, Korean studies were to be suppressed; it was old-fashioned conquest and subjugation.

The tremendous advances in British attitudes and administration must be seen as part of the general advances in Western civilization. Perhaps we may take as the starting point of the European advance the work of Dutch prodigy, Hugo Grotius (1583–1645), the father of international law. In 1604, in order to justify the action of one of its admirals in seizing a Portuguese vessel, the Dutch East India Company asked Grotius to write on the lawfulness of capturing merchant ships. His treatise 'On the Law of Prize and Booty' maintained that the oceans were free to all nations and that the Dutch were entitled to compensation for Portuguese attempts to exclude them. One must question Grotius' impartiality and note that the treatise ignored the people of Mexico and South America, but it was a milestone in the development of the notion that nations should be subject to the Rule of Law, and his 1625 work, *De iure belli ac pacis* (*On the law of War and Peace*) dealt with the whole law of mankind and stressed that the law of war had to be mitigated by equity. Of course, the recognition, development and implementation of these ideas was to take centuries, and the process is still far from complete, but the fact that the law of most European countries was based on Roman law made possible a degree of progress; and at Trafalgar, for example, it was taken for granted that the British warships should rescue the French sailors whose ships they had sunk.

The eighteenth century saw the Age of Reason – the writings of the French philosophers such as Rousseau, the American Declaration of Independence, and advances in science and historiography. When the Second British Empire began, the nature of man and society was being intensively discussed, the scientific spirit was widely respected, and the British parliament possessed some of its finest orators. It was an auspicious background, especially as the Industrial Revolution was about to transform Britain's trading potential.

Japan, on the other hand, began her empire in a period of civil wars and farmer uprisings, with the press manacled, the Rule of Law strangled at birth and power effectively concentrated in the hands of Satchō. Also of considerable importance was the fact that modern historiography had not yet developed. The historian was still viewed narrowly as an official serving the government, while the main histories studied, for example, by the Meiji leaders, were the great epics of ancient China. A poignant pointer was provided after the Saga uprising of 1874 when Soejima Taneomi, Japan's first foreign minister of note, wrote a poem presumed to be an epitaph for Murayama Chohei, one of the executed leaders (Matano 1914,

Vol. 2: 37). A fine classics scholar, Soejima does not mention Saga or modern Japan, but writes of two great warriors of ancient China, Haikō and Ko-o. The great Shin dynasty has fallen, and the 'countries' which brought about its downfall now turn against each other and fight for control of the River Ha which symbolizes control of 'the world' (*haken*).

In this poem Soejima tacitly acknowledged that the Saga uprising was about *haken*. For the Shin dynasty, we must read 'the Shogunate'. Once the Shogun had been overthrown, the allies embarked on a series of struggles to decide *haken*. Satsuma and Chōshū, old enemies, came to the brink more than once, but, faced by certain disaster, drew back. Soejima's poem might be taken as an epitaph, not only for Murayama, but for all the power struggles of the Bakumatsu and early Meiji period. Indeed, it might be taken as an epitaph for Japanese imperialism as a whole, for though that imperialism was economic imperialism, dressed up in the garb of Emperor system ideology, it could also be summed up simply as a struggle for *haken*, the depiction of which required the epic powers of a Shiki rather than the analytical powers of a modern historian, for conquest itself seemed as natural and self-explanatory as in ancient China or in the seventeenth century, and the epic historian might perhaps be forgiven for feeling that analysis merely gets in the way of the narrative.

## Fiji

Much of the Second British Empire was acquired as a result of the world shrinking and the Crown being forced to act to control its own nationals. New Zealand, Malaya and Fiji are all cases in point. Let us briefly consider the annexation of Fiji (Calman 1950) as it coincides with the Japanese opening of Korea. Earlier proposals to annex Fiji had been rejected by parliament, primarily because of the expense involved, but by 1874 the situation had become an ugly one. Freebooters, largely British, had introduced firearms, acquired land for trinkets and started plantations. They then scoured other island groups kidnapping the natives to work on the plantations. The Deed of Session provided that no more land could be alienated, and the first few years of British rule were largely given over to the land courts which disallowed most of the 'sales' made prior to 1874. Needless to say, this represents a tremendous advance on seventeenth-century imperialism and the 'base desertion' of 1784. The establishment of

British rule in Fiji was a highly responsible act which averted certain disaster at the hands of the freebooters.

The nineteenth-century humanitarian movement was of tremendous importance. Its early victories were mostly in the empire – the slave trade, emancipation, female infanticide, widow burning, etc. – then it turned inward and campaigned within Britain to achieve, for example, factory laws to protect women and children. If one reads the confidential reports and comments of the Colonial and Indian offices, one can have little doubt that they had a distinguished list of permanent officials in the humanitarian mainstream. Generally speaking they were firmly on the side of the indigenous populations. On the other side of the equation were planters and traders pushing for a 'forward' policy. It was rather like our contemporary clash between environmentalists and developers. Of course, both humanitarians and developers would try to whip up support in parliament and in the press. The missionaries would also enter the fray, and not necessarily on the side of the angels. It all added up to a system of checks and balances with a highly professional bureaucracy at the centre. Needless to say, the men on the spot – the traders and planters – would often try to force the government's hand; it was not all that rare for local officials to join these trading interests in what amounted to a conspiracy against the home government, and to confront it with a *fait accompli*. However, they had first to get past Colonial Office officials highly sceptical about their character and motives. A colonial 'system' depends on its bureaucracy.

In Meiji Japan the bureaucracy was just getting established. Many of the people whom historians generally refer to as 'bureaucrats' stayed in the bureaucracy only a few months or even weeks. They were essentially followers of one politician or another, and the rest of their career would be spent on the politician's personal staff or working for one of the related newspapers or companies. They would be no less the politician's *kobun* (follower) during their stint in the bureaucracy than they were when on his personal staff. Thus, instead of a professional bureaucracy dedicated to the protection of the indigenous peoples, the 'bureaucrats' (extending up to the head man) were members of the same clique as the merchants and military people and were among the worst oppressors.

Meiji Japan was not, of course, without sincere, humane men. The Emperor himself was clearly a case in point. But there was no significant humanitarian movement as such willing to take up the cudgels on the part of the oppressed and capable of gaining significant victories over the government. Though class distinctions had been abolished at law, the ethos was still feudal. The cholic or depressed *samurai* could no longer restore his spirits by carving up a peasant, but if he became a prison officer he had a fairly free hand, and part of the attraction of colonies was that they were dealing with 'inferior' peoples.

Japanese imperial excesses and the ultimate tragedy must be traced back to the failure to establish the Rule of Law within Japan, to the lack of a humanitarian movement, and to the fact that the feudal ethos with its concept of *samurai* 'rights' was carried to Korea. It should be stressed that it was not just the *samurai* who clung to their feudal pretensions. Granting the Eta legal equality provoked widespread agrarian uprisings, and the real battle for Eta rights did not begin until after the Second World War. In Japanese thinking, Korea had been often grouped with Ezo and the Ryūkyūs, and the fate of the Koreans was to be very similar to that of the Ainu and Ryūkyūans. This was not just a question of 'policy' but extended to the conduct of individuals.

It is now platitudinous to say that the Japanese businessmen flying off overseas to do battle are the new *samurai*. It is not rare to have Japanese businessmen in their cups put it even more bluntly: the war never ended, only now the weapons are economic. Be that as it may, this doctrine of the businessman as the *new samurai* is highly misleading. Most of the economic imperialists such as Godai, Inoue and Iwasaki had been former *samurai*, and the doctrine that those who enriched themselves were serving the nation had been widely disseminated, especially by Fukuzawa. Keio's Lloyd gave the following testimony:

> There was a time, before I knew as much of the Japanese character as I do now, when I invariably found it difficult to listen with patience to the loquacious student who would explain to me that he wished to serve his country by making himself a very rich man.
>
> (Lloyd 1909: 66–7)

This enriching process very frequently centred around getting into money – lending and extracting huge interest from tenant farmers. Lloyd also wrote thus of *bushido*:

> The name is quite new – I never heard it used until a few years ago – but the thing itself is as old as the hills of Japan. . . . I

have found the spirit of *Bushido* as strong among the young men preparing themselves for business life as amongst the cadets and officers of the Naval Academy.

(ibid.: 16)

It is sometimes convenient to divide Japanese imperialists into ideological and economic imperialists, but, as Lloyd implies, it is very easy to exaggerate this distinction. In England, in an upper-class family with two sons of similar beliefs and interests, one frequently went into the army and one into the Church; in Japan we would be likely to find them going into the army and the *zaibatsu*.

## THE 1873 SEIHEN

Japanese historians writing about the 1873 *Seihen* have to face up to the later atrocious Japanese record in Korea. The struggle to overthrow the Bakufu had begun in earnest in the late eighteenth century. It was marked by the sort of ferocity usually reserved for religious wars. There could be no moral justification for turning this savagery outwards against Japan's hapless neighbours. Yet, as our study of Kurume clearly indicates, the desire to divert this ferocity was certainly one part of the motivation in 1873. When this fact is viewed against the totality of the story down to 1945, the truth becomes too awful to behold, and surely it is this which keeps driving Japanese historians back to Saigō's heart and to the shrill insistence that Saigō and Japan merely planned a punitive expedition against Korea.

## SUMMARY

'Modern' Japanese imperialism was an anachronism. During Japan's long period of seclusion, the world had, though unevenly, moved forward, leaving Japan back in 1600. Its 'modern' imperialism belongs to the seventeenth century, alongside that of Spain in Mexico and Peru, and England in Ireland, and a gross distortion occurs immediately one attempts to discuss it using nineteenth-century liberal terminology. Though her neighbours had committed no crimes they became the recipients of Japanese ferocity. The old feudal ethos, now formally a thing of the past in Japan itself, was turned outwards, and most Koreans, like the Ryūkyūans and Ainu, were 'assimilated' into the ranks of the Eta.

209

A major objective of the 1875 opening of Korea was to gain control of its rice, and this was then funnelled into Japan and beyond by Chōshū-linked companies in which Inoue Kaoru was the major figure. When the Koreans went to Japan to protest at the wanton dislocation of their economy, they found that the Minister they had to talk to was Inoue Kaoru. Here three points need to be made: this vital rice story has received relatively little attention from Japanese historians; the Korean rice scandal followed a similar story with much the same cast within Japan itself, typifying the unity of the internal and external narrative; and this disgraceful story had its counterpart in India in the 1770s. Britain, however, moved decisively in India to establish the Rule of Law, and to separate trade and government. Within Japan, on the other hand, Satchō scotched the growth of the Rule of Law, and what was to become known as 'Japan Incorporated' was already a reality: government, *zaibatsu*, military, bureaucracy and usually parliament and the media, combined in the cause of economic exploitation. The Japanese people at home found it increasingly impossible to defend their own basic human rights, so the conquered peoples had little or no hope of having their plight taken up within Japan itself by strong, sympathetic groups in the parliament, bureaucracy, media, law courts or populace at large.

The Second British Empire began and developed against an auspicious background: two centuries of experience as a colonial power, the Age of Reason in Europe, the spread of the scientific spirit, the nineteenth-century humanitarian movement and the steady growth of full parliamentary government. Equally important was the development, following the Indian experience, of a professional civil service highly sceptical of, and prepared to thwart, the machinations of planters and traders. Many of these parliamentarians and bureaucrats accepted the Rousseau doctrine that 'man is born free'; they were in the humanitarian movement mainstream. Though the horrors of Ireland and of India in the period 1764–84 can never be obliterated from memory, and though the very name 'Opium Wars' remains an embarrassment, the British Empire can still boast comparison with the Roman for its positive achievements. The world inevitably grew smaller, and had the British Empire not come into existence a great number of indigenous populations would have been faced with ultimate anarchy and extinction.

Japanese imperialism, by comparison, could not have had a more inauspicious backdrop. Meiji Japan was born out of a long and bitter power struggle, and that struggle continued without a break.

A Don Peasant army, conscripted to break the power of rival *samurai* factions, committed barbaric atrocities, and the story was repeated seventeen years later when this new 'modern' army was launched against China.

To protect its power base in the face of a growing democratic movement, Satchō hoisted the iniquitous Emperor system upon the nation. Japanese imperialism was basically economic imperialism, but the Emperor system overlay meant that there could be no question of 'trade, not dominion', for that system was based on *kokugaku* teachings that the Emperor and Japan were divine and destined to rule the world. The extreme racism, the failure of the Rule of Law to take root within Japan itself, the sheer weight of numbers of nefarious adventurers, Japan's own slide into a brutally repressive regime, the lack of a strong humanitarian movement, and the fact that the Japanese Empire was acquired and controlled against a background of almost non-stop war all combined to make Japanese imperialism a synonym for repression.

Surely it is the word 'repression' which contains the key to the 'unfathomable savagery' of the war-time atrocities. The ferocity of Japan's own internal struggles, the use traditionally made of torture, the extreme racism, the notion of *hinin* and the vertical nature of Japanese society, were all major factors; but the extreme and unnatural repression to which the Japanese people were themselves subjected meant that violence was always lurking just below the surface.

Having thus shone the spotlight on the nature of Japanese imperialism, let us return to the analysis of its origins which should now stand out in sharper relief, and follow through with three threads which show clearly what was happening and what was about to happen.

First, Japanese colonial policy was largely worked out in Hokkaidō and the Ryūkyūs. Hokkaidō provides solid evidence of what was in store for Korea. It also shows that there was no substance in the claims that Saigō was mainly concerned with the Russian threat, and it enables us to understand the nature of the 'Colonial Office'. There was simply no trained bureaucracy and few officials championing the rights of the colonized. There was no system of checks and balances which is at the heart of a modern colonial system. Instead the Colonial Office officials were from the same clans as, and very close to, the military and economic imperialists; and they were very keen to get their share of the plunder.

Second, we must follow the struggle to set up the Rule of Law. That struggle was lost and the Satchō government remained above the law. If they were to be above the law in Japan itself obviously they would be even more free of restraints outside Japan, and would lack the moral stature and the will to restrain their lawless countrymen.

Finally, we must hone in on the economic imperialists. From the outset, Japanese imperialism was economic imperialism of the most blatant and extreme kind. The Seisho (government-linked companies) were a Japanese phenomenon. When Western historians state that the Japanese government had no plans for aggrandizement, one must remember that not only Mutsu and Inoue, but virtually all the top politicians and bureaucrats were major holders in the companies that were to be 'asked' to take over these colonial resources. It is therefore quite preposterous to write of the *government* having no thoughts of aggrandizement.

It will, perhaps, help to clarify this picture of Japanese imperialism – and give reassurance to those inclined to worry overly about the future – if we try to picture the Second Japanese Empire. It should be close, not to the First Japanese Empire, but to the Second British Empire. All the indications are that by the end of the century Japan will have huge overseas holdings of land, mines and property. As the north–south divide solidifies, it should be a fully paid-up member of a Northern Club based around the EEC, America and Japan. It may be possible to maintain permanently the economic imperialists' dream of wealth without responsibility – the sort of situation normal to the Philippines where most of the wealth drains off to America, Japan and China – but a more likely scenario is that some regions will try to regain control of their own resources, and this will then lead back to old-fashioned direct imperialism.

The positive aspects to this story are: that Japan will already have great wealth and will not have to take the local rice and gold; that it will be able to invest heavily and introduce new products, as the British did in Malaysia (tea, coffee, rubber); that the Japanese language, like English in India, will be seen to be the road to advancement; that Japan now has an advanced education system which will draw masses of students to its shores; and that Japan now has a fine legal system, a sophisticated bureaucracy, an executive more or less subject to the Rule of Law, and a widespread humanitarian movement. In short, any Second Japanese Empire will be based on all those elements which Japan so sorely lacked on first emerging from her long isolation.

The likely scenario was summed up nicely by the *Sydney Morning Herald*'s Canberra correspondent Milton Cockburn, in an article dated 28 September 1990, under the benign heading 'Leading a Giant gently by the hand towards leadership'. Referring to a recent visit to Japan by Prime Minister Hawke, he wrote:

> Mr Hawke's comments appear to have created no controversy and little debate in a country which is still supposedly coming to terms with the trauma of large-scale Japanese investment. . . . The nub of the message which Mr Hawke conveyed in public *and private* was this: Australia would not object if Japan did seek to forge a role of political and *strategic* leadership in *the region we share*. . . . Part of Mr Hawke's thinking appears to stem from the belief that Japanese investment in South-East Asia is now so substantial that in the event of instability, *it is inevitable that Japan will be forced to take steps to protect its investments, its strategic concerns and its citizens*. On this thinking, it is better for Japan to do so as an allied nation – perhaps some time in the future as a defence ally – than from its stance of isolation.

This is a classic description of how most modern empires have begun. To repeat Harlow's words, 'A metropolitan state cannot halt a moving frontier: it can only disengage by abdication.' There are likely to be many 'moving frontiers' in the unstable regions where Japanese economic penetration is proceeding apace. 'Trade (and investment) without dominion' is likely to prove as difficult an ideal in the next century as it was in the last. Hence the Australian 'Labour' Prime Minister has made clear his prior commitment to help legitimize future Japanese aggression.

Of course, this embryonic Bob Hawke diplomacy is not without its precedents. In the thirties Bob Menzies' foreign policy was essentially one of appeasement. 'Responsible' Australian officials were delighted that Japan was expanding north, not south, and got their message across to the Japanese loud and clear. However, in the interests of Australia's international image, it should be noted that there were Australian groups with a deeper moral sense and a more profound grasp of international realities – e.g. the wharfies (dockers) who refused to ship pig iron to feed the rampaging Japanese military machine.

Oriental history would suggest that Japanese and American 'friendship' will be unlikely to survive the loss of their common enmity for Russia. Yet both retain their commitment to 'liberty', 'civilization' and 'free trade', so future Japanese moves for their 'defence' and the establishment of a Second Japanese Empire should underline the Reischauer doctrine of 'natural allies' and demonstrate that Japan has at last graduated with honours from the language classes initiated by Perry in the 1850s.

Language will be of the greatest importance, for empire is anathema to the average Japanese. Indeed, one is reminded of Sato Shinen (1769–1850) (see p.63 *et seq.*) with his Hondo Hisaku (Secret Plan for Unifying the World) and his recognition of one great problem: the Japanese people. The Japanese people were prosperous and just enjoyed living their own lives. The idea of war did not appeal to them, and if they knew his plans, they would think him crazy, or they would get angry and think of him as a criminal; thus a positive programme of education and indoctrination was required. It is still deemed a necessity.

# 9

# THE POWER STRUGGLE
# IN HOKKAIDŌ

Japanese historians make the 1873 *Seihen* revolve around Saigō. Hence it becomes necessary to examine the claim that, for Saigō, the *aite* was not Korea but Russia, and that it was 'the Russian menace' which dictated his policies. The most commonly advanced 'proof' was the way Saigō had *tonden hei* set up in Hokkaidō to provide a first line of defence against Russia. So let us turn back to the story of Hokkaidō, particularly noting the role of Saigō and of Satsuma.

As we saw in chapter 3, Satsuma's wealth was based on its colonies, but it was notorious for the cruelty of its rule in the Ryūkyūs. During his exile there, Saigō was adopting the standard attitude when he regarded the locals as barbarians, and he was soon writing to Ōkubo describing the local government as 'more cruel in its treatment of the local population than Matsumae is in its treatment of the Ezo-jin' (Inoue 1970, Vol. 1: 7–8). It was a strict Satsuma law that its people living in the Ryūkyūs, be they officials or exiles, could marry there, but the marriage would be annulled when they returned home (ibid.: 80–1). They could call the children of the marriage to Satsuma, but not the ex-wife. Thus Saigō called his son in 1869 and his daughter in 1875, but their mother lived alone until her death in 1902 (ibid.: 83). None of his wives had much of a life, and shortly after he married his third wife, he took a *geisha* mistress (ibid., Vol. 2: 12–13). Such extreme claims have been made for Saigō's high moral standards that one should note this evidence that he was a child of his times.

Saigō's 1869 comment about Matsumae indicates that he was long aware of the treatment of the 'barbarian' Ainu. Ezochi, Korea and the Ryūkyūs were not infrequently grouped together (see chapter 3) as areas suitable for development by Japan, and Saigō's attitude to the people of the Ryūkyūs, and Kuroda's subsequent treatment of

215

the Ainu, may perhaps be taken as indications of his attitude to the Koreans. In short, they were not regarded as equals.

## THE HAKODATE WAR

The noted local historian Kaiho Mineo (1982) has provided an incisive analysis of this period.

The Matsumae clan was part of the northern alliance, but pro-Emperor forces soon seized control. When Enomoto took Matsumae, the clan chief and seventy of his men escaped to Tsugaru, but 500 were left behind. Leaderless, inexperienced and poorly armed, they soon surrendered.

Enomoto set up a republic which was 'like a democracy within an outlaw group' (ibid.: 297). Voting was confined to his officers, all locals and other ranks being excluded. The residents were squeezed mercilessly to provide money and 'volunteers'. Around Hakodate, up to 2,000 were subject to forced labour (ibid.: 299–301).

When the Matsumae clan leaders returned, they issued a proclamation which amounted to an apology for fleeing and leaving the people to their fate, but this was little more than a device for calming the people. Once back firmly in the saddle, they took a terrible revenge on their abandoned troops who had had no real option but to co-operate to some extent with the occupying forces. Sixteen young *samurai* with shaven heads and placards around their necks stating their offences were placed backwards on horses, paraded slowly through the town, then executed. Their heads were then displayed on bamboo poles. The clan records are not clear, but it seems that about fifty suffered this fate. Another 450 were branded as traitors, many fleeing or staying in hiding.

The loss of the clan's special rights, combined with this savage and unnatural reprisal, meant the end of the Matsumae clan. Its clansmen played virtually no role in the Kaitakushi. Soldier settlers were introduced, but when the Kaitakushi was abolished in 1881, they numbered less than 1,000 (Iguro and Katayama 1967: 292), so Matsumae's 500 *samurai* represented a considerable force. Their elimination surely suggests that the government was concerned with internal security, and not with the 'Russian menace'.

As we saw in chapter 3, the role of the Matsumae clan was one which developed slowly over centuries. Its *samurai* were responsible not for external defence, but for internal law and order. Once the Matsumae clan fell and its *samurai* were eliminated, others had to be brought in to perform this policing role. Bearing in mind the overall increase in population, there was no great build up in such forces.

## THE ESTABLISHMENT OF THE KAITAKUSHI

On 16 April 1868 the Ezochi Saibansho was set up. The Miami historian Harrison (1953), who never visited Hokkaidō, wrongly translates this as 'circuit judge', but it was the term for the administration set up in the open ports. A month later, the name was changed to Hakodate-fu, then in 1869 the Kaitakushi (Colonial Office or Pioneering Office) was set up to take charge of Ezochi, which was given a new name, Hokkaidō, to emphasize that it was now an integral part of Japan. Historians have generally been sympathetic to the Kaitakushi. Harrison's conclusion (ibid.: 141) that it laid 'an excellent foundation' is a fair summary of the standard Japanese histories. Yet such a conclusion merely illustrates the pervasive influence of official histories and fostered legends, for the Kaitakushi was a brutal, dismal failure. Blakiston, a long-time Hakodate resident, was close to the mark when he described it as 'based on wrong principles or no principles at all: it was utopian and impracticable' (1883: 50). As he pointed out, it was going against human nature to develop the inland before the coast was properly settled, and there should have been more emphasis on fishing, harbours and coast roads. Such successes as were achieved, at Date, for example, were achieved in spite of the Kaitakushi and not because of it.

As we saw in chapter 3, Saga had long been interested in Ezochi. Thus its ex-lord, Nabeshima Kansō (1814–70) was appointed Chōkan (Colonial Secretary); despite his poor health, his followers persuaded him to accept. Matano (1914: 438–41) makes a point which is fundamental to our understanding of the Kaitakushi years. In January 1869, Nabeshima asked Etō and Soejima to return to Saga to reform the clan. Their reforms stressed *fukoku kyōhei*; for this purpose, the clan needed three or four steamers to trade between Tokyo, Osaka, Nagasaki, Shanghai and Ezochi. One ship had to be engaged full-time on the Hokkaidō run, carrying its products as far as Shanghai. The profits, they declared, would be great, and there could be no better way to build up a rich country. When Etō returned to Tokyo, the ailing Kansō went with him to take over the Kaitakushi. His appointment must be seen as the result of an initiative by the Saga clan which was clearly motivated by the desire to develop its own trading network.

Kansō's deputy was Shimizutani, the noble who had been in charge at Hakodate before fleeing from Enomoto. The *hankan* were Shima Yoshitake of Saga, Iwamura Michitoshi of Tosa, Matsumoto Jirō of Shōnai (Yamagata), Okamoto Kensuke and Takeda Nobuyori. With the exception of Iwamura, all were old Hokkaidō hands. When Kansō's health soon forced him to resign, Shimizutani was passed over for Higashikuse and resigned. Shima became the deputy, with most of the other officials also being Saga men (Iguro and Katayama 1967: 181ff.).

The fullest account of these early days is *hankan* Matsumoto's reminiscences, *Nemuro mo Hoshi Kusa*. In old age, Matsumoto was also interviewed by the leading Hokkaidō historian Kōno Tsunekichi, whose works were collected and published in 1982 by the present doyen of Hokkaidō historians, Takakura Shinichirō, under the title *Saisen Kai Shiryo* (Takakura 1982: 304–40; Saisen was Kōno's pen-name). Matsumoto related how initially the Kaitakushi had no offices of its own, and had to borrow Court rooms with no places for files, so every evening Shima took all the documents home (ibid.: 307ff.). Even when Higashikuse was appointed, Shima remained the real head, for the officials simply ignored the Chōkan and took all their problems to Shima. Harrison therefore concluded, quite wrongly, that 'the directorship of the Kaitakushi was in reality an honorary position' (Harrison 1953: 66).

Higashikuse was an activist who had devoted his life to the *sonnō* cause. In 1842, at the age of nine, he had been appointed as official playmate to the future Emperor Kōmei, then eleven, and he had continued to serve him until his death (*Hokkaidō no Yoake* 1965: 62–3). In the last days of the Bakufu, he had negotiated with Parkes in Ōsaka, and English sources testified to the favourable impression he made (Daniels 1967: 148–9). With the *ishin*, he was appointed to the Foreign Office, and was given responsibility for both the Hyōgo and Yokohama *saibansho*. It was because of the various problems with foreigners at both Hakodate and Karafuto that Ōkubo persuaded a somewhat reluctant Higashikuse to take over the Kaitakushi (Takakura 1982: 45–79). Far from being a nominal position, it was a case of getting the best man for the job.

Higashikuse's diaries and letters (*Hokkaidō no Yoake* 1965: 65) show that, once in Hokkaidō, he moved quickly to establish his own authority, and that he dealt personally with the problems involving foreigners, clans and migrants. But he had no real power base of his own. He had earlier clashed violently with Etō and Shima over the running of Tokyo-fu (Matano 1914, Vol. 1: 399–414). In April 1868, when Tokyo-fu was established, a noble, Karasumaru Mitsunori, was made governor, but for some time the position existed in name only (ibid.: 399–400). Karasumaru and Higashikuse soon found themselves engaged in a power struggle with the Meiji government's Kaikei Kyoku (Accounts Department) which was squeezing money out of Tokyo's wealthy citizens. Three of its senior officials, Etō, Shima and Mito's Kitashima, penned a joint reply to the nobles' protests, threatening to resign if the powers of the Kaikei Kyoku were not confirmed. Their reply bristled with indignation at criticism from 'these people of high rank', and was of a bluntness quite unexpected from subordinate officials (ibid.: 408). The government response was to amalgamate Tokyo-fu with the Kaikei Kyoku – a strange decision as one was a local body and the other an organ of the central government. They were separated again the following year (ibid.: 413–14) and the Treasury set up.

This clash augured ill for relations between Shima and Higashikuse when both were appointed to the Kaitakushi. When they sailed for Hokkaidō in the autumn of 1869, Shima clearly expected to repeat his earlier victory and to retain real control. He went off to build Sapporo, while Takeda went to Soya, Okamoto to Karafuto and Matsumoto to Nemuro. Iwamura stayed on at Hakodate to assist Higashikuse. Though he had no direct power base, Higashikuse belonged to the group of nobles with strong ties with Chōshū and with the nationwide network of extremists typified by Kurume's Maki and Tosa's Takechi (see chapter 11). The Iwamura brothers were from Hata-gun, Takechi's stronghold, and must be ranked among the Takechi supporters. Thus Iwamura should perhaps be regarded, at least initially, as aligned with Higashikuse. Matsumoto, on the other hand, was from Shōnai which, after the Boshin War, was treated with magnanimity by Saigō and Kuroda (Takakura 1982: 307ff.). He owed his Kaitakushi appointment to Kuroda and was clearly *kisatsu*.

In building Sapporo, Shima arrogantly ignored Higashikuse's directions and far exceeded his budget. In January 1870, the Chōkan sailed for Yokohama to obtain more money and to bring Shima to heel (ibid.: 56ff.). He reached Yokohama on the sixteenth, saw the government leaders on the seventeenth, had Shima's dismissal agreed to on the nineteenth, and on the twentieth was on his way back to Hokkaidō with 103,000 *ryō*. Shima had undermined his own position by corresponding directly with, and giving orders to, the Kaitakushi officials in Tokyo (ibid.: 289–90), and by seeming to interfere with the other *hankan*; even so, in having him removed, Higashikuse had shown that he could act with great firmness and despatch.

Iwamura had been one of Shima's critics (ibid.: 297–301), and with his removal, he became in effect the number two man. In March he was sent to Sapporo to pay off the remaining workers (Iguro and Katayama 1967), and in August he was sent back to resume building. Higashikuse arrived to inspect on 2 September 1870, and in his diary confessed that he was impressed by the scale of Shima's achievements (Takakura 1982: 60). Iwamura was more critical (ibid.: 297–301), claiming Shima had spent far too much on public buildings and official residences instead of on housing for permanent settlers.

The removal of Shima effectively ended the Saga dominance of the Kaitakushi. Shima, Ōkuma and Sano had formed a close-knit group in the Bakumatsu period, and after Shima's exploratory work, Ōkuma had helped promote Saga interest in Ezochi (*Ōkuma Kō 85 Nen Shi* 1925: 86). The ousting of Shima was a blow to Saga, and must have been a factor in Ōkuma's and Sano's hostility to the proposed 1881 *haraisage*.

Until 1871 the Kaitakushi directly administered only 20 per cent of the island (Iguro and Katayama 1967: 187ff.), the rest having been turned over to the clans. When this was discussed at a conference on 22 July 1869, only Iwamura had opposed the proposal, pointing out that the clans were both self-centred and exhausted. When volunteers were called for, several clans came forth, hoping for profits from the taxes on fisheries. They included Mito, Sendai, Ichinoseki, Saga, Tokushima and Tosa, but Satsuma, Chōshū, Kaga and Shizuoka were notable abstainers. The government was therefore reduced to ordering the top ten clans to participate. Certain religious orders, the Emperor and the army were also allotted regions.

The role of Satsuma must be stressed. Like Kanazawa, it simply refused to take over its allotted areas, pleading distance and climate. Because of the paucity of sources, very little research has been done on the clan administrators, but from the Higashikuse papers (Takakura 1982: 61) we learn that when he toured in mid-1870 he saw a depressing scene. Tokushima, for example, had control of a coastal area stretching east from Atsubeshi River, but they had not laid a hand on it.

Perhaps the most striking failure was that of Saga, because it did make a serious effort. Higashikuse recorded (ibid.: 52) that Hizen people arrived on 28 November 1869, and proceeded to Akkeshi. Kushiro, Kitami and Akkeshi were all part of Saga's state enterprise (Matsumoto 1974). The largest Saga group migration was from the Imari branch clan which sent 286 migrants who arrived in Kushiro and Akkeshi just before the clans were abolished. They found no prospect of work, and in 1872, 165 were sent on to Sapporo. Perhaps Blakiston, a somewhat jaundiced British observer, was correct when he claimed that the basic trouble was that the Kaitakushi kept the best areas for itself, and that the government was deliberately trying to impoverish and cripple the semi-independent *daimyō*, who were obliged to introduce farmers, whereas agriculture should have been left to a later stage after the coast had been developed (Blakiston 1883).

## THE DISMISSAL OF HIGASHIKUSE

As the clans' administration had been a failure, the system was changed in 1871 and their areas brought under direct Kaitakushi control. Karafuto, which had been a separate department, was also brought under the direct control of Sapporo. In the summer of 1871 Kuroda went to the United States for three months. He met up with Capron, who was being sent to Japan with a party of young Americans to advise the Kaitakushi. It seems they travelled together and bought up a mass of highly expensive machinery which the agricultural assistant Dun described as being as useful as a fifth wheel on a waggon (Dun n.d.: 13–14). In view of the corruption prevailing in both countries, they must be suspected of keeping handsome commissions. Be that as it may, it seems clear that, before he went to America, Kuroda had been assured that he would be put in charge of the Kaitakushi.

The details of Higashikuse's dismissal are not all that clear. According to Ōsaka (1962: 65ff.), Soejima came to Hokkaidō and toured with Higashikuse. When he confided to him that he was to be transferred, Higashikuse accompanied him back to Tokyo to try to save his position. It seems clear that Higashikuse did not go of his own volition. He was made Chief Chamberlain, a position he occupied for thirteen months before going with the Iwakura

Mission, but that does not gainsay the fact that he was ousted from Hokkaidō. At that time, Matsumoto was called to Tokyo to confer. On the boat down, he met Kirino Toshiaki, Saigō's lieutenant, who had been sent to Hokkaidō to assess the situation, especially in relation to possible Satsuma settlements (Matsumoto 1974: 113). Kurino's Hokkaidō tour would reinforce the view that, well before the decision was announced, Satsuma was planning to take over in Hokkaidō. From the outset, there had been clashes between the Kaitakushi and the army over its allotted areas. Thus in October 1869 Shima wrote to Matsuura in Tokyo telling him to get back from the army its three choice *gun* near Sapporo. The appointment of Kuroda may perhaps be regarded as the triumph of the army over its old foes, the Kaitakushi officials. That Kuroda was made Jikan (Deputy Chief), and was not raised to Chōkan till August 1874 (*Hokkaidō no Yoake* 1965: 72ff.), was a sure indication that there was considerable opposition to the change.

Despite the prettified official histories, the personal relations were marked by considerable nastiness. During the Boshin War, Saionji called at a field hospital attending the Satsuma wounded. Yamagata received him politely, but Kuroda refused to meet him, letting it be known he did not think much of nobles (Toyoda 1983: 11–12). Matsumoto also told a strange story of how Kuroda, on returning from Karafuto in 1870, landed at Soya, then made his way in disguise overland to Hakodate, avoiding all the receptions Higashikuse had arranged (Takakura 1982). It would seem to have been a studied insult to Higashikuse.

We are, however, looking at more than mere personal vindictiveness. It would seem that Higashikuse's removal was the result of a considered Satsuma campaign, which left Kuroda in charge in Tokyo and Iwamura in Sapporo. The campaign coincided with the turbulent events of 1870–1, when Sawa and the young nobles led the opposition to the Satchō *batsu*. Rather than viewing Hokkaidō history as a separate story, the dismissal of Higashikuse must be seen as a manifestation of the tightening Satchō grip on the country, and even as an integral part of the 1871 *coup d'état*.

Tosa aided Satchō in their *coup*, and that strengthened Iwamura's hand. He and Kuroda were of the same age, and equal in ambition. The stage was now set for these two to engage in a trial of strength. Again it was partly a personal struggle, and partly a contest between the Chief in Tokyo and the man on the spot in Hokkaidō. But above and beyond that, it must be seen as part of the Tosa-led fight against Satchō – a battle which led into, and was part of, the 1873 *Seihen*.

## THE DISMISSAL OF IWAMURA

The clash between Iwamura and Kuroda was a re-play of that between Shima and Higashikuse. In 1872 Iwamura, without proper reference to Kuroda, exceeded his budget by about 30,000 *yen* (Iguro and Katayama 1967: 218ff.). When asked to apologize, he refused and submitted his resignation. This was not accepted. When Kuroda came to Sapporo for a conference of regional governors, the two clashed violently. In 1871 there had been thirty-five Kaitakushi officials, but a year later there were 306 (ibid.: 119–21). Iwamura now demanded the dismissal of 'all surplus people', and the ending of the policy of creating positions just to give people jobs – a clear reference to Kuroda's practice of providing sinecures for Satsuma *samurai*. Kuroda responded by announcing that the *kisatsu* Matsumoto was being transferred to Sapporo 'to supervise Iwamura'. This angered Iwamura greatly. After the conference, to avoid Matsumoto, Iwamura went off on a long tour, during which he received a letter of dismissal.

Iwamura left Hokkaidō in January 1873. Matsumoto also submitted his resignation, for his subordinates were all loyal to Iwamura, and he had become completely isolated. Kuroda soon came north to put down an uprising in Esashi, and instead of accepting Matsumoto's resignation dismissed 128 officials in Sapporo and Nemuro (Takakura 1982: 139). The way was thus cleared for a complete Satsuma take-over. In the 1873 *Seihen* Kuroda was to be on the Ōkubo–Iwakura side. That *seihen* was largely a Tosa–Saga-led attack on the growing Satchō monopoly of wealth and power, and Kuroda's own *coup* in Hokkaidō must be regarded as part of this wider story. In 1881 Mitsubishi was to combine with Ōkuma to block the 'sale' of Hokkaidō to a mainly Satsuma company, so one should note Iwamura's close Mitsubishi ties.

A small collection of Iwamura's correspondence (Banno and Itō 1978–9) contains about a score of letters from Iwasaki Yatarō. For most, the year is unknown, but they clearly indicate a regular, intimate correspondence. One name which crops up in these letters is Ono Yoshisane (ibid.: 67–8, 73). To say simply that he and Iwamura were cousins does not truly reflect the degree of relationship, for the two families had multiple alliances over a number of generations.

Ono served in the Meiji government from April 1870 till the end of 1873, when he resigned to enter business. Like Inoue, his resignation was also connected to the Osarisawa case. He was arrested and subjected to severe questioning. Inoue was also called to the court and questioned, but in a letter to Yoshitomi pointed out that he had been treated politely and not grilled like Ono (*Segai Inoue Kō Den* 1933, Vol. 2: 101–2). While in the Treasury, Ono also helped substantially to promote Mitsubishi. It was another cousin, Hayashi Yūzō, Iwamura's brother, who arranged the transfer of the clan's Kansai property to Iwasaki; the official Iwasaki biographies point out that the details are not known, but that it was an excellent deal (*Iwasaki Hisaya Den* 1961: 88–91).

A small local history makes the somewhat sweeping claim that it was Yoshisane who laid the real basis for Mitsubishi's wealth and power (*Sukumo Jimbutsu* 1968: 41–8). It points out that when he left the government he became an adviser to Mitsubishi which consulted him on all matters. It would seem that while still an official, Yoshisane not only advised Yataro to get into shipping and helped him obtain government support, but also, along with other officials, put in the capital to buy one of the earliest ships. This was illegal, but it was not difficult to circumvent the law. The sweeping claims made by this history might be attributed to over-zealous local patriotism, but they are substantiated by the official Iwasaki Yatarō biography. It states that during his early days in Osaka, before Mitsubishi was started, Yatarō

> gained a close friend, Ono Yoshisane. . . . In January 1874 Ono resigned from the Government and thereafter he played a key role in Mitsubishi as 'sōdan yaku' [consultant]. He did not formally become a member of Mitsubishi, but as Yatarō's representative he took charge of important negotiations with the Government and with other companies. There are extant about 150 letters from Yatarō to Yoshisane. Many of them relate to highly confidential business matters. At Mitsubishi he received special treatment and must be ranked in importance alongside the top executives, Ishikawa and Kawada.
>
> (*Iwasaki Yatarō Den* 1967, Vol. 1: 639–40)

At the end of volume 1 (p. 758), in discussing sources, the authors amend the figure for the number of letters, saying there are 150 letters to people who are not family members, and of these 100 and some tens are addressed to Yoshisane. This amended figure merely drives home Yoshisane's unique role which cannot be adequately rendered by 'consultant' or any other word in English. He was their pipeline to the government, a major ideas man, and their negotiator with the business world. He can perhaps be compared to Inoue and his role with Mitsui.

In 1881 Yoshisane took part in the formation of the Japan Railways which was about to link Tokyo and Aomori. He became president of the railway and remained in charge for twenty-one years until it was sold to the government. But again he must be regarded as Mitsubishi's man. By 1881 Mitsubishi already controlled the seaways around Hokkaidō. It had also established banking facilities, and, as we saw in earlier ages, control of shipping and credit would surely lead to control of trade. Getting control, through Ono, of the railway to Aomori must be regarded as another link in the chain binding Hokkaidō to Mitsubishi. The Kuroda–Godai *haraisage* of 1881 must be seen as a counter-attack against Mitsubishi.

In 1886 Iwamura was to return to Hokkaidō as chief administrator and instituted policies which favoured the big capitalists at the expense of the small settlers (Iguro and Katayama 1967: 236–40). In 1888, however, Kuroda became prime minister and promptly had Iwamura transferred. Hereafter Iwamura was mostly at the Imperial Household Ministry from which position in 1896 he arranged the transfer of the Sado gold mines and Ikuno copper to Mitsubishi (*Iwasaki Hisaya Den* 1961: 356ff.). Unlike Hayashi, Iwamura was a true conservative. Their family history nicely illustrates the continuity of the story, for Hayashi's son opposed the military in the thirties and became deputy prime minister under Yoshida after the war, whereas one of Iwamura's sons became Tōjō's most successful minister. His particular responsibility was law and order. (*Iwamura Yoshio Den* 1971) After the war he was imprisoned as a war criminal.

Historians, both Western and Japanese, have generally treated the triumphant Satchō oligarchy with such politeness that the natures of their 1871 *coup*, of the *seihen* of 1873 and 1881, and of their subsequent government, have all been distorted beyond all recognition. Thus the leading study of the 1873 *Seihen* concentrates on Saigō's 'heart' and does not touch on Hokkaidō, while Ōkubo's authoritative study of the 1881 *Seihen* dismisses Hokkaidō as irrelevant and concentrates on the personal rivalry of Itō and Ōkuma. But the policies which were to be applied in Korea were worked out in Hokkaidō. Equally as significant, as will be discussed later, Iwasaki, Godai and Mitsui were all trying to penetrate Korea before the *ishin*. Far from being irrelevant, Hokkaidō gave a clear warning of the kind of political–commercial struggles between the leading clans which would arise once Korea was opened. Advantage in Korea, and later Manchuria and China, was going to depend on who was in charge in Tokyo when the opening was effected. This basic fact, it would seem, has never been pinpointed by Japanese historians, but surely it goes to the heart of the 1873 *Seihen*. The clashes involving Shima, Higashikuse, Iwamura and Kuroda cannot be brought down to the level of power struggles between ambitious individuals. Essentially, they were contests for commercial empire.

Though source material is scarce, let us therefore look at an example of this early commercial rivalry.

## TOKYO-FU'S ATTEMPT TO TAKE OVER NEMURO

Not a great deal of detailed research has been done on commercial rivalry in the early Meiji period. To illustrate some of the cross-currents, let us take just one example, Tokyo-fu's attempt to take over Nemuro. We are mainly dependent on Matsumoto's accounts (1974: 65–87; Takakura 1982: 317ff.), and must remember that he was not a disinterested party.

Matsumoto was in charge of three *gun* – Nemuro, Nofu and Hanasaki – which had an established fishing industry. A group of Tokyo merchants, anticipating large profits, carried on a campaign to have this region placed under the Tokyo local government (ibid.: 318). Eventually they obtained the support of Higashikuse, who wrote to Matsumoto in mid-1870 informing him of the decision. Matsumoto had been off touring, and returned to be greeted by glum-faced officials and fishermen who would both lose out to new people from Tokyo.

Matsumoto set off for Hakodate, catching up with the touring Higashikuse north of that city. He pointed out that Nemuro was quite unsuitable for migrants, and that Tokyo was only interested in the lucrative fisheries. Higashikuse seemed to share his anger, but advised acceptance, saying it was the government's orders. Matsumoto repeated that he was unable to accept the decision, whereupon Higashikuse announced that he was posting Matsumoto to Otaru. Matsumoto pointed out that Iwamura was in Sapporo and that there was no need for a *hankan* in neighbouring Otaru. He argued by analogy with Takeda, the Soya *hankan* who had resigned when Soya was transferred to the Kanazawa clan.

Eventually he agreed to proceed to Hakodate and to wait there for Higashikuse.

In Hakodate, he soon got together with the deputy *hankan* Sugiura, a Shizuoka clansman he had known from old. Kuroda also passed through Hakodate with his deputies on his way to Karafuto, and expressed great sympathy. He praised Matsumoto for his 'model administration', and went off to talk to Higashikuse. The result was that Higashikuse ordered Matsumoto back to Nemuro, saying he was determined that the three *gun* would stay under the Kaitakushi.

Matsumoto was welcomed back by the fisherfolk 'as though back from the dead'. The new officials had already arived from Tokyo, so a cat-and-mouse game followed until in October word came from Tokyo that the transfer had been cancelled. Matsumoto concluded: 'Thus at long last the fisherfolk of the three *gun* were able to feel good and to relax.'

Tokyo-fu was urged to take over Abuta-*gun* as an alternative, as its good climate and soil made it far more suitable for migrants; but it showed no interest, a clear indication that its main interests were commercial, and that as far as migrants were concerned, all they wanted was a dumping ground. That winter, a police officer, Kitagaki Kunimichi, visited Nemuro and reported that it was not suitable for migrants. This report helped Matsumoto have the Tokyo migrants moved on in the summer of 1871 (ibid.: 319).

The historian must largely rely on sparse, highly personal accounts such as this, but one can detect some of the undercurrents. Matsumoto and Sugiura were clearly working closely with the old-established Hakodate merchants with fishing interests in the east. There are constant references to services such as providing accommodation and transport, selling off furniture, entertaining, etc., so it seems probable that Matsumoto had a financial stake in keeping out the Tokyo newcomers. But the wide story of what interests were involved requires far more research.

Kuroda's struggle with Higashikuse would seem to have been more than a contest between two individuals. Higashikuse, one of 'the seven nobles', had close Chōshū ties, and though the evidence is sketchy, it would seem that the commercial struggle for Hokkaidō, which was to climax in 1881, began straight after the *ishin*. Mitsui and Ono were both *goyō* merchants to the Kaitakushi (Miyamoto 1981: 323ff.). When Inoue's Senshūsha was set up in late 1873, Inoue was soon writing, stressing the importance of Hokkaidō products such as herring (*Segai Inoue Kō Den* 1933, Vol. 2: 523–5).

227

Clearly Chōshū was interested in the Hokkaidō trade, but the story does not seem to have been researched. The Hokkaidō official histories are of little help, as are the official biographies. Ōkura, for example, became a key figure in Hokkaidō, but his 1924 official biography is just a mass of inconsequential trivia. Miyamoto (1981: 139ff.) writes of the Osarisawa mine, and later of Inoue's key protégé, Nakano (ibid.: 254), without even mentioning Inoue. We must remember this when Miyamoto tells us (ibid.: 323ff.) that in the New Year of 1872 Nagasaki merchant Mitsukawa Shingō sent the Kaitakushi a paper on Hokkaidō pointing out that the China trade had fallen into foreign hands because of the lack of capital. The Kaitakushi therefore sent representatives to Shanghai and Amoy to investigate, and in October a group of eight merchants led by Enomoto Rokubei obtained permission to trade directly with China. They were given a subsidy of 100,000 *yen* and the loan of a steamer, *Hokkai Maru*. Their Hōninsha, with Enomoto as president, began its operations in May 1873, trading between Hakodate, Osaka and Shanghai. In the uprisings of 1874–5, the government recalled both its ship and its subsidy, and the Hōninsha had to close down. But other officials were soon sent to China, and in October 1876 the Kōgyō Shōkai was set up under Kasano Kumakichi. Kasano was to die in 1879, and Godai then took over direct control of the company. It would seem it was really a Godai company from the outset. From his childhood, Godai was Kuroda's 'aniki' (see chapter 10), and it would seem logical to believe that Godai was closely involved in Hokkaidō from the time when Kuroda took over.

Though the evidence of *zaibatsu* struggles in early Hokkaidō is sketchy, a leading merchant, Kashima Manpei, seems to provide a connecting link between Mitsui, the colonization of Chiba, and the Tokyo interests wanting to get control of the Nemuro fisheries. So let us turn to the subject of poor relief and the role of Kashima.

## THE PROBLEM OF POVERTY IN TOKYO

A major aspect of the 1873 *Seihen* was Etō Shimpei's attempt to make Satchō officials subject to the Rule of Law. The term 'human rights' was not yet in use, but Etō was struggling to guarantee basic human rights. The need for that struggle is clearly illustrated by the Hokkaidō story. *Goyō* historians are lavish in their praise for the Meiji leaders, but their personal rapacity is an important element in the Meiji story. Far from the 1873 *Seihen* being, as Tokutomi would have us believe, a dispute between two factions both guided by the highest principles, much of the trouble came from an unprincipled grab for the spoils of war.

In his *Recollections* (Kanjō Shogun Kaisō-roku), Miura Gorō (1925: 75–6) pointed out that after the Boshin War, 'the Court' distributed rewards – Satsuma and Chōshū both receiving 100,000 *koku*. The troops, however, received very little. Instead of looking after his men, Yamagata merely allotted three *ryō* each for burial expenses; even then, many corpses were simply thrown into a long trench, one on top of another. It was not until 1891 that a Miura-led movement had the bodies sorted out and headstones put up. The continuing widespread corruption in the form of lavish distribution of travel funds, etc., and the scandals exposed, kept the demobilized troops in a state of anger. At one stage, about 3,000 took to the mountains and the clan leaders fled for their lives. Kido rejected Saigō's offers of assistance and returned home to regain control.

While the Satchō leaders were thus rewarding themselves, conditions in Tokyo were a shambles. The population of Edo had often been given as 3,000,000, but Etō put it at 2,000,000, of whom 1,310,000 had been clan retainers, with the remaining 690,000 dependent upon them (Matano 1914: 389). But with the civil war, the clans had withdrawn, and their properties remained unoccupied and unsaleable. Thus Etō estimated that in 1868 nine-tenths of Tokyo's population were *hinmin* (ibid.: 384). Beggars and untouchables swarmed through the city. Rents were high, fires numerous, the bureaucracy corrupt, the courts slow, and rice distribution in the hands of middlemen given to hoarding. Etō addressed himself vigorously to these problems. Detailed laws were drawn up to prevent fires, including the forbidding of single occupancy; rules were drawn up to eliminate rice middlemen, and a system of poor relief was revived. Officially, the money was to provide work, but the people of Edo lacked the craft skills of their Kansai counterparts, so it was not clear what work could be made available. These plans and Etō's financial demands on the Tokyo citizens brought him into conflict with Tokyo local officials Karasumaru and Higashikuse.

The relief question was tied up with that of law and order, so the government wished to register everyone before trying to find them work. The main hope was to get them out of Tokyo and settle them on the land.

The poor consisted of two types: those who had been poor under the Bakufu and those who were reduced to poverty by the fall of the

Bakufu. The latter may be sub-divided into *samurai* who had lost their stipends and city people who had depended on the Bakufu for a living. On 4 August 1868 the Grand Council of State issued a notice urging *rōnin* to return to their former clans and to re-register (Kitahara 1975). These *rōnin* had played an important role in the overthrow of the Bakufu, but whereas the Satchō leaders were now a new power elite, the *rōnin* had quickly been reduced to the status of unemployed poor no different to the followers of the defeated Bakufu. On 27 October 1868 a proclamation announced that former Tokugawa followers and other *furyō no hai* would soon be investigated. For the *rōnin* it was a cruel blow.

On 14 October 1868 the Army Department had been made responsible for unemployed *samurai*, but on 8 March 1869 they were made the joint responsibility of the army, the Accounts Department and the Department of Law and Police (ibid.: 54–5). The purpose of this change was revealed two days later when it was proclaimed that people without means of support were to be sent to Koganehara in Shimōsa (Chiba) to pioneer new lands. The despatch of the poor elsewhere would not only remove a financial burden but would also clear out the dangerous *rōnin* class.

On 15 March 1869 the Tokyo-fu presented the government with a detailed plan for Koganehara. The new area was to be amalgamated with the neighbouring prefectures and so cease to be the responsibility of Tokyo. Farmers, traders and other moneyed people were to be attracted by land grants, as it was impossible for the poor alone to start a new settlement. Those who had committed crimes were also to be sent as colonists and turned into productive farmers. Escapees were to be severely punished (ibid.: 56–7).

All Tokyo residents were to be registered by the twentieth. Those with no previous Tokyo registration were to be placed in a separate book. The wording refers to '*sewa*' (being looked after), but in practice this meant being sent to Koganehara. It was estimated there were 100,000 Tokyo *rōnin* with no previous registration.

On 19 March a Kaikon-Kyoku (Pioneering Department) was set up with wide-ranging powers. The task was a daunting one. A survey of August 1869 found a population of 503,700, which it divided into four classes: the propertied classes, the poor, the extremely poor and the destitute needing institutionalization. The respective figures were 196, 670, 201, 760, 103, 470 and 1,800 (ibid.: 59).

In May 200,000 *ryō* had been set aside for the Pioneering Office (ibid.: 62), and the Koganehara plan expanded to a grand scheme to develop the whole of Shimōsa. Representatives of trading companies were brought into the organization (ibid.: 65–6). Recruitment mostly took the form of rounding up and corralling the Tokyo poor. Four former clan residences were used to house them while waiting to set out. During the waiting period they were given simple work and divided into *samurai* and *heimin*. The *samurai* were then sub-divided into Shogun and Emperor supporters. By the end of 1870, when recruitment virtually stopped, 8,200 of the Tokyo poor had been handled by this Pioneering Office, and of these 6,149 were sent to pioneer, many after a stay of only a couple of days at one of the above residences (ibid.: 63–4). Only 20 per cent of these pioneers were *samurai* (ibid.: 91).

Kitahara concluded (ibid.: 70) that though the term *shigansha* (volunteer) was used, compulsion was widely employed. The Bakufu dependants were mostly of the lower classes, such as messengers, so they did not take kindly to the new life, and a high proportion became fugitives (ibid.: 72ff.). There was also a high infant mortality rate due to infectious diseases. Crop failures added to the problems, so in September 1871 the company was reduced to asking the government for a loan of 70,000 *ryō*. That year the government also urged the Colonial Company to undertake the drainage and development of two large marsh lands in Shimōsa (ibid.: 83), but the company successfully resisted this government pressure. In December the new territories were handed over to the local small prefectures, and the sale or return of the former clan residences was begun. By mid-1872, Tokyo-fu was able to wash its hands of the whole business, leaving it to the Colonial Company and to the small neighbouring prefectures. In November 1871 laws for Poor Relief were laid down for all prefectures, but these were merely regulations for fire and other emergencies. Basic responsibility for Poor Relief remained with the central government, where it passed to the newly instituted Treasury.

A *bussan kyoku* had also been set up in 1869 on the initiative of Ōki (ibid.: 77–8). Some of the poor were set to work cultivating tea and mulberries, for this work required no training, and tea and silk provided the most certain exports. But it would seem the plan failed, for in 1872 these lands were sold off. It had been hoped that these enterprises would provide the funds for three asylums set up in 1869, two for those too young or too old to work and one for beggars rounded up off the streets (ibid.: 73). The inmates of this workhouse could not leave until they had been trained and had acquired a little money. Of the 955 who entered, seventy-nine died in the first month and 307 escaped (ibid.: 74–5). The Western press predictably applauded the government's efforts. On 6 January 1872 the *Weekly Mail* gave a review of 1871 in which its bitterest attacks were reserved for the lower *samurai*, an idle lot who were 'a canker in the very heart of the country'.

Kitahara (1973: 78) notes that in response to a Grand Council of State notice of 22 July 1869, 400 men and women were recruited for Hokkaidō, and that when they sailed on 9 September 1869, the 400 included forty-four ex-inmates of the Mita workhouse. Compulsion had been used in sending people to Koganehara, and it would seem that Tokyo's early migrants to Hokkaidō were subjected to a mixture of coercion and misrepresentation.

Kitahara's study does not cover Hokkaidō, but he notes that in June 1870, when the three Nemuro-*gun* were switched to Tokyo-fu, there were great hopes of sending the Tokyo poor; then in August this transfer was cancelled, and all Tokyo's efforts came to naught (ibid.: 82). Here it would seem that Kitahara was being naive, for Tokyo's interest in Nemuro was clearly commercial, not humanitarian.

Much research remains to be done on this story, but it would seem that the Tokyo merchants interested in Nemuro were the same as those involved commercially at Koganehara. A connecting link is provided by Kashima Manpei (1822–91). It seems that little research has been done on Kashima, but a potted biography is provided by *Nippon Zaikai Jimbutsu Retsu Den* (1963), a large, glossy publication which must be treated with caution as it contains some factual errors. It states that as a youth Manpei worked for a merchant, then, with the opening of Yokohama, he went into foreign trade and made a fortune from cotton. In 1867 he combined with Mitsui's Minomura to go into money-changing, and with the Restoration went with the ex-Shogun to Shizuoka as the Mitsui representative. He was a founding member of the Koganehara Kaikon Kaisha, and in 1869, 'on government orders', he opened a trading post in Hokkaidō. He set up an exchange business there, then developed the wild areas around Kushiro, dealing in herring, fish oil and seaweed. Back in Kanto he ordered cotton machinery, setting up a factory in Takinogawa village. In 1876 he was successful in making cotton cloth, and late in life he retired to Ōji in the Takinogawa district.

We are, of course, getting into a grey area where proof gives way to speculation, but this brief sketch provides us with important clues.

The Dai-Ichi Bank, which, after 1875, simultaneously opened up Korea and Tohoku, was backed by Mitsui which had been trying to get into Korea even before the *ishin*. The export of cotton cloth was likewise dominated by Shibusawa and Ōkura, and Ōji paper by Shibusawa and Mitsui. It would seem that we are looking at one interlocking story – that Chiba, Tōhoku, Hokkaidō and Korea were all parts of early Meiji colonization, and that in all cases, not too far away in the background, was Mitsui.

Hokkaidō history has been so submerged by official histories that the true story rarely emerges. We saw in chapter 2 how for at least a century and a half before the Restoration, Ezochi, an important part of a wide trading network, was the scene of an extreme form of modern commercial capitalism dominated by the Ōmi merchants. In Kaiho's words, it was 'armed commercial capitalism' (1974: 169). There was no Rule of Law, but Matsumae *samurai* policed the land for the rich merchants, while labour was provided by the Ainu and seasonal workers from Tōhoku. With the Restoration, the Ōmi merchants were squeezed out, and in 1881 we seem suddenly to find the fierce struggle for commercial supremacy between Mitsubishi and Godai, with the eighties seeing Mitsui and the Ōkura-gumi coming to the fore. But this surely was no sudden confrontation. If we look again at the seemingly personal struggles involving in turn Shima, Higashikuse, Kuroda and Iwamura, we can, despite the 'histories', begin to detect a pattern of commercial rivalry. Saga was quickly eliminated and lost the economic toe-hold established in the Bakumatsu period. Higashikuse's elimination was no doubt in part due to the Sawa-led political upheavals, but probably more fundamental was the fact that Higashikuse was *Chōshū-kei* and was backing the attempts of Tokyo merchants such as Kashima to take over an important area in Hokkaidō; and behind Kashima was Mitsui. The 1881 *Seihen* was merely the climax of a commercial struggle which had begun as soon as Ezochi was taken back from Enomoto. It should be remembered that Kuroda was born near *aniki* Godai and remained close to him. The idea of making Hokkaidō a part of the Satsuma commercial empire was not something which popped up spontaneously in 1881, but was inherent in its 1871 move for control of the Kaitakushi.

Iwamura, as we have seen, had strong Mitsubishi ties. There was no doubt a strong personal element in the clash between Kuroda and Iwamura, but Tosa, like Saga, had been interested in Ezochi in the Bakumatsu period, and later Mitsubishi moved quickly to establish itself there. Surely the driving out of Iwamura and his supporters should be viewed as an early battle in the Mitsubishi–Satchō wars of the eighties.

In short, after the Satchō *coup* of 1871, Satsuma took control of the Kaitakushi and moved to drive the opposition out of Hokkaidō and to make it a Satsuma sphere of influence, both politically and commercially. This entry into Hokkaidō represented a dramatic change of heart from 1868 when it flatly refused to take up the areas allotted to her, so the differences should be noted. The 1868 plan called for Satsuma, like the other clans, to bear the expenses herself and to send her own settlers. But when Satsuma took over the Kaitakushi, the central government bore all the expenses, and Satsuma sent not settlers or soldiers but well-paid officials who were not called upon to brave the elements or to live permanently in Hokkaidō.

## HOKKAIDŌ MIGRATION

Let us take up again the story of the Tokyo poor who migrated to Hokkaidō. When Higashikuse and the *hankan* sailed for Hokkaidō in 1869, they were accompanied by about 300 migrants, 100 each for Nemuro, Soya and Karafuto. As we have seen, they included forty-five from the Tokyo workhouse set up for those too broken-down to go to Koganehara. Matsumoto (1974: 61) summed it up by saying that his people could not be thought of as ordinary human beings. Before their departure, Matsumoto had urged Shima to suspend this migration, pointing out that in Nemuro there was neither housing nor work; the migrants were not trained as farmers; and the land was inhospitable and under snow for most of the year. Thus they would merely eat up the limited food supplies and catch the local diseases. The government was portraying its programme as philanthropic, but it was no act of philanthropy to send penniless, untrained people to such an environment.

Shima replied that the Colonial Office had nothing to do with the decision, but was merely following orders, so any complaints had to be taken up with the Tokyo authorities. Matsumoto therefore went to see Yuri Kimimasa, but Yuri claimed it was too late to back down as the government had given its approval and the migrants had been selected. Yuri painted a more favourable picture of the migrants, claiming some had sold their homes and others had obtained brides specifically to go to Hokkaidō.

There seems to be little detailed information about these settlers. One can compare them, for example, to British Indian indentured labourers going overseas. Though there were abuses and misrepresentation, the Indian labourers had a written contract with provision for a free return passage after a certain number of years, and stipulations about wages, food, housing and medical care. But it would seem that the Hokkaidō migrants, though they had committed no crime, were really convict labour with no contracts and no legal guarantees of any kind. Far from a contractual right to a free return passage, it seems obvious that the position was the same as with the Koganehara migrants: those who left were fugitives and as such subject to the full weight of the law. Indeed, for the government, the advantages of Hokkaidō were essentially those which Van Dieman's Land (Tasmania) presented to the early Australian government, for Nemuro, Soya and Karafuto were places from which it was virtually impossible to escape.

Not surprisingly, Matsumoto's two sets of reminiscences made in old age vary somewhat in detail. The account in *Nemuro mo Hoshi Kusa* (ibid.: 59–64) says that at first the migrants were housed in rented huts by the sea. They were extremely disorderly, threatening the fishing community and stealing their *sake*, so with the help of fifteen tradesmen he set them to build a three-cell prison. But according to the Kōno account (Takakura 1982: 317), Matsumoto, realizing that his charges were lazy good-for-nothings, set them to build a prison as soon as they arrived. This caused great indignation among 'the good citizens', so, out of his own pocket, he built a hospital and set aside one room for schooling. He does not explain how he came to have this money in his pocket, but it strengthens suspicions that he had his own arrangements with Hokkaidō merchants.

Whichever version one takes – and the second seems the more likely – the cells were soon occupied. They proved effective, and long incarceration was not necessary. In the Hokkaidō winter, even after one night in an unheated cell with no covering, the miscreants were too frozen to walk. In Matsumoto's words, 'it was cruel in the extreme, but there was no alternative'. That first winter seventeen of the ninety-nine died. We are not told how many of the seventeen had spent a night in jail. Nemuro was an old settlement with a fishing industry, so appalling though conditions were, they were not as bad as in the even more isolated Soya and Karafuto. Again we are given few details, but that first winter twenty-two of the Soya party and thirty-five of the Karafuto party died, making a total of seventy-four out of 300, or 25 per cent (Matsumoto 1974: 65–87).

Of course, the death rate may well have been far greater than indicated by the official figures. Thus the *Japan Weekly Mail* of 28 October 1871 (pp. 604–5) declared that 'more care must be exercised in regard to the people sent up than was the case last year when *the greater part* of those who left in November perished miserably of cold and hunger'.

In September 1870, during the struggle with Tokyo-fu, Kuroda praised Matsumoto for his 'model administration':

> Your handling of the situation was very good, so there was no violence. At Soya, the Karafuto migrants became uncontrollable, and to restore order it became necessary to shoot and kill. Also many got the local diseases and about 35 died. . . . Among the Soya migrants 22 died of local diseases. There were also those who raped the wives and daughters of local officials, and the Akita clan Long House was destroyed and used for firewood. Because of this I have returned all the Soya–Karafuto migrants to the jurisdiction of Tokyo.
>
> (ibid.)

One cannot imagine half-starved, half-frozen men in the Hokkaidō winter being in any condition to commit rape. Nor was Hokkaidō an unhealthy place like West Africa with a high death rate among officials. Indeed, many missionaries such as Batchelor (1902), first came to Hokkaidō from China for their health. The high death rate was surely due not to unnamed 'local diseases' but to shocking conditions and a feeling that the migrants were expendable. Kōno adds a few details (Takakura 1982: 66–7). Soya was 'a running sore'. Higashikuse's diary noted that on 17 September 1870 seventeen Soya officials were dismissed. On 10 October 1870 Matsumoto came to see him about the Soya problem. No details of their talks are given, but that same month the Soya migrants were given permission to return to Tokyo. They were each given 15 *ryō* and told they should report back in spring.

The whole migration 'plan' had been an utter disaster. In Nemuro, the migrants had clearly been sent off, partly to clear the poor out of Tokyo and partly to establish Tokyo's claims to the profitable fisheries. Once those claims collapsed, they showed no interest in neighbouring areas suitable for migrants. The Nemuro migrants hung on till May 1871, when sixty-seven were shipped out to work at Banaguro. The adults were given three *ryō*, the children two, and all were given a set of clothes. It seems that this is all they had to show for eighteen months. About a dozen were able to stay on and be absorbed in Nemuro.

In 1872 Matsumoto was to pass Banaguro by boat on his way to the Sapporo Conference. Seeing his former charges, he went ashore for a re-union. He remarked that they were under the control of two strong Mito *samurai* who had worked for him in Nemuro (ibid.: 65–87). It is hard to imagine them volunteering to do construction work in Hokkaidō rather than returning to Tokyo. It would seem that they had no right to a free return passage and had not saved the fare. One point raised by Capron in an 1873 report (Iguro and Katayama 1967: 143–4) was that the fare from Tokyo to Sapporo was higher than that to San Francisco. It would seem that the law regarding 'fugitives' still applied and that the two Mito stalwarts were really armed guards.

Two other lots of migrants should be noted. In 1876 ten Chinese agricultural workers were brought to Hokkaidō on a three-year contract. One of those contracts is preserved in the Hokkaidō University *Shiryō Shitsu* (Ryō Ishō 8.1.1876). It provides for a free room, utensils, farming implements and a free return passage at the end of the contract but not if they left early. They had to work every day except national holidays. Though the Chinese example proved instructive, the experiment was not repeated as having foreigners living in their midst posed social problems. The experiment is of interest as it contrasts with internal migration where there were no written contracts, no free return passage and no legally enforcible rights. It was possible simply to dump the urban poor in Hokkaidō.

As we have seen, Sada gave as one of his reasons for invading Korea the fact that Korean labourers could be sent to work in Hokkaidō. Which system did he envisage – that for the urban poor or the written contracts of the ten Chinese? China was an independent country which could back its own migrants, but once Japan had occupied Korea its position was going to be similar to that of Hokkaidō and the Ryūkyūs. Koreans sent to labour in Hokkaidō would clearly have been part of the internal migration 'system'.

## HIROSHIMA MIGRATION

It should be noted that as the Kaitakushi period drew to a close, the human rights situation of the migrants remained as grim as ever. In

1882, 436 migrants arrived in Eastern Hokkaidō (311 for Nemuro and 121 for Kushiro) (*Nemuro City History*: 390–5). They included 233 from Aki, a group of eighty families having sailed from Hiroshima on 7 September. Because of cholera on board they were delayed at Hyōgo, and when they reached Nemuro it was already late October. All these migrants had been recruited from the destitute poor. They had been promised that they could take up either agriculture or fishing, and that there would be all sorts of openings. When they arrived, however, it was already too late for farming and fishing, and as Nemuro was experiencing a depression, there were no jobs. On 25 December 1882 the Nemuro prefecture applied to Saigō, the Minister for Agriculture and Commerce, for relief. Saigō refused. They were put on public relief, but by the end of 1883, 138 had died. For the men, the figure was 123 out of 243.

The City History (p. 395) places the blame on the nature of the migrants – the scrapings of Hiroshima who did not want to work so that all the urgings and assistance of the local authorities were of no avail. This attitude tells us a great deal about Japanese official histories – that the victims themselves are criticized and that Satsuma's Saigō, who let them die, escapes censure, though lack of funds must be traced back to Satsuma sloth and corruption.

## THE SATSUMA 'CONTRIBUTION'

Japanese historians sometimes write casually of a feudal system having existed in Ezochi. This is highly misleading, for feudalism presupposes a body of serfs tied to one area, whereas Ezochi was a trade-based colony in which the natives had been enslaved to provide labour. As even the clan leaders had originally been traders, merchants and officials were on more intimate terms and there had been relatively little of the 'respect officials, look down on the people' attitude so typical of Japanese feudalism.

Satsuma's policy may be described as an attempt to impose a kind of feudalism, with an official *samurai* class lording it over permanent settlers from the conquered clans. It recalls the many settlements after Sekigahara, where the victors sent their men into Tosa, Fukuoka, etc. to form a new hereditary, ruling warrior class, while the defeated *samurai* were forced back onto the land. The failure of the Kaitakushi was the failure of this feudalism to take root, for the new official warrior class were drones who left both farming and soldiering to the defeated clans. Hokkaidō was not yet ready for extensive agricultural development, but remained dependent on trade, with most migrants drifting off the land to find work in the coastal trade (Blakiston 1883: 60).

Japanese *goyō* histories are, as ever, evasive, but we have extensive foreign witness to the character and 'achievements' of the Kaitakushi under Satsuma. Harrison (1953: 116) who had access to the Capron Papers in the Department of Agriculture Library, Washington, quoted Capron as sardonically estimating that at the Ishikari salmon fisheries there was one official to every ten salmon netted, and at Nanae farm, one supervisor for every labourer.

Hokkaidō University has a large collection of letters and documents relating to the *yatoi gaijin*. Though some of these people were not unbiased, their witness still adds up to a damning indictment. Wheeler, Clarke's deputy, summed it up in a letter to his mother dated 19 May 1879: 'Officers! Officers! Officers! – are Japan's burden – the practical object of the government is their support.'

On 19 July 1873, Samuel Askins, the American captain of the *Kuroda* from 20 November 1872 to 21 March 1874, wrote to Kuroda about his 'filthy ship':

> Two Captains on board of one Ship is one to [sic] many. . . . When Sailors are permitted to go on shore as soon as the Anchor is let go, and remain there till the Ship sails, and come on board in a very intoxicated state, go to the forecastle and remain there for several days. The Boatswain should be dismissed from the Ship immediately, he is a man that takes care of nothing, he has destroyed more rigging and other material in two months than i [sic] would in 218. When i [sic] remonstrate with him, the answer is the Kaitakushi have plenty of money . . . with such doings as we have here, the largest Shipowner in America would be drove to Bankruptcy in 18 months . . . i [sic] have been at sea forty two years and have never seen such very bad discipline.

Among the *yatoi gaijin*, the most eminent was Lyman, a leading American geologist who had served with distinction in India (Hokkaidō University Library: Henry to Mori Arinori 8.7.1872). A highly cultured man, he was to be for years the dining companion and correspondent of such academic greats as Basil Hall Chamberlain and David Murray. Lyman wrote to Capron about 'what foreigners call "the Japanese sickness" – a poor excuse for idleness' (ibid.: Lyman to Capron 5.12.1874). He specifically excluded his field workers from this description. He wrote an even more sweeping indictment in a letter to 'the Honourable Sangi' dated 6 April 1874. This letter, written in the heat of anger, was never sent but, significantly, has been preserved for posterity. Lyman had proposed to, and been accepted by, one of the ladies in the Sapporo girls' school. Neither the school nor the Kaitakushi wished to put a ban on international marriages, but they found it arrogant that Lyman should come in and expect to marry anyone he chose. They sought a compromise, but Lyman would not accept the girl they offered. He went to battle and finally obtained official permission to marry the girl of his choice. Then, however, the officials exerted pressure on the girl and her family and made her reject him. This must be borne in mind when reading Lyman's letter.

> I have the gravest complaints to make against K. Kuroda, Kaitakijikwan and make bold to ask for his dismissal from the present responsible post.
> 1. He has most wastefully expended to the extent of seven millions of rios in three years, it is said, the money appropriated for the improvement of Hokkaidō, with so little return to show therefore as to make it clear that he has either connived at robbery of the government or that he has through intellectual incapacity been unable to prevent it. He has, for example, in the building of a single road, allowed about half a million dollars to be stolen outright, twice as much as by a liberal estimate would have built the road. Most costly and palpably useless engineering works have been carried out with his consent, and not a single important officer has been seriously punished for complicity with such wholesale robberies. On the contrary one at least of the chief managers of such works is well known to be a favourite of his. It is perfectly plain to all disinterested men that he is either a knave or a fool; and on either account is wholly unfit to act as the head of a department.

Even allowing for Lyman's palpable anger, it does seem that there was, on the one hand, 'the Japanese sickness', and on the other, widespread institutionalized corruption orchestrated by the men who were to lay claim in 1881 to all the government property in Hokkaidō.

Capron himself was given to pointed barbs. When Kuroda was made a Major General during the Formosa campaign, he commented that 'the position was intended to give him a little higher rank as I understand, but I think it will turn his head, and the Kaitakushi may suffer by being turned over to some of those common fellows' (ibid.: Capron to Lyman 23.7.1874).

For the courtly Capron, this was strong language. The *Japan Weekly Mail* also carried British reports which were no more flattering. On 11 May 1872 (pp. 266–7) it gave Troup's Consular Trade Report for 1871 which declared: 'The [Hokkaidō] trade is hampered by the action of a herd of ignorant officials whose only object is to get as much as possible out of it for themselves.'

On the large issues, Capron's advice seems to have been sound, but it brought him into conflict with the high officials concerned with self-aggrandizement. He wanted the application of the American Homestead Law which allowed free occupation of 20 to 160 acres if taken up within six months of applying. After a stay of two years, occupiers would be entitled to all the deeds of the land (see Preliminary Report on the Development of Hokkaidō 2.1.1972).

He also spelt out his opposition to 'forced immigration', pointing out that the rapid changes taking place in Japan 'must necessarily involve radical changes in the whole labour system of the Empire'. This would seem to confirm the impression that the migration from Tokyo, for example, was far from voluntary. More controversial were his plans for American and European migrants. It may, of course, be argued that the government was right to insist on maintaining a homogeneous society, but it must be noted that the Kaitakushi officials were not occupying the high moral ground.

In 1875, Matsumoto, then in charge in Sapporo, returned to Nemuro (Takakura 1982: 329) to settle some trouble there. While he was away, Enomoto and Ōtori applied for, and had approved, huge land grants along the Toyohira and Ishikari rivers respectively. The approval was granted by Ōyama Shige, who had been promoted in March. He denied any impropriety and challenged them to arrest him for theft if he had broken the law. But Capron opposed the grants, pointing out that alienating such large areas would pose problems for the future. Lyman also entered the fray (Harrison 1953: 78), advocating a tax on undeveloped land. The central fact was that Enomoto and Ōtori had no intention of developing their holdings, but intended to keep them until the inferior surrounding areas had been settled. They could then sell them and make a fortune without having lifted a finger. The effects of such grants were, of course, disastrous, for it was difficult enough to get settlers without denying them access to the best lands. Matsumoto went on to claim that Enomoto used a dummy to get possession of the former Wada village where Nemuro *tonden* were placed, and concluded by saying 'Enomoto did many bad things' (Takakura 1982: 330).

Ōsaka's account (1962: 85–6) is in substantial agreement with Matsumoto's. Ōtori and Yoshida Kiyonari had been sent to the United States to buy agricultural equipment – in itself somewhat suspicious as both were devoid of any expertise. In September 1873, following new rules for land sales, Enomoto and Ōtori applied for grants in the name of their sons. Kuroda then applied for a huge grant for himself. In the face of a public outcry, Ōtori then handed back half his grant and Kuroda withdrew following a bitter protest from Matsumoto. However, their applications had lighted the fuse for extensive land *haraisage*.

What was good for Satsuma was not good for Japan. The Kaitakushi officials blatantly and arrogantly sacrificed the national interest. The Hokkaidō grants were no one-off thing, but were to be repeated in other parts of Japan. After the 1873 *Seihen*, Satchō were to proceed at full speed to take over much of the mineral wealth of Japan (see below), and these land grants must be viewed as part of the same story. The 1873 and 1881 *Seihen* were not constitutional or diplomatic crises, but literally fights to the death for power, wealth and self-awarded honours.

## THE AINU

In late 1875 Kuroda and Inoue Kaoru were appointed to lead the mission which forced open Korea. Their selection was most significant: Inoue was to direct the economic exploitation of Korea, while the choice of the Kaitakushi Chōkan is a fairly plain indication that, as many *kokugaku* and other writers had long since suggested, Korea was thought of as being rightfully a Japanese colony like Ezochi and the Ryūkyūs. The policy to be applied in Korea – including the huge land grants – was essentially that which evolved in Ezochi, so it is pertinent to look at Kuroda's relations with the Ainu.

In 1876 Matsumoto broke with his Satsuma patrons and returned to Shōnai to live the life of a farmer. He gave Kōno five additional reasons – including the land grants – for his decision but his main reason was disgust at Kuroda's treatment of the Ainu (Takakura 1982: 332). By the Karafuto treaty of 21 September 1875, Japan vacated Karafuto in exchange for Russian evacuation of the Kuriles. Matsumoto accepted direct responsibility for the welfare of 842 Karafuto Ainu who were transferred to northern Hokkaidō. He saw them happily settled in, then went off touring. In July he received a letter telling him that they had been rounded up like pigs, forced to board a ship for Otaru then sent inland to work in the Ishikari coal mines. Matsumoto promptly resigned.

His letter to Kuroda burned with indignation and anger (Matsumoto 1974: 169). The Russian treaty specifically states that the natives could either stay or go to Hokkaidō, yet Kuroda had insisted that they go. The treaty further specified that if they went to Hokkaidō they were to be allowed to live where they chose and would be exempt from taxes for ten years. Yet they had been hunted down and forced on board like animals. To send them up the Ishikari River to work in the Yubari coal mines was treating them like convicts serving life sentences. But what crimes had they committed? To justify his action, Kuroda had described them as barbarians. They were, however, good citizens leading peaceful, communal lives. They had asked him to name their new village and he had called it Andō village (Place of Safety and Relief). Now they were forced inland away from the warmer coastal regions, and it would be difficult to survive the long, savage winters. How could he possibly face these people again?

Kuroda held up the notice granting him permission to return home, and followed him to Hakodate. Matsumoto, however, remained hidden in the surrounding hills and when Kuroda finally sailed, watched the ship through his binoculars. Then, after a banquet in town with his friends, he sailed for Akita. He never again served the government.

Soon after signing the Karafuto treaty, Kuroda was chosen to lead the Korean mission. His treatment of the Ainu, in blatant defiance of all the written and verbal undertakings, was a chilling indication of what lay in store for Korea.

Japanese accounts of the 1873 *Seihen* do not even touch on Hokkaidō – the various power struggles, the huge land grants, the treatment of the defeated clans and the Ainu, etc. – but debate *ad nauseam* Saigō's *seikan-ron* and the question of whether such an honourable man really intended to attack Korea. The direction in which Japan was moving is indicated by the above account of Hokkaidō, and the soul-searching analyses of Saigō's character are little more than red herrings.

## 'SAIGŌ'S *TONDEN HEI*'

Saigō Takamori was an all-purpose cleansing and beautifying agent. It is standard practice to invoke his name when *taigi meibun* is called for, be it justification of the Boshin War, the 1871 *coup*, *seikan-ron*, Hokkaidō policy or the Seinan War. Hokkaidō was to become known for its *tonden hei* and, as with *seikan-ron*, one often reads of 'Saigō's *tonden hei*', the implication being that Satsuma took over the Kaitakushi because of its concern for the defence of the north. So let us look more carefully at these soldier settlements and general migration into Hokkaidō.

The major colonizing effort was that of Sendai, the leader of the northern coalition. Partly because its lords were young, Sendai and its large Watari branch clan vacillated during the Bakumatsu period. *Kaikoku* and *jōi* factions debated so bitterly that the clans were 'like an ants' nest' (*Date City Publication* 1970: 7). At Toba-Fushimi the clan did not move, and so was branded *sabaku*, yet it saw no reason to be dictated to by Satchō, and led seventeen northern clans in proposing that, instead of everything being settled by Satchō, there should be a national conference to decide future policy. Satchō, of course, refused to share their newly-won power, and ordered Sendai to attack Aizu. The clan despatched an envoy to Kyoto to ask that Aizu be pardoned, but Satsuma's Sera, a rough and violent man, arrived in Sendai with 500 troops (ibid.: 8–14). When he upbraided them for 'defying the Emperor', the hot-headed young Sendai *samurai* returned the abuse, pointing out that they were opposing, not the Emperor, but the Satchō monopoly of power. This confrontation between Sera and the Sendai clansmen comes to the heart of Meiji history: at a time when national unity was essential, Satchō brutally and cynically took absolute control, set one clan against another, and accused any who challenged them of being disloyal to the Emperor. Aizu, the most loyal of all the clans, was branded as the most traitorous.

The Boshin War was marked by a series of betrayals, with Sendai eventually sending messengers to its branch clan in Uwajima to arrange for it to change sides.

As a leading 'traitorous' clan, Sendai and its branch clans lost much of their land and income. On the initiative of its Karō, Tamura Akimasa, the Watari branch clan decided to restore its fortunes by migrating to Hokkaidō. It applied for the area of Saru-*gun*, but in December Shima wrote to the officials in Tokyo pointing out that he had sent repeated urgent requests that various areas be set aside as imperial lands yet he had had no reply; 'now these characters from Sendai had presented their request to the government' (Takakura 1982: 289–90). He therefore instructed them, after due consultation with the appropriate officials, to secure the rejection of the Date request.

Despite Shima, their application was not rejected, but they were told that since they were rebels, they did not deserve such a good climate and were therefore allotted the less favourable adjoining region (*Date City Publication* 1970: 139ff.). The first settlers landed in Muroran on 19 March 1970 (Date Kinenkan), and made their way overland by Ainu tracks to present-day Date. Ishikari Tobetsu and Date were to be the only really successful continuous settlements founded in this period. Date's success was due to the fact that virtually the whole clan migrated, clan loyalties and organization were preserved, and they had long since been *samurai*–farmers back in Sendai, accustomed to coping with harsh, cold conditions. Recognition of their achievements came as early as the summer of 1870 when Higashikuse made an inspection, and was ultimately crowned in 1892 when Date was made a count.

The concrete Date achievements were many: they were the first in Hokkaidō to use the plough, to plant indigo, to sell beans to Honshu, to have horses and cow pastures and to run an agricultural co-operative (*Date City History* 1949: Intro.). They were also the first, on the urging of the foreign teachers, to plant beet and to set up sugar mills. These later became a model for Japanese colonists in Korea and Manchuria. In short, Date was both a model experimental station and the prototype for the *tonden hei*, the soldier settlements ostensibly meant to provide soldiers in case of invasion.

Not surprisingly, the *Date City History* proudly points out that Satsuma was the first to return its allotted regions, and that this and similar refusals make the success of the bankrupt Date clan even more remarkable. It might also have added that history should recall 'Date *tonden hei*', not 'Saigō's *tonden hei*', and that when hordes of Satsuma men did arrive, they occupied not land but heated offices.

## GENERAL MIGRATION

The story of general migration remains confused. The Higashikuse documents reveal that as early as 26 October 1869 Sendai and Shizuoka POWs arrived in Hakodate (Takakura 1982: 51). We are given no information about their numbers or their fate, but they were guarded by two *shotai* and so probably numbered 200 men. It would seem that some early 'convicts' were really POWs from the defeated clans. Their untold story typifies the piecemeal nature of the sources and the paucity of serious research. Important contributions, however, have been made by Nagai (1966) and Seki (1971).

Seki's charts reveal that in the seventies there was a total of sixteen groups which migrated to Hokkaidō. Of these eight were from Miyagi (Sendai); all these were *shizoku* or *tonden*, and all arrived in 1870–1. Five more such Sendai groups were to come in the period 1885–99, and in the years 1900–10 three farmer groups also arrived from Sendai. Thus for Sendai there was a fifteen-year gap after 1871, no Sendai group settlements of any kind taking place while Kuroda and Satsuma were in charge. The Sendai settlers were essentially post-war refugees who had been dispossessed by the Satchō victors. Though this post-war group migration was probably drying up by 1871, and individual migration was becoming easier, it would seem that once Satsuma took control, Hokkaidō became far less attractive to Sendai migrants.

Of the other eight groups which arrived in the seventies, five came in 1871. They included one each from Nagasaki and Shimabara (Amakusa). They were described as farmer groups and settled in Hitaka. The Amakusa settlement soon ran into trouble. When its crops failed, Capron pointed out that they had been given poor land (Iguro and Katayama 1967). The officials replied that if the first settlers were given the best land, later settlers would not follow. Capron, of course, argued that if the first settlers failed then others would not come.

In the case of these Nagasaki and Shimabara settlers, there may have been an element of religious persecution. The description 'farmer' seems simply to have meant *heimin*, for such groups were not infrequently referred to as 'the scrapings of the city'. The other 1871 groups were the ill-fated Saga *shizoku* group which never took root, a Hyōgo *shizoku* group, and an Aomori group which was really composed of Aizu *samurai* who had been deported to bleak, inhospitable Tonami (Ōsaka 1962: 483).

The other three examples of group migration in the seventies were mixed Tohoku *tonden* or *shizoku* groups in 1875–6 and 1878, and an Aichi *shizoku* group in 1878. This must be regarded as a most unimpressive record, and one which makes it necessary for us to question both the origins and the objectives of the *tonden hei* system.

Official publications (Iguro and Katayama 1967: 157) claim the name came from Han China, and that the scheme was partly modelled on a similar Russian system. Such publications note that there had been similar small settlements before the Restoration, then usually skip over to 'Saigō's 1871 initiative' which was later taken up by Kuroda to provide defence against Russia. It is true that the Russian 'threat' was regularly emphasized at convenient moments, such as in 1873 when Kuroda wished to draw attention away from Korea. The facts, however, strongly indicate that the soldier settlements were to meet not any remote foreign threat but rather the far more immediate internal danger. Indeed, 1875, when the first Kuroda *tonden* were established at Kotoni, was the year in which Russia and Japan settled their differences in the north. In 1874, Enomoto, who was very close to Kuroda, went as envoy to Russia, and it was agreed that Russia should have Karafuto and leave the Kuriles to Japan. This was clearly intended as a long-range solution. A short time later Kuroda went off to lead the mission which opened Korea. The 'northern question' was obviously settled in order to clear the way for action in Korea. Both Russia and Japan were addicted to secret diplomacy, and it is logical to assume that Japan's impending opening of Korea was discussed and agreed to during the negotiations over the northern islands. Thus it was a most peculiar time to institute soldier settlements to meet 'the Russian threat'.

Capron's term of office had not been stipulated, but he resigned in 1874 and left Japan in June 1875 (ibid.). Thus his departure coincided with the Russian treaty. It also marked a distinctive turning away from America towards Russia. Capron's relations with the Japanese were apparently none too cordial towards the end. His unpublished autobiography (Ōsaka 1962: 388–9) overflows with indignation, for example at his lack of control over expenditure. Capron was not replaced and the American connection was gradually wound down. Largely due to Enomoto, Russian culture and advisers were brought in: Russian huts, heaters, sleighs, clothing and plants were all experimented with (*Hokkaidō no Yoake* 1965: 83–4). From 1879 the Japanese participated in the market set up in Vladivostok. In the years that followed, there was a significant migration of permanent Japanese settlers to the Siberian Maritime Provinces where they engaged in industry, commerce and some agriculture (*The Times* 18.3.1902). Sapporo is closer to Vladivostok than to Tokyo, and many believed with Kaneko that the development of Russian Asia would be of great benefit to Japan (ibid.: 7.7.1902).

One small episode perhaps illustrates the fact that after 1875 Japanese–Russian relations became quite cordial. In the early eighties Saigō Jūdō gave the Russian envoy his six-year-old son, Jūri, to take back to Russia where he became a great favourite at the Court (*Furukawa Jūjun Den* 1971: 110ff.). Unfortunately, the envoy was transferred to America and the boy died there. But it does seem to have been an extension of the Japanese custom of giving children in adoption to make alliances.

Thus the story of Russian relations, especially from 1875, strongly suggests that the handful of soldier settlements Kuroda set up after 1875 had nothing to do with defence against Russia. Indeed, one of the early Americans, Antisell, had pointed out (Iguro and Katayama 1967: 114–15) that Sapporo was a strange place to build a capital if the purpose was defence against Russia. The distribution of Kuroda's *tonden* is even stranger if they were meant to guard against external attack. The first, in 1875, placed at Kotoni just outside Sapporo, was plainly to guard the local government, while the next two, at Yamakane and Hassamu, likewise bordered Sapporo (ibid.: 280–3).

We are brought back to the fact that Hokkaidō was no ordinary society. For centuries there had been 'armed capitalism'. New police had to be brought in to replace the Matsumae *samurai* who performed this function. The oppressed Ainu were semi-slaves, the recruited labourers were largely the victims of coercion and misrepresentation; convicts (and POWs) were a significant element; both Matsumae followers and Enomoto supporters had become fugitives; and the prostitutes were kept under lock and key, under strict police surveillance, save on special festival days (Blakiston 1883: 20). There had been serious rioting from the time of the first arrivals, climaxing in June 1873 with a riot by over-taxed Hiyama fishermen which forced Kuroda to send for troops from Akita (Iguro and Katayama 1967: 278).

It should be noted that Capron had been a colonel in the Maryland militia, which was often used to suppress trouble with the Irish migrants, and he urged Kuroda to set up a force, modelled on the American militia, which could be called out in time of trouble (ibid.: 97; Harrison 1953: 84). In view of the advice, and of the obvious need, some of the new arrivals were formed into *tonden kempei* to protect private citizens (Iguro and Katayama 1967: 279–80). This clearly meant citizens with property, not day labourers.

When the Kaitakushi was abolished, there were less than 1,000 such troops. Most had come in before Satsuma took over in 1871. Then there was a four-year gap. In 1875, when a treaty was signed with Russia and a new, cordial period in Russo-Japanese relations began, Kuroda built the first of his three *tonden* around Sapporo. They were armed with rifles and a few cannons (ibid.: 292), and were clearly much the same as the American militia. It was a far cry from the teachings of men such as Hayashi Shihei and the priest Gesshō who preached the need for coastal defence. There is nothing in the Hokkaidō story to suggest that, in this period, either Saigō, Satsuma or Japan as a whole was obsessed with the 'Russian menace'.

Nagai makes the point that right down to the Second World War, Hokkaidō migration was predominantly from Tōhoku and Hokuriku (Nagai 1966: 2–4). The 1920 Census showed that of a total population of 55,780,000, 5,100,000 (or 9.1 per cent) had migrated to other prefectures. The lowest percentage of internal migrants was from Kyūshū. Seki's figures show that of the 329 groups which migrated to Hokkaidō to 1912, only fourteen, including one from Kagoshima, came from Kyūshū. Neither Nagai nor Seki ponder the question of Kyūshū migration, but surely the central fact is that Kyūshū migration was towards the Asian mainland – Korea, China, Manchuria – and also to Taiwan. Even Tokyo, the other great Mecca for internal migrants, was, for Kyūshū people, a remote, inaccessible place, whereas Korea was just a short journey away by local boat. *Seikan-ron* was not about punishment, but about commerce and migration. Hideyoshi's vision of large-scale migration to Korea had never been forgotten. It was to be taken up, for example, by 'the enlightened sage of Mita', who was to urge that as many Japanese as possible should migrate to Korea to engage in mining, industry and agriculture. He suggested a nice round figure of 5 million as sufficient to lead Korea 'gradually but surely into the path of progress and prosperity' (Seung : 277). Though earlier writers did not usually spell it out so explicitly, the urgings of *kokugakusha*, etc. to 'restore' Japan's position in Korea were really little different from Fukuzawa's enthusiasm for taking 'civilization' to every nook and cranny of Korea.

## SUMMARY

The now-standard work on the 1873 *Seihen*, Mōri's *Study of the 1873 Seihen*, has as one of its major themes the claim that Saigō did not want to attack Korea. Other aspects of Mōri's thesis were subsequently challenged, but this claim met with general acceptance. It is, however, most disturbing, for it raises questions about the direction in which Japanese history writing is moving. Mōri gets quite immersed in considering 'Saigō's heart', and agonizes over flimsy documentary evidence which can be neither authenticated nor exposed as false. Yet neither Mōri nor any other historian dealing with the 1873 *Seihen* examines the Hokkaidō story. One cannot separate the Hokkaidō and Korean stories: both represent Japanese expansion, and the policies to be applied in Korea were worked out in Hokkaidō. In particular, Hokkaidō affords us the opportunity to study Satsuma colonial policy in operation. That is the real evidence – evidence far more solid and substantial than the highly dubious documents on which most historians build their case.

The Hokkaidō story does not support the official legend of Saigō being obsessed with the Russian 'menace'. Satsuma provided neither pioneers nor soldiers, but used the Colonial Office to provide sinecures for the Satsuma drones. Its corrupt officials endangered and delayed development by locking up great land-holdings in their own names. The establishment of soldier settlements came to a stop in 1871, and was not resumed until after Japan and Russia reached a lasting agreement in the north. That fact, and the geographical distribution of the new settlements away from the coast, clearly indicates that the main purpose of the *tonden hei* was to provide a militia to help maintain internal order.

The defeated clans had little option but to provide the labour and the farmer–soldiers for Hokkaidō. But as part of its 1871 *coup*, Satsuma in effect also took over Hokkaidō. Saga was driven out, then all the nobles, and then Tosa. Satsuma and *kika-Satsujin* provided the officials. The old Ōmi traders were squeezed out and Satsuma was in a position to control the economy. But though Shima, Higashikuse and Iwamura had all been driven out, that did not mean Saga, Chōshū and Tosa were prepared simply to abandon Hokkaidō to Satsuma. The Mitsui men may have failed to take over Nemuro, but Mitsui, like the Ōkura-gumi, would go on to become a major force in Hokkaidō. Because of its products and because of its position in the trading network, Hokkaidō was too important to leave to Satsuma. Mitsubishi used its powerful shipping lines to make Hokkaidō a major target. When the Kaitakushi was wound up in 1881, the Mitsubishi threat was countered by virtually presenting Hokkaidō to Godai's company. It would be an exaggeration to say that the exact blue-print for this company already existed in 1871, but it is all too clear that Satsuma took over Hokkaidō in 1871 to provide comfortable jobs for its unemployed *samurai* and to establish Hokkaidō as a Satsuma sphere of influence, both political and commercial. The idea of Satsuma taking over the facilities and resources of Hokkaidō was not an idea that just occurred in 1881.

What the Hokkaidō story emphasizes is that the great clans were engaged in a bitter struggle to establish their own spheres of influence, and this struggle led into the 1873 *Seihen*. There was fairly general agreement that Korea could and should be taken. But whose sphere of influence was it to be? The 1873 *Seihen* must be viewed as having been largely a fight over the spoils of wars yet to come.

# 10

# THE RULE OF LAW

As the word *seihen* implies, the 1873 crisis must be regarded as a milestone, for it was followed immediately by a movement to secure parliamentary government and, eventually, by the establishment of the iniquitous Emperor system. The 1873 *Seihen* had little if anything to do with this struggle for a parliament; but as it largely revolved around the struggle to set up an independent judiciary, that aspect should be set in historical perspective.

Japanese historians such as Matsumoto (1969) frequently bring the fight for the Rule of Law down to a naked power struggle in which Etō used the Justice Ministry to gain power for himself. Matsumoto is correct in stressing that Etō sought to expand central power at the expense of local, but he ignores the fact that this was the only way to curb arbitrary local officials and to make them subject to the law. Even without the usual gross distortions, this concentration on Etō's personality makes it seem that this struggle ended with his death. It was, of course, carried on by his loyal lieutenants within both the judiciary and the Justice Ministry. By ignoring that subsequent struggle, historians, both Japanese and Western, have not only distorted the nature of the 1873 *Seihen*, but have also concealed the true character of the Satchō *batsu* and the political system they instituted.

Most Western historians are particularly at fault in that, instead of investigating events and then reaching their conclusions about the characters involved, they tend to start with pre-conceived character judgements, then use those judgements as a basis for interpreting events. Thus Gluck relates how palace advisers such as Sasaki and Motoda objected to the inclusion of Inoue Kaoru in the Emperor's northern trip of 1878: 'The palace advisers accused Inoue of "scandalous behaviour" which may have referred to his financial

252

views, his Westernism, his recent visit to Paris, or his Chōshū origins' (Gluck 1985: 75). Gluck has simply accepted 'victor's history'. If one accepts Inoue's righteousness without question, one is pre-judging a great part of Meiji history. Gluck must have known that Inoue was despised by Saigō and Etō, and boycotted by Ōkubo, as well as being loathed by Sasaki and Motoda. We also have Ōkuma's testimony that his reputation was 'unspeakably bad' both with the public and at court (*Ōkuma Kō 85 Nen Shi* 1925, Vol. 1: 695–7); Ōkuma further related how he was reluctantly persuaded by Iwakura to plead Inoue's case with the Emperor, and though he eventually talked him round, he had never known the Emperor to be so hostile to anyone (ibid.: 706–10). Even the official Inoue biography (*Segai Inoue Kō Den* 1933, Vol. 3: 8–10) admits this widespread opposition to his reinstatement. The announcement of his appointment was both cool and shamefaced: 'As it is difficult to get the perfect, faultless person, in the present emergency situation, as it cannot be helped, Inoue has been appointed.'

This tendency to begin with pre-conceived character judgements and then to use those judgements as the basis for the analysis of events can be seen even more dramatically in Akita's 1967 *Foundations of Constitutional Government in Modern Japan 1868–1910*. There is not even a brief reference to the Third World style corruption and extortion, or to the struggle to establish the Rule of Law. This classic example of *goyō* scholarship begins with the judgement that the Satchō *batsu* were intellectually and morally superior; their opponents are referred to dismissively as 'the outs', while the enlightened government is depicted as being concerned at the dangers of sharing power with 'irresponsible and selfish elements' (Akita 1967: 3). Akita begins with this conclusion, and uses it as the basis for his analysis of events; that analysis then leads inevitably to his major conclusion: 'The quality of Meiji leadership was unique. And it was this quality of leadership, perhaps as much as any other factor, that gave distinctive and incomparable tone and substance to the Meiji era' (ibid.: 177). As a corollary, the vicious and oppressive Emperor system is made to sound quite reasonable. Rarely can a historian have got everything so completely wrong.

Akita dismissed the *seikan-ron* as the idea of 'chastising Korea', and this failure to grasp the nature of the 1873 *Seihen* helped set him off on his circular course. Gluck's flippant asides and Akita's sweeping pre-judgements demonstrate how easy it is to conceal or ignore issues by concentrating on one or two characters. Individuals, of course, can be important, and Etō did play a vital role in 1873. But his character must not be allowed to personify the struggle for the Rule of Law. A man must be judged by his whole life, and his character cannot be analysed on the basis of the events of one year. Let us restore some kind of balance by looking, not at Etō but at the life of the man who became known as the Father of Japanese Law.

## MINKEN

The *minken* movement is usually depicted as having begun with the resignation of the caretaker government whose members then sought to regain power by leading a popular movement to achieve a parliament (e.g. Gotō 1966). This interpretation, however, ignores the first stage of the *minken* movement.

Matano (1914: 106ff.) tells the story of how the word *minken* came into being. In 1870 the Seido Kyoku (Law System Office) was set up within the Great Council of State to translate foreign laws, especially the French, and to compile legal codes. For a year Etō was in charge. The chief translator would translate a section which would then be discussed by a committee. When Mitsukuri Rinshō translated '*droit civil*' as *jinmin kenri*, a heated discussion took place – 'What's this about people having rights?' he was asked. It was quite an alien concept and received a hostile reception. Mitsukuri defended his translation while Etō acted as peacemaker. Etō suggested that the phrase be put on one side – neither accepted nor rejected – but within a few years it had been shortened to *minken* and had passed into the language. In popular usage, it became equated with the struggle for a popularly elected parliament; but its civil rights origins must not be forgotten. Until 1873, the civil rights movement centred around the judiciary, not the legislature, and must be equated with the civil rights movements in America and South Africa rather than a struggle for a popular parliament.

Later *minken* was joined by *kokken* – a prime piece of sophistry. The two were placed in juxtaposition, and *kokken* (*koku* being country or nation) was made to sound the antithesis of *minken*. The implication was that the people had to choose between *minken* and *kokken*. It was, of course, a giant confidence trick, for *kokken* had nothing to do with rights, being a contraction of *kokka kenryoku* (the power of the state). It was made to seem that *minken* reduced *kokken*, so its advocates were disloyal; it managed to cultivate the illusion that the only way to preserve the strength of the nation was to keep in power the Satchō *batsu*, 'the Emperor's servants'.

Blacker has pointed out that the word *kenri* was not Mitsukuri's own invention, but was

> taken from William Martin's Chinese translation of Wheaton's 'Elements of International Law', where the words *kenri* and *gimu* were used to translate the terms rights and duties. The word was rather an unfortunate choice, since the character *ken* carried a strong connotation of 'might' rather than 'right', previous compounds containing the character all having had this meaning. The word therefore made it all the more difficult for the Japanese to grasp the meaning of rights.
>
> (Blacker 1964: 105)

Blacker went on (pp. 114–15) to accept Fukuzawa's view that many *minken* advocates were frivolous and ignorant, and that they should have first developed their own private rights and then moved for a parliament; for in all other countries, parliaments had been set up to protect existing rights. Blacker, however, would seem to have been too much under Fukuzawa's influence, for this is precisely what Etō had tried to do.

In the Ono case, the central issue was freedom of movement. Old feudal restrictions had been removed, but the Chōshū *batsu* in Kyoto refused to let the Ono family escape from its clutches by moving to Tokyo. In both the Ono and Osarisawa cases (further details below), the key principle which Etō was trying to make widely known was the new principle that citizens had the right to appeal to the courts against rapacious officials. Some historians have argued that the average citizen was little interested in the fate of wealthy families such as the Onos. But the principles involved, such as freedom of movement, were equally as important for the poor; inevitably, however, it was the wealthiest and well connected, and not the poor, who tested the efficacy of the new laws. Had they won, the exercise of these rights would soon have spread. It was precisely because the first stage of the *minken* movement – the civil rights movement in the narrower, non-parliamentary sense of the word – was overwhelmed and battered to death by the Satchō *batsu*, that the defeated forces regrouped and entered upon the second stage of the *minken* movement, namely the struggle for a parliament. It is the height of irony to suggest that they should first have acquired those basic rights which the ruthless military government was determined to deny them.

Likewise one must question Blacker's contention that the choice

255

of the word *kenri* was unfortunate. In China, the people had traditionally had the right to overthrow a bad ruler, but this right was alien to Japanese teachings. If the Satchō monopoly were to be broken, this fundamental right to drive out a bad government had to be established. The word *kenri*, with its overtones of strength, probably struck just the right note.

To understand the need for a civil rights movement, one must look at the brazen and monumental corruption which was of a type later to become associated with newly emerging Third World countries. The Satchō *batsu* acted as though above the law, and Etō's attempt to make them subject to the Rule of Law was an important element in bringing on the crisis of 1873.

In early Meiji, the Treasury was a huge ministry performing the functions later taken over by the Home, Communications, Agriculture and Commerce Ministries and also the Accounts Investigation Department. It was so powerful that not even the Great Council of State could control it. Ōkubo became Treasurer, with Inoue, Yoshida Kiyonari and Shibusawa his major assistants. When Ōkubo left with the Iwakura Mission, Yoshida was soon transferred to the provinces, leaving Inoue and Shibusawa in charge. Inoue and Yamagata had the further task of guarding Satchō interests while the Mission was away. The Iwakura Mission returned, however, to find both Inoue and Yamagata in disgrace, the 'caretaker' government firmly entrenched, and their own position that of outsiders. So let us look at the major scandals which almost brought Chōshū to its knees.

## THE YAMASHIROYA AFFAIR

It was the Yamashiroya affair (see Matano 1914, Vol. 2: 37ff.) which brought disgrace to Yamagata. Nomura Michimi had been an officer in the Chōshū Irregulars where his close friends included Yamagata, Fujita Densaburō and Katsura Tarō who, on cutting off his *chomage*, a feudal symbol, entrusted his sword to Nomura – a sure sign of an intimate relationship (Tokutomi 1916: 302–3).

After the Boshin War, Nomura opened a shop in Yokohama and took the name Yamashiroya. Thanks to Yamagata, he became *goyō* merchant to the army – a guarantee of a successful business. But the support of the 'Chōshū Army' went further, for Yamashiroya was given interest-free loans totalling 649,000 *yen* – from army funds. Rapidly expanding the business, he entered the silk trade only to suffer severe losses when prices slumped dramatically. On the pretext of studying the market, he went off to Paris where he spent so lavishly on actresses and horse races that reports were sent back to Japan not only by Sameshima from Paris but also by Terajima in London (Matano 1914, Vol. 2: 41).

The Satsuma officers were incensed at the way Chōshū was turning the army into its own private domain, and Yamagata was obliged to telegram Yamashiroya to return. Kirino declared that Yamashiroya should be prevented from trading, and sent troops to surround the premises. Etō, however, insisted to Saigō that the case had to be handled by the Justice Ministry, not the army – in other words, that the Rule of Law had to be established. When he sent a top official, Shimamoto, to the Army Ministry to investigate, Yamagata attempted a cover-up, blandly claiming that all the money had been repaid. Shimamoto's investigations soon showed that this was untrue, and on Etō's orders he proceeded to examine the whole of the army finances. The trial was obscured somewhat when Yamashiroya burnt all his papers and committed *seppuku*, but the Satsuma officers still demanded that all the corrupt Chōshū elements should be driven out. Instead, Saigō confirmed Yamagata as Army Minister, merely having him resign as Chief of the Emperor's Troops. Saigō, however, had himself made Field Marshal. It would have required a wide-sweeping purge of the Chōshū faction to eliminate the corruption, but it was only a year since the Satchō *coup* – too soon for a major confrontation between the two dominant clans.

Histories of the *seihen* sometimes give the impression that, apart from Saigō, Satchō were united against their enemies. Saigō, however, had the support of the Satsuma lower *samurai*, and they were as hostile to Chōshū as were Etō and most other clans. It must be borne in mind that the squalid Yamashiroya story involved not just a couple of individuals but the Chōshū army leadership as a whole, and was played out at a time when the Treasury could not find adequate funds for the Justice and Education Ministries, and when an estimated 90 per cent of the Tokyo inhabitants were living in poverty.

## THE MITSUYA AFFAIR

The Mitsuya affair (see ibid.: 45ff.) was even more bizarre. Under the Bakufu, Mitsuya Sankurō had been an Edo *goyō* merchant to Chōshū. After the Kyoto *seihen* of 1863, Chōshū had to withdraw from Edo, and Mitsuya was left holding 3,200 *ryō* of Chōshū money. Before Mitsuya could forward this sum, it was confiscated by the Bakufu. When the Chōshū forces re-entered Edo in triumph, they demanded the repayment of the 3,200 *ryō* plus a donation of 5,000 *ryō* to the government and 30,000 to Chōshū (Morikawa 1976: 22). Even though Mitsuya scraped together this amount, the Chōshū forces, 'just like a band of mountain bandits' (Kajinishi 1960: 37–42), still planned to execute him. When Yamashiroya and two others passed along a warning, Mitsuya shaved his head and escaped disguised as a priest. Some time later he was pardoned, probably as a result of substantial bribes, and once more became a *goyō* merchant with close ties to Yamagata and Inoue.

As there were no banks, the government money was simply stored, interest-free, with friendly merchants such as Yamashiroya and Mitsuya, who would use it to make a profit and then give their sponsors a 'rebate'. Thus Yamagata placed the army money with Mitsuya, who began rapidly to overtake Mitsui and Ono. However, a Mitsuya assistant named Watanabe used it for his private speculation and lost 700,000 *yen*. Yamagata was forced to investigate, but a series of loans were raised and the trouble was papered over. Then, again through the fault of Watanabe, a further 50,000 *yen* was found to be missing. Yamagata conferred with Inoue and Shibusawa who arranged for Mitsui to pay in the 50,000 in return for a ten-year interest-free loan of 600,000 *yen* from army and Treasury funds. Mitsui was also made the army *goyō* instead of Mitsuya. As security, Mitsuya handed over to Mitsui fifty-three properties he possessed in select parts of Tokyo. Of course, these properties were to be returned unconditionally at the end of ten years. When the time came, however, Mitsuya's son-in-law died suddenly and the receipts could not be found. It seems he had dissipated company money and had then sold the receipts back to Mitsui (ibid.). Mitsuya approached both Mitsui and Yamagata, now (1884) Home Minister, but they both evaded the issue. Eventually Mitsuya went to court, but could prove nothing without the receipts. (There can be little doubt that Yamagata was also on the Mitsui payroll. He had acquired several valuable properties: his villa, *Tsubakiyama*, stood on 18,000 *tsubo*, and he also had mansions in Odawara, Koishikawa and Kyoto.)

In 1889, Treasurer Matsukata appointed Mitsubishi's Kawada as President of the Bank of Japan. When a financial panic occurred in 1890, the Mitsui Bank found itself in trouble. Kawada agreed to help on condition that Fukuzawa's nephew, Nakamigawa, be given a top Mitsui position (*Nakamigawa Hikojirō Den* 1939: 313ff.). Asabuki, another key Fukuzawa lieutenant, also transferred (Ōnishi 1928), and an influx of Keio people followed. As Asabuki had once served the Mitsuya family, they hoped he would now plead their cause, but Mitsui still showed no inclination either to pay compensation or to return the properties.

In 1900, the Mitsuya case was suddenly revived. Nakamigawa had become director of Mitsui Heavy Industries and became involved in a bitter power struggle with Masuda, the director of the Mitsui Light Industries. His attempts to tidy up Mitsui affairs also brought him into conflict with the Chōshū figures who controlled its affairs from 'behind the curtain'. From 29 April to 19 May 1900, the *Nijū Roku Shimpō* published a series of articles criticizing Mitsui. This paper, under Akiyama Teisuke, obviously had inside information, and one of its major stories concerned the Mitsuya case. Eventually the police suspended publication, but this suspension notice was published in the paper, causing further trouble.

In cases such as this, it is almost impossible to separate fact from legend, but it would seem that behind Akiyama were Inoue, Itō and Yamagata who were determined to eliminate Nakamigawa for having interfered with this Chōshū preserve. Eventually, Itō negotiated between Mitsui and the paper, but all Mitsuya received was 10,000 *yen* for properties worth millions. Akiyama made no attempt to take up the story of this shabby treatment – a fair indication that his attacks on Mitsui had not been inspired by abstract concepts of justice. Nakamigawa was ultimately defeated and died in 1901 at the age of 47. Mitsui's Keio people were then driven out (*Nakamigawa Hikojirō Den* 1939: 313ff.).

The Mitsuya case makes it all too clear that the corruption was deep and enduring. Etō had made a valiant attempt to apply the law, seeking to have the case investigated by his top official, Shimamoto, but Iwakura, Sanjō and the Chōshū clique had succeeded in blocking his path (Matano 1914, Vol. 2: 45ff.). Once Etō resigned, the investigations were suspended. The cover-up clearly involved Inoue and Shibusawa at the Treasury, and Sanjō and Iwakura as heads of government. Huge sums of money were involved, and it is difficult to avoid the conclusion that corruption was so deep and widespread that it could be controlled only by destroying the government. Morris was hardly exaggerating when he declared that Saigō's 1873 departure 'signified a final break with the Meiji oligarchs whom he now regarded as hopelessly corrupt and misguided and with whom he could no longer possibly co-operate in good conscience' (Morris : 257). As we have seen in chapter 7, 'Naganuma's' 1906 study stressed the importance of this issue of public morality. There is nothing substantial in the way of documentary proof, but the popular legends depict Saigō wanting a foreign war to help sweep away the prevailing corruption and restore a spirit of public service. It was certainly ominous that it was the Yamashiroya affair which inspired Saigō to have himself made Field Marshal – a title which surely conjured up visions of Saigō as a modern Shogun.

## SAGA AND NAVAL CORRUPTION

Yamaji Aizan, a noted contemporary political commentator, perhaps made a valid point concerning Inoue: he admitted that Inoue had taken possession of Osarisawa mine for himself, but pointed out that 'everyone was doing it' (Yamaji 1908: 58ff.). He also declared that in 1908 it was still not physically safe to criticize Inoue in writing.

Though the most spectacular cases of corruption related to 'the Chōshū Army', the navy administration was also involved in graft. Here the Saga people played a key role. During the 1873 *Seihen*, Ōkuma and Ōki were the most troubled as to which side to align with (Tsuda 1927: 297). They finally supported the Iwakura side, but it would seem that the deciding factor was that Ōkuma's own corruption tied him to Itō and Inoue. Apparently, Ōkuma was already a rich man when he came up to Edo. He immediately acquired a large mansion next to Itō, and, like his neighbour, lived in considerable splendour with a horde of retainers. The story of the early navy gives some indications as to how his wealth was obtained.

Widespread corruption did not begin with the *ishin* but was endemic in the Tokugawa system. This fact may be illustrated by a study of the Saga Navy (Hideshima 1917). The central figure was Ōkuma's close associate, Sano Tsunetami, whose duties included buying ships and machinery. His recollections are reproduced at length in Hideshima's work. They are jumbled, self-serving and confusing, but if supplemented by Ōkuma's own self-serving *Recollections*, the general picture becomes reasonably clear.

Ōkuma admitted that both he and Sano had many detractors, but he would have us believe that the main charges were that they had become Christians and were excessively dissolute (*Ōkuma Kō 85 Nen Shi* 1925: 402–17). He denied the former and excused the latter on the grounds that Saga students in Nagasaki usually spent freely. Much of the money came from great clan merchants such as Taketomi who thus placed future clan officials under a load of obligation. Ōkuma, a master weaver of myths, steered clear of the subject of corruption, but Sano's 'apologia' took up some of the specific charges, noting in passing that the same things were said about Ōkuma (Hideshima 1917: 399).

Sano was entrusted with 30,000 to 50,000 *ryō* to buy a steamship and arms from the Dutch. The Bakufu officials, however, demanded about a 40 per cent payment as a kind of tax (ibid.: 386–7). Sano argued that this was inappropriate where the purchase was not for trade but for national defence. He therefore wined and dined the Bakufu officials to convince them not to impose this tax. When his lavish spending came to the notice of the clan inspectors he was recalled to Saga and tried. Though he feared he would be ordered to commit *seppuku* he was merely placed under house arrest for thirty days. By clan law he should have been banned from holding office for thirty years, but in less then half a year he was re-instated as official in charge of navy training, though not of naval purchases. He had been saved by Kansō's customary magnanimity and by the fact that he could not easily be replaced.

At about this time, another matter came to light. Sano had been entrusted with 30,000 *ryō* to buy a furnace from the Dutch, but had paid over only 12,500 *ryō*. Sano explained the matter away by referring to the different value of gold and silver coins. As such transactions were conducted by word of mouth, one cannot seek documentary proof, but their acknowledged payments from the rich merchants, Sano's arrest and conviction, and their lavish spending leave little doubt that Sano and Ōkuma were guilty of large-scale corruption. The Bakufu officials must also be adjudged guilty, for at a time when Japan was alleged to be threatened by the West, they delayed the purchase of war-ships while they were wined and dined in Nagasaki's famed *geisha* houses.

In 1870 Sano was appointed to the Army Ministry, with responsibility for building up a navy. Here again he was suddenly dismissed for corruption (ibid.: 395–7). He was accused of buying up leaky old ships for the navy at ridiculously high prices – in other words, of keeping a large commission. His superior, Chōshū's Maebara Issei, was sympathetic, and he was re-instated in the spring of 1871 and soon promoted.

His re-instatement, like the failure to prosecute Yamagata, was not proof of innocence, but merely indicated the extent of the corruption and the fact that the executive was above the law. In 1914 the Siemens affair was to bring down the Prime Minister, navy supremo Yamamoto Gombei. That case revealed that navy corruption was widespread, deep-rooted and of long duration. It would seem to have continued in an unbroken line, not only from the early Meiji period but even back to the fifties.

## THE BUDGET PROBLEM

These army and navy scandals were played out against the background of a wider struggle between Etō at the Justice Ministry and Inoue at the Treasury. To set up a nation-wide judicial system, Etō needed money, but Inoue tried to abort these plans by declaring that no finance could be made available. At the Education Ministry, Etō had been succeeded by his Saga colleague, Ōki, who likewise had his estimates cut to the bone while the army, though wallowing in corruption, received what it requested (Matano 1914, Vol. 2: 1ff.). Etō therefore sent in a long letter of resignation in which he accused Inoue of being a mere book-keeper with no knowledge of economic policy. He further pointed out that a strong, prosperous country was impossible unless the people enjoyed a sense of security; in other words, a strong independent judiciary was necessary for the generally agreed objective, *fukoku kyōhei*. He listed the laws being drawn up and the courts set up. His projected reforms included a review of marriage and family law, for people were marrying in the morning and divorcing in the afternoon, and orphans were being cheated out of their inheritance (ibid.: 8–10).

The anti-Ōkubo side in the 1873 *Seihen* are sometimes depicted as reactionary champions of feudalism, but Etō's letter of resignation – and, indeed, the whole struggle to establish the Rule of Law – plainly demonstrated that though he had no European language, Etō had absorbed the essence of Western civilization far better than most of the so-called Western scholars. Etō was fully backed by the Justice Department officials, who were to display great courage and dedication.

The Great Council of State tried to mediate, but Inoue refused to alter his position, and rallied his own forces in both Tokyo and the prefectures. A great number of prefectural governors were Chōshū protégés, so naturally they supported Inoue (ibid.: 25–6). Until the time of Etō's reforms, local governors had been in charge of justice, with only the death penalty requiring the approval of the central government. The jails were often described as 'valleys of death' and it was virtually impossible for the citizens to oppose the oppression of corrupt local officials who consequently did not welcome a change which would make them subject to an independent judiciary.

When Sanjō prevaricated, Etō's deputy, Fukuoka Takachika, and other officials also resigned, bringing the Justice Department to a virtual standstill. When the Cabinet asked them to withdraw their resignations, they did so, for this request amounted to a victory. At this stage Ōkuma was recalled to Tokyo and put in charge of investigating the Budget. After two months, he reported that it was possible to meet the estimates of the Justice and Education Ministries. By the time he made his estimates, the crop situation had improved, so that explained part of the discrepancy, but even so Inoue had clearly been either grossly incompetent or deliberately obstructive.

When the Budget struggle ended in defeat, Inoue and Shibusawa resigned.

## THE OSARISAWA AFFAIR

Inoue's resignation was not just a result of the Budget struggle. It would seem fair to say he was hounded out of office by Etō, who had the strong backing of Saigō and of Tosa (Matano 1914, Vol. 2: 52ff.).

After the Boshin War, the Nambu clan had its *roku* reduced from 200,000 to 130,000 *koku*, and was ordered to pay 70,000 *ryō* into the Treasury. When the clans were abolished in 1871 their debts and assets were taken over by the central government. The Nambu clan owed a leading merchant, Murai, a large sum of money, but in the Delphic language of the day, the receipt could also be read to mean that Murai owed the money to the clan. Despite the avowals of all concerned, and the clear logic of the situation, Murai was ordered to pay this sum to the Treasury. When Murai was unable to pay, the government seized his property, including the Osarisawa copper mine which his family had worked for generations. Murai begged to be allowed to go on working the mine and to repay the 'debt' over five years; Inoue, however, refused, and the mine was sold off to his Chōshū friend, Okada Heizō, who was permitted to pay in twenty-four annual instalments.

As a vital step towards establishing the Rule of Law, Etō's Justice Ministry had introduced laws giving citizens the right to sue corrupt and oppressive officials. Murai now took Inoue to court and it became a test case. Etō put Shimamoto on the case, and he confirmed that the money was owed to, and not by, Murai. He also noted the generous terms for Okada, and the fact that the clan had other wealth such as timber which could have been used for paying any outstanding debts without seizing the mine, a traditional source of clan income.

Inoue resigned soon after Shimamoto submitted his report, but went to Osarisawa and brazenly put up a sign: 'This mine is the property of Inoue Kaoru' (ibid.: 59). Unfortunately, Japanese historians can be equally brazen, and it is not rare to find the case discussed without Inoue's name even being mentioned. The case, however, should be regarded as a symbol of Chōshū corruption, and was very much a part of the fabric of events leading up to the 1873 *Seihen*. Etō's disgust knew no bounds. He wanted to imprison Inoue. Kido, however, was just back from abroad, and he and Sanjō rushed to Inoue's defence, claiming that others in the government had to be consulted. Etō lacked the power to proceed alone, and even Gotō and Ōkuma, though both outwardly sympathetic, warned that it was impossible to punish one as highly placed as Inoue.

Nevertheless, Etō took the case to court in May 1873. The Chōshū *batsu* had the case prolonged, and once Etō resigned over the *seikan* dispute, the top officials on the case were all transferred: Kōno Togama to the Genrō-In, Ōshima to head the Kōchi court and Kobatake to the High Court. In other words, the Executive had asserted its supremacy over the Judiciary, and the trial became a travesty of justice. It continued until 1875 when Inoue, though still on trial, was appointed as Kuroda's deputy on the expedition to open Korea. Proceedings were then hurried up to enable him to depart (*Segai Inoue Kō Den* 1933, Vol. 2: 103–4).

Eleven of the accused, including top officials Shibusawa, Ono Yoshisane and Okamoto Kensaburō, were found guilty of two unintentional errors: they had mistaken a loan for a debt, and they had not obtained a written agreement for the sale of the mine and its facilities. As punishment, there were a few minor demotions and some nominal fines, Inoue's being thirty *yen*. The Treasury was ordered to return to Murai 25,000 *yen* he had paid as part of his 'debt', but the mine remained with Inoue. Later it was sold to Mitsubishi.

Attention should be drawn to the presence of Ono Yoshisane among the accused, for he was already playing a central role in Mitsubishi. In 1874, Gotō's eldest daughter was married to Iwasaki Yatarō's younger brother, Yanosuke, who was to become company president on Yatarō's death in 1885 (*Iwasaki Hisaya Den* 1961: 170). Thus though Gotō was outwardly sympathetic to Etō, he could hardly have welcomed a campaign which would have eliminated Ono, one of their own key members. The usually commendable Iwasaki biographies relate how Okada Heizō obtained the Osarisawa mining rights in 1872, and how the mine was bought by Mitsubishi in 1888, but there is absolutely no mention of Inoue (ibid.: 347ff.). Matano's 1914 biography of Etō is a work of the highest standard, but he had interviewed, and was perhaps somewhat under the influence of Ōkuma. The picture of Gotō and Ōkuma being sympathetic to Etō must be treated with caution. Though they doubtless professed sympathy, and though they were later to participate in many battles against Mitsui and Chōshū, they had their own network of contacts with the accused officials such as Ono, and one can hardly believe that they wanted them convicted.

This is later confirmed by Ōkuma's biographers who state that Ōkuma did all he could to get Inoue off the Osarisawa hook (*Ōkuma Kō 85 Nen Shi* 1925: 493–4). If one looks at the roll-call of the accused – Inoue, Shibusawa, Ono, etc. – and of their backers such as Sanjō and Iwakura, the case is clearly seen as a David and Goliath struggle, especially after Etō's resignation. This leads us back to the popular legend that Saigō planned to make himself Shogun. It is not illogical to believe that Saigō felt that only by taking direct control could he sweep away the corrupt forces and set up a state based on the Rule of Law. The careers of Washington and Napoleon were well known in Meiji Japan, and Saigō's close associate, Etō, was trying to set up a legal system based on the Code Napoleon. It is not difficult to picture Saigō taking Napoleon as a role model. There is no substantive proof that this was so, but this interpretation cannot be dismissed out of hand.

## THE KYOTO AFFAIR

The nature of the struggle to establish the Rule of Law is best illustrated by the Kyoto affair (see Matano 1914, Vol. 2: 68ff.)

which broke out in May 1873, a month after Etō resigned as Justice Minister. It was, however, a direct result of Etō's reforms, especially Law Sixteen which gave citizens the power to challenge officials in the Justice Ministry Court. Previously, of course, the local governors had control of justice, and if oppressed citizens protested, they faced summary arrest.

An outstanding feature of the Meiji 'peace settlement' was the way in which the Satchō *batsu* gave their own merchants special privileges in Kansai, while at the same time exploiting the old business houses. Thus Satchō were largely able to take over the Kansai business world. The rich Ono family, to avoid the excessive exactions, decided to take advantage of the new right to move freely and applied to have their registration transferred from Kyoto to Tokyo, but this application was rejected.

The Kyoto governor was Nagatani Nobuatsu, a noble. Effective power was in the hands of his deputy, Makimura Masanao, a Chōshū man closely allied to Kido. He had helped Kido obtain a fine mansion which had belonged to Konoe (Tominari 1972: 221). There Kido stayed in great splendour, maintaining several *geisha* mistresses. On his death in 1877, they were all taken over by Itō Hirobimi, but for this 'he was not praised by the world' (Kume 1931: 404ff.). Kaya, the most famous of the *geisha*, was about to make her debut and her dress bill came to 3,000 *yen*, which Itō paid. That same year, when the Seinan War ended, the Fujita-Gumi simply terminated on the spot the contracts of 1,000 coolies it had taken to Kyūshū. After a noisy dispute, they received 3.5 *yen* each – a grand total of 3,500 *yen* (Miyamoto 1960: 125ff.).

This Chōshū-dominated Kyoto government resented any diminution of its powers, and did everything possible to prevent the establishment of the new courts, even blocking physical access. In January, Etō sent a strong-man, Kitabatake Harafusa, to head the court, and in May his battle with Makimura became a national issue when the Onos took their case to the court. When Makimura disdainfully told the court to drop the case, Kitabatake angrily replied that the Rule of Law had been established and that the case would proceed. As the local government ignored its proceeding, Ono won by default. The local government, however, still refused to let the Onos move, claiming it was an administrative matter which had nothing to do with the judiciary. When the Kyoto court sought the backing of the Justice Ministry, it developed into a struggle to determine whether Japan really did have an independent judiciary.

266

Etō sought support within the Great Council of State, but months passed with Sanjō refusing to act against his Chōshū friends.

As Nagatani and Makimura both continued to refuse to answer summonses to appear in court, Nagatani was sentenced in his absence on 5 August 1873 to thirty days imprisonment and Makimura to twenty (ibid.: 86). Instead of complying, they sought permission to come to Tokyo to argue the case. On Etō's insistence, Sanjō refused to accept their letter, and on 17 August they agreed to pay a fine – the standard alternative for top officials and nobles. The Justice Ministry still pushed on with the case, but the Kyoto government rallied their Chōshū and noble supporters. Despite this political pressure, Nagatani and Makimura eventually stood trial in Tokyo. The Justice Ministry agreed to set up a kind of jury which included Tosa stalwarts Hijikata, Sasaki and Takeuchi (ibid.: 96), but these all had strong Chōshū ties. Since Makimura acted with such extreme arrogance in court, it was decided to place him under arrest while the trial continued. At this point, however, political considerations took over. The Korean question had climaxed with the resignation of Saigō, Etō, etc. On 25 November 1873 Iwakura celebrated his now undisputed supremacy by ordering the release of Makimura, who had been under arrest for just one week. The Justice Department, of course, protested vigorously against this political interference, and when their protests went unheeded, all the top figures such as Shimamoto and Fukuoka Takachika resigned.

By the end of the year, the case was more or less over. The Onos were permitted to move to Tokyo, but their triumph was to be short lived. Eight members of the Kyoto government were punished, four receiving 100 days imprisonment and fines of 30 *yen*, and four others forty days. For the Justice Department it had been a Pyrrhic victory. Their ranks had been decimated, and Iwakura had demonstrated that the judiciary was not independent but subservient to the Executive. The Rule of Law had not taken root; it was patently clear that it was not possible to sue corrupt officials, and that Satchō were again free to take the spoils of war.

Destroying the Rule of Law had almost been Iwakura's first act on forcing out Saigō and Etō, and judicial independence must be regarded as one of the great issues of the 1873 *Seihen*. This does not, however, preclude other interpretations. The personal conflicts, the clan *batsu* struggles and the issue of public morality are manifestly relevant. Nor were the Satchō *batsu* simply interested in abstract constitutional issues. Had Etō triumphed, and the Rule of Law been established, the Satchō *batsu* could not have seized the Osarisawa mine and other spoils of war. These five factors – personal conflicts, clan *batsu* struggle, public morality, the Rule of Law and obtaining the spoils of war – should not be seen as conflicting interpretations of the 1873 *Seihen* but rather as a closely interwoven pattern of indivisible factors.

It should be noted that there is here a related question of considerable importance which Japanese historians seem not to have addressed. The central fact of the story is that both the Ono-kumi in Osaka and the Murais in Namba were Ōmi merchants. Though Osaka historian Miyamoto Mataji has written a multi-volume account of the Ono-kumi which highlights the relationship with the Murais in Nambu, it stops far short of a general analysis of the Satchō relationship with the Ōmi merchants. Indeed, it seems fair to say that over the years Miyamoto has developed into the spokesman for the Osaka business community. The central fact of the story is that both the Onokumi in Osaka and the Murais in Nambu were Ōmi merchants. Bearing in mind that the Ōmi clans were close to the Shogun and that Ōmi was the home of Ii Naosuke, the Shogunate minister responsible for the great crack-down on dissidents in 1858, the way in which the Ōmi merchants were eliminated from Hokkaidō, the Ōmi position destroyed in Nambu, and the Ono *kumi* smashed in Kyoto surely suggests a deliberate Satchō policy of breaking the power of the Ōmi merchants as part of their move to seize economic as well as political control of Japan. The typical *goyō* phrases about the Ōmi merchants being 'unable to adopt to the modern world', like the official histories' description of the Hokkaidō migrants who died of cold and hunger as 'unsuitable . . . the scrapings of the cities . . . unwilling to help themselves', should drive home the lesson that Japanese history is still heavily slanted in favour of the 1868 victors whose descendants form the backbone of the modern Japanese Establishment. These internal stories, along with the Satchō grab for mines, trade and land, must be regarded as a prelude to, and an integral part of, Japan's bid for commercial Empire.

## THE TRIAL OF ETŌ SHIMPEI

The message that the Rule of Law had not taken root was driven home in brutal fashion at the trial of Etō and Shima (Okumura 1975: 57ff.). The 1873 *Seihen* had tightened the Satchō control of government and commerce. Though Ōkuma and Ōki remained within the government, they had effectively cut themselves off from their own clan, and did not return home for years. The Saga people, now outsiders, grouped themselves into two anti-government factions, one still supporting *seikan* and one mostly hostile to Westernization (ibid.: 60). When an uprising seemed imminent, both Etō and Shima returned to Saga, either to calm or to lead these two factions. Fighting broke out but lasted only a week. The savagery of the fighting was indicated by the number of suicides (Matano 1914, Vol. 2: 487ff.). Short Western swords were of little use for *seppuku*, so the defeated warriors helped each other with strangulations and hangings. Though the leaders fled, mostly to Satsuma and Tosa, they were soon rounded up and taken back to Saga for trial.

A court was set up within Saga Castle. It was presided over by Tosa's Kōno Togama, an Etō protégé at the Justice Ministry, so his appointment was probably to give an air of impartiality. Other Tosa men were involved in defeating Etō, Iwamura Takatoshi having been sent as governor just before the uprising and Tani Tateki being ordered to send troops from Kumamoto. Ōkubo was probably trying to create a lasting Saga–Tosa hostility. It should, however, be noted that the Tosa men he used had all been supporters of the extremist Takechi faction, and, as such, anti-Gotō; and they had all refused to resign in 1873 with Gotō and Itagaki (see chapter 9).

Matano (1914, Vol. 2: 571ff.) provides a lucid analysis of the trial, demonstrating that it was a travesty of justice. Etō was brought back to Saga on 7 April, the trials took place on the eighth and ninth, and the executions on the thirteenth. Thirteen were executed, but the accused numbered thousands. In all, 150 received sentences of from two to ten years' hard labour.

Ōkubo's diaries make it clear that even before reaching Saga, he had already decided who was to be punished and what the sentences were to be. Kōno was acting, not as an independent judge, but as an executive officer moving with all possible speed to carry out Ōkubo's orders.

Despite Etō's new legal codes, the trial made no pretence at following Western legal procedures, but reverted to the old system which depended on getting a confession before the case was taken to court. Though there is no evidence that torture was in fact used, the defendants knew that torture was normally used until a confession was extracted. 'Confessions' were read out in court, but it seems clear that they were not authentic. Many were read out in a voice so low that the defendants could not hear what it was they had allegedly confessed to. Others claimed that their depositions had been changed. They therefore refused to thumb-print these 'confessions' and a furious struggle ensued in court as the authorities tried to get their prints onto the documents. This struggle continued until Etō convinced his followers that it was pointless.

In 1870 the government had promulgated a new penal code based on Chinese and Japanese models, especially the Tokugawa. It reduced punishment (ibid.: 105ff.) to four classes: death, exile, imprisonment and whipping. There were three categories of each. The death penalty could be execution followed by putting the head on public display, simple beheading, and hanging. Displaying the head to the public gaze was to be ordered only in cases of treason. Burning at the stake was abolished, as was the death penalty for robberies under 100 *yen*.

Etō's new code of June 1873 did not go as far as he would have liked, but the displaying of heads was abolished and imprisonment substituted for hanging – a highly dubious advance considering the number of prisoners who promptly died of 'sickness'. But a year after these reforms were introduced, Etō and Shima had their heads cut off and stuck up for all to behold. Photographs of their heads were then taken and sold throughout Japan.

Etō's sentence was an act of savagery, and reeked of vengeance. It effectively disposes of Tokutomi's picture of the 1873 *Seihen* as a gentlemanly struggle between men of principle. When the sentences were pronounced by his protégé, Etō was stunned. He tried to speak, but was taken from court to be executed a few days later (ibid.: 576). He died a poor man. His family, of course, were shunned. Of his Tosa 'friends' only Hijikata made any attempt to help the destitute family, and it was left to Shimamoto, his right-hand man at the Justice Ministry, to come forward openly to help the Etōs return to Saga.

Saga had received a blow from which it never recovered, and became an insignificant backwater. Even more devastating for Etō was the vicious, gloating final message from Ōkubo implicit in this sentence: his carefully nurtured legal reforms and the Rule of Law were dying with him. The Satchō government was once more above the law.

## THE ONGOING STRUGGLE

Though the 1873 *Seihen* and the subsequent execution of Etō were blows from which the judiciary never recovered, the struggle did not die with him but was carried on courageously both by judges in the courts and by officials within the Justice Ministry.

Though it was to be a losing war, it is worth noting some of the battles.

## The Seinan War trials

After the Seinan War, the Commander-in-Chief, Arisugawa, issued orders authorizing the use of torture. It had been a very nasty war, and it would seem that the orders were based on the desire for revenge rather than on the need to extract information (*Itō Hirobumi Den* 1940, Vol. 2: 87–8). However, wartime atrocities had been widely reported in both the local and foreign press, so the further use of torture would make treaty revision even more difficult. The Cabinet therefore decided that 'only in the case of the present crime against the nation, its use was most undesirable'. Kōno Togama was again the presiding judge, and he was directed to be magnanimous. The decisions to be magnanimous and not to use torture were based on political expediency and were not creating precedents. In other words, the trials confirmed that there was no independent judiciary.

## Kuroda's violence

Kuroda had long been notorious for his drunken violence. It seems that in March 1878 he came home drunk and hacked his wife to pieces; but the affair was hushed up by his clansman, Police Chief Kawaji (Iguchi 1965: 100–5). Two months later Ōkubo was assassinated. In a written statement, the assassins gave five reasons for their action; one was the fact that Kuroda had murdered his wife. Though the murder may never be proved it plainly was widely believed to have taken place.

The character of Kuroda helps highlight the nature of both the 1873 *Seihen* and the subsequent Satchō governments. During the 1881 *Seihen* Kuroda is said to have written to Nagayama telling him to recruit a ten-man hit squad from among the *tonden hei* and to send them to Tokyo. Nagayama and his friends, however, restrained him (Ōsaka 1962: 506). In 1885 plans to make him Minister of the Right ran into strong opposition. Sasaki described him as an unqualified, widely disliked drunkard (*Itō Hirobumi Den* 1940, Vol. 2: 455). Kuroda at first accepted the appointment then wrote to Sanjō on 21 November 1885 declining because he did not want to defile the position (ibid.: 468–70). Around this time Kuroda was guilty of particularly wild and violent behaviour including threatening Inoue with a pistol. When apologizing, he explained that he had frequently sought medical help for his drinking problem but that the doctors had declared his condition was difficult to treat. Sanjō put it succinctly in a letter to Itō on 9 December 1885 when he described Kuroda's conduct as 'abnormal, out of the ordinary, and truly dangerous'.

Yet when it was time to replace Itō as Prime Minister, Kuroda was pushed forward as the senior Satsuma man. Most reluctantly Ōkubo's son, Makino Nobuaki, became his Private Secretary, but only on the strict condition that he never had to socialize with this dangerous character (Makino 1948, Vol. 1: 187–8). Makino later drew a vivid picture of Kuroda as a pathetically isolated, deeply disturbed man. He also stated that Kuroda never once asked him to investigate any question or to provide him with information. He summed him up as a man without any policies of his own (ibid.: 194).

That a violent, unstable, unpopular man, devoid of political policies should be pushed forward as Prime Minister clearly shows that the over-riding principle which guided the Satchō leaders was not the national interest but the maintenance of the Satchō balance. This was not a principle which emerged in the eighties but was one which was central to the 1873 *Seihen*, for the caretaker government had been determined to oust the corrupt Chōshū *batsu*, while Ōkubo, Iwakura and Sanjō's conduct must be seen as an attempt to reinstate Chōshū and to maintain the Satchō balance.

## Mitsukuri Rinshō

Apologists for the Satchō power struggle generally depict their opponents such as Etō as irresponsible and backward. They ignore the fact that within the judiciary were many men of high principle, courage and ability. These opponents of Satchō are better understood if we look at the career of Mitsukuri Rinshō.

Rinshō was largely raised and taught by his grandfather, Genpo. When Genpo was born in 1799, his clan, Tsuyama in modern Okayama prefecture, already had well-established traditions of Western studies. Utagawa Gensui (1755–97), the clan doctor, had turned to Western medicine and in 1793 published the first translation of a Dutch anatomy textbook. Gensui's adopted son, Genshin, helped produce a Dutch–Japanese dictionary in 1796, then wrote many textbooks on Western medicine. Gensui's adopted son, Yōan, produced textbooks on botany and chemistry, and his writings are widely regarded as the real beginnings of modern scientific studies in Japan (Jiromaru 1970: 28ff.). It should be noted that not only in medicine and science, but also in the social sciences, the 'translator' was not merely a linguist but a leader in that field.

Mitsukuri Genpo became a disciple of Utagawa, and practised medicine, then in 1839 he was appointed as an official translator to the Bakufu (Kure 1914: 35ff.). His writings were to cover a wide range of subjects including geography, geology, military studies, mining and foreign affairs. He acted as an interpreter when Perry arrived in 1853, and a month later he was sent to Nagasaki to help negotiate with the Russians (ibid.: 140–5). Genpo, who was in favour of opening the country (ibid.: 130–1), was also consulted by the leading *daimyō* such as Kansō and Shungaku (ibid.: 256).

Genpo's successor, Shūhei, likewise became a noted translator–adviser. He went to Europe with the Takeuchi mission of 1861 and with the mission sent to Russia in 1866. His eldest son studied at London University, and another, a noted scientist, obtained a doctorate at Johns Hopkins (ibid.: 246).

Rinshō's father died young, so the main influence in his life was his grandfather, Genpo. At twelve he was already reading Dutch fluently. He also began to study English under Tosa's Nakahama Manjirō (Ōtsugi 1906: 3ff.). He soon established himself as both teacher and translator. Half the fourteen students sent to England in 1866 were Rinshō's students, but he himself could not be spared. In 1867, however, he was the youngest member of the party to the Paris Exhibition where he made good progress with his French.

Unlike Shūhei and Fukuzawa, Rinshō went to work for the new government. He was appointed to the newly-created Education Ministry, then followed Etō to the Justice Ministry. In order to translate foreign codes, especially the Code Napoleon, he studied not only French but also the law, taking advantage of the experts such as Barnard, brought from France. Fukuzawa urged him to practise law (ibid.: 169–70), but he brushed this aside, dismissing Fukuzawa as *kanemōke shugi* (money orientated).

Though he stayed with the government, Rinshō was no lackey of the Satchō *batsu*. It was rather a case of fighting from within. After Etō's execution, he took a particularly courageous stand. In October 1875 his stirring translation of *Kokusei Tenpen Ron* (*On Overthrowing the Government*) was published and led to a flurry of articles in the popular press. Even such a distinguished historian as Ienaga Saburō (1960: 107–8) commented that it was difficult to understand why a bureaucratic scholar such as Mitsukuri should translate and publish such a work. Ienaga's condescension was unwarranted, for the anti-Satchō case had never been put with such lack of ambiguity and compromise:

> The nation and the Government are not one and the same thing. Even though the Government is changed, that does not mean the nation is no longer the same. . . . When the Government pursues its own selfish purpose and suppresses the freedom of the People, the People should take up arms and drive out that Government.
>
> (Ōtsugi 1906: 83)

Predictably, all this caused a great commotion within government circles. Rinshō was protected by the Justice Minister, Ōki Takato, who insisted he was 'just a translator'. But that same year Rinshō also translated Caspar Hopkins' *World Government* which began with a chapter on natural rights, then went on to discuss tyranny, oligarchies and republicanism. Obviously, Rinshō was belabouring the theme of natural freedom.

In the years that followed, Rinshō, as bureaucrat and teacher, went on to become widely accepted as 'The Father of Japanese Law'. In 1887, when the Meiji Law School was set up, Rinshō, Ōki, Barnard, Namura and Tsurata were made honorary members of the faculty. Both Barnard and Namura made speeches in which they praised Rinshō as the real father of Japanese law (ibid.: 97). In 1888 he was made a Doctor of Law; two years later he was made Principal of the French Law School and a non-titled member of the House of Peers (ibid.: 87–8). He developed stomach cancer in 1896 but continued to work. When the doctors urged him to rest, he replied that a soldier dies on the battlefield, a bureaucrat in his office. It is said that the day before he died, he went to his office, and on his way home he called in at the Mombusho. He was then fifty.

Ōkuma was to give a balanced verdict on both Etō and Mitsukuri (ibid.: 127): it was Etō's aim to bring Japan into line with world civilization, while Mitsukuri's great contribution was to guide the bureaucrats to a new appreciation of legal administration and concepts.

One is reminded of Morris's phrase, 'the nobility of failure'. The Meiji judges and bureaucrats in the Justice Department made a valiant but ultimately unsuccessful attempt to set up an independent judiciary. Nonetheless, they made an invaluable contribution. Modern legal concepts and practices were introduced and accepted; fine law schools were set up; and, despite the Executive, the judiciary never entirely lost its traditions of high-principled service. All this made possible a smooth transition to a modern, independent legal system after the Second World War.

The 1873 struggle must be viewed against this wider background. Obviously, at that time, 'translator' Mitsukuri with his *minken kenri* was not yet the Father of Japanese Law; but neither was he a mere linguist. The 1873 struggle for the Rule of Law cannot be brought down to a personal contest between Etō and Ōkubo. Behind Etō were men like Mitsukuri and Shimamoto who carried on the fight for many years. Ultimately, Etō's character, like that of Saigō, is irrelevant: the Satchō *batsu* in 1873, in its determination to place itself above the law, must clearly be seen as fighting not just Etō but the whole judiciary; and if we are to understand the Satchō rule of Japan itself, and the form of imperialism it imposed on conquered peoples we must bear in mind the question asked rhetorically of Mitsukuri, the young translator: What's this about the people having rights?

# 11

# THE TOSA CLAN, GODAI AND THE OPENING OF KOREA

Most histories of the 1873 *Seihen* treat it as a political crisis which took place in Tokyo. Yet it was largely an economic struggle, and the movement to attack Korea was likewise based on economic motives. This emerges clearly if we look at Tosa clan and at Satchō's Godai and Inoue.

## TOSA AND THE 1873 *SEIHEN*

In the 1873 *Seihen* Tosa split into two camps. Gotō, Itagaki and Kataoka, who were to play a leading role in the *minken* movement, followed Saigō out of the government, but Sasaki, Tani, Hijikata and Kōno Togama all stayed on. This was partly a division along class lines, the former being high-ranking *samurai*, the latter lower ranking. It was also a continuation of the 1863 *Seihen*.

Gotō was a nephew of Yoshida Tōyō (1816–62), an administrator who was forced into retirement in 1854 and opened a *juku* outside Kōchi. There his students included Gotō and Iwasaki Yatarō who was to found Mitsubishi. Tōyō was restored to favour in 1858, and was the driving force in the administration until his assassination in 1862. There is little in Tōyō's writings to suggest he was a profound or original thinker. His teachings revolved around *fukoku kyōhei* and commercial expansion with strong *kokugaku* overtones. His seven-year plan stressed both mercantile and naval expansion. Thus a letter to Yōdō dated 8 September 1861 discussed the setting up of a *Bunbukan* (Institute of Literary and Military Studies) and the purchase of a steamship; then once their people were trained, they could buy warships, occupy islands in the South Seas, and when the time came to fight the Western nations then enjoying trading rights in Japan, it would be seen that this

276

merchant marine training had not been a waste (Otsuka 1929: 268–70).

With his emphasis on trade and on learning from the West, Tōyō is generally described as 'progressive' – a description warranted by his attempts to break down the old, complicated system of classifying *samurai* and to open more positions to talented lower *samurai*. But his ambitious new *Bunbukan* and his own magnificent new home and lavish life style (Hirao 1964: 137ff.) aroused the opposition of both conservatives and extremists for they meant increased taxation and forced labour. The immediate cause of his downfall, however, was his support for *Kōbu-gattai* (national unity). The Emperor Party was already committed to overthrowing the Bakufu, restoring the Emperor, and driving out the 'barbarians'. When they could not convert him, the Emperor Party assassinated Tōyō on 8 April 1862 and stuck his head on a post. Little attempt was made to track down the assassins, but as they were of low class, power now passed to the high-born conservatives. A year later the pendulum swung back with the Satsuma-led *coup* in Kyoto. Gotō came to power in Tosa, and Itagaki rounded up most of Tōyō's assassins. As usual, it was trial by torture. No one confessed but, contrary to established custom, they were found guilty, their crime being that of disturbing the public peace and unsettling the people. The leader, Takechi, and several others were ordered to commit *seppuku*.

Takechi's lieutenant, Kōno Togama, was tortured and imprisoned, but not executed. Among the Takechi supporters who escaped punishment were Sakamoto Ryōma, Sasaki, Tani and Hijikata. Ryōma had escaped from the clan before the assassination, while Hijikata had accompanied the seven nobles to Chōshū. Sasaki kept a famous diary (*Sasaki Takayuki Nikki* 1970) which is regarded as a major Meiji document. However, it was edited and rewritten in his old age, and seems to have been substantially amended. Sasaki claimed that he was of a much higher social class than the Takechi faction, which was composed of country *samurai* and members of the village headsmen class, and this inhibited him from joining them. His case, however, is most unconvincing. He knew neither his father nor grandfather, and his grandmother, a farmer's daughter, was not 'the real wife'. He grew up in poverty, and his only family contacts seem to have been his *heimin* relatives. He went to the same fencing school as Takechi and was also taught by Takechi's uncle, Kamochi Masazumi, a *kokugakusha* of some note. The authoritative *Kokugakusha Denki Shūsei* (Vol. 2: 1353–5) lists Takechi, Sasaki and Yoshimura

Toratarō among Masazumi's nine main disciples. Yoshimura was one of the leaders of the ill-fated Tenchū-gumi uprising. That Sasaki and Takechi were both taught by Masazumi meant they were steeped in the same *kokugaku* traditions. With the Restoration, several hundred 'volumes' of Masazumi's works found their way into the Palace Library where they sit to this day. In 1879 much of it was published by the Kunai-sho, helping to spread his honour throughout the land. It is reasonable to suppose that Sasaki was involved both in placing these works in the Palace Library and in having them published.

On 4 December 1861, as the political struggle was approaching its climax, one of Sasaki's sisters married Miyasaki Takegorō, a close relative of Takechi's and a fervent kinnō-ka (*Sasaki Takayuki Nikki* 1970, Vol. 1: 349–50). This marriage indicates that there was no great social gap between Sasaki and Takechi; it would also seem to be a public confirmation of a firm political alliance. On the other hand, throughout this period Sasaki became completely estranged from his old upper-class *samurai* friends (ibid.: 415–16). His diary also makes clear that most of Takechi's supporters lived in the countryside, and that he, Tani and Hayashi attended key meetings in Kōchi, acting as a kind of *sambō* (ibid.: 354).

Likewise, Tani was not the high-born *samurai* he is often depicted to be. Until Tani was eleven, his father was a country teacher; then he – and later Tani – was appointed to the clan school and was promoted to *samurai* status for his work there. Hirao aptly describes the Tanis as 'newly emerging', and, as with Sasaki, there was no great social gap between Tani and the Takechi faction (Hirao 1935: 95ff.).

In 1873 Sasaki was not present at the key meetings, but his second-hand reports are often quoted. He described the *seikan* party as emotional, expansionary and militaristic, and the anti-*seikan* party as rational, non-militaristic and opposed to overseas expansion (Tsuda 1915, Vol. 1: 292–3). This description is contrary to all logic and the known facts. The Takechi party was firmly allied with Maki, with the most extreme nobles such as Anegakōji, Sawa and Sanjō, and with the Chōshū extremists such as Kusaka, the brother-in-law of Yoshida Shōin who, in his *Lectures on Mōshi* (*Kōmō Yowa*), had advocated an attack on Korea back in the mid-fifties. When Sanjō and Anegakōji had ridden up to Edo to present the edict demanding that the Bakufu expel the 'barbarians' within a certain time, Takechi and his men rode by their side; when Anegakōji was assassinated on 20 May 1863, Hijikata and Higo's Yamada Shindō were staying with him as bodyguards (Hirao 1979–80, Vol. 1: 95–6); and when the seven nobles fled to Chōshū, Sawa, wishing to join an uprising, put a lamp in his bed and escaped in the dead of night (ibid.: 97). Hijikata and Higashikuse went in pursuit but failed to overtake him. Hijikata went on to guard the nobles in both Chōshū and Dazai-fu, where he was later visited by Sasaki. The closeness of Sasaki's own Chōshū ties was illustrated after Chōshū was declared *chōteki*. The Tosa lord sought to return his young Chōshū bride, but Sasaki successfully attacked his plans as immoral and impolitic for Chōshū might well rise again (*Sasaki Takayuki Nikki* 1970, Vol. 4: 42ff.). Thus the extreme Emperor Party was one that cut across clan boundaries.

Its leaders – Maki, Anegakōji, Kusaka and Takechi – had all died violent deaths within a few years of each other, but the old loyalties remained. In 1873, Sasaki and his companions were not so much men of principle agonizing over matters of high policy, as extremists and habitual conspirators, bound by old loyalties and enmities. Gotō was firmly allied to Etō and Itagaki to Saigō, so the Takechi faction members, the long-standing opponents of Gotō and Itagaki, gravitated to the other side which revolved around their old allies, Sanjō and the Chōshū extremists. In short, in 1873 Tosa divided along 1863 lines, and though the Takechi faction were fanatical imperialists, they thus found themselves in the anti-*seikan* camp.

As we saw with Kurume, *hanbatsu* struggles were not simply a matter of struggles between clans but also involved bitter, on-going struggles within clans, and these bitter internal struggles cutting across principles and beliefs were an important ingredient of the 1873 *Seihen*. Both the Tosa factions were, in Tokutomi's words, 'splendid imperialists', the only real difference being that the Takechi faction stressed 'strong troops' while the Gotō side was more concerned with 'a prosperous country'. That the Takechi faction were fanatical imperialists emerges quite clearly from their ties with Maki, Kusaka, etc., and Sasaki's own position is spelt out in an opinion paper dated 21 May 1869 (ibid.). It deplored the fact that *kōdō fukkō* had not yet been attempted. It stressed the high origins of Japan and its superiority to the rest of the world, and specially emphasized the need to develop Ezochi, 'the Northern Gate of the Imperial Country', pointing out that it was close to both Manchuria and Shantung.

The evidence is thus overwhelming: Sasaki and the Takechi faction strongly supported imperial expansion. Their stance in 1873 was determined by Tosa history. After the battle of Sekigahara,

Yamanouchi, a Tokugawa favourite, had been brought in as lord, and his followers became the Tosa upper *samurai*. Generally they remained loyal to the Tokugawas. The followers of the former lord, Chōsogabe, who met an ignominious death, became lower *samurai* or a special new rank, *gōshi*, a kind of farmer–*samurai*. They never lost their pride as *samurai* and never forgot Sekigahara. Instead of feeling loyalty to the Tokugawas and the Yamanouchis, it became easier for them to relate to the Chōshū challenge to the Bakufu. Many fled the clan, at great cost, and joined forces with Chōshū. Many died with the men of Chōshū, Kyoto and Kurume. These traumatic events reached their climax in 1863, and in 1873 the Tosa leaders divided along 1863 lines. *Seikan* was virtually a non issue.

This Tosa story also graphically illustrates the fundamental importance of economic factors in the 1873 *Seihen* and in the subsequent opening of Korea. That story revolved around three men: Gotō, Sakamoto Ryōma and Iwasaki Yatarō. When Gotō came to power in Tosa, he continued Tōyō's policies, and set up the *kaiseikan* which opened early in 1865 (see Hirao 1935: 93ff.). It was half school, half trading company. The scale was to be heroic: trading, whaling, mining, medicine, a modern navy, foreign instructors and Western buildings were all included. But all the people could see was the expense, and so the institute was called *ahōkan* (the fools' building).

The opposition to the *kaiseikan* was widespread. The merchants fiercely opposed its monopolies, the people the increased taxes. The purchases, especially of ships and arms, far exceeded revenue so the clan was soon in debt to Nagasaki and foreign merchants (Kajinishi 1963: 62ff.). Sasaki and Tani were among the critics. Sasaki argued that they should start with simple wooden buildings (Tsuda 1915, Vol. 2: 318ff.) and once results were produced they could put up grandiose headquarters. Tani (Hirao 1935: 93ff.) likewise stressed that it was taking money from the people who normally engaged in trade. The aim should be to create a harmonious community.

With the cost of living rising rapidly and the burden on the people growing, the clan issued paper money. Tani wrote a paper deploring this step; he correctly predicted that it would disrupt the economy and lead to more paper money. On the pretext of promoting trade, but largely to escape his critics, Gotō went on to Nagasaki where he continued his free-spending ways. He also entered into an alliance with Sakamoto Ryōma.

Ryōma was a Takechi follower who left the clan late in 1861, ostensibly to study swordsmanship. He arrived in Hagi the following February as Takechi's messenger and became acquainted with Kusaka (Hirao 1978: 13fn.). He returned briefly to Tosa, but he fled the clan in March 1863 and so was not involved in Tōyō's assassination. Later he went up to Tokyo to assassinate Katsu, but was converted by him to the need to open the country and build a navy (*Iwasaki Yatarō Den* 1967: 321ff.).

When Katsu started a Bakufu navy school in Hyōgo, he made Sakamoto its head. In 1865 this school was closed because it was full of anti-Bakufu extremists. Thereupon Sakamoto took his followers to Nagasaki and set up in business with the backing of Satsuma which, not wanting to advertise its own trading operations, used Ryōma to transport its goods. In 1866 he helped bring Satchō together, and also opened a trading branch in Shimonoseki with Satchō backing.

When Gotō, their old enemy, arrived in Nagasaki, many of Ryōma's followers wished to assassinate him, but Sakamoto persuaded them that the best course was to convert Gotō and to use him to change the clan's position. In this he was successful, Gotō agreeing to back his company. Ryōma, for his part, agreed that his force should in effect become the Tosa navy. Thus in 1867 both Sakamoto and Nagaoka were reinstated as Tosa *samurai*, and the *Kaientai* (sea force) and *Rikuentai* (land force) were formed. They were not to be directly under clan control, but were to be available if required, and were to carry out Tōyō's policy – develop trade, build up a mercantile and naval fleet, and occupy uninhabited islands.

Much has been written about Ryōma, largely because he seems to have been a genuinely attractive and romantic figure. In 1978 Tosa's prolific historian, Hirao Michio, published a 992-page collected edition of Ryōma's correspondence and other writings. One would have thought that a new dimension had been added to Ryōma studies, but in fact the volume demonstrates that 'primary sources' can be hagiographical.

Nevertheless, Hirao produces a vital piece of evidence in the form of a long letter dated 6 March 1867 (Hirao 1978: 178–89) from Ryōma to Indo Hajime, an old Chōshū acquaintance (ibid.: 73–6, fn. to letter 16), and a man of considerable importance within Chōshū; it would seem it was their commercial ambitions which brought Indo and Ryōma together. Ryōma's letter of 6 March 1867 discussed co-operating with Indo over developing Takeshima island. Hirao gives a note (ibid.: 188) on Takeshima which closely follows the *Kawade Rekishi Dai Jiten* description of Takeshima as a small, rocky island, only 23 square kilometres, reaching a height of 115 metres, and situated 55 nautical miles from Kankoku's (Korea's) Utsuryō island. There was no vegetation save for grass growing near the top, but fish were plentiful, so the area was important for Japanese fishermen. Both Japan and Korea claimed ownership, so Japan's title was not established until 1905.

This description, however, is at odds with Ryōma's letter which refers to making a survey of Takeshima's *timber* and fishing. Clearly Ryōma was referring not to Takeshima but to Utsuryō-tō. The Kawade Encyclopaedia's note on Utsuryō-tō explains that it was also known to the Japanese as Takeshima or Matsushima. It, too, was a rocky island with steep cliffs, no natural harbour, and little vegetation, but it was large and had a plain of sorts.

At the end of the seventeenth century the Bakufu recognized Korean rights and forbade the Japanese from using it. But again the Koreans left it unoccupied, so gradually Japanese fishermen and smugglers resumed their activities. The Hamada clan's smuggling activities were discovered in the Tempo period, and again Japanese coastal ships were forbidden from going so far. In the Ansei period, Chōshū planned to settle the island, and in the Meiji period there were plans to settle Matsushima until it was discovered Matsushima was really Utsuryō-tō and therefore not suitable for settlement. In 1881, the Koreans negotiated to prevent Japanese fishing and smuggling, but these activities continued until 1896 when the Russians were given timber rights and the Japanese driven out. It was annexed by Japan in 1905 and returned to Korea in 1945.

Ryōma wrote that the island had camphor trees and was suitable for wax and mulberry trees. He described his vision of the island being developed by *rōshi (rōnin)*, who would grow crops and harvest the riches of the sea. Yet it is clear that Utsuryō-tō itself was not his main interest. More than once he mentioned Inoue Bunta (Kaoru) who had told him about Takeshima and its topography. Recently he had again discussed the island with him. His plan was to use the Ozu ship (*Iroha*) to survey the island. He found it regrettable that people were just concerned with immediate matters, and would not take an interest in such 'great and distant plans'.

If one considers the island's history, its inhospitable nature and lack of a harbour, it is clear that its economic development was an unattractive proposition which would never have attracted a joint Tosa–Chōshū enterprise. Ryōma's 'great and distant plans' surely referred to building up the island as a jumping-off place for the penetration of Korea. In 1896 the Russians did move in to develop its timber, but the move seems to have been strategic, for the Koreans had asked for Russian protection and their entry into Utsuryō-tō was not because it was a promising business venture but because it helped establish them as Korea's protectors.

Any lingering doubts about these plans to occupy Takeshima are removed if we turn back to the writings of Yoshida Shōin. The *Nippon Shisō Taikei* (Vol. 54: 224–5; 238–9) contains two letters Shōin wrote in the mid-fifties to Katsura (Kido) then up in Edo. Both letters urged the occupation of Takeshima and its development as a base from which to launch the invasion of Korea and Manchuria. Shōin's use of the expression *Takeshima-Ron* (the Takeshima concept) and his references to other advocates, such as a certain clan doctor, make it clear that this was not just Shōin's own idiosyncratic idea but was a plan with wide support within Chōshū. It should also be noted that Shōin was urging that this imperial expansion should be carried out, not by the central government, but by the Chōshū clan. This helps alert us to the fact that the great Meiji *seihen* were not debates over whether the mainland should be attacked, but were concerned essentially with who should lead the charge.

Again one must stress the continuity of the story. Only a little over a decade after Shōin described these plans to Kido, Inoue Kaoru, a close associate of Kido, tried to get Tosa to co-operate in the occupation of Takeshima. More research needs to be done on the Takeshima story. It will surely confirm that the *Takeshima-Ron* was a continuous, on-going debate.

It should also be noted that these letters to Kido stressed that they had to plan the first stages carefully, while thinking of great and distant objectives. Shōin had breached Japan's seclusion laws by trying to stow away with Perry. He had been apprehended, caged, then imprisoned. While in prison he wrote his famous *Yūshūroku* (*A Prisoner's Record*) (Shōin 1854) which argued (pp. 105–7) that Japan's 'defence' required that Japan attack Russia, drive her out of Asia, and take over her Asian possessions, such as Kamchatka and Ohtsuka; she also had to 'wake up' the Ryūkyūs, attack and occupy Korea, then take Manchuria in the north and Taiwan and the Luzon Islands in the south. He also advocated setting up Japanese colonies in Australia. The fact that he produced no detailed plans cannot be taken to mean that this was a passing whim. It was the first stages of expansion which had to be planned in detail. Whether one looks at the Nogi–Hirohito line, or the young officers of the thirties or the more obvious Ito–Inoue–Yamagata line, Shōin must be seen as a central figure in the on-going imperial story.

Many post-war revisionist historians simply ignore such evidence of Japan's long-range imperialist plans. Others mention Shōin, then suggest he and his type were just lone voices crying in the wilderness. To counter this line of defence, let us again look at Saga, then quickly trace Shōin's Chōshū legacy, bearing in mind all the while that virtually every clan was split into conflicting factions, with their own vocal advocates, and that we are concentrating on Satchō, Tosa and Saga because they dominated Meiji Japan and because they have been the subject of more intense research.

As we have seen, Etō Shimpei, the dominant leader during the absence of the Iwakura Mission, was an early advocate of attacking Korea and Russia. The idea of making Peking the Japanese capital remained the essence of his foreign policy, but he later veered to the view that Japan should initially split China with Russia, then after ten years of developing the southern half she should turn on her erstwhile Russian allies and drive them from the north (Matano 1914: 288 *et seq.*). Herein we can see the seeds of later history. In 1871 Etō presented Iwakura with a 'Foreign Policy Plan' which argued that Britain would come under attack from Germany, Russia and America, and that she would be unable to hold her possessions. Thus he suggested that Japan should maintain outwardly friendly ties with Britain, while secretly cultivating close ties with these three powers; then her chance would come.

Perhaps Etō's closest disciple was Yamanaka Ichirō who studied under Etō as a youth and later stayed with him in Tokyo. In 1871 Yamanaka took a party of youths to study in France and Germany, where he himself remained to study government. On his return in 1873 he presented the government with a long paper on her relations with the West. Yamanaka stressed the importance of a twenty-five or fifty-year plan in preparation for the day when Asia and Europe would be linked by rail. In spelling out the 'Strike South' school of thought he drew particular attention to Australia and the South Islands. Whereas Japan had a population of forty million, Australia had only four, and while it was twenty days by ship to Victoria, northern Australia could be reached in ten. As Britain also possessed India and Canada, she would be unable to develop Australia properly. Therefore Japan should train 100,000 men and send them to settle in Australia just as colonists were being sent to

Hokkaidō. They should be paid a wage and forbidden either to return to Japan or to move on elsewhere. As Britain declined, the day would probably come when Russia could do as it pleased in Asia, so it was far better to reach agreement with her and to strike south. Thus, even in the case of Australia, the plan was not one for normal colonization or migration but for conquest, with early Japanese settlers playing a key role.

During the 1874 Saga uprising, Yamanaka was Etō's right-hand man and at the age of twenty-seven he was executed along with Etō (Matano 1914, Supplement: 47 *et seq.*). Neither this Yamanaka plan, nor Australia's own efforts to recruit Japanese labour in the 1870s came to anything largely because of Japan's own internal upheavals and because Japan's expansion was to be a step-by-step one via Korea and Taiwan. Yet Yamanaka cannot be dismissed as a 'lone voice'. Matano's outstanding biography of Etō came out in 1914 – only forty years after the execution of Etō and Yamanaka, twenty years after the China War, four years after the annexation of Korea, two years before the notorious Twenty-One Demands were presented to China, and in the middle of the series of secret treaties with Russia. Matano's work is excellent history, yet like those of the Black Dragon Society, the Jiyūtō and Tokutomi Ichiro it must be regarded as politically motivated. Thus it is of the highest significance that this outstanding history included the forty-six page Yamanaka report in its entirety (Matano 1914, Supplement: 54–100). Yamanaka's ideas and outlook must be viewed as the views and outlook of Etō, in 1873 effectively the leader of the Japanese government; and Matano's book as a whole makes it clear that those views were being endorsed in 1914 by Matano and the wide body of opinion he represented. The history of the intervening forty years would also strongly suggest that it was not a question of old ideas being suddenly revived in 1914; the story would surely indicate that those views never went out of fashion.

Thus Shōin and Chōshū thoughts were far from unique. However, the Chōshū Shōin line was of special significance as it leads us through Nogi to Hirohito, through Inoue to the great *zaibatsu*, through Yamagata to the army, and through Itō to the premiership. We left Inoue in early 1867 successfully selling to Tosa's Ryōma the idea of occupying Takeshima. In 1875 we were to see the extraordinary spectacle of Inoue's Osarisawa case being quickly disposed of so that he could go to Korea as Kuroda's deputy. This decision was partly due to Inoue's position as 'bagman' for the new

Meiji establishment but it must also be linked up with this picture of Inoue in 1867 and be seen as a recognition of his on-going role in pressing for a solution of 'the Korea problem'.

Let us take the Chōshū story a little further through the medium of Katsura Tarō – not to be confused with Kido, also earlier known as Katsura – who was to be Prime Minister during the Russian War. In 1874, a year after their traumatic struggle against 'foreign adventures', the reinstated Ōkubo–Iwakura government sent a military expedition against Taiwan. Both Japan and China claimed suzerainty over the Ryūkyūs, and when some Taiwanese massacred some Ryūkyūan sailors, Japan seized this opportunity to demonstrate that the Ryūkyūs came within her sphere of influence. She was able to punish 'the barbarians' and extract an indemnity from China. Kido, however, had opposed the expedition because it was completely inconsistent with their 1873 stance, because it over-stretched their finances and because it represented an expansion led by and benefiting Satsuma. Kido therefore resigned from the government and returned to Hagi.

Not long after Katsura's death in 1913 a committee was formed to compile an official biography, but later the task was handed over to pundit Tokutomi Iichirō whose 1131 pages of Katsura trivia was published in 1916. Among the rare enlightening flashes is the account of how Kido, on returning to Hagi, sent Katsura a telegram saying his mother was seriously ill. Fearing that he would be seen to be joining Kido's anti-war party, Katsura stayed on in Tokyo, and when he did return to Hagi his mother was already dead. Tokutomi points out that Katsura had faced the choice of family versus state at a time of great significance. 'It was important at this stage not to make a mistake in the State's long-range plans for the next hundred years' (Kōshaku Katsura Tarō Den: 338). In other words, Tokutomi was pointing out that the Taiwan expedition was not just a war involving a few 'barbarians', but was meant to launch a hundred years of imperialism.

In 1875, with Ōkubo now firmly in charge, the decision was made to open Korea by force. This decision was succinctly summed up by the official biography of Itō Hirobumi (1940, Vol. 2: 1). In February 1875 Foreign Minister Terashima sought to re-open negotiations with Korea. When his advances were rejected, it was decided to make a show of force 'under the name of carrying out maritime survey work'. It should be noted that the Itō biography was published in 1940, a bumper year for good, honest, uncluttered history writing.

When the 'surveying party' proceeded up the Han River towards Seoul, it was, of course, fired upon. The Korean defences were soon destroyed, but this Korean 'aggression' provided the pretext for the Kuroda–Inoue Mission which forced Korea to sign treaties 'opening' the country. The economic slaughter now began. It forms a stark contrast to the West's treatment of newly-opened Japan. There the rice trade was effectively under government control, foreigners were prohibited from acquiring mines, land or railways, and the nation controlled its own currency and banking. In all these matters, Japan's economic aggression in Korea was to be blatant and unrestricted. Inoue himself was to be the key figure in controlling the trade in Korean rice.

Partly because his reputation was so obnoxious, and partly because it suited his trading activities, Inoue went off to England where he remained in virtual exile (ibid., Vol 2: 3) until Ōkuba's assassination in 1878. Then he immediately contacted clansman Katsura, who had been studying in Germany and the two hurried back to Japan together.

Ōkubo, Saigō and Kido had now all departed the scene, and Satchō was being pressured on the one side by the Mitsubishi –Fukuzawa–Ōkuma forces, and on the other by the *minken* movement. In December 1878, largely as a response to this new, uncertain situation, the Sambo Hombu Kyoku (General Staff Bureau) was separated from the Army Ministry and made directly responsible to the Emperor. Previously, the chain of command had run from the Emperor through the Dajōkan (Council of State) to the War Ministry and then on down to the General Staff Bureau. This meant that the Dajōkan controlled both the civilian and military branches. Henceforth, with their iron grip on the armed forces, Satchō would always be in a position to act independently of the civilian government if ever civilian control slipped from their clutches.

In his unpublished 1960 Yale doctoral thesis, 'The Japanese Emperor: A Study in Constitutional and Political Change', W. M. Tsuneishi described the new chief of staff as 'being in charge of national defence and strategy'. Whilst this is not an inaccurate description, a more evocative picture is provided by Tokutomi (Katsura Den: 381–2) who described the new office as being entrusted with 'the hopes and plans of the military state'. This involved the drawing up of plans for both local defence and external conquest. Offices were set up in Kansai and Kanto. The latter was to control the Tokyo and Sendai *chintai*, and was responsible for information and planning for Hokkaidō, Karafuto, Manchuria, Kamchatka and Siberia. The Kansai office was to control the other four *chintai* and to make plans for China and Korea in readiness for the day of reckoning. Katsura was appointed as Kansai chief. Naturally, he took his allotted duties quite literally. Thus in 1879 he made a secret tour of North China, and on the basis of this tour he drew up detailed plans of attack. In 1916 Tokutomi (1916: 386) noted regretfully that he was unable to reveal these plans as they were still a military secret.

The 1880s saw the building of the Kure naval base and Ujina port in Hiroshima. Katsura's Kansai office also had the responsibility for obtaining information about the geography and military preparedness of countries west of China. It seems unclear how much was achieved further west but certainly the years 1879–94 saw the detailed, unremitting preparations for the China War. Intelligence was a major factor. *The Times* in London (25.9.94 8a) pointed out that Japan was a police state with an intensive network of spies both at home and abroad. 'Japan is, in short, one great intelligence department, and they are proving in an unexpected way that knowledge is power.' *The Times* also reproduced (3.9.94 4ab) the somewhat chilling words of the war declaration: 'We, the Emperor of the Empire of Great Japan, having ascended the throne by virtue of a lineal succession unbroke for ages eternal, fully assured of heavenly aid, do announce to all our brave and loyal subjects that we hereby declare war against China.' *The Times* went on to state that all foreign residents in Japan agreed it was a war of aggression for trumped-up reasons, 'The Chinese have all along been anxious to avoid hostilities.'

I hope to cover this ground in detail in a later volume. Yet even this brief account of the forty year period 1854–94 should establish the fact that we are not dealing with 'lone voices' and isolated, haphazard events, but with the relentless, almost inevitable development and implementation of deeply felt teachings and far-ranging plans. We are brought back to Beasley's claim that 'Japanese imperialism dates from the Sino-Japanese War of 1894–5. . . . There is no evidence that in declaring war on China in 1894 its government had any expectation of territorial gain.' It is not enough to describe these statements as superficial and mistaken. There is something quite shocking and deeply disturbing in the sight of a historian of Beasley's stature taking up a position so palpably false. It goes beyond matters of historiography and raises questions about the role of the historian and the relationship between academia and the government.

One cannot understand an historical event by freezing the camera at the point and pouring over the print from every possible angle. Stripping away the myths surrounding an historical event is rather like solving a murder. First, you visit the scene of the crime and try to assess what you see. Then you must go back and delve into the lives of all involved and find out what they had been up to before the crime. One must also investigate what happens after the crime, and take note of those who benefited. Thus armed, you go back once more to the day and place of the crime.

In like manner, let us now return to early 1867, noting along the way Conroy's deposition that Japan 'had no long-range plans for taking over Korea, and that in the period up to 1900 "economic" factors were negligible, insufficient, unimportant'. We left Inoue Kaoru initiating Tosa's Ryōma into the mysteries of Takeshima-*Ron* (see p.283). Ryōma, a Takechi disciple, was now working in closely with Gotō and his rival Tosa faction. In other words, both the main Tosa factions were in favour of 'opening' Korea. Yet far from abandoning *sakoku*, Korea had recently repulsed both the French and Americans, so any Japanese penetration had to be by stealth or force. In other words, both the Tosa factions and the Chōshū forces represented by Kido and Inoue, favoured *seikan*. But neither Gotō nor Ryōma, Kido nor Inoue, were bound to the extreme *kokugaku* teachings which sought to build up military might to make the Japanese Emperor the ruler of the world. They were already modern, pragmatic men primarily concerned with trade and economic imperialism. Ryōma, who had worked closely with Chōshū, was soon to be assassinated, and Tosa's economic arm came to be dominated by Iwasaki and his company, Mitsubishi. Iwasaki, a more abrasive, uncompromising character, was to replace Ryōma's spirit of co-operation with one of fierce competition.

The war between Mitsubishi and the Chōshū-aligned *zaibatsu* was to be a crucial factor in the Meiji story. In the 1873 *Seihen*, Inoue and Gotō were to be on opposite sides, but historians who seek an explanation in 'principles' are surely misreading the situation. In 1873, as in 1867, Inoue and Gotō were economic imperialists who were bent on opening Korea and China. But by 1873, Inoue had been driven out of the government, Yamagata was in disgrace, and the position of Chōshū as a whole endangered. Neither Inoue's Senshū-sha, Fujita-gumi or Mitsui Bussan had yet been set up. Tosa, however, was riding high: the caretaker government revolved around the Etō–Gotō alliance. Whereas Saigō and the caretaker government had a marked antipathy to Mitsui, Gotō and the Tōyō–Gotō faction were closely involved with Mitsubishi. Thanks to the legacy of Ryōma and the reorganization of Iwasaki, Tosa's economic arm was well prepared to embark on the economic penetration of Korea. Little wonder that Gotō and Itagaki staked their future on attacking Korea while Inoue, Yamagata, etc. were equally determined to prevent Tosa and Saga from leading the charge into the mainland.

It should also be noted that Ryōma's letter of 6 march 1867 went on to discuss Ezochi and his long-held ambitions to create a new country there – a further proof of Tosa's pre-Ishin interest in Ezochi and multi-directional commercial expansion.

Space prevents a chronicling of the Mitsubishi story. Let us merely note the close early ties with Gotō. The story goes that Iwasaki was banished from his village after a fight and went to live in a village near Tōyō's *juku*. He got to know Gotō, and when Gotō was given an essay to write on foreign trade, he had Yatarō write it for him. Tōyō was much impressed by the essay, but at once concluded that it had not been written by Gotō. When Gotō confessed, Yatarō was admitted to the school despite his lowly status (*Iwasaki Yatarō Den* 1967: 196ff.). Tōyō promoted Yatarō's career, but with his assassination, he returned home and farmed for four years. In 1867 he was appointed to the Nagasaki *kaiseikan*, and within a year became its head due to his business ability and connections with Gotō.

In April 1867, not long after he arrived in Nagasaki, Yatarō led a party to explore Utsuryō-tō (ibid.: 430ff.). In later years, Gotō's widow claimed that he had ordered the sending of the party; the plan, of course, goes back to Ryōma, but the interest of Gotō and Iwasaki confirms the belief that it was a question of considerable importance. Sasaki Takayuki was now clan representative in Nagasaki, part of his task being to restrain Gotō's spending. Later in 1867, Yatarō conspired with a Korean merchant, and obtained Sasaki's permission to send a trading ship. The ship, however, sank in a storm. Many details of this story are obscure (ibid.: 434–5), but in this display of enterprise and disregard of legal niceties, Yatarō was surely acting as a representative of Gotō and the *kaiseikan* and was carrying out clan policy. Shortly after Yatarō's transfer to Ōsaka, another vain attempt was made to open up Korea (ibid.: 594–5).

Yatarō also tried to develop the North Sea trade (ibid.: 215ff.). In 1868 a ship was put to sea in the name of the Walsh brothers, American traders well known in Nagasaki. It flew the American flag and had two American officers. It carried its cargo of rice, axes, coal, etc. to Hakodate, then proceeded to Kamchatka. A second voyage was made in September. This time the expedition carried a letter from Nagasaki Governor Sawa to Hakodate Governor Shimizutani. But by this time Shimizutani had already fled and Hakodate was occupied by Enomoto. The ship was detained and was able to escape only with the co-operation of the British. This despatch of ships even before the northern war was finished shows that Tosa was acting resolutely as a trading and maritime power.

Nor should we overlook Tosa's interest in the South Seas – an interest trumpeted by Tōyō. In 1863 Takeuchi and Iwamura met Gotō who spoke grandiosely of colonizing Borneo, Sumatra and the Celebes (Hattori 1949: 153). His listeners were soon caught up in his enthusiasm. The scheme was not forgotten and in the mid-seventies Gotō and Takeuchi were to negotiate with Jardine-Matheson to buy land in Borneo. When negotiations broke down, Gotō bought Takashima coal mine instead.

We may safely conclude that Tosa, a traditional maritime state, wanted to embark on a policy of economic imperialism, occupying islands in the South Seas to feed tropical goods into a trading system extending up to Ezochi and on to Russian Asia. Likewise there can be no doubt that the line represented by Tōyō, Gotō, Itagaki, Ryōma and Iwasaki was trying to penetrate Korea in the Bakumatsu period, and that with the *ishin* it would play a leading role in forcing open Korea and introducing modern Japanese commercial capitalism. Pre-war biographers were wont to claim for their man the honour of having started the *seikan* agitation. For example, Kawada's 1939 biography of Kataoka insists that in 1870 Kataoka and Hayashi were already urging war against Korea and that this cry was later taken up by Gotō and Itagaki. (Kataoka was also of *umamawari* class, and though he made common cause with Tani on the issue of fiscal responsibility, he later aligned himself with Itagaki and Gotō – perhaps another case of class solidarity.) Sasaki, however, recorded that by mid-1870 Itagaki was already a fervent advocate of *seikan* (*Sasaki Takayuki Nikki* 1970, Vol. 4: 365–6).

Trying to pin-point who took the lead in advocating *seikan* is a somewhat sterile exercise. The idea of attacking Korea had long been commonplace, and, with the *ishin*, there was a great groundswell of opinion. The Ryōma–Gotō–Itagaki–Iwasaki line had long been pro-*seikan*, and even before the Restoration Tosa's commercial arm had made repeated attempts to penetrate Korea. What was to happen in Korea was what was meant to happen. When Korea was annexed, an Iwasaki son-in-law became its first Minister of Agriculture and Commerce, and Mitsubishi quickly became not only a dominating trader but also a great landowner. A major reason for the Satchō opposition to Saigō's 1873 mission was the fact that Chōshū leaders were in disgrace, the clan had little voice in the government, and its commercial arm was also in confusion. Other clans, but most notably Tosa, would have been in the best position to take over the all-important mainland trade. The 1881 *Seihen* was to revolve around a stop-Mitsubishi campaign, and a similar element was also present in 1873. For Sasaki, Hijikata, Kōno and Tani the triumph of the Tosa commercial arm would have brought no joy. They would have had no place to stand in either the Meiji or Tosa governments. Their support of Sanjō, Chōshū and Ōkubo was clearly based not on principle but on self-interest.

## GODAI

That economic motives were of fundamental importance in the opening of Korea and in the 1873 *Seihen* is also graphically illustrated by the career of Satsuma's Godai Tomoatsu.

Writing on Japanese history perhaps reaches an all-time low when dealing with Godai. Iwata's 1964 biography of Ōkubo fails even to mention Godai, while Hoover's 1973 study of Godai reached the bizarre conclusion that Godai was a self-sacrificing idealist. Japanese analyses are little better. The glossy, encyclopaedic, but inaccurate *Zaikai Jimbutsu Retsu Den* (*Biographies of the Leading Personages of the Business World*) (pp. 87–98) likewise writes of Godai the idealist who was opposed by unenlightened militarists and by jealous people back in Satsuma who had been 'left behind'.

A somewhat more balanced picture is provided by the 1933 biography by Godai's heir, Godai Ryūsaku. Naturally, it is not impartial, but it contains revealing snatches of correspondence, and makes manifest the all-important fact that Ōkubo was Godai's main friend and ally, while Godai was Ōkubo's 'brain' (Godai 1933: 400). As has been noted, Japanese historians tend to observe strict divisions into political, diplomatic and economic history. The story only emerges when we jettison such divisions and regard Godai and

Ōkubo as a combination. It is likewise impossible to separate their public and private lives.

Ryūsaku, however, makes little attempt to illuminate the network of contacts so essential to our understanding of what Godai was up to. For example, the first reference to Moriyama Shigeru is for 1877, when Godai and Moriyama jointly entertained a certain traveller (ibid.: 394). Then we pass over to Godai's death (ibid.: 549). Those who watched at his bedside were, 'of course, first of all his wife Toyoko, his relative Moriyama Shigeru and his wife Masako . . .'; other regular visitors included Kuroda, Saigō and Matsukata. It was Moriyama who attended to the funeral arrangements and public announcements (ibid.: 553).

Neither this biography nor, it would seem, any serious Japanese history, has taken up the question of Godai's relationship with Moriyama. Godai married his sister at the start of the Meiji period, but it would seem he got to know the sister through Moriyama, and not vice versa. The 'documents' and biographies maintain a discreet silence, but it is evident that Godai and Moriyama were the closest of friends from the Bakumatsu period, and remained so till Godai's death. This is, of course, the same Moriyama who went to Korea as Sada's deputy, later brought back the 'monkey' poster which precipitated the 1873 *Seihen* crisis, and in 1875 was deeply involved in the strategy which brought about the opening of Korea. Despite the lack of documentary proof, one must suspect that Godai was generally involved in Moriyama's Korean activities, and, at least in 1875, Godai, Moriyama and Ōkubo acted together to bring about the opening of Korea.

There are two other biographies of Godai, but neither help to link Godai to the opening of Korea. The first, by a Satsuma Shimazu, is a glossy, privately produced volume which is not for sale. Though lurid and grossly inaccurate, it cannot be ignored, as Reischauer personally presented a copy to Yenching Library – perhaps just a nice little illustration of how difficult it is to be both historian and diplomat.

The standard biography is that by noted Osaka historian Miyamoto Mataji. A first reading of this work suggests it to be a masterly biography. But if re-read after one has become familiar with the period, it stands revealed as a highly nationalistic work of considerable dishonesty. In an earlier work, Miyamoto (1960: 122) wrote that Matsukata always spoke contemptuously of Godai, referring to him as *kozō* (urchin). Yet now (Miyamoto 1981: 506) he claimed that after Ōkubo's death Matsukata became Godai's closest friend. One can accept that in Godai's last years, Matsukata showed considerable concern for his health and arranged for a top army doctor to treat him; he was also among those who watched at his death-bed and helped wind-up his affairs. But Satsuma had a considerable investment in Godai, just as Chōshū did in Fujita and Tosa in Mitsubishi. Yet he died owing a million *yen* and left no permanent *zaibatsu*. No wonder Matsukata was concerned! One must question whether Miyamoto was not trying to clean up Godai's image.

Miyamoto's treatment – or non-treatment – of the Godai–Moriyama connection must likewise be regarded as strange in a historian so familiar with the intricacies of the period. On page 187 he mentions that in the New Year of 1870 Godai married the younger sister of his good friend, Moriyama Shigeru. Then Moriyama is not mentioned again till page 503, where Miyamoto quotes Ryūsaku's description given above. As Miyamoto has referred to Godai's pre-*ishin* attempts to trade with Korea, it is difficult to see how he could fail to grasp the significance of the close Godai–Moriyama connection in the story of Japan's opening of Korea. The answer, however, becomes patently clear when one digests the book as a whole. For example, Miyamoto manages to discuss the Osarisawa mine without even mentioning Inoue, merely giving a thumb-sketch of Inoue's cover man, Okada Heizō (ibid.: 190). His account of the Ono collapse, and the subsequent Furukawa acquisition, is in a similar vein. This alerts us not only to the fact that his accounts of how Godai acquired his mining empire are liable to be of little value but also to the broader truth that this is a biased piece of *goyō* scholarship calculated to endear both Godai and Miyamoto to the Kansai business world.

We have discussed at some length the problem with Japanese sources. There is an urgent need for a large body of historians to produce countless biographies so that we can accurately piece together what was really happening. That Korea in 1875–6 was forced open by Japanese commercial imperialists might almost be described as a self-evident truth. Yet Japanese myth-making proceeds apace, with no attempt, for example, to link Godai to the opening of Korea. All we have in the way of biographies are his son-in-law's *Life*, Shimazu's lurid account, Miyamoto's *goyō* scholarship and Hoover's hagiography. Yet even from these the story may be deduced.

Godai's early career was characterized by cloak and dagger activities which seldom found their way into 'documents', for much of Godai's correspondence, like that of his contemporaries, ended with the injunction, 'without fail burn this letter' (see Godai 1933: 228, 327). However, two letters survive from early 1867, and they make it quite clear that Godai, like Ryōma and Iwasaki, was engaged in covert operations to open trade with Korea. A letter dated 3 January 1867 from Nagasaki to Katsura Hisatake stated that he was being urged to return to Kagoshima, but that he was resisting this pressure because he was busy arranging trade with Korea (ibid.: 92–3). He also mentioned that there were problems back home, but declared that it would be difficult to put them in a letter, so he would tell him about them when he got back. 'Difficult' probably means 'dangerous', and we may perhaps deduce that Godai was not acting on behalf of the clan, but trying to penetrate Korea for his own profit.

Another letter, dated 21 January 1867 and addressed to Katsura Uemon, again referred to trade with Korea (ibid.: 98). He had discussed it with Arikawa Yakurō, who was reacting very positively, but Godai now felt that if this type of trade were conducted privately it would be unlikely to continue over a long period, no matter who undertook it. For the sake of the nation, he wanted someone to undertake this task and to consider seriously the pluses and minuses.

Despite these pious protestations the simple fact would seem to be that Godai, like Ryōma, first tried to get into Korea as a private trader, and that only when he reluctantly concluded that it would be impossible for a private operation to continue for any length of time did he then talk of 'the good of the nation' and, by inference, of getting the government to open Korea. Godai also entered the Foreign Office, and was a Foreign Office official when the Sada–Moriyama Mission was sent. It would seem that he had found the man he was looking for to open Korea in his good friend Moriyama Shigeru (1842–1913), a Yamato *shishi* who seems not to have attracted a biographer despite the importance of his role in opening Korea.

Let us look a little more closely at Godai's career. He was the second son of a noted Confucian scholar with *samurai* status. The elder brother also became a scholar. Both were conservative and opposed the opening of Japan (ibid.: 12–13). Godai apologists dismiss Godai's Satsuma critics as jealous and behind-the-times, but it should be noted that his own family shared in the disgust he inspired. As a youth he had his own close gang of friends who grew up in the same neighbourhood, Shirogatani. These included Kuroda, who was five years younger and had an *aniki* relationship with Godai. The 'documents' do not flesh out this relationship, but as Godai was already a wealthy man when Kuroda launched his career one may speculate that it was promoted by Godai. Other members of Godai's childhood gang were Yoshida Sadanori and Orita Heinai, the two *Kaitakushi* officials who were to put in for the Hokkaidō *haraisage* in 1881. Miyamoto gives the impression that it was merely fortuitous that Godai formed his Kansai company about this time (Miyamoto 1981: 221–2); but bearing in mind Satsuma's extreme clannishness, and the sharpness of its internal divisions, one must surely dismiss such suggestions of 'chance' and picture Godai as the leader of a childhood gang which survived into adult life and became a major factor in both Hokkaidō and Korea.

Godai was first sent to Nagasaki in 1857. There he was to become acquainted with such future notables as Gotō, Iwasaki, Ryōma, Ōkuma and Mutsu. There are many gaps in the story, but if one considers the size and special nature of Nagasaki, one must conclude that like any group of 'foreigners' in a distant colony, the *shishi* from various clans who stayed to become old Nagasaki hands all got to know each other quite well. Thus, though not documented, it seems inevitable that Godai and Hirotsu were already close acquaintances.

Godai's career is remarkable for its consistency. In 1862 he bought a steamship for his clan in Shanghai (ibid.: 32; Godai 1933: 44–5). It was widely believed that Godai schemed with Glover to keep a large slice of the commission.

It was Glover who helped get a party of fourteen students to England in 1865 (Miyamoto 1981: 40ff.). They included Mori Arinori, Samejima and Tōgō. All had to be smuggled out of Japan using false names. The whole mission was sponsored by Britain to develop commercial and political ties with Satsuma, so while the students were housed in private homes and got on with their studies, Godai toured around looking at industries.

Early in July a certain Shirakawa Kenjirō came to England with a Belgian noble, Comte des Cantons de Montblanc, whom he introduced to Godai. After meeting an early Bakufu mission, Montblanc had come to Japan in 1863 or 1864, and lived briefly in Yokohama and Edo. He became acquainted with a young man named Saitō Kenjirō who lived in Kumagai and took him back to Paris where he became something of a fixture at parties. Montblanc often used the Japanese version of his name, Shirayama, so Saitō changed his name to Shirakawa (White River).

Having tried unsuccessfully to extract commercial concessions from the Bakufu representatives, Montblanc crossed to London to meet Godai. He took Godai and other officials on a tour of the Continent, and on 28 August 1865 they signed a contract to form a joint trading company. This was amended in December, but both versions made Montblanc and France Satsuma's main trading partners responsible for the trade in goods from all over Japan. Their joint company was also to be responsible for developing Satsuma mines and the Okinawa trade. As Godai and his party had been smuggled out of Japan by the British and brought to Europe to develop Satsuma–British commercial ties, and as the Satsuma students were staying in British homes and being trained in British institutions, the contract to give a virtual monopoly to Britain's main rival must be seen as a most unscrupulous double-cross which would no doubt have brought great personal profit to Godai. Yet Hoover (1973: 110) comments fatuously that 'Godai and other Satsuma officials failed to recognize the intricacies of European foreign relations.' Even the young students understood, and were deeply embarrassed by, those negotiations and several wrote home urging that the contracts should not be ratified. Mori Arinori seems to have been particularly scathing in his attacks on Godai. Terashima, who was dealing with the Foreign Office, likewise seems to have been most unimpressed by Godai's activities, and once Godai left the government, he was never close to either Terashima or Mori Arinori (Miyamoto 1981: 64).

Eventually, the Montblanc contract was repudiated. Despite Miyamoto's protestations to the contrary, it does seem that Montblanc was something of a confidence man who never had at his disposal the sort of funds required for his grandiose schemes. Meanwhile, Godai had become disenchanted with Shirakawa, whom he now found to have 'dubious characteristics' (*Satsuma Kaigun-shi* quoted in Miyamoto 1981: 52). Hence he stopped using him as an interpreter, and, on returning to Japan, he wrote to Machida Hisanari in London on 6 May 1866 warning him to be careful in his dealings with interpreter Shirakawa. Probably Shirakawa's crime was to repeat, or threaten to repeat, Godai's underhand dealings. For Godai, Montblanc now represented a problem. He was

297

appointed as adviser to the Satsuma party at the Paris Exhibition
(Miyamoto 1981: 62–3), and one may surmise that Shirakawa
was also involved. Despite the collapse of the trading contract,
Montblanc and Shirakawa stubbornly returned to Japan. They
travelled back with Iwashita, who had been in charge of the
Satsuma Paris Exhibition display. Godai went to Shanghai to meet
them (Godai 1933: 98). In October we find them all in Nagasaki.
Godai had met Kido at Baseki the previous October to urge that
Chōshū join their company. Kido was enthusiastic, but Chōshū was
in no position to join such a venture (*Sasaki Takayuki Nikki* 1970,
Vol. 2: 519ff.). Now Montblanc was introduced to Tosa people, for
at this time Godai was negotiating with Kii over the *Iroka*. Sasaki
recorded calling on Iwashita on 1 October 1867 only to find him out;
but there he met 'a certain Shirakawa' (no first name given) who was
just back from France. They and some friends went off to a restaurant
and talked till the small hours of the morning (ibid.). On the third,
Shirakawa *nanibō* took them to meet Montblanc. A certain Satsuma
man named Asakura acted as interpreter. On the sixth, Shirakawa
and a Frenchman called, but on the seventh Asakura Seigo – he has
now learnt his full name – told them that Shirakawa had suddenly
left the previous night for Kagoshima. Sasaki noted that he found
this most suspicious, but more meetings with Montblanc and three
other Frenchmen followed over the next few days.

It seems clear that Montblanc had become an embarrassment to
Godai. However, he was found work with the French legation, and in
the early days of Meiji he was able to assist with incidents involving
foreigners, thus helping to save Godai's face (Miyamoto 1981: 63ff.).
Eventually he returned to France. Shirakawa disappeared from the
story, and from Japanese history books. Sasaki claimed in his notes
for the end of 1867 that later in the year, Shirakawa, now using
the name Saitō Kenjirō, had been assassinated in Satsuma, and
added that many suspected him of having been a Bakufu spy (*Sasaki
Takayuki Nikki* 1970, Vol. 2: 645–6).

The Shirakawa story is worth relating, not as a titillating digres-
sion, but to emphasize two points: first that we are dealing in
cloak and dagger matters, and second that there are great gaps
in our knowledge. Many of these same individuals, such as Godai,
were to enter the Foreign Office. Many are to be regarded –
though in varying degrees – as adventurers tied to no law. Not
surprisingly, their early negotiations with Korea took on much the
same characteristics.

What really happened to Shirakawa? Sasaki referred vaguely to a report of his assassination in the Yomiuri Shimbun, but as they would be referring to reports of what happened in faraway Kagoshima, it would not have proven too much. One can merely speculate. That Shirakawa was a Bakufu spy seems most unlikely. His background is never mentioned, which would surely mean he was not of *samurai* origin. The linking of their names – Shirakawa and Shirayama – and the way in which Montblanc took him to Europe and paraded him at parties would surely suggest that their relationship was personal. Godai's early warnings against Shirakawa would rather suggest some form of threats or blackmail. As interpreter, Shirakawa would have been privy to most of Godai's shady plans and dealings and in a position to exert pressure once things turned sour. Bearing in mind that relations with Satsuma had in effect broken down, and that he and Montblanc had only recently arrived in Nagasaki and were holding daily meetings with a variety of people, that he should suddenly leave for Kagoshima was most suspicious, especially as Sasaki was to meet the Frenchman again on succeeding days. The logical deduction is that Shirakawa was either assassinated or abducted that night. We are not looking at normal diplomatic or commercial negotiations, but at a group of ruthless adventurers operating at a time of civil upheaval. This description must likewise cover their operations to force open Korea. The reality of the situation has simply been buried by Japanese 'diplomatic' histories.

The 1869 Sada–Moriyama Mission originally intended to take along a business man, but it was eventually decided to take along a Foreign Office official, Saitō Sakae, who had business experience and had served in Nagasaki (Sada 1903: 39). We are told nothing else about this Saitō, and he simply fades from the picture. Despite the importance of his role, we learn nothing of his commercial recommendations or of his subsequent career. There is a distinct possibility that this Saitō Sakae was Saitō Kenjirō. Perhaps for safety's sake he fled from Nagasaki and joined up again with Montblanc in Tokyo. As he spoke French, and as Montblanc was assisting the Meiji government in its dealings with foreigners, it should not have been too difficult to get him into the Foreign Office, and as Korea's dealings with Westerners had largely been with French priests, a French-speaking member offered definite advantages. Changing the name as one rose in the world was a general practice, so Kenjirō could easily have become Sakae. It is most peculiar that this Saitō disappears so quickly, but this disappearance becomes understandable if it were Kenjirō, for his presence would completely expose the dubious nature of this mission. The reported assassination could have taken place a couple of years later.

If all this seems too fanciful let us recall the manner in which the fourth member, Hirotsu, was added to the party. Sada merely described him as a Nagasaki doctor, deliberately obscuring the fact that he was his own cousin and a member of a distinguished Kurume family, and that he was a Kurume *kikiyaku* still on the clan payroll and obliged to report back to that clan. Whoever he was, Saitō Sakae would seem to have had an interesting history, and even if he were simply a Foreign Office official appointed because of his official or business experience in Nagasaki, he must surely have been well known to Godai and probably was involved in some of his operations, even his early attempts to penetrate Korea.

In the years 1868–75, Japanese negotiations with Korea were essentially handled by five men: Moriyama, Sada, Saitō, Hirotsu and Ueno Kagenori. Sada and Saitō soon dropped out of the picture. Ueno Kagenori was another Godai protégé. He had gone to Nagasaki in 1856 to study Dutch, and had later switched to English. In his garrulous old age, Masuda recalled how when he went to Europe with his father on the Ikeda Mission, they met up in Shanghai with young Ueno who had stowed away to Shanghai early in 1862 hoping to go on to Europe, but had become stranded there (Nagai 1939: 41). They rejected his pleas to be taken on to Europe, but helped him get back to Nagasaki. There Godai took him under his wing, providing him with clothes and money and arranging a clan pardon. For two years (1865–7) he was then stationed in Ōshima as interpreter for the English engineer, Waters, who was setting up sugar factories using machinery Godai had bought in Europe (Miyamoto 1981: 159–61). One may reasonably assume that Godai was behind this appointment. With the *ishin*, he was attached to the Yokohama *Saibansho*. When Godai and Terashima, through Glover, bought the machinery of the Hong Kong mint, Ueno was sent to collect it. Later he became a central figure in the Korean negotiations. His debt to, and ties with, Godai no doubt remained intact, and as Godai was Ōkubo's 'brain' (and pocket), one must picture Ueno reporting back not only to the Foreign Office but also to Godai.

Thus the Sada–Moriyama Mission may be viewed as having had two components representing respectively the military and the economic imperialists. Sada and Sawa were extreme members of the Emperor Party as exemplified by Maki. They wanted to take Korea as a first step in 'restoring' Japan's position in the world. Moriyama had also been a *shishi*, but he had been a member of Katsu's Hyogo naval academy, and no doubt Matano (1914: 155ff.) was correct in describing him as being a realist, in the Ryōma tradition, mostly interested in trade; by 1869 he was very close to Godai who was living with his sister in Osaka. Hirotsu had close ties with extremists and army men, but he seems to have been a modern, pragmatic man. It was Godai who promoted the Kansai career of Hirotsu's son, Ryūrō (whose reminiscences are given in *Sennin no Omokage* 1961: 327ff.), and even back in 1869 Hirotsu was probably a commercial rather than a military imperialist.

Sada was to meet Itagaki again on 18 February 1899 at a meeting of a history society (Sada 1903: 51–2). They had a long discussion about the authenticity of certain unspecified 'Korean documents', with Sada insisting that they had been fabricated by Japanese officials. Itagaki stubbornly argued that they were authentic, for Soejima had vigorously pressed his case on the basis of the documents in question. As Itagaki and Soejima both resigned straight after the *seikan* debate, there can be little doubt that the document Sada referred to as fake was the infamous monkey poster. Hirotsu was in Pusan at the time when Moriyama left to take the poster back to Tokyo, where he gave it to Ueno to argue before the government. So the three people involved were Godai's close associates who had been pressing since 1869 for an attack on Korea. There is no reliable witness to vouch for its authenticity, and it came at just the right time, May 1873, to stir the government into action before the Iwakura Mission returned.

Korean historians, of course, regard the poster as completely ludicrous. The officials for whom it was intended were in close daily contact and, being aware of Japanese ambitions and frustrations, they had studiously kept them at arms' length. It beggars belief that they would suddenly provide those officials with such a perfect pretext to act. Though it is extremely unlikely that documentary proof will ever be uncovered, the poster story is so manifestly absurd that Sada's testimony must be regarded as fairly convincing proof that it was a scheme hatched by Godai's three associates. Bearing in mind that Hirotsu was a writer, and that three generations of his family were noted writers of fiction, one must nominate Hirotsu as the most likely author of

301

this little bit of fiction known to every Japanese high-school student.

One must also speculate that Godai was involved in the scheme. This may seem to be contradicted by the fact that Ōkubo, Godai's political *alter ego*, led the opposition to Saigō's mission. However, Godai's group had no reason to predict that Saigō himself would insist on going to Korea. What they had in mind was probably something along the lines of the 1875 mission led by Godai's *chikuba no tomo* Kuroda. Indeed, it is logical to speculate further that Saigō insisted on going personally partly because he was determined to forestall a Kuroda–Inoue style mission. It should also be noted that Mōri has effectively demonstrated that when he returned to Japan, Ōkubo was not particularly concerned with the *seikan* question. According to Kido's diary (Mōri 1978: 128), the day before the Iwakura Mission left Tokyo, a meeting at Iwakura's attended by Sanjō, Saigō and the Sangi, spent an hour discussing the order in which steps should be taken against Korea. The issue was brought to the fore because in May five American ships had been fired on at Kōka-tō and had been forced to withdraw. It would seem that there was general agreement that the groundwork should be laid for future positive action against Korea, but that no major initiative was to be taken till the Mission returned. Thus before long Saigō sent his spies to Korea and Manchuria, and Soejima went to China to sound it out about Korea.

It was a very dejected Ōkubo who returned to Japan in 1873. In the United States they had been led to believe, partly by Mori Arinori, that if they had the right letters of accreditation, they could renegotiate the treaties on the spot. Thus Ōkubo and Itō had hurried back to Japan. But Soejima was very critical, and what they received, after the stay of fifty days, was little more than a face-saver for Ōkubo (ibid.: 172ff.). They were given limited powers to negotiate with certain specified countries, but no power to sign treaties. Their Grand Tour continued, but they came back like tourists with tales to tell but no one to tell them to. On 15 June 1873, just after his return, Godai wrote Ōkubo a letter beginning 'this time you have returned suffering a great defeat' (ibid.: 154). He also sent him 4,000 *yen*. We have here a clear picture not only of Ōkubo's dejection but also of his financial ties with Godai.

Two months later, on 15 August 1873, just before he left for Kansai, Ōkubo wrote to Murata and Ōyama in Paris, describing himself as just filling in time till Iwakura returned: 'in truth I am in a situation about which nothing can be done . . . I have been caught in the coils of the spider [Etō] and there is nothing to be done'. He saw no reason for optimism, but had no time to elaborate, so referred them to the newspapers for details. Mōri points out that the editorial note to *Ōkubo Toshimichi Bunsho*, Vol. 4, states that this mainly refers to Saigō's impending trip to Korea, but Mōri searched through collected newspapers for the first seven months of the year and found only one reference to *seikan*. On the other hand, the newspapers went into great detail about the Inoue case and also agricultural uprisings against conscription. Hence it is fairly clear that Ōkubo's head was filled with thoughts of the Justice Ministry, of 'the spider' Etō, and of Inoue who had let the Satchō side down so badly. Mōri reaches the logical conclusion that until mid-August Ōkubo was not anti-*seikan* and did not regard the question as being of central importance (ibid.: 156ff.). So till August 16 when Ōkubo left for Kansai, he expressed no opposition to Saigō's trip and probably felt none. When and why did he change?

Mōri attributes the change mostly to Itō and Kido and pictures Ōkubo being gradually dragged into their plans to oust Etō. As he did not want to clash with Shimazu (whose role in the 1873 *Seihen*, though fascinating and controversial, is only marginally relevant to the main story), and as he was not anti-*seikan*, Ōkubo resisted the attempts by Itō and Kido to push him back onto centre stage. His central problem, Mōri reasoned (ibid.: 166), was whether, in his anxiety to get at Etō, he should go as far as becoming involved against Saigō and his Korean mission.

A major strength of Mōri's analysis is his honesty. Though he credits Itō and Chōshū with pushing Ōkubo into an anti-*seikan* stand, he admits that he has no source to back this claim. Though his closely reasoned argument certainly accords with 'the logic of the situation', it should also be noted that Ōkubo apparently changed his stance after going to Kansai and staying with Godai. Like Mōri, we must point out that there is no documentary evidence, but we would suggest that though Godai was involved in the original poster scheme, he and Ōkubo had gradually to face up to the fact that, knowingly or not, Saigō had trumped the poster plot. With Chōshū in disarray, and Saga and Tosa dominating the government, a Saigō mission would have been disastrous for the Godai–Ōkubo–Chōshū political and commercial ambitions. Thus they slowly came round to the view that, for them, a Saigō mission had to be stopped at all costs.

Mōri also significantly advanced the analysis of the 1873 *Seihen* by highlighting the Chōshū grab for spoils – an advance received somewhat sourly in many quarters (ibid.: 185).

He quotes Kido's diaries to show that as soon as Kido returned on 23 July, he held a series of meetings with other Chōshū leaders. It would seem that Kido's main concern was the Kyoto case, for Makimura was his *funkei no tomo*. Kido had secured for him the Kyoto appointment, and he had reciprocated by acquiring for Kido a Kyoto mansion and a slush fund from Mitsui. Makimura now visited him on 20 and 24 August.

In August, Kido also went three times to the Foreign Office to see Ueno, the official who had proposed sending troops. On the twenty-first, four days after the decision to send Saigō, he called on him but did not directly express his opposition. However, he did so when he met Sanjō two weeks later, and he followed up this visit with an opinion paper. When this brought no response, he handed in his resignation, but Sanjō persuaded him to stay on till Iwakura's return on 13 September. His resignation would seem to be the result of a feeling of isolation and impotence rather than of the Korean question as such. On the fifteenth he again wrote to Itō saying he was not trusted by either Iwakura or the caretaker government, and he for his part trusted neither, so he wished to resign (ibid.: 193ff.). It was still the Makimura case which rankled most, and on the twentieth he again wrote to Itō expressing his fury at the rough way in which authority had been used: 'not even under the Bakufu did you have officials of high rank being treated thus'.

Kido's diary tells us little about the split of 14–17 October. The first two days' entries simply referred to his guests, while that for the seventeenth mentioned Makimura but neither Saigō nor Korea. On the twentieth, two days after Sanjō's stroke, he sent the Dajōkan a long paper on the Makimura case; and on the twenty-fifth, the day after Etō, Itagaki, etc. resigned, Iwakura ordered the Justice Ministry to free Makimura – an act which prompted mass resignations. In Mōri's words, 'The Rule of Law had been trampled underfoot . . . Kido and Itō had defeated the Justice Ministry and also the Law' (ibid.: 201).

Inoue likewise lost no time in capitalizing on the Satchō victory. Itō had taken over as Construction Minister, a position which carried

considerable patronage. Thus when Etō had taken over the Sa-in on
4 August 1871 he had wanted Gotō to relinquish the Construction
Ministry to become its President (Matano 1914: 625ff.), but it was
only with the greatest difficulty that he persuaded Gotō to forego this
patronage. Now it was back in Chōshū hands. Inoue wrote to Itō on
1 November 1873; he began by declaring that recent events were 'the
cause for congratulations for the sake of the country' (Mōri 1978:
201–2). This fortunate outcome was due to Itō's persuading Iwakura
and to Sanjō's illness. Although it was still early days, he would like
humbly to request that the Minister of Construction remove the taxes
on various mines (the names have been blotted out). He also referred
to the Asuka mine which till now had been worked by 'small people'.
They had not been able to work it efficiently, but, as it was a mine
of great potential, he suggested that the Construction Ministry take
it over then later pass it on to his company. He also mentioned a
further mine (its name has also been obliterated) which he wanted
Itō to *haraisage* to his company.

Here Mōri has surely come to a vital aspect of the *seihen*. The
situation he has revealed is one where the various interpretations
come together: bitter personal rivalries, a fierce power struggle, the
successful attempt to topple the Rule of Law, and the subsequent
grab for riches. The bitter struggle was not about constitutional
niceties *per se*; the Satchō *batsu* once more placed itself above the
law and proceeded with its lawless money grabbing.

Unfortunately, at this point we must part company with Mōri. He
does not develop the above theme, but, desiring perhaps to remain
in the historical mainstream, he goes on to concentrate on 'Saigō's
heart' and to provide the national *taigi meibun*. So let us restate the
situation in words no Establishment Japanese historian would use:
it was a classic example of a newly emerging Third World country
where a corrupt, oppressive military government trampled the law
underfoot, and seized the wealth of the land for itself and its friends.
Goyō historians still portray people like Inoue and Godai as being
motivated by 'the good of the country', but it was not in the national
interest to turn the conquered clans into Satchō colonies. Nor was it
a question of men with capital and expertise moving in to develop
backward regions. Inoue had no mining experience or expertise,
and his only wealth was what he had appropriated as spoils of war
or had misappropriated in gross abuse of his official position. The
government was later to hire foreign experts and to lend them to
help develop the expropriated mines. The services of these foreign

experts, and government assistance in the form of tax concessions, bank loans, etc., could just as easily have been provided to the original owners and managers who had the experience which Inoue and others lacked. It was colonial despoliation and exploitation of an extreme form.

Mōri's otherwise excellent study loses much of its potential impact because he largely exonerates Satsuma and depicts Ōkubo as some kind of puppet. Satsuma, however, must be regarded as a full partner with Chōshū in the colonial exploitation of much of Japan. Let us return for a moment to Godai.

As early as 1868, voices were raised against Godai back in Satsuma because of his lavish lifestyle which was out of all proportion to his salary and status. The popular rumours eventually forced the government to act, and on 15 May 1869 he was removed from the accounts department and sent to Yokohama (Godai 1933: 222ff.). Ōkuma led a movement to have him retained, but two months later he resigned. Ōkubo accepted his resignation on the day on which it was received and gave him an official farewell present of 750 *yen*, though he had been an official for just thirty-one months. He obtained his first mine, a Yamato-kuni copper mine, in May 1870 (ibid.: 269). Other mines soon followed, usually in someone else's name. He had drawn close to the Ono-kumi and persuaded them to back his mining expansion (Miyamoto 1981: 294–5). This backing enabled him to set up in Kansai his mining organization, Kōseikan, which began operations on 1 January 1873, and immediately sent people out to examine mines throughout Japan.

Saigō resigned after the meetings on 14 and 15 October. On the eighteenth, Godai wrote to Zeisho Atsushi saying that it was of great importance not to lose the present opportunity, and so on the twentieth he would be setting up a residence in Tokyo, and in that residence he would set up 'Handa no mise' to deal with the Fukushima silver mine (Godai 1933: 222ff.). Early in 1874 he was able to establish a Kantō branch of the Kōseikan which presumably incorporated the 'Handa no mise' (Miyamoto 1981: 294–5). He finally obtained possession of Handa silver mine in July 1874. In November, due to a sudden change in government regulations, the Ono-kumi went bankrupt and Godai was left in sole control of the Kōseikan. Graciously, he did not push his demands for other Ono mines and they were parcelled out among other friends of the government.

The main outlines of the story seem clear enough, but as it is the sort of story that Japanese historians rarely disinter, let us look a little more closely at the Handa mine.

## Handa Silver

Handa silver was usually ranked with Sadō gold and Ikuno silver as one of the three great mines of the Edo period. In 1664 it became a Bakufu 'jikiyama' (directly managed mine). Later it was placed under the administration of the Sado *bugyō* and for 140 years officials and administrators, as well as miners, were sent from the Iwami and Ikuno silver mines. Its organization was the same as that of Sadō, with a wide array of officials who were usually rotated annually (Saitō 1984: 4–5).

Towards the end of the Bakufu there were nine mines in the mountain, but due to problems with water, fire, etc. their profitability declined so rapidly that in 1864 the Bakufu ceased operations (ibid.: 9). Thereafter, some of the mines were carried on by the Hayata *gonō* family who had been *dai shoyā* for generations and had a long experience in mining. Hayata Dennosuke (1791–1874) was also a noted Shingaku scholar with his own large *juku*. Shingaku emphasizes cultivating the heart and putting ideals into practice, and the Hayatas seem to have been partly acting in the interests of the miners and local community (see *Fukushima Dai Hyakkajiten*).

In February 1869, the Hayatas wrote a long letter to the Meiji government giving the history of the mine and pointing out that it would again be of great value to the nation if funds could be made available for repairs and help provided with rice supplies, for rice prices had increased ten times (Shōji 1981: 325ff.). There was little in the way of positive response, but in 1872 the Construction Ministry sent a party of foreign experts and Japanese officials to survey Tohoku mines. They spent three days at Handa. In September 1873, the Mining Law was published making all mines government property but providing for a system of licences to encourage private management. In April 1874, another official, Ōshima Takatō, made an inspection of the area, and it seems that Godai heard of the Ōshima report (Saitō 1984: 9). It would seem that the government itself had been planning to take over. In July 1872, the survey leaders, Godfrey and Tsuda Hiromichi, stayed with Hayata Dennosuke and Tsuda's diary speaks of uncertainty about the mine, but mentions one place which the government should take over first and then expand from there (ibid.: 31). However, Godai suddenly entered the picture, and on 19 July 1874 he was able to write to Katsura Hisatake: 'As expected, it was very complicated, but at last it has passed into my hands' (ibid.: 29). He also added gleefully that it seemed to be better than Ikuno.

This prediction was soon borne out. Backed by government assistance such as the loan of its foreign experts, production was increased from 4,160 *momme* in 1874 to 1,877,378 *momme* in 1884, as against 789,900 for Sadō and 415,118 for Ikuno (ibid.: 41; 1 *momme* is 3.75 grammes). Handa was thus out on its own.

*Goyō gakusha* often argue that what was good for Godai was good for Japan, but the argument is extremely weak.

The above account, based on the highly illuminating histories of the Handa mine by Saitō and Shōji, needs further clarification. Far greater cynicism is called for. It is highly unlikely that Godai just happened to hear of the Ōshima report. We have seen how, straight after the *seihen*, Inoue wrote to new Construction Minister Itō naming various mines he wanted the government to take over and then later hand over to his company. Surely the situation was the same with Godai. His Kansai mining organization had been set up at the start of 1873, and had promptly sent out agents all over Japan looking for mines to buy up. Straight after the *seihen* he had set up a branch in Tokyo with the Fukushima mines in mind. Ōshima Takatō, a Nambu clansman (*Kawada Shobō* 1972) had been abroad with the Iwakura Mission from 1871 to 1873 studying Western mines, so he must have been known to Ōkubo and Itō. Bearing in mind the fame of the Handa silver mines, surely the logical scenario is that Ōshima was sent on his Tohoku tour after full consultation between Itō, Okubo and Godai, and that the government, well before taking over Handa, had already agreed to pass it over to Godai. That it was no sudden move by Godai is clearly indicated by Godai's letter of 19 July: '. . . *at last* it has passed into my hands' (Godai 1933: 558–60).

It would take many volumes to describe how Japanese corruption worked (and still works). It would be a worthy topic, for as Japan gets established as the world's economic superpower, corruption – political, economic and academic – is likely to be a major export. Here let us merely note the expression *seishō* (government-backed companies). When government ministers and bureaucrats helped establish new companies they were not just assisting their friends but were also making fortunes for themselves; they must be regarded as, in effect, major shareholders of the new companies. We have seen how Godai presented Ōkubo with money when he returned from Europe. He also gave him a coach and horses – the equivalent of a modern gift of a Rolls – and in 1875 when 'the Emperor gave a large gift' to Ōkubo, he used it to build a magnificent brick residence. Godai was largely responsible for 'supervising' the construction of the gardens, and he and Ōkura took over complete responsibility for all furnishings and interior decorations (Tokutomi 1927: 389ff.). Ōkubo's diary boasted that the guests were all left speechless at the splendour of the house. Ōkubo apologists claim that such a place was necessary to impress foreigners, but Ōkubo was familiar with the White House and surely realized the difference between using 'the Emperor's' money on a building which would belong to the state and one which was to be his personal property. It probably indicates that Ōkubo viewed himself as a permanent head of state, but neither the money from the Emperor nor that from Godai can rightly be regarded as gifts.

Ōkubo showed more finesse than Inoue and lacked Inoue's gross insensitivity, but he was hardly less corrupt, vain and avaricious. The Meiji leaders built up the ideal slush fund by putting cash, land and property in the name of the Emperor. It sounds so much nicer to say that Ōkubo built his own magnificent home with money presented by the Emperor rather than declaring that state funds were diverted for this purpose. Likewise the coach and horses and house interior were not one-off gifts but part of what would have been life-long dividends from Handa silver mine, etc. Little wonder that, to use Akita's droll expression, 'these people were not prepared to share government with selfish and irresponsible elements'!

If one goes today to Saga, one finds that Ōkuma's home is kept up as a museum, while there is little to remind one of Etō Shimpei. Yet Etō is still respected, while Ōkuma certainly is not. Likewise go to Satsuma and you'll find 'Saigō *sensei*' is still revered while Ōkubo's name brings a cold response. As we have seen, from the late eighteenth century there were three Satsumas: the high flyers in Edo, the simpler, austere *samurai* back home, and the common people groaning under a grievous burden of taxation. Ōkubo, Kuroda and Godai are not to be taken as representing the whole of Satsuma nor are they fitting symbols of Japan, but they do represent one very important element which is always threatening to take over completely and to erase all the simpler, finer images of Japan.

Thus Godai was disreputable, Kuroda grotesque, and Ōkubo inextricably linked with both. Godai was the pimp extraordinaire who, according to Shimazu (p. 73), provided Satsuma officials with both money and mistresses, and whose new million-*yen*, four-storeyed home was big enough to house three mistresses in separate wings like the Emperors of old. When he died, the house and grounds were large enough to accommodate 5,000 mourners. The timber for the house was provided by Maruyama Shinden, a merchant who had made a fortune from Hokkaidō timber, for Kuroda sold it to him cheaply and let him transport it free of charge in Kaitakushi ships – a fair indication of why it cost more to sail to Hokkaidō than to California.

Kuroda was forty when he first spotted Maruyama's only child, a girl of seventeen. The Shimazu version (pp. 317–23) has an inflamed Kuroda carrying her off at the point of a pistol, then raping her; but it is more likely that she became his second wife by an ordinary, everyday arrangement (Maruyama could hardly refuse after all those years of patronage).

*Minei* (private management) meant in practice rejecting the local applications from people with long experience and expertise, and handing the mines over on most generous terms to their own Satchō and related friends: Handa, etc. to Godai, Nambu's Osarisawa to Inoue, Akita's Ani and In-nai and Tochigi's Besshi to Furukawa. The wealth simply drained out of Tōhoku which degenerated into a poor and backward region. The long-range consequences were serious not only for Tōhoku but also for Japan as a whole. In 1934 alone an estimated 10,000 Akita girls were sold, mostly into prostitution, for the price of a *koku* of rice (Imamura 1969: 169ff.). It was this extreme rural poverty, especially in Tōhoku, which fuelled the fanaticism of the Young Officers in the thirties.

It is abundantly clear that had the Ōkubo–Iwakura side not triumphed in the 1873 *Seihen*, Inoue would not have kept Osarisawa, Godai would not have laid his hands on Handa, and the Ono-kumi would not have been brought down and Furukawa built up to take over their assets. It should also be noted that 1873 was the year in which Mitsubishi acquired Okayama's Yoshioka mine, and it was this mine, not shipping, which laid the basis of Mitsubishi wealth (*Iwasaki Yatarō Den* 1967, Vol. 1: 310–17; *Iwasaki Hisaya Den* 1961: 344ff.). Thus 1873 was a key year for the redistribution of Japan's mineral wealth, which generally occurred as a result of the 1873 *Seihen*. Surely one must go further: this redistribution of mineral wealth was basically part of the ongoing distribution of spoils from the Boshin War, and this fight over the spoils from wars past must be seen not merely as a result but also as a major cause of the 1873 *Seihen*.

Once these facts have been grasped, it is not hard to understand the nature of Japan's penetration of Korea. Hokkaidō and Tōhoku had provided a full dress rehearsal.

# 12

# CONCLUSION

A true understanding of the 1873 *Seihen* is essential to the understanding of Japanese imperialism. So let us first summarize the results of our research into that *seihen*, then move on to the wider question of Japanese imperialism.

There are four main traps awaiting the historian writing about the 1873 *Seihen*: the tendency to begin the analysis with 1868; the belief that 'it's all there in the documents'; the practice of regarding the two opposing factions as consistent, unified groups; and the temptation to reduce the crisis to one all-embracing theory.

American 'bridge-building' historians do the Japanese people a grave disservice. From the beginning of the Meiji era, Western writers have tended to align themselves with the Japanese government and to act as propagandists for the Establishment. Paradoxically, this tendency increased after the Second World War. Akita, Conroy and Gluck are prime examples. Akita's picture of the noble Satchō leaders' concern at the thought of sharing power with 'selfish and irresponsible elements' is simply grotesque, and leads him to applaud every act and mechanism of oppression. Unfortunately, these are not just Akita's own idiosyncratic views. The prestigious *Sources of Japanese Tradition* (de Bary 1964, Vol. 2: 133–4), for example, endorses this blanket approval of the Meiji leadership with its 'tenacious adherence to traditional ideals and virtues' and its 'strong sense of moderation, cohesion, and national loyalty'. Not surprisingly, such works as Akita's and Lebra's starry-eyed account of Ōkuma have been translated into Japanese.

The question of to what degree the Meiji leaders were true Japanese patriots and to what degree they were essentially serving themselves and their own clan is one of considerable complexity. The general verdict of Western historians such as Beasley (1973: 145ff.)

312

has been that the Meiji leaders were motivated by a true national patriotism and that 'the Meiji Period stands out as a golden age of Japanese history' (Bolitho 1977: 30). But it must surely be noted that their concept of the national good coincided to a remarkable degree with their own personal interests and with those of their own fief. It is a theme which needs to be developed in subsequent volumes, but the tentative conclusion must be that they were prepared to sacrifice the national welfare for the sake of their own personal, clan and class interests.

The Western contribution to the Korean debate has been a negative one. Conroy sets the tone for his work when he describes the Sada mission as the 'fact-finders'. Quite ignoring the way in which the government controlled the media and manipulated records, he goes on to exonerate the Japanese government from having had any long-range plans to take over Korea. More insidious is Gluck's thesis that Emperor system ideology emerged only after 1890 and did not penetrate deeply into the Japanese psyche; thus after the Second World War it simply disappeared, leaving the New Japan. This is a distortion of major importance, for Japan's obsession with becoming, in economic terms, 'Number One', must be regarded as having more than a passing relationship with the *kokugaku* teachings that Japan is the centre of the universe and that all other peoples are inferior and subordinate.

Gluck is a perfect example of the dangers of taking a certain year – in this case 1890 – as a starting point, and ignoring the evidence of early ages. Island nations are, by definition, insular. The Japanese islands have the advantage, or disadvantage, of great natural beauty – of mountains, mists, and of living close to a turbulent nature. This gives a feeling of being near to the source of things and lends itself readily to a semi-mystical nationalism. When such a country is cut off from the rest of the world for 250 years, there is a natural tendency for this mysticism to take over, and when it is reinforced by a planned policy of indoctrination, the result is a religious or semi-religious belief that the country is the centre of the world. Once the Tokugawas introduced their policy of seclusion, they had to justify cutting the country off from China and India, the source of much of its religious, cultural and political traditions. Here the Chinese doctrine of China as 'the Middle Kingdom' was adopted to make Japan the centre of the world, and the stress was laid on 'Japanism' and the natural purity which existed before it was corrupted by a heavy coating of Chinese culture. Inevitably, such doctrines were racist, with the Indians in particular being regarded as an inferior species. It should be stressed that the main targets of these racial teachings were not Europeans but other Asians.

The disciples of men such as Motoori and Hirata spread out into every corner of Japan, so that *kokugaku* teachings literally became national teachings. When they spoke of a 'Restoration', they meant restoring the Emperor not only to centre stage within Japan but also as the centre of the universe. The term for Emperor was of prime importance. Thus when the Meiji government sent representatives to Korea in the name of this 'Emperor', they were not simply restoring the relations which had existed under the Bakufu, but were advancing the doctrine that the Japanese Emperor was superior to the Korean, and that the Korean state was subordinate to the Japanese. This Emperor doctrine – later enshrined in the Emperor system – had been debated and taught over a long period of time. The Foreign Office was dominated by *sonnō* fanatics such as Sawa, Maruyama and Sada. The Korean rejection of their overtures was neither rude nor illogical, but was essential to their survival. These early attempts to make the Koreans deal with this 'superior' Emperor must be regarded as the first step in Meiji Japan's aggression towards Korea. This aggressive intent is further advanced by Sada, then Saigō. Japanese historians usually pay scant attention to this long background, and prefer to start with 1868 and to concentrate on 'Saigō's heart'. But Saigō, like Sada, belonged to this 'Emperor' school. Those such as Mōri Toshihiko, who insist that Saigō wanted peace with Korea, ingenuously evade this central issue: the 'rudeness' the Koreans were guilty of was their refusal to acknowledge this 'superior' Japanese Emperor and their own subordinate position. Saigō's 'peace' meant not only that Korea should acknowledge her subordinate position but also that she agree to open the country to Japanese traders. That she would agree to Saigō's 'peace' was simply beyond the realms of possibility.

Westerners such as Chamberlain commended Satchō for their unprecedented *volte-face* in using the *sonnō jōi* movement to gain power, then ditching their allies and opening the country. Though this duplicity may have been unprecedented, it was a precedent which was soon equalled. In 1873, the Iwakura–Ōkubo–Chōshū side argued strongly against the Saigō Mission and 'foreign adventures'. Having used this issue to drive out the caretaker government, they then themselves invaded Taiwan (1874) and Korea (1875–6). It was, however, a predictable act of duplicity, for if one has followed the longer story, it becomes obvious that both sides in the *seikan* dispute favoured attacking Korea, but both wished to be in charge when this penetration was undertaken.

This long-range study of Japanese history also makes clear the underlying geo-political factors which made it highly likely that, once *sakoku* was ended, Japan would try to expand on the mainland. Japan is a mountainous country subject to natural disasters and with no natural internal communications system. Korea is a far flatter country with a high percentage of good farming land. Since at least the fourteenth century, the Japanese had tried desperately to obtain Korean grains, especially rice. Very largely this activity was left to the *wakō*, pirates operating in conjuncture with the Western *daimyō* and the great merchants. Officially, the Japanese authorities remained clean, but the *wakō* are better seen as an instrument of state policy.

It is important to remember that Korean antipathy to Japan is not just a result of its 1910–45 rule, or even of its penetration from 1868. It was primarily because of Japanese depredations that the new Korean king moved his capital inland in 1392. Thus even 600 years ago Japan had the status of traditional enemy. Then came the unspeakable horror of the Hideyoshi invasions followed by Korea's own *sakoku*, largely directed at Japan. It was largely because Japan posed a constant threat that Korea accepted a subordinate relationship with China. For Meiji Japan, a prime object of her diplomatic policy was therefore to make Korea 'truly independent' (of China) and thus render her vulnerable and exposed. When *sakoku* ended Japan was back where it had been in the late sixteenth century: once again, civil war had ended, leaving a large, unemployed army; there was a business slump, so most businessmen favoured a move into the continent; the grain supplies had been seriously dislocated; and there was a need to rally the nation behind the new central government. Not surprisingly the Meiji government was to adopt the same solution as Hideyoshi.

The Japanese are very fond of metaphors about rivers, so it is not inappropriate to refer to the flow of Japanese history. Few who have travelled down the Danube would describe it as blue, yet if you freeze the camera at one spot, and get the light just right, one may perhaps 'prove' that it is blue. One cannot dispute Tokutomi's assertion that both sides in the 1873 conflict were 'splendid imperialists'. But only by freezing the camera at 1873 can we build up the illusion that we have here two altruistic groups of patriots dividing over matters of principle and high policy.

If one is forced to take a limited time-span, the starting point must be 1866 not 1868. The years 1866–73, beginning with the assassination of Kōmei and ending with the 1873 *Seihen*, which leaves the two main regicides firmly in power, must be seen as an integrated period, The *Satchō*-Usurpation of Power. The 1873 *Seihen* should be viewed as the consolidation of the assassination gains and the culmination of that seven-year period.

It is important, however, that we go far beyond the period 1866–73, travelling up and down the river of history until the many vivid cameo scenes begin to form a connecting pattern. For example, we can picture Iwakura Tsunetomo being forced to resign in 1758 when the Bakufu arrested radical teacher, Takenouchi Shikibu, whose influence extended right up to young Momozono Tennō. We can pass over to 1791 when another young man, Tomonobu adopted into the Iwakura family, carries on its *sonnō* traditions and for six months acts as host of activist Takayama Hikokurō. Again we can picture a meeting between Hikokurō and the bitter young Emperor Kōkaku, who had been 'adopted' from a junior branch – the founder of the modern line. We can skip over to 1866 and observe another young man adopted into the Iwakura family, espousing *sonnō* principles as he conspires to assassinate the Emperor. Our last cameo scene in this series occurs in 1883. Iwakura lies on his death bed (Iwakura Tomomi 1977 edn, Introduction: 2–3). The last person he calls is Inoue Kaoru, 'bagman' for the Meiji Establishment – the founder and manager of *zaibatsu*, the much-detested wheeler-dealer who maintained his power by making sure that all the people who counted got their slice from the major confiscations. A thread of betrayal runs through modern Japanese history. 'The Meiji Ishin' was a sedulously propagated myth, but the ideals of *ishin* had been real. Even today Japan suffers because the fact that the *ishin* was smothered at birth has never clearly been recognized. By the end of the century Inoue was writing (Stead 1904: 308) of 'the ruling classes'. At first one was tempted to take this as a delicious self-parody, but Inoue was quite seriously giving this as a description of their small-town men from the west who had taken over the country.

In post-war Japan, the feeling of betrayal still continues, not so much in relation to their own politicians – there expectations were low – but in relation to America which began so brightly then changed course and insisted that Japan be rich, hypocritical, polluted and armed. The old myths survive, intangible but strong – the 'glorious' Meiji leaders' descendants have in truth become 'the ruling classes'. Their political invincibility is in part a tribute to the power of legends absorbed in childhood.

The second trap to be avoided is the belief that 'it's all there in the documents'. Quite simply, it is far from all there. The 'documents' must be regarded as a mere supplement, and handled with great care. Saigō is a case in point. He has left some hundreds of poems and some little essays, but they are vague and general. We must look at the logic of the situation and argue from what actually happened. The salient fact is that there was no prospect of Saigō's 'peace' initiative succeeding. Obviously, the Koreans would not have apologized for the palpably fictitious 'monkey' poster, and, even more fundamentally, they would not have recognized the superior position of the Japanese Emperor. Inevitably, any discussions would have led to the Emperor being 'insulted'. Saigō would either have died in Korea or have returned to trumpet Korea's 'insults'. Either way his mission would have been a prelude to war. Sada refused to return to Korea, save at the head of an army, and despite the lack of documentary evidence, one must conclude that this was also in Saigō's mind. Quite probably, he had thought along these lines ever since he had been urged on by Maki in 1863.

Japanese historians agonize over Saigō's three letters to Itagaki, either denying their authenticity or arguing that they did not represent his true mind. Yet the major point of *haragei* would seem to relate to his determination to die. The Koreans were not barbarians. Fishermen from western Japan were regularly washed ashore in Korea and were routinely returned. Other envoys went to Korea and were not harmed. The Americans tried to build up a picture of savage Koreans attacking an American ship, but its intrusion upstream into the heart of the country was an action which no country would have tolerated. In other cases Korean behaviour towards shipwrecked ships had been quite civilized. There is no reason to believe that they would have killed Saigō.

For Saigō the danger was not death in Korea but being forced to stand down for Foreign Minister Soejima. Tōyama's tribute in the pre-war edition of Maruyama's biography makes it clear that Soejima was in the *kokugaku* mainstream; he was earlier than Saigō as an advocate of *seikan*, and provides a link running through from the early Meiji years to the 1930s. Even so Soejima was a very fine scholar, especially of the Chinese classics; and classical Chinese was the language of the Korean court and of Korean diplomacy. Soejima had been successful in cultivating good personal relations with both the Chinese and the Russians. Thus if anyone had a chance of achieving a face-saving formula to the question of Emperor terminology, and then extracting some commercial concessions from the Koreans, it would have been this distinguished, cultured and skilful diplomat. Probably Saigō was afraid not of Soejima's failure but of his success. Hence Saigō stressed the great danger to be encountered in Korea and argued that Japan could not afford to see Soejima killed. Rather than being killed in Korea, the logical scenario would have been for Saigō to return from Korea to report that the Emperor had been insulted, then to go back to Korea at the head of an army which would then move on to take Manchuria.

The *bun* and *bu* explanation of the 1873 *Seihen* at first seems merely an officially propagated legend. Early Western witnesses such as Mounsey and Reed (1880: 339) reported that Saigō had planned to make himself military despot under the Mikado like Yorimoto and Ieyasu, and this was clearly the interpretation which Ōkubo presented and Westerners generally accepted. Here we must lament the lack of documents. Saigō, it seems clear, engaged in *haragei* even with Itagaki, and left no revealing documents. Ōkubo kept a diary, but the months in which we are most interested are missing. So one is reduced to arguing from the logic of the situation. Ōkubo soon presided over invasions of Taiwan and Korea, so he was not anti-*seikan* and not overly concerned with the various issues he listed such as fear of England and Russia. Yet his fight with Saigō and Etō was literally a fight to the death. This in itself suggests that this was no mere constitutional crisis, and supports the idea that Saigō's mission would lead to a military dictatorship. There is a definite logic in this belief. If Saigō went back to Korea with an army, and then moved into Manchuria, such a war would have involved increased taxes and led to even more *ikki*. On returning to Japan, Saigō would have had to re-establish internal order. Surely Ōkubo believed, and was right to believe, that there would be tremendous pressure on Saigō to declare himself Shogun. Bearing in mind Saigō's disgust with the corruption of the Meiji government, and its lack of public credibility, it is easy to picture Saigō being swept along by the tide of events.

Saigō's model was not necessarily a past Shogun. Washington and

Napoleon were both well known and highly regarded in Japan, and Napoleon was perhaps the most likely role model. Saigō was close to Etō, and must have been fully aware of what Etō was trying to achieve at the Justice Ministry. The Japanese carpet-baggers had to be subjected to the Rule of Law, and a modern legal code set up before the foreign powers would agree to treaty revision. That in practice meant translating the Code Napoleon. Thus it would probably not have been too difficult to persuade Saigō that he should act as Japan's Napoleon to end corruption and to preside over the establishment of the Rule of Law. The uncompromising ferocity of the confrontation with Ōkubo, Iwakura and Chōshū cannot be explained in terms of difference over policy towards Korea, but makes eminent sense if viewed in terms of the above scenario. This military versus civil factor should be seen as one part of the overall picture – a factor which remained vital down to 1945.

We cannot wander off too far into the realms of speculation, but it should be stressed that had Saigō become military dictator, it was unlikely to have made much difference to the subsequent course of events on the mainland. Korea was widely regarded as on a par with Hokkaidō and the Ryūkyūs, and Saigō's Satsuma colleagues worked out in Hokkaidō the policies which were later applied to Korea. Japan acted in accordance with the teachings of the *kokugakusha* and in line with age-old geo-political factors. She wanted Korean grains, especially rice, a base from which to expand into Manchuria and China, and a market where Japan could initially act as middleman for Western goods, then, after a few years, send her own textiles. Kyūshū people would not brave the cold of Hokkaidō, but Korea offered a viable alternative. Saigō may have been able to head off some of the worst excesses, but the Hokkaidō story indicates that even that was unlikely. Bolitho (1977: 24) sums Saigō up as 'a bully', while the perspicacious novelist Shiba Ryōtarō (1975) suggests that, from the *ishin* onwards, Saigō was suffering damage from a blow to the head. As the Seinan War was to demonstrate, Saigō was not ultimately in charge but was swept along by the tide of events. The same, too, would surely have been true had he gone on his mission to Korea.

The third trap to be avoided is that of simply taking the two opposing sides as representing consistent, unified positions. Both sides were as diverse as, for example, the American Democratic Party, but without its enduring cohesiveness. One must look at the position of various individuals and sub-factions.

This is a point well taken by Ōkuma writing in 1895 (Enjōji 1895, Vol. 2: 636ff.). He noted that the *seikan* struggle had not just been about Korea and its insults. The various *seikan* leaders had sought to use the Korean question for their own purposes. Etō, for example, hoped to use it to break the Satchō *batsu*, while Itagaki hoped it would restore public morality. Gotō, on the other hand, was mostly interested in trade, and was already planning to leave government for the business world. Ōkubo and Iwakura were well aware of these various ulterior motives, hence their implacable opposition to the Saigō mission.

Indeed, issues and principles often become of limited relevance as we look at individuals and groups. Like Ōkuma, Ōki Takatō, for example, agonized over his position in 1873 before eventually sticking with Ōkubo and Iwakura. In 1881 he was to split with Ōkuma and again go along with Satchō. The natural assumption would be that here was a man agonizing over principles and issues. Miyage Setsurei, however, was a perspicacious contemporary observer and he described Ōki as a fellow devoted to guarding his own position (Miyage 1949, Vol. 1: 357). This seems to be borne out by a sad little biography to be found in the Saga Public Library. Ōki's son, a right-wing politician of some note, wanted to produce a biography of his father, but so isolated had Ōki become, that the son had to approach Ōkuma, who agreed with ill-concealed reluctance, pointing out that though he and Ōki were relatives, they had been completely alienated in their later years. Ōki's father had been a drunken wastrel, and he and his mother had had to return to the grandparents. He grew up proud and aloof and determined to rise in the world. Having got to the top, he was determined to remain there. He was to present the government with many opinion papers, but these seem to have been mostly the equivalent of modern paliamentary sweetheart questions. When Satchō wanted to pursue a certain course, they would ask Ōki to present an appropriate paper. Thus in 1873 it would seem that Ōki's doubts were caused by the uncertainty as to the ultimate victors.

As we have seen, the Tosa divisions in 1873 were along 1863 lines. Gotō and Etō had become a firm combination, while the Takechi supporters were tied to Sanjō and the old Chōshū extremists. The Takechi group – Sasaki, Tani, Hijikata, etc. – were strong imperialists, but they found themselves inevitably but briefly in the anti-*seikan* corner.

Chōshū was fighting desperately to restore its position, so Itō,

Inoue and Yamagata had to rely on Ōkubo and Iwakura. But both Itō and Inoue must be regarded as part of a wider group which included Godai, Kuroda and Ōkuma. Saigō and Itagaki were disgusted at the corruption and the decay of old *samurai* virtues. These five must be regarded as the prime exponents of that corruption. At times they were bitter rivals, as with Ōkuma and Inoue in Nagasaki in 1868, and again in 1881. But generally they worked together and should be seen as a group. In the Bakumatsu period, currency reforms always presented the officials with rich pickings, and so with the Meiji period this is the group which took control of the mint. People such as Okada Heizō and Masuda Takashi, who began as Godai men, sought his permission, before moving over to Inoue. They tended to know the same merchants such as Takashima Yoshiemon, and when they came to divide up Japan's mineral wealth, they maintained a nice balance. Ōkuma had isolated himself by refusing to back Inoue's Treasury estimates and by reporting that there was enough finance available to provide the Justice and Education Ministries with adequate funds. But when the crunch came, it was impossible for him to align himself with Etō and Saigō and their campaigns to eliminate corruption and to establish the Rule of Law. He belonged with Inoue, Itō, Godai and Kuroda.

The last trap we must note is that of seeking one single, all-embracing theory to explain the 1873 crisis. It was the product of a number of interlocking causes. The personal conflicts were obviously important, as was the campaign to break the power of the Satchō *batsu*. Etō's campaign to establish the Rule of Law was vital, but it was not a thing apart but one aspect of Etō's fierce personal contest with Inoue and Ōkubo and also one manifestation of his war on Satchō, for it was Satchō which had placed themselves above the law. Again, the personal, clan-*batsu* and Rule of Law struggles were not about abstract issues. As Itagaki and Saigō stressed, they were closely related to the question of public morality.

Westerners writing about Japan are prone to treat corruption as a victimless crime, but as in any newly emerging nation, it went to the heart of the government's credibility and stability. Excessive corruption has been a common factor providing the rationale for military take-overs. Widespread corruption and the decline of old *samurai* virtues were not new problems which suddenly emerged in 1868. As we have seen, at least since the late eighteenth century Satsuma was deeply divided between those living in luxury in Edo and those leading spartan lives back in Satsuma. But corruption by newcomers provokes more disgust than that by traditional ruling classes, inevitably leading to barbs about 'monkeys wearing crowns'. Thus corruption must be seen as a central issue, being both a cause and a manifestation of the personal and clan clashes, the impetus to Etō's Rule of Law campaign, and, probably, to a belief on Saigō's part that Japan needed a Napoleon.

The events of 1874–5 rob the *nai-gai* theory of much of its validity. Even so, given the human animal's capacity for self-deception, one cannot simply dismiss the Ōkubo concern for internal law and order. The caretaker government reforms such as conscription and giving full legal rights to the Eta aroused widespread opposition, so 1873 was marked by *ikki* on a gigantic scale. Even so, had there not been the underlying, implacable power struggles, this question and the timing of Saigō's mission were the sort of issues which lent themselves to compromise. Concern was called for, but it is difficult to avoid the conclusion that Ōkubo was largely rationalizing his opposition to Saigō's mission. Closely related is the question, never far in the background in these Bakumatsu and early Meiji periods, of to what extent these conflicts were basically class struggles. It is an aspect which must remain outside the scope of this history, and we can merely note its obvious relevance. But our analysis of Kurume history leaves no doubt as to one aspect of the *nai-gai* debate: Kurume and many other clans, even with the *ishin*, were still tearing themselves apart. But here the reasoning of Sada and the *seikan* party was that this aggression should be turned outwards. There can be no doubting Sada's sincerity when he advanced this argument.

We are thus left with a compromise position which recognizes at least some validity in all the standard theories. Nevertheless, we differ from Japanese historians in four important respects. First, the year 1873 must be seen against the background of unchanging geo-political factors which largely determined the last 600 years of history. From ancient times, Japan had cultural and commercial ties with mainland Asia, mostly through western Japan. *Sakoku* meant an unnatural suspension of those ties – suspension enforced by the Tokugawas to prevent western Japan from becoming too strong economically and militarily. Once *sakoku* was ended, it was inevitable that western Japan in particular would want to restore the trade on which their wealth was largely based. But the old problem remained: the western clans had to be tightly controlled from the centre or they would build up their own bases in Korea and China and pose a constant threat to the Japanese government. For Satsuma and Chōshū, of course, Restoration largely meant the restoration of their old commercial supremacy, but this restoration also sharply revived their position as traditional enemies of each other and of various other clans. The essential nature of the struggle was determined by these age-old factors. In this sense, individual Meiji leaders were of little significance. These age-old factors were likewise going to determine the form of trade and wealth which would be central to these conflicts. Mountainous Japan was again bound to cast its eyes on Korean grains, especially rice; shipping was obviously vital, while control of mines, especially precious metals and copper, were going to be a key to wealth and power. The 1873 *Seihen* must be seen as part of this long on-going story which continues at least till 1945. One must analyse the motives and the roles of the leading participants not as individuals who are going to determine the course of history but as representatives of the various forces and currents which were bound to come to the fore with the Restoration.

Second, one must lay far greater stress on the National Learning than modern Japanese historians are generally prepared to do. *Kokugaku juku* existed throughout Japan. They taught an extreme form of racism and nationalism. Modern Japan's imperialist expansion was to be at least semi-religious. Satchō had made its unprecedented *volte-face*, and had turned its back on its erstwhile ideologue allies, but the teachings had not faded away. Throughout the nation there were great numbers of both *samurai* and *heimin* who felt that the *ishin* had been betrayed, and it was their presence not too far in the background that gave to 1873 its implacable, somewhat hysterical character. The Satchō victors had not been welcomed in the first place. In the words of newspaper man Black (1962, Vol. 2: 242), they took over a nation 'in the sulks'. It took the further military *coup* of 1871 to establish Satchō power, but the government's credibility had never really been established. The 1873 crisis was not just between two factions within the government; rather should it be viewed as the outcome of a government with little credibility acting somewhat hysterically in the face of widespread national disapproval. The future of the Japanese people was at stake. The *seihen* largely comes down to disagreements over how to control the people. The two main solutions touted – setting up a strong Satchō police state or embarking on a series of foreign wars – by no means exhausted the list of viable solutions facing Japan as a nation in 1873. But they probably do represent the only ways in which the narrowly based government could have maintained its monopoly of wealth and power.

Third, one must insist that the struggle to establish the Rule of Law was a factor of tremendous importance. Etō's defeat in 1873 was a defeat for the Japanese people and for the peoples of the lands Japan later conquered. An essential feature of a feudal system is that the rulers are above the law. It was Japan's tragedy that Satchō were able to preserve this aspect of feudalism, and to combine it with a form of conscription which left generations of its people trapped in a situation from which there was no escape.

Finally, we must stress what no Japanese historian, even Mōri, is prepared to stress: the *seihen* largely revolved about the spoils of war. When a civil war ends, there is an inevitable period of dislocation. It takes time to distribute the fruits of victory. After the Boshin War it took about twenty years to transform the small-town men from the west, but by the mid-eighties they were the new aristocrats with titles, ribbons, speech-writers, fine landed estates, villas, top *geisha* and all the paraphernalia of a permanent ruling class. It was the year 1873 which put the seal on this transformation. Etō's Rule of Law threatened both the permanence of Satchō's political power and the fine sweep of its economic aggrandizement. With Etō out of the way, Inoue was able to keep Osarisawa, to organize first his Senshūsha then Mitsui Bussan, and to tie up much of the vital rice trade. Godai was able to move his mining operations up to Tokyo and to take over Handa silver mines and various other mines. The Ono *kumi* was effectively broken and replaced by the Furukawa *zaibatsu*, a front organization for Mutsu and numerous other 'statesmen' and officials; and 1873 saw Mitsubishi take over Okayama's Yoshioka mine which financed its subsequent shipping expansion. Quite clearly this sudden accumulation of mining and other wealth was a result of victory in the 1873 *Seihen*. It must also be regarded as a major cause of the *seihen*.

Yet the 1873 *Seihen* was not just about the spoils of wars past. It also centred around the spoils of wars yet to come. In government circles, the idea of imperialistic expansion was more or less agreed upon, though there were divisions over timing and direction. The wars were to be largely commercial, to be fought over rice, minerals, markets and farming land. But who was to lead this change? Had Saigō gone to Korea, Chōshū would have remained on the outer circle; at the time there was no Mitsui Bussan or Fujita *gumi*, and no Shibusawa network. Likewise Godai was still relatively small, and, in any case, he, no more than Inoue and the Chōshū-line companies, could have hoped for little from an anti-Satchō government. But how different was the story when Korea was opened in 1875–6! Inoue tied up the rice trade, Shibusawa the banking, Ōkura the textiles. Over a decade of *zaibatsu* fratricidal strife gradually gave way to the realization that there was enough for everyone, and we move on to Saionji's cosy Cabinet of 1906. Thus Furukawa was 'invited' to take over Korean mines and Mitsubishi became the biggest Korean landowner. But 1906 was light years away from 1873. Then the accepted hero was Clive of India, and the question was what group in Japan would form the equivalent of the Japanese British East India Company. Far more was at stake than Osarisawa or Handa and the other spoils of 1868. Inoue, Kuroda, Godai, Ōkuma, etc. surely realized that what was at stake was not just the spoils of past civil wars but also the distribution of the spoils of wars soon to come on mainland Asia.

This study has given a brief outline of relevant aspects of earlier Japanese history, but the true nature of the 1873 *Seihen* will emerge with full clarity only when the events from 1874 to 1945 are analysed in detail. The *seihen* must be seen as part of an on-going current of events. To help put the *seihen* in perspective let us briefly indicate future lines of research.

The years 1874 and 1875 require a full volume, centring around the Taiwan expedition and the opening of Korea. The Taiwan question is closely related to the Ryūkyūs so the story of Satsuma's colonial rule there needs to be traced in detail. The opening of Korea was probably plotted at the Osaka Conference which sought to bring Kido and Itagaki back into the government. The pretext of opening Korea in 1875 was as false and contrived as the 'monkey' poster of 1873. The mission was led by Kuroda, a member of Godai's childhood gang, and included two Kaitakushi officials who were likewise members of that same gang. The deputy was Inoue, whose Osarisawa court case was speeded up to permit him to depart. Inoue's main interest was Korean rice. He was able to organize Mitsui Bussan, which took over his own company, Senshūsha, and soon gained a virtual monopoly of Korean rice. The proper understanding of the opening of Korea requires a detailed study of the Chōshū clan in the early Meiji period, especially its rice trade, for Inoue's control of Chōshū rice and Mitsui Bussan's monopoly of Korean rice must be seen as one ongoing story.

The 1881 *Seihen* also requires a full volume. Japanese studies tend to be narrowly political, but again, economic aspects are of fundamental importance and Hokkaidō needs to be put back into the centre of the story.

Subsequent developments requiring detailed treatment are the shipping wars of the eighties, the election of 1892 and accompanying judicial struggles, the growing influence of the Fukuoka and Kumamoto Rightists, the annexation of Korea, and the colonial policies imposed upon it.

Obviously, the full telling of this story requires many volumes. Only then will the 1873 *Seihen* be seen clearly not as one historical event which happened and was then over, but as part of a rapidly moving current of history. The *seihen* was a temporary interruption – a mere hiccup – in Japan's perhaps irresistible movement into Korea, Manchuria and China. Ultimately, what was at stake in 1873 was a large Asian empire, but the immediate question was which of the embryonic *zaibatsu* were to gain control of Korean rice, markets, mines and land. It was because the stakes were so high that Satchō opposed the attack on Korea in 1873, but reversed themselves in 1874 and 1875 once they were back firmly in the saddle – a reversal as dramatic as their unprecedented *volte-face* in dumping their ideologue allies soon after the *ishin*.

In 1876, after Japan had deliberately provoked an incident by sending its 'surveyors' up the Han River towards Seoul, Korea was forced to sign the Kangwha Treaty which, in the words of Korean historian Kuk Ju Shin (1966: 4 [résumé]), 'marked the beginning of Japan's full-scale, modern capitalistic invasion of Korea'. There can be little doubt that what most of the Japanese leaders – those 'splendid imperialists' – had in mind in 1873 was just such a 'full-scale modern capitalistic invasion of Korea'.

To hasten the process of turning Korea into a semi-colony, a goodwill mission of over eighty officials was invited to Japan (ibid.: 66ff.). Despite popular opposition, the King went ahead with the mission as Korea was interested in viewing Japanese production, especially of modern arms. They wished to pay their own expenses, but they were met by the Japanese 'government'; that is to say they were transported in a Mitsubishi ship and stayed in a Mitsui residence. Moriyama, Godai's friend, was in charge of arrangements. The busy schedule prepared for them, including meeting the Emperor, left no time to view matters of military and economic interest. They were showered with presents, and, from the Japanese viewpoint, the mission was a great success, for they reported favourably on Japan and their treatment there and helped secure the signing of two supplementary treaties. From the Korean viewpoint, however, the mission was a disaster, for it created a body of Koreans beholden to Japan and led to the two supplementary treaties which pushed Korea into a semi-colonial status. The existence of this pro-Japanese faction was essential for the achievement of Japan's objectives, for it helped to give legitimacy to the Japanese line that they represented progress and enlightenment, and that all who opposed them were backward, prejudiced and living in the past. As so frequently happens, the imperialistic power, having gained control of the economy, then felt obliged to take over political control to preserve those gains. The pro-Japanese faction, their 'contribution' made, was thereupon promptly ditched, and the Koreans were reduced to a servile condition in an oppressive, racist police state.

As in 1873 and 1875, Russia was pushed forward to justify the Japanese 'advance'. Thus it should be noted that the Montono–Iswalsky Agreement of 1907 had secret clauses designed to protect Japanese and Russian special interests in Manchuria, Korea and Mongolia against US encroachments (Kashima 1965: 45–51). Three more treaties were to follow, the last having a secret clause pledging to wage war against any power 'trespassing on their vital interests'. The contents of these four treaties were not known to the world until revealed by the 1917 Revolutionary Government.

It is deeply disturbing that, in the West, the standard account of Japanese–Korean relations is still the Conroy version: once upon a time the Japanese government sent to Korea a party of fact-finders under a Foreign Office official named Sada. For almost half a century since war's end the Japanese government has been able to defy the majority of its own people and to deny both the nature and the meaning of its recent past. Whereas other ex-colonial powers now generally accept the sins of the past, in Japan the search for *taigi meibun* still continues. As Japan climbs ever higher as the world's economic superpower, one must expect that the unrelenting indoctrination will begin to bite. In the 1870s Japan launched its imperial expansion with attacks on Korea that were unprovoked, unjustified and carried out with great cynicism and duplicity. Yet official Japan is moving even further from accepting this basic truth.

Japan's history is not a matter of mere academic interest. 'History' is how a nation looks at its future. Once more Japan, quite consciously, is completing the first stage of economic imperialism, to whit, the acquisition of great holdings of land, property and resources in other countries. Almost inevitably, there will come a time when the Japanese people are asked to defend some or all of those investments. Japan's present history textbooks must be regarded as a preparation for that day.

# BIBLIOGRAPHY

*Note: Any political, economic or social history of modern Japan is of some relevance, so the following list is highly selective.*

## JAPANESE WORKS

Official biographies present a problem as they are usually compiled and published by a committee, with neither author nor publisher. So unless there is a clear author they are placed under the name of the subject.

Banno Junji and Itō Takashi (eds) (1978–9) *Iwamura Michitoshi Kankei Bunsho*, Chūgaku Zasshi Dai
*Date City History* (1949), Date city authorities
*Date City Publication* (1970), Date city authorities
Endo Shusaku (1982) *Chinmoku*, Kodansha
Enjōji Kiyoshi (1895) *Ōkuma Haku Sekijitsu Tan*,
*Fukushima Dai Hyakkajiten* (encyclopaedia)
*Fukuzawa Yukichi Zenshū* (1960), Hokuseidō Press
*Furukawa Jūjun Den* (1971), Furukawa Company
Gabe Masao (1979) *Meiji Kokka to Okinawa*, Sanichi Shobō
Go Seinosuke official biography (1943) (Hakushaku *Go Seinosuke Den*)
Godai Ryūsuke (ed.) (1933) *Godai Tomoatsu Den*, Nishikawa Yoshiemon
Gotō Yasushi (1966) *Jiyū Minken Undō no Tenkai*, Yūhikaku
Haraguchi Kiyoshi *Chōshū Han Shotai no Hanran*, Ochanomizu Shobō
——(1968) *Nippon Kindai Kokka no Keisei*, Iwanami Shoten
Hatsuse Ryūhei (1980) *Uchita Ryūhei no Kenkyū*, Kyushu Daigaku
Hattori Shisō (1949, 1954) *Meiji no Seijika Tachi* (*Meiji Politicians*), Iwanami Shinsho
*Dai Jimmmei Jiten* (1953) *Heibon Sha* (Encyclopaedia of Japanese historical figures)
Hideshima Naritada (ed.) (1912) *Saga Kaigun Shi*, 2nd edn 1972, Hara Shobō
Iwanami Shoten (1970) *Nippon Shisō Taikei*
Hirao Michio (1935) *Shikaku Tani Tateki* (Kanjō), 2nd edn 1981, Toyoma-to
Hirotsu Rankei (1911) *collected writings* Honjo Naotaro (ed.)
——(1964) *Yoshida Tōyo*, Yoshikawa Kobunkan

——(ed.) (1978) *Sakamoto Ryōma Zenshū*, Kofu sha Shoten
——(1979–80) *Zenshū*, Kōchi Shimbun-sha
Hitomata Masao (1975) *Sugiyama Shigemaru*, Hara Shobō
*Hokkaidō no Yoake* (1965), *Hokkaidō's Dawn* – official publication
Iechika Yoshiki (1981) 'Meiji Rokunen Seihen to Ōkubo Toshimichi no
  Seiji Teki Ito – Mori Toshihiko Setsu ni Tai Suru Gimon' in *Nihon Shi
  Kenkyū* 229
Ienaga Saburō (1960) *Ueki Emori Kenkyū*, 2nd edn 1976, Iwanami Shoten
Iguro Yatarō and Katayama Keiji (1967) *Hokkaidō no Ishizue Yonin*,
  Miyamasho Company
Imai Sakae (1866) *Shūya no Yume-gatari*
Imamura Yoshitaka (1969) *Akita Ken no Rekishi*, Yamakawa
Inoue Kiyoshi (1970) *Saigō Takamori*, Chūō Shinsho
——(1953) *Nihon no Gunkoku Shugi*, Iwanami Shoten
Inoue Kaoru official biography (1933) (*Segai Inoue Kō Den*)
Naigai Shoseki, 5 vols
Isa Hideo (1951) *Ozaki Yukio Den*, Osaki Yukio Den Kai
*Itō Hirobumi Den* (1940), Tōsei Company
Itoya Toshio (1974) *Shiden Itagaki Taisuke*, Shimizushoin
*Iwamura Yoshio Den* (official biography) (1971)
*Iwasaki Hisaya Den* (1961) Mitsubishi official publication
*Iwasaki Yatarō Den* (1967) Mitsubishi official publication
Jiromaru Kenzō (1970) *Mitsukuri Shūhei to Sono Shūhen*, Sanyō Insatsu
Kaiho Mineo (1974) *Nippon Hoppō-shi no Ronri*,
——(1982) 'Hakodate sensō to Kaitaku nōmin' in *Hokkaidō no Kenkyū* 4
Kajinishi Mitsuhaya (1960) *Seishō kara Zaibatsu*, Chikuma Shobō
——(1963) *Seishō*, Chikuma Shobō
Kata Tetsuzō (1940) *Shokumin Seisaku*, Diamondo Sha
*Kawade Shobō: Nippon Rekishi Dai Jiten* (1972),
Kawada Mizuko (1939) *Kataoka Kenkichi Den*, 2nd edn 1978,
Kawashima Chōnosuke (Suminosuke) (1911) *Kurume han Nanki*,
Kemuyama Sentarō (1907) *Seikanron Jissō*, Waseda University Press
Kimura Ki (1979) 'Meiji Tennō to Genrō' in *Rekishi Dokuhon*, December
Kitahara Keiko (1975) 'Meiji Shōnen Tokyo-fu ni Okeru Kyūmin jūsan'
  in *Meiji Kokka no Tenkai to Minshū Seikatsu*, Kōbundō
*Kokugakusha Denki Shūsei*
Kokuryūkai Hen (1966) *Tōa Senkaku Shishi Kiden* (*Chronicles of the Men of
  Spirit who Pioneered the Penetration*), Hara Shobō
*Kōshaku Katsura Tarō Den*, Tokutomi Iichirō
Kuk Ju Shin (1966) *Kindai Chōsen Gaikō Shi Kenkyū*, Yūshindō
Kume Masao (1931) *Itō Hirobumi Den*, Kaizō Sha
Kure Yuzō (1914) *Mitsukuri Genpo, Igaku Hakase*, Dai Nippon Tosho K.K.
Makino Nobuaki (1948) *Kaisō Roku*, Bungei Shunshū Sha
Maruyama Kanji (1936) *Soejimi Taneomi Haku*, Dainichi sha
Maruyama Masahiko (1899) *Maruyama Sakura Den*, Maruyama Masahiko
Matano Hansuke (1914) *Etō Nampaku*, 2nd edn 1968, Hara Shobō
Matsumoto Seichō (1965) *Showa Shi Hakkutsu*, Bungei Shunshu
Matsumoto Seinosuke (1969) *Tennō-sei Kokka to Seiji Shisō*, Miraisha
Mikami Taku (1940) *Takayama Hikokurō*, Heibonsha

Misaka Keiji (ed.) (1979) *Gesshō no Kenkyū*, Matsuno Shoten
Miura Gorō (1925) *Kanjū Shogun Kaisō-roku*, Seikyō-sha
Miyadera Toshio (1953) *Zaikai no Oni Sai*, Shiki
Miyage Setsurei (1949) *Dō Jidai Shi (History of our Times)*, Iwanami Shoten
Miyaji Masahito (1985) 'Haikan Chiken no Seiji Katei' in Banno Junji and Miyaji Masahito (eds) *Nippon Kindai Shi ni Okeru Tenkanki no Kenkyū*, Yamakawa
Miyamoto Mataji (1960) *Osaka Jimbutsu Shi*, Ōtena Shunshō
——(1981) *Godai Tomoatsu Den*, Yūhikaku
Mōri Toshihiko (1978) *Meiji Rokunen no Seihen no Kenkyū*, Osaka Shiritsu Daigaku Hōgaku Kai
Morikawa Tetsurō (1976) *Nippon Gigoku-shi*, Seiwa
Nagai Hideo (1966) 'Hokkaidō Ijū to Ken fu no Jōkyō' in *Atarashii Dōshi*
Nagai Minoru (ed.) (1939) *Jijō Masuda Takashi Ō Den*, Seibudo Insatsu
Nagata Tomitomo (1966) 'Yanagawa to Satsuma' in *Atarashii Dōshi* 9 January
*Nakamigawa Hikojirō Den* (1939), Chūchō Kaizō
*Nemuro City History*
*Nippon Zaikei Jimbutsu Retsu Den* (1963), Seiko
Okamoto Ryōichi (1969) *Kokumin no Rekishi*, Buneidō
*Ōkuma Kō 85 Nen Shi* (1925)
Okumura Momoko (1975) *Shima Yoshitake*
Ōnishi Rikei (ed.) (1928) *Asabuki Eiji*, Nisshin Insatsu
Ōoka Shōhei (1957) *Nobi*, Secker and Warburg
Ōsaka Shingo (1962) *Kuroda Kiyotaka to Horace Capron*, Hokkaidō Times
Ōsaki Katsuzumi (1943) *Ōkuni Takamasa*, Dai Nippon Yū ben kai Kōdansha
Ōtsugi Fumihiko (1906) *Mitsukuri Rinshō den*, Maruzen
Otsuka Takematsu (ed.) (1929) *Yoshida Tōyō Ikō*
Sada Hakuho (1903) *Seikan-Ron Reminiscences*, reprinted in *Meiji Bunka Zenshū*, Vol. 22: 35–52
Saitō Jirō (1984) *Handa Ginzan no Rekishi*, Vols 1–5
Sasaki Takayuki (1970) *Nikki*, Tokyo University Press
Seki Hideshi (1971) 'Ijū: Kaitaku-zu no shisaku ni tsuite' in *Atarashii Dōshi* 48, 31 October
*Sennin no Omokage* (1961) City Hall
Shiba Ryōtarō (1972a) 'Sako no Ue no Kumo' in *Shiba Ryōtarō Zenshū*, Vols 24, 25, 26, Bungei Shunshū
——(1972b) 'Junshi' in *Shiba Ryōtarō Zenshū*, Vol. 23, Bungei Shunshū
——(1972c) 'Yō ni Sumu Hibi' in *Shiba Ryōtarō Zenshū*, Vol. 27, Bungei Shunshū
——(1975) *Tobu ga Gotoku*, Bungei Shunshū
Shiraishi Kitarō (1933) *Shibusawa Eiichi Ō*, Tōkō Shoin
Shōji Kichinosuke (1981) 'Minei Handa Ginzan' in *Fukushima Ken Rekishi Shiryō Kan* publication *Kenkyū Kiyo* 3: 56–89
*Sukumo Jimbutsu* (1968) Town Office
Tabohashi Kiyoshi (1940) *Kindai Nikkan Kankei no Kenkyū*, 2nd edn 1972, Sōko Shobō
Tahara Tsugo (1963) *Hirata Atsutane*, 2nd edn 1986, Yoshikawa Kōbunkan

Tai Kito (1927) *Nippon Ron*, 2nd edn 1972, Shakai Shiso Sha
Takakura Shinichirō (ed.) (1982) *Saisen Kai Shiryō*,
Takeno Yōko (1979) *Han Bo-eki shi no Kenkyū*, Minerva
Tanaka Akira (1984) *Datsu A no Meiji Ishin*, NHK Books
Tanaka Sōgorō (1939) *Seikan Ron, Seinan Sensō*, Hakuyō
Taniguchi Sumio (1964) *Okayama Ken no Rekishi*, Yamakawa
Teraishi Masamichi (1976) *Tosa Ijin Den*
Tezuka Yutaka (1956) *Meiji Shoki Keihō Shi no Kenkyū*, Keio Tsushin
Tokutomi Iichirō (Soho) (1916) *Kōshaku Katsura Tarō Den*, 2nd edn 1967, Hara Shobō
——(1926) *Saigō Nanshū Sensei*, Minsyū-sha
——(1927) *Ōkubo Kōtō Sensei*, Minyū-sha
Tominari Hiroshi (1972) *Kido Takayoshi*, San-ichi Shobō
Toriumi Yasushi (1979) 'Meiji Tennō to Genrō' in *Rekishi Dokuhon*, December
Tōyama Shigeki (1950) 'Seikan ron, Jiyū minken ron, Hoken ron' in *Rekishi Gaku Kenkyū*
Toyoda Go (1983) *Saionji Kinmochi to Meiji Daitei Hōgyo*, Kodansha
Tsuda Shigemaru (1915) *Kinnō Hishi Sasaki Rōkō Sekijitsu Dan*, 2nd edn 1980, Tokyo University Press
——(1927) *Meiji Seijo to Shin Takayuki*, 2nd edn 1970,
Uchimura Kanzō (1932–3) *Zenshū*, Iwanami Shoten
Watsuji Tetsurō (1950) *Sakoku, Nihon no Higeki*, 2nd edn 1964, Chikuma Shobō
Yamaguchi Muneyuki (1973) *Maki Izumi*, Yoshikawa Kōbunkan
Yamaji Aizan (1908) *Gendai Kinken Shi*, 2nd edn 1975, Shūko Shobō
Yim Jong-Han *Jongshin Dae*, Hanrim Publisher
Yomiuri Shinbun Sha Kaibu (1972) *Rengō Sekigun*, (*The Red Army*)
Yosano Akiko Shikashu (1970) *Kimi Shini Tamao Nakare*, Hakuko-sha
*Yoshida Shōin Zenshū* (1936) Iwanami Shoten
Yoshikawa Kōbun Kan (1981) *Meiji Ishin Jimmei Jiten*, (historical encyclopaedia)

## Supplementary biographies and local histories

This term is used loosely to include critical studies of individuals. Those relating to Hokkaidō, Kurume, Tosa and Korea have been listed separately under that section. As many of the biographies are compiled by committees with no author given, the biographies are listed alphabetically according to the subject's name, not the author's.

### *Business leaders*

*Fujikawa Sankei Den*, Kuwada Hidekazu (1940), Suisan K.K.
*Fukuzawa Yukichi*, Koizumi Shinzo (1966), 2nd edn 1985, Iwanami Shinsha
*Hakuseki Yukichi*, Hani Gorō (1937), 2nd edn 1961, Iwanami Shoten
*Kashima Morinosuke Jiden* (1964)
*Magoshi Ryōhei Den*, Otsuka Eizo (1935), Kyōdō Insatsu

# BIBLIOGRAPHY

*Mori Tsutomu*, Yamaura Kaniichi (1940)
*Okura Kihachirō Den* (1924)
*Shibusawa Hideo Jiden* (1964)


## Chōshū

*Ayukawa Yoshisuke Den*, Kosawa Chikamatsu (1974), Yamaguchi Shimbun
  Sha
*Murata Munajirō: Shinagawa Den* (1910), Tokyo
*Nippon no Meicho*, Yoshida Shōin (1973), Chūo Kōron
*Yoshida Shōin*, Naramoto Tatsuya (1951), 2nd edn 1985, Iwanami Shinsho
*Yoshida Shōin*, Tokunaga Shinichirō (1976), Seibidō
*Yoshida Shōin*, Tokutomi Iichirō (1893), 2nd edn 1981, Iwanami Shinsho


## North and Central Kyūshū

*Asia Shugi to Tōyama Mitsuru*, Ashizu Uzhiko (1965), 2nd edn 1984, Nihon
  Kyōbun Sha
*Hirota Kōki* (1966), Chūo Kōron Jigyō Shuppan
*Inoue Kowashi to Meiji Kokka*, Sakai Yukichi (1983), Tokyo University
  Shuppan Kai
*Kiyoura Keigo Den*, Inoue Masaaki (1938), Fuji Insatsu
*Kokudō Sasa Sensei Kikō* (1936) (A collection of Sasa's letters and writings
  published by a committee headed by Tōyama and Sugiyama)
*Miyasaki Kyōdai Den*, Uemura Kimio (1984), Ishobō
*Tōyama, Mutsu, Komura*, Sugimori Hisahide (1966), Mainichi Shimbunsha
*Yamaza Enjirō*, Hitomata Masao (1974), Hara Shobō
*Yokoi Shōnan*, Matsuura Rei (1976), Asahi Shimbunsha


## Saga

*Etō Shimpei*, Sugitani Akira (1962), Yoshikawa Kōbunkan
*Kaikoku Gojūnenshi*, Ōkuma Shigenobu (1908), 2nd edn 1970,
*(Saga) Kyōdō Shi Ni Kagayaku Hito-bito (People who Shone in Saga History)*
  (1973), Kyoiku Tosho K.K.
*Sano Tsunetami: Yomigaeri Hakuai Seishin (Come Alive Again, Humanitarian Spirit)*
  (1985), Saga Education Committee


## Satsuma

*Godai Tomoatsu Hishi (Secret History of Godai Tomoatsu)* (1961)
*Kawaji Dai Keishi*, Nakamura Tokugorō (1932), Japan Police Newspaper
  Company
*Kōbunkan Jimbutsu Kuroda Kiyotaka*, Iguro Yatarō (1977)
*Kōshaku Matsukata Masayoshi Den*, Tokutomi Iichirō (ed.) (1935)
*Ōkubo Toshimichi Nikki* (1927)
*Saigō no Higeki (Saigo's Tragedy)*, Kawai Teikichi (1976), Gakugei Shorin

*Saigō Takamori*, Tanaka Sōgorō (1958), Yoshikawa Kobunkan
*Saigō to Ōkubo to Hisamitsu*, Kaionji Shōgorō (1978), Asahi Shimbun Sha
*Seinan Sensō no Genin to Shite no Fukuzawa Yukichi to Ōkubo Toshimichi no Tairitsu*
(*The Origins of the Seinan War as a struggle between Fukuzawa and Ōkubo*),
Sakamoto Moriaki (1971), Hyogen Sha

### Other biographies

*Hashimoto Sanai*, Yamaguchi Muneyuki (1962), 2nd edn 1985, Yoshikawa
Kōbunkan
*Inugai Mokudō Den*, Washio Yoshinao (ed.) (1940)
*Iwakura Tomomi*, Ōkubo Toshiaki (1973), 2nd edn 1977, Chūō Koron
*Katō Takaaki Den* (1928), Katō Takaaki Den Kankō Kai
*Ozaki Yukio Autobiography*, Gakudō Jiden (1937)
*Yuri Kimimasa Den*, Shishaku (1940), Yuri Masamichi

# Kurume

### Primary sources

Hirotsu Shunzō (Hironobu) (1873) *Jishu no Ken* (*The Right to Self-
Determination*), Yamashiroya Sahei and Yamashiro Masakichi
Honjō-Ikkō (1888) *Kurume Han Ichi-Yūtan* (*One Night's Story*)
Sada Hakuho (ed.) (1875) *Seikan Hyōron*
Sada Hakuho (1897) *Arima Shi Shinsei Shi-shi* (*A Modern History of Lord
Arima*), Yoshikawa Heishichi
*Saikai Chōshi Koden* (*A Brief Account of a Loyal Samurai of Western Japan*),
Chikugo Shidan-kai

### Secondary sources

Asano Yokichi *Tsuge Zengo-Den*
*Kurume Jimbutsu Shi* (*A History of Kurume Personalities*) (1981)
*Kurume Shi-shi* (*History of Kurume City*) (1982)
*Kurume Shishi* (*Annals of Kurume City*) (1932) Kurume City Office
Ogawa Tsunedo (1979) *Maki Izume no Kami no Kenkyū*, Shintō-shi Gakukai
Ogawa Tsunedo (1983) *Seisei Dōdō. Maki Izumi no Kami no Shōgai* (*Like a
Bold Soldier. Life of Maki Izumi no Kami*)
Tanikawa Kenichi (1977) *Saigo no Jōi-tō* (*The Last 'Drive out the Foreigner'
Party*), Sanichi Shobō
Utaka Hiroshi (1934) *Maki Izumi no Kami*, Sasaki Shinichi

# Hokkaidō

Emori Susumu (1983) 'Matsumae han no Ōsaka kura yashiki' ('Matsumae
clan's Ōsaka storehouses') in *Hokkaidō no Kenkyū* 3: 175–258

Hasegawa Seiichi (1982) 'Tohoku daimyō and Ezochi' in *Hokkaidō no Kenkyū*
4: 55–90

*Hiroshima. Machi no Ayumi (Progress of the City)* (1972)

*Hokkaidō Prefecture: Foreign Pioneers* (1968)

Homma Yūji (1970) 'Karafuto timber' in *Atarashii Dōshi* 38, 15 March

Kaiho Mineo (1983a) 'Unified government Matsumae clan and Ezochi' in
*Hokkaidō no Kenkyū* 3

Kaiho Mineo (1983b) 'Establishment of Japanese political control' in
*Hokkaidō no Kenkyū* 3: 2–35

Kimi Takahiko (1973) 'Shizuoka clan control of Tokachi' in *Atarashii Dōshi*
47, 2 September

Kitauchi Isao (1982) 'Gaiatsu to dōka shugi' ('Foreign pressure and
assimilation') in *Hokkaidō no Kenkyū* 4: 1–30

Kobayashi Masato (1983) 'Matsumae clan's authority and problems
of communication in early modern period' in *Hokkaidō no Kenkyū*
3: 142–73

*Kushiro City History* (1957)

Matsumoto Jirō (1974) *Nemuro mo Hoshi Kusa*, Miyama Shobō

Sasaki Toshikazu (1983) 'Ezo fuzoku jū ni ka getsa zu' ('Paintings showing
Ezo scenes for the twelve months') in *Hokkaidō no Kenkyū* 3: 365–95

Satō Tadao (1980) *Shimbun ni Miru Hokkaidō no Meiji Taishō*, Hokkaidō
Shimbun Sha

*Shin Hokkaidō Shi (New Hokkaidō History)* (1969–81)

Suzue Eiichi (1983) 'Establishment of villages in Japanese section of Ezochi'
in *Hokkaidō no Kenkyū* 3: 77–140

Takakura Shinichirō (1960) *Outline of Chishima History*, Nampō Doho
Engo Kai

Takeuchi Umpei (1943) *Hakodate Kaisen Shiwa (Chronicles of the Hakodate
War)*, 2nd edn 1980, Miyama Shobō

Tanimura Issa (1937) *Capron Shogun*, Yamaguchi Sōkichi

Yajima Satoshi (1983) 'Hokkaidō Festivals' in *Hokkaidō no Kenkyū* 3:
327–64

## Tosa

Hagihara Nobutoshi (1967) *Baba Tatsui*, Chūō Kōronsha

Hirao Michio (1970) *Ishin Ansatsu Hiroku (Secret Records of Restoration
Assassinations)*, 2nd edn 1978, Shin Jimbutsu Orai Sha

——(1974) *Mukei Itagaki Taisuke*, Kochi Shimbun Sha

Nishimura Sanetsugu (1941) *Ono Azusa Den*, Tokyo Tōyama

*Takeuchi Tsuyoshi: Autobiography* in *Meiji Bunka Zenshū* 22

## Korea

Kashima Morinosuke (ed.) (1970) *Nippon Gaikō Shi (History of Japanese
Diplomacy)*, Kashima Kenkyū sho Shuppan Kai, Vols 1–4

——(1973) *Nippon Gaikō Shi: Sōkotsu Hen (Brief Diplomatic History of Japan)*,
Kashima Heiwa Kenkyūjo

# BIBLIOGRAPHY

Nakano Yasuo (1984) *An Chong Kon*, Aki Shobō
Yagi Nobuo (1978) *Nippon to Kankoku*, Zaidan Hōjin Nikkan Bunka Kyōkai
  (Society to Promote Japanese–Korean Cultural Ties)

## Northern Honshū

*Fukushima-ken Jimmei Jiten* (1914)
*Handa Ginzan Kōgyō Enkaku Shi* (*Chronicle of Handa Silver Mine Enterprise*)
  (1885), Handa Ginzan Kōsei Kan
Morio Ryōichi (1978) *Kurume Kaikon Shi* (*History of Kurume Pioneering*)
*Nasunogahara Kaitaku Shi Kenkyū Kai*, Yearly, collected articles published
  annually since 1975 by Nasunogahara Kaitaku Shi Kenkyū Kai
Shōji Kichinosuke (1969) *Handa Ginzan no Ukeyama to Jikiyama Keiei* (*The
  Delegated and Direct Management of Handa Silver Mine*)
*Tochigi-ken Shi* (1984) Vol. 8 (kin-gendai 3)
*Yamagata Ken Dai Hyakkajiten* (1983)
*Yamagata Ken Shi* (1971) Nogyō 4, Takushuku hen

## 1873 and 1881 *Seihen*

Inada Masatsugu (1960) *Meiji Kempō Seiritsu Shi* (*History of the Setting up of
  the Meiji Constitution*), Yūhikaku
Ōkubo Toshiaki (1954) 'Meiji 14 Nen no Seihen' ('The 1881 Seihen') in
  *Meiji Kenkyū* series Ochanomizu Shobo 1
Yamamuro Shin-ichi (1984) *Hōsei Kanryō no Jidai* (*The Age of Legal
  Bureaucracy*), Mokutai

## Other histories

Banno Junji (1982) *Taishō Seihen: 1900 Nen Taisei no Hōkai* (*The Taishō Crisis:
  the Collapse of the 1900 System*), Minerva Shobō
——1983 'Fukoku ron no seiji shi teki kōsatsu 1874–81' ('Investigation of
  the political history of the theory of a prosperous country') in *Matsukata
  Zaisei to Shokusan Kōgyō Seisaku*
Hani Gorō (1956) *Meiji Ishin Shi Kenkyū* (*A Study on the History of the Meiji
  Revolution*), Iwanami Shoten
Hanmachi Shōji (1982) *Tetsudō no Nihon-shi* (*History of the Japanese Rail-
  ways*), Bunken
Hattori Shisō (1950) *Meiji no Kakumei*, Nippon Hyōron
Ishii Takashi (1974) 'Development of Japanese–Russian relations in early
  Meiji period' in *Rekishi Gaku Kenkyū* 407
——(1975) *Meiji Ishin no Butai Ura* (*Behind the Scenes of the Meiji Restoration*),
  Iwanami Shinsho
Itagaki Taisuke (ed.) (1910) Jiyūtō Shi, 2nd edn 1981, Iwanami Bunkō
Kaionji Chōgorō (1978) *Saigō to Ōkubo to Hisamitsu*, Asahi Shimbunsha
Kajinishi Mitsuhaya (1959) 'Meiji no Shihon ka zō' ('Portraits of Meiji
  Capitalists') in *Nihon Bunka Kenkyū* 7

Kamiya Jirō and Soda Kōichi (1977) *Bakumatsu Ishin 300 Han Sōran* (*A General Account of 300 Clans in the Bakumatsu and Ishin Periods*), Shin Jimbutsu Ōrai Sha

Kashima Morinosuke (1973) *Nippon Gaikō Shi: Sōkatsu Hen* (*Brief Diplomatic History of Japan*), Kashima Heiwa Kenkyūjo

Kojita Yasunao (1981) 'Meiji 14 no seihen to Kansai boeki sha' ('Meiji 14 crisis and the Kansai Trading Co.') in *Nihon shi Kenkyū* 229: 23–55

*Meiji Tennō Ki* (1969), Yoshikawa Kōbunkan, Vols 1–4

Muroyama Yoshimasa (1984) *Kindai Nippon no Gunji to Zaisei* (*Modern Japan's Armaments and Economic Policy*), Tokyo Daigaku Shuppan Kai

*Nippon Jin no Jiden* (*Japanese Autobiographies*) (1985), Heibon Sha

Noda Kazuo (1969) *Zaibatsu*, 2nd edn 1983, Chūō Kōron

*Rekishi Dokuhon* (1977) 'Meiji Tennō to Ishin no Gunzō' ('Portrait of the Meiji Emperor and the Ishin leaders'), special issue December

——(1978) 'Bakumatsu Ishin Dōran no Gunzō' ('Portrait of the group active in the Bakumatsu and Ishin disturbances'), 8 October

Sakamoto Takeo (ed.) (1974) *Kuge Jiten*, Kokusho Konkō-kei

Sawada Akira (1966) *Meiji Zaisei no Kihon-teki Kenkyū* (*A Basic Study of Meiji Economic Policy*), Kashima Shobō

Shiba Ryōtarō (1972d) 'Ryōma ga Yuku' in *Shiba Ryōtarō Zenshū*, Vols 3–5, Bungei Shunshū

——(1972e) 'Saigetsu' in *Shiba Ryōtarō Zenshū*, Vol. 23, Bungei Shunshū

——(1972f) 'Kashin' in *Shiba Ryōtarō Zenshū*, Vols 30, 31, Bungei Shunshū

Suzuki Tadashi (1968) *Ansatsu Hiroku* (*Secret Report on Assassination*), Hara Shobō

Tada Kōmon (ed.) (1968) *Iwakura kō Jikki* (*Iwakura's Diaries and Papers*)

Tanaka Akira (1965) *Bakumatsu no Chōshū* (*Chōshū in the Bakumatsu Period*), 2nd edn 1981, Chūkō Shinsho

——(1984) *Meiji Ishin no Haisha to Shōsha* (*The Victors and the Defeated of the Meiji Ishin*), N.H.K. Books

Tanaka Sōgorō (1947) 'Nihon no Jijū Minken' in *Yusankaku Rekishi Shinsho* 2

Torio Koyata (1885) *Butsudō Honron*, Narise Onsho

Tōyama Shigeki (1962) *Meiji Ishin*, Iwanami Zensho

Umemura Mataji and Nakamura Takafusa (eds) (1983) *Matsukata Zaisei to Shokusan Kōgyō Seisaku* (*Matsukata's Economic Policies and Plans for Expanding Industry*), Todai Shuppan Kai

Watanabe Masao (1976) *Nippon Jin to Kindai Kagaku* (*The Japanese and Modern Science*), Iwanami Shinsho

## ENGLISH WORKS

Akita, G. (1967) *The Foundations of Constitutional Government in Modern Japan 1868–1900*, Harvard University Press

Alcock, R. (1863) *The Capital of the Tycoon*, Longman, Roberts and Green

Arberry, J. (1946) *Asiatic Jones*, Longmans Green

Batchelor, J. (1902) *Sea-Girt Yeso. Glimpses of Missionary Work in North Japan*, Church Missionary Society

Beasley, W. G. (1973) *The Meiji Restoration*, Stanford University Press
——(1987) *Japanese Imperialism 1894–1945*, Clarendon Press, Oxford
Behr, E. (1989) *Hirohito. Behind the Myth*, Hamish Hamilton
Benedict, R. (1946) *The Chrysanthemum and the Sword*, Houghton Mifflin
Black, J. P. (1962) *Young Japan 1858–79*, Oxford University Press
Blacker, D. (1964) *The Japanese Enlightenment: A Study in the Writings of Fukuzawa Yukichi*, Cambridge University Press
Blakiston, T. W. (1883) *Japan in Yezo*, Japan Gazette
Bogarde, D. (1988) *The Complete Autobiography*, Chatto and Windus
Bolitho, H. (1977) *Meiji Japan*, Cambridge University Press
Calman, D. (1950) *History of the Indians in Fiji*, unpub. thesis
Cannon, G. H. (1964) *Oriental Jones*, Bombay Asia Publishing House
Chamberlain, B. H. (1905) *Things Japanese*, John Murray
Conroy, H. (1960) *The Japanese Seizure of Korea 1868–1910*, Philadelphia University Press
Craig, A. (1961) *Chōshū in the Meiji Restoration*, Harvard University Press
——(1968) 'Fukuzawa Yukichi: the philosophical foundations of Meiji nationalism' in R. Ward (ed.) *Political Development in Modern Japan*, Princeton University Press
Craig, W. (1967) *The Fall of Japan. The March of History* series
Curzon, G. (1894) *Problems of the Far East*, Longmans Green
Daniels, G. (1967) *Sir Henry Parkes*, London University Press
De Bary, T. (ed.) (1964) *Sources of Japanese Tradition*, Columbia University Press
Dun, E. *Reminiscences in Japan*, unpub. ms.
Gluck, G. (1985) *Japan's Modern Myths*, Princeton University Press
Griffis, W. E. (1876) *The Mikado's Empire*, Harper
Hackett, R. (1968) 'Political modernisation and the Meiji Genro' in R. Ward (ed.) *Political Development in Modern Japan*, Princeton University Press
Hamilton, A. (1904) *Korea*, Heinemann
Harlow, V. T. (1952) *The Founding of the Second British Empire 1763–1793*, Longmans
Harrison, J. A. (1953) *Japan's Northern Frontier*, University of Florida Press
Hirotsu Rankei (1911) *Collected Writings*, Honjo Naotaro
Hokkaidō University Library collection of letters
Hong Yi Sup (1973) *Korea's Self Identity*, Yonsei University Press
Hoover, W. D. (1973) *Godai Tomoatsu (1836–1885). An Economic Statesman of Early Meiji Japan*, unpub. Ph.D. thesis
Hulbert, H. B. (1905) *History of Korea*, Hilary House
Iwata Masakazu (1964) *Ōkubo Toshimichi: the Bismarck of Japan*, University of California Press
Kashima Morinosuke (1965) *Diplomatic History of Japan*, Tuttle
Kawahara Toshiaki (1990) *Hirohito and His Times*, Kodansha
Kido Koichi, (1984) *The Diary of Marquis Kido 1931–1945*, University Publications of America, University of Maryland Press
Kiyooka Eiichi (ed.) (1985) *Fukuzawa Yukichi on Education*, Tokyo University Press
Knightley, P. (1975) *The First Casualty*, Harcourt Brace Jovanovich
*Kodansha's English Language Historical Encyclopaedia*

Ledyard, G. (1971) *The Dutch Come to Korea. An Account of the Life of the First Westerners in Korea (1665–1666)*, R. A. S. Korea

Lloyd, A. (1909) *Everyday Japan*, Cassell

Morris, I. (1964) *The Nobility of Failure*, Penguin

Mossman, S. (1873) *New Japan, the Land of the Rising Sun*, John Murray

Oxford, W. (1973) *The Speeches of Fukuzawa. A Translation and Critical Study*, Hokuseidō Press

Prasad, S. A. (1984) *The Japanologists: A History*, Samudraiah Prakashan

Ratti, O. and Westbrook, A. (1973) *Secrets of the Samurai*, Tuttle

Reed, E. (1880) *Japan: its History, Traditions and Religions*, John Murray

Sadler, A. L. (1937) *The Maker of Modern Japan. The Life of Shogun Tokugawa Ieyasu*, Tuttle

Sansom, G. (1963) *A History of Japan*, Dawson

Satow, Sir E. (1968) (original edn 1921) *A Diplomat in Japan*, Oxford University Press

Simons, J. E. (1954) *In the Arms of the Japanese*, Heinemann

Stead, A. (ed.) (1904) *Japan by the Japanese*, Heinemann

Synn Seung Kwon *The Russo-Japanese Rivalry over Korea 1876–1904*

Takekoshi, Y. (1930) *The Economic Aspects of the History of the Civilization of Japan*, Dawson, 2nd edn 1967

Trotter, A. (1975) *Britain and East Asia 1933–37*, Cambridge University Press

Ward, R. (ed.) (1968) *Political Developments in Modern Japan*, Princeton University Press

Warner, D. (1974) *The Tide at Sunrise*, Angus & Robertson

Watanabe Shoichi (1980) *The Peasant Soul of Japan*, Kodansha

## Biographies and critical studies

Hackett, R. (1971) *Yamagata Aritomo in the Rise of Modern Japan 1838–1922*, Harvard University Press

Hudson, W. *Memoir of William Wheeler*, unpub. ms.

Jansen, M. (1961) *Sakamoto Ryōma and the Meiji Restoration*, Princeton University Press

Kuwada, G. (1937) *Biography of Benjamin Smith Lyman*, Sanseido Company

Maki, J. M. (1975) *William Smith Clark: A Yankee in Hokkaidō*, unpub. ms.

Michell, D. *Clark of Sapporo*, unpub. ms.

Pooley, A. M. (ed.) (1915) *The Secret Memoirs of Count Hayashi*, Eveleigh Nash

Sakamoto Moriaki (1971) *Saigō Takamori's Poems and Posthumous Words*, Hyogen sha

Sansom, K. (1972) *Sir George Sansom and Japan – a Memoir*, Diplomatic Press

## Other histories

Akamatsu, P. (1972) *Meiji 1868*, George Allen and Unwin

Arnesen, P. J. (1979) *The Medieval Japanese Daimyō*, Yale University Press

# BIBLIOGRAPHY

Batchelor, J. (1928) *Autobiography Waga Kioku o tadorite (According to my memory)*

Bellah, R. N. (1957) *Tokugawa Religion*, Beacon Press

Bishop, D. M. (1983) *Shared Failure: American Military Advisers in Korea, 1888–96*, R.A.S. Korea, Vol. 58: 53–76

Borton, H. (1955) *Japan's Modern Century*, 2nd edn 1970, Ronald Press

Bowen, R. W. (1980) *Rebellion and Democracy in Meiji Japan. A Study of Commoners in the Popular Rights Movement*, California University Press

Cable, E. M. (1938) *The United States Korean Relations 1866–1871*, R.A.S. Korea, Vol. 27: 1–230

Hibino, Y. (1928) *Nippon Shindo Ron (The National Ideals of the Japanese People)*, orig. edn 1904, Cambridge University Press

Honjo, E. (1965) *Economic Theory and the History of Japan in the Tokugawa Period*, Russell and Russell

Ki-baik Lee (1967) *A New History of Korea*, 2nd. edn 1984, Harvard University Press

Ku Dae Yeol (1985) *Korea under Colonialism: the March First Movement and Anglo-Japanese Relations*, Seoul Computer Press

Lee Sun-Keun (1962) *Some Lesser Known Facts about Taewongun and his Foreign Policy*, R.A.S. Korea, Vol. 39: 23–46

Lehman, J. P. (1978) *The Image of Japan: From Feudal Isolation to World Power, 1850–1905*, George Allen and Unwin

Lensen, G. A. (1959) *The Russian Push Towards Japan. Russo-Japanese Relations 1697–1874*, Princeton University Press

MacDonald, D. S. (1959) *The American Role in the Opening of Korea to the West*, R.A.S. Korea, Vol. 35: 51–65

Malozemoff, A. (1958) *Russian Far Eastern Policy 1881–1904*, California University Press

Nish, I. (1985) *The Origins of the Russo-Japanese War*, Longman

Oliver, R. T. (1954) *Syngman Rhee: The Man Behind the Myth*, Dodd Mead

Pyle, K. B. (1969) *The New Generation in Meiji Japan – Problems of Cultural Identity 1885–1895*, Stanford University Press

Snow, H. J. (1910) *In Forbidden Seas. Recollections of Sea-Otter Hunting in the Kuriles*, Edward Arnold

Spaulding, R. M. (1969) *Imperial Japan's Higher Civil Service Examinations*, Princeton University Press

Steeds, D. and Nish, I. (1977) *China, Japan and 19th Century Britain*, Irish University Press

Totman, C. (1980) *The Collapse of the Tokugawa Bakufu 1862–1868*, Hawaii University Press

Treat, P. (1946) 'The Causes of the Sino-Japanese War', *Pacific Historical Review*, June

Webb, H. (1968) *The Japanese Imperial Institution in the Tokugawa Period*, Columbia University Press

# INDEX

341

wartime atrocities 171–82, 211
Watanabe (Mitsuya employee) 258
Watanabe Shoichi 176
Watari branch clan 244–5
Waters 300
Watsuji Tetsurō 34, 37
Westbrook, A. 174, 175
Western writers 12–26, 312–14;
  early 12–22; modern 22–6
women 183
workhouse 231–2, 234
World War II *see* Second World
  War

Xavier, F. 43

Yamada Hōkoku 69, 69–70, 103
Yamada Shindō 278–9
Yamada Shingo 118
Yamagata Yoritomo 130, 222, 290,
  321; Boshin War 289; Mutsu 19;
  scandals 132, 256, 257 (Fujita
  145; Mitsuya 258, 259)
Yamaguchi 43
Yamaguchi Muneyaki 16; Maki 81,
  82, 83–5, 87
Yamaji Aizan 260
Yamamoto Gombei 262
Yamanaka Ichirō 284–5

Yamanouchi Yōdō 46, 280
Yamashiroya (Nomura Michimi)
  256–7, 258, 260
Yamazaki Ansai 46, 55
Yano Motomichi 127
Yasuba Yasukazu 118
Yi Song-gye (Taejo), General 35
Yokoi Shōnan 87, 121
Yomiuri Shinbun Sha Kaibu 185
Yorinori, Kurume Lord 82
Yorishige, Kurume Lord 73, 83,
  85, 108, 109, 115
Yoritō, Kurume Lord 82, 83
Yosano Akiko 188
Yoshida Kiyonari 242, 256
Yoshida Sadanori 296
Yoshida Shigeru 27
Yoshida Shōin 11, 175, 188,
  278, 283–4
Yoshida Tamba (Shikie) 107, 108
Yoshida Tōyō 149, 276–7, 290
Yoshikawa Kōbun Kan 106, 126
Yoshimune, Shogun 56, 61
Yoshimura Toratarō 277–8
Yoshinobu (Keiki), Shogun 91,
  108, 141
Yuri Kimimasa 24, 234

*zaibatsu* 7